LONDON 1500–1700

London 1500–1700

The making of the metropolis

Edited by
A. L. Beier
Roger Finlay

Longman
London and New York

Longman Group Limited
Longman House, Burnt Mill, Harlow
Essex CM20 2JE, England

Associated companies throughout the world

*Published in the United States of America
by Longman Inc., New York*

© Longman Group Limited 1986

First published 1986

British Library Cataloguing in Publication Data

London 1500–1700: the making of the metropolis.
1. London (England)—Social conditions
I. Beier, A. L.   II. Finlay, Roger
942.105   HN398.L6

ISBN 0 582 49436 2

Library of Congress Cataloging in Publication Data

Main entry under title:

London 1500–1700.

Includes bibliographies and index.
1. London (England)—Social conditions—Addresses,
essays, lectures.   2. London (England)—Economic
conditions—Addresses, essays, lectures.   3. London
(England)—History—16th century—Addresses, essays,
lectures.   4. London (England)—History—17th century
—Addresses, essays, lectures.   I. Beier, A. L.   II. Finlay,
Roger.
HN398.L7L585 1985   306′.09421   84–29703
ISBN 0–582–49436–2

Set in 10/12 pt AM Comp/set Garamond
Produced by Longman Group (FE) Limited
Printed in Hong Kong

Contents

List of figures

List of tables

Contributors

A. L. Beier is Lecturer in History in the University of Lancaster. He is the author of several papers on the sixteenth and seventeenth centuries, a booklet on *The Problem of the Poor in Tudor and Early Stuart England* (1983), and is currently completing a volume on the vagrancy question in England, 1560–1640.

J. A. Chartres is Senior Lecturer in Economic History in the School of Economic Studies in the University of Leeds. He has published *Internal Trade in England, 1500–1700* (1977) and a major contribution to *The Agrarian History of England and Wales*, Vol. 5 (J. Thirsk, ed, 1985), as well as many articles.

Brian Dietz is Senior Lecturer in Modern History in the University of Glasgow. He has edited *The Port and Trade of Early Elizabethan London: Documents* (1972), and contributed to *The Reign of James VI and I* (A. G. R. Smith, ed., 1973), and *Wealth and Power in Tudor England* (E. W. Ives, R. J. Knecht and J. J. Scarisbrick, eds, 1978).

Roger Finlay is Assistant Librarian in the John Rylands University Library of Manchester. His research at the ESRC Cambridge Group for the History of Population and Social Structure was published as *Population and Metropolis. The Demography of London, 1580–1650* (1981).

M. J. Kitch is Reader in the School of English and American Studies in the University of Sussex. He is the editor of *Capitalism and the Reformation* (1967) and *Studies in Sussex Church History* (1981) and the author of papers on sixteenth- and seventeenth-century history.

Stephen Macfarlane is a member of the faculty in the Social Science Division at Bennington College, Vermont. He received a D.Phil. from Oxford University for a thesis entitled 'Studies in Poverty and Poor Relief in London at the End of the Seventeenth Century'.

Margaret Pelling is Assistant to the Director of the Wellcome Unit for the History of Medicine in the University of Oxford. Her publications include *Cholera, Fever and English Medicine* (1978) and, as editor (with F. Maddison and C. Webster), *Linacre Studies* (1977).

M. J. Power is Lecturer in the School of History and a member of the Institute for European Population Studies in the University of Liverpool. He has contributed to *Crisis and Order in English Towns* (P. Clark and P. Slack, eds, 1972) and to *Wealth and Power in Tudor England* (E. W. Ives, R. J. Knecht and J. J. Scarisbrick, eds, 1978).

Beatrice Shearer is Adult Education Officer in the Diocese of London. She is completing a thesis on 'Demographic Change in London and Middlesex, 1550–1700' at the ESRC Cambridge Group for the History of Population and Social Structure.

Paul Slack is a Fellow and Senior Tutor of Exeter College, Oxford. He has written (with P. Clark) *English Towns in Transition* (1976) and edited (with P. Clark) *Crisis and Order in English Towns* (1972). His *The Impact of Plague in Tudor and Stuart England* is due to appear in 1985.

INTRODUCTION
The significance of the metropolis

A. L. Beier and Roger Finlay

Why should one study the economic and social history of early modern London? The question might seem odd, considering that London was by far England's largest city in the period, and by 1750 the largest in Europe and the fourth largest in the world. The question would certainly have seemed out of place to an earlier generation of historians who believed that towns were uniquely important agents of change in the West. This traditional view, concisely stated in Pirenne's *Medieval Cities* (1925), assigned to urban centres a critical role in the origins of modernity. From the towns, Pirenne argued, there emanated the commercial practices and spirit that undermined feudalism and gave rise to capitalist economies. From the same source came modern political forms, including democratic and bureaucratic systems of government, and the new ideologies of civic humanism and Machiavellianism.[1] As the homes of bishoprics and the universities, the towns were also religious, professional and cultural centres. They played a crucial role in Renaissance culture, and were leading lights in the Reformation.[2]

But while the concentration of great numbers in one place makes a town, scholars no longer accept that it explains history. For instance, some now think that serfdom declined mainly because of dysfunctions within traditional medieval society rather than because of the influence of towns, and that the origins of capitalism lay in the rural as much as in the urban sector. If anything, great cities like London were conspicuous by their absence at the coming of the industrial revolution.[3] Urban historians also question whether pre-modern towns were the birthplaces of democracy. They have found that late medieval and early modern towns were often run by oligarchies, when not by local lords.[4] Nor can bourgeois social and cultural pre-eminence be assumed any longer. In Braudel's view urban patriciates committed 'the treason of the bourgeoisie' in allying themselves socially and politically with the landed classes rather than pursuing their own class interests.[5] Renaissance culture, moreover, was not purely bourgeois: from around 1500 it became distinctly aristocratic and courtly in tone.[6] Finally, behind the glitter, Pirenne's brave new urban world was often tarnished with social problems, including vagrancy, disease and class hatred.[7]

The most significant critique of the importance of towns is Philip Abrams's contribution to the collection *Towns in Societies* (1978).[8] Abrams questioned the whole concept of the city, on the grounds that sociological theory and historical research had failed to demonstrate the unique historical role of towns: instead of making a case most writers had simply assumed that urbanism was a special historical phenomenon, while those that had attempted to develop an urban typology had produced either broad, empirically suspect distinctions such as pre-industrial and industrial, or monographs lacking conceptual awareness and rigour. The way out of the impasse, Abrams argued, lay in rejecting the assumption that cities were special social entities and instead in examining them in their historical context.

The case of early modern London confirms that lumping towns together is an unsatisfactory way to proceed. London was, in fact, quite different from other cities. Within the British Isles, no town remotely approached it in size or importance: London alone accounted for half the increase in England's urban population between 1500 and 1700.[9] And while there were continental counterparts to the English metropolis, none of these grew as fast as London did, and most, unlike London, slumped in the seventeenth century (see Fig. 1).

It is also the case that many of the changes traditionally associated with urbanization were not solely the result of urban expansion in England. Capitalistic methods of production in agriculture and industry have been shown to have been as much rural as urban in origin. Population growth, migration, and disease mortality – all admittedly very high in London – are to be found in many other parts of the country. Similarly, although the growth of domestic and foreign trade is most striking with respect to London, it also affected much of the rest of England, particularly in the seventeenth century.[10]

Having rejected notions that London's development was typical or unique, we may raise specific historical questions about the metropolis and its phenomenal growth in the period. For by the standards of the day, as Fig. 1 shows (opposite), London's growth was remarkable. The new population figures provided by Roger Finlay and Beatrice Shearer in Chapter One suggest that it grew from a middling city of 120,000 in 1550, to 200,000 in 1600, 375,000 in 1650, 490,000 in 1700, and to

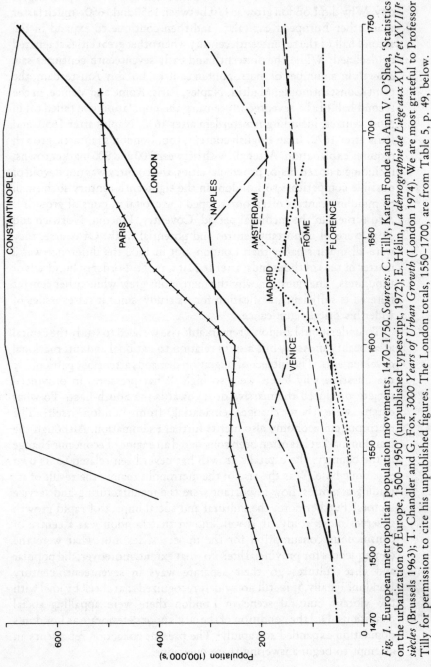

Fig. 1. European metropolitan population movements, 1470–1750. *Sources:* C. Tilly, Karen Fonde and Ann V. O'Shea, 'Statistics on the urbanization of Europe, 1500–1950' (unpublished typescript, 1972); E. Hélin, *La démographie de Liège aux XVIIe et XVIIIe siècles* (Brussels 1963); T. Chandler and G. Fox, *3000 Years of Urban Growth* (London 1974). We are most grateful to Professor Tilly for permission to cite his unpublished figures. The London totals, 1550–1700, are from Table 5, p. 49, below.

675,000 in 1750, when it surpassed Constantinople as Europe's largest city. Why did London grow so fast between 1550 and 1650 – much faster than other European capitals – and then continue to expand in the second half of the seventeenth century when other great cities stagnated or declined? While the sixteenth and early seventeenth centuries saw growth in a number of metropolitan centres, notably Amsterdam, the giant Constantinople, Madrid, Naples, Paris, Rome and Venice, in the second half of the seventeenth century the population rise tailed off in most centres, including Amsterdam after 1630, Naples after 1650, and Paris after 1670. In an English context, too, London's fantastic growth requires explanation. After all, with between 700 and 800 market towns, including a dozen major provincial cities, the country was not devoid of possible competitors to London. In the eighteenth century such small to middling centres often outstripped the capital in rates of growth.[11] And earlier, in the medieval period, Coventry, Lincoln, Norwich and York were all important centres and potential rivals. Of course, they were all much smaller than London, but in 1500 the difference was a matter of tens of thousands; after 1600 it was of the order of hundreds of thousands. The question why the metropolis grew while other centres faltered is sufficient justification for its study, since it raises issues of wider historical significance.

To understand London's remarkable rise we need to study the capital as a locality in itself, but also in relation to national and international developments. The subject of migration demands attention, particularly the question why levels were so high. What pressures in provincial society produced the massive drift towards the South-East? To what extent were these changes emanating from London itself? The metropolitan economy also merits further examination. Although the London market has often been considered an engine of economic change in the country, the capital's growth has never been related to its own economic base. Was the rise of the metropolis mainly the result of its trading activities; how important were the manufacturing and service sectors? Furthermore, the cultural and social impact of rapid growth deserves more study. It is well known that London was a centre of conspicuous consumption for the upper classes, but what were the consequences for provincial life? To what extent, moreover, did popular and élite cultures go their separate ways in seventeenth-century London? Finally, it is still not widely recognized that cheek by jowl with the vibrant cultural scene in London there were appalling social conditions. Did the condition of the city's poor deteriorate as London's population expanded so rapidly? The present collection represents an attempt to begin answering these questions.

I

London life 300 years ago was quite different from anything known in England today. Its immense growth occurred against a background of upheaval and limited advance in the national economy, thus demonstrating the social implications of high population density in a pre-industrial setting. Massive urban growth in the absence of factory industrialization might strike an unfamiliar chord, yet by 1650 there was a largely free-market economy in London organized around small manufacturing enterprises. The success of this system in catering for a high level of consumer demand shows that the metropolis had outgrown its traditional gild structures. Now there were few limits to the market economy apart from Government fiscal policy.[12] Thus the loosening of restrictions and attitudes geared to consumption and production considerably predated the industrial revolution.[13] The present Introduction explores some of the reasons for these changes; above all, the processes of political and economic centralization.

But early modern urban growth in the case of London was by no means a story of unimpeded progress. The pattern of work was irregular and subject to crises caused by epidemics, wars and trade depressions. The poverty of many inhabitants was so great that 'leisure' was frequently a norm rather than a preference. Their experience contrasted sharply with the quite phenomenal wealth of the fortunate few, the great merchants and members of the aristocracy. There were immense problems of child care, health, broken marriages, alien immigration, and ageing. Even the wealthy experienced some of these vicissitudes of London life. The authorities had to attempt to deal with these conditions, which were so serious as to make the metropolis totally foreign to the modern eye. It is within that paradox that much of the fascination of London history lies.

It is a surprising fact that, despite London's national and international importance and the questions surrounding its development in the period, it has not inspired the new generation of urban historians. This neglect is not peculiar to English historiography, for full-length studies of continental capitals are also few. Some aspects of London history have, of course, been examined. The capital's economic significance, above all, has been demonstrated: the role of its market in stimulating agricultural and industrial changes; its importance in shaping the course of overseas trade and as a centre of consumption for the privileged classes; and its centrality for the nascent professions. In addition, several writers have produced pioneering studies of London's topography and housing; others have immeasurably improved our knowledge of the merchant community; and still others have shown the capital's dominant position in influencing the course of the Great Rebellion.[14] But it is still the case that little work has been undertaken on the causes of London's phenomenal rise, compared with the attention given to its consequences.

Two main explanations have been advanced for the relative dearth of the literature on London. One is the sheer size of the metropolis, which may have been offputting to scholars. Yet there is no shortage of works on regions containing a similar-sized population. The other is a suggested inadequacy of source materials. As the chapters in this volume indicate, however, the kinds of records used in studies of provincial England also exist for London. There are some variations due to differences in institutional structures, but the size of London means that its archives are in general correspondingly richer. Its corporation, gild and parish records all represent outstanding collections for the study of metropolitan history. Like most other localities, it is also represented in central government sources – indeed exceptionally well represented, because of the strong links between the city and the Government. Thus the reasons usually given for the lack of work on the capital do not stand up to scrutiny.

One possible reason for London's comparative neglect has been the tendency towards a 'total' approach in local historical studies, which requires that all possible aspects of a community's existence be analysed. This would clearly be a daunting task in London's case. But if we cease to regard the city as a reified totality, then the need to document all features of its life becomes less pressing.[15] This collection attempts to be comprehensive by covering major themes and questions, but its main purpose is to bring together important new work on the subject. From the outset it was decided to eschew reprinting published work, valuable as it might be. So as well as being original to this volume, these essays convey the result of current work. As essays, they also aim to indicate possible directions for future research.

For convenience, the subject has been divided into three main parts. The first describes the enormous growth of London's population, showing that by 1700 the city had become quite unrecognizable from its counterpart of two centuries earlier. This section also focuses on the signal role of disease and mortality in demographic change. The second analyses the economic changes that made possible London's expansion, emphasizing the importance of developments in the metropolis itself as well as in wider economic spheres. The third consists of case studies of social conditions in London, paying special attention to the ways that pre-industrial metropolitan society evolved after 1660. These essays demonstrate that social problems persisted, however the capital was administered, and consider some of the ways that urban society adapted to external changes.

Some topics receive limited attention in this volume because they have been comparatively well covered elsewhere. This category includes topography, merchants, the gilds, financial and legal institutions, fiscal and other Government policies, and popular culture.[16] The political and administrative aspect deserves a separate volume by itself, and is a subject which has been more thoroughly examined than most others in metropolitan historiography.[17] It has proved impossible to secure papers on some topics, such as the role of the gentry, education and schooling, the position of women, public order and crime, housing, and religion.[18] These omissions (and the list is far from complete) indicate many subjects deserving further research, which would enhance, and perhaps modify some of the preliminary conclusions presented here.

II

An outline of the growth of London must begin with a reassessment of N. Brett-James's *Growth of Stuart London* (1935), to which all subsequent studies owe a great debt.[19] The core of the book consists of cartographic reconstructions of the city in 1603, 1658 and 1708. These provide the basis for maps illustrating the expansion of the metropolis, which have been reprinted and redrawn many times.[20] How far they accurately capture the course of London's growth, however, is open to question. The latter two maps probably reflect the capital's size fairly well, for they were based on fresh surveys leading to the contemporary engravings by Faithorne and Newcourt published in 1658 and by Hatton in 1708. The dating of the map usually ascribed to 1603 is more controversial. This was based on Stow's *Survey of London*, which was reprinted that year, but it is now thought that London was surveyed only once before 1640, which resulted in the copper engravings from *c*. 1553–9; all subsequent maps of the period are considered to have been based on this survey.[21] It may also plausibly be argued that Stow was essentially an antiquarian: while his best-known work on London appeared just a few years before his death in 1605, his descriptions are mixed with reminiscences about the city of his youth half a century earlier.[22]

The enlargement of the metropolis in the second half of the sixteenth century still has to be adequately described. The dissolution of the monasteries brought about a massive increase in buildings and land, but the extent of the townscape does not appear to have expanded until around 1580.[23] Then it was rapidly extended despite government efforts to halt it.[24] Michael Power's study of the 1660s demonstrates the social effects of rapid growth. It shows how contrasts existed between various parts of London as wealthier citizens tended to inhabit the centre of the city and the poor lived in the suburban parishes. He also finds that householders with higher-status occupations possessed more hearths, which suggests larger houses with main street frontages. Both wealth and occupational zoning were prominent in the central parishes, although the poor were by no means absent from these areas. Thus the tremendous extension of the capital accelerated residential patterns of an earlier date without fundamentally altering them.

Demographic trends are perhaps the best available indicator of London's growth. The relative uniformity of the source materials means that population studies are not subject to many of the inconsistencies of topographic history. The expansion of the area within which the municipality collected the bills of mortality corresponded very closely, moreover, to the extent of the metropolis as defined by its distinctively high levels of fertility and mortality. Roger Finlay and Beatrice Shearer present new figures on the growth of population from 1560 onwards, which they reconstructed from information derived from parish registers and from various surveys of numbers of households and communicants extant for almost the whole city. They show that while population grew continually London's expansion was by no means uniform, and demonstrate how the 'incipient divorce of City and metropolis' took place from the seventeenth century.[25] In particular, the central area of the city within and without the Walls maintained fairly constant numbers, while London as a whole increased four-fold in population. This was entirely due to the growth of the suburbs, which mushroomed relative to the city itself. Differential rates of growth between the various suburban areas have also been found. It is often assumed that migration from the City centre to the suburbs accompanied upward social mobility, yet the reverse was nearer the truth in early modern London. New migrants to London generally settled first in the suburbs, which consisted of highly variegated communities and made the metropolis by 1700 a vast conurbation. The expansion of the eastern suburbs was particularly awesome, rising fourteen-fold between 1560 and 1680, but growth was also sharp elsewhere.

Mortality was the principal motor of demographic trends throughout London. Death rates in early modern England were directly related to settlement size, and the population was continually unable to replace itself in a great urban area. Unsanitary conditions meant that disease was both endemic and epidemic. The most dramatic was plague. Paul Slack's chapter draws attention to the intensity of the five major outbreaks from 1563 to 1665, each of which claimed about a fifth of the population, and to the city's failure to check their spread. He also shows how Londoners reacted to the crisis conditions and how their social position influenced their responses. Even in the absence of epidemics, disease pervaded the metropolis, so that mortality rates did not fall after the disappearance of plague. Margaret Pelling's essay examines Londoners' reactions to such conditions, focusing particularly on the problem of sexual diseases and the role of barber-surgeons in treating them. These afflictions hit all social groups, a shared social experience that contrasted sharply with the great differences between rich and poor in wealth, housing and expectation of life.

Short-term demographic fluctuations therefore had a huge effect on both the overall size of the metropolis and the living conditions of Londoners. Yet the city grew rather than declined in numbers, and its crises were of temporary duration. This remarkable ability to recover was due to two principal features of London demography. First, the single population was exceptionally large, so that in all but the very worst periods surplus labour was available to continue the functioning of the metropolis. Secondly, immigration was phenomenally high and made up for the high mortality levels, which the remarkably high marital fertility levels in the capital did not entirely counter, because the married population was relatively small.[26]

It is difficult to put a precise figure on the total numbers of immigrants. A minimum estimate of 8,000 a year has been suggested for the period from 1650 to 1750, and John Graunt's total *c*.1650 was 6,000 a year. The minimum total proposed here is derived from burial and baptismal figures for 1604–59, which showed an average annual deficit of 3,500. If, as Finlay and Shearer suggest, London's population grew from 200,000 in 1600 to 375,000 in 1650, the mortality deficit required at least 7,000 persons to come and settle in that interval, which is nearly as high as the estimate for 1650–1750. In reality, of course, many more descended upon London who were not recorded because they did not die in the capital. This floating population, which included rich and poor at a time of high rates of migration, might increase the total by as much as 50 per cent to some 10,000 a year.[27] But to gauge the full impact of immigration to London we should attempt to calculate, as Wrigley did for the later period, what proportion of the nation's surplus birth-rate was absorbed by the capital. Between 1600 and 1650 the proportion was nearly half – 48 per cent, if it is assumed, as for the later period, that the 7,000 immigrants represented survivors of a birth population which can be estimated to have been at least half as large again, that is 10,500, and that the total of births in the country outside London ran at about 22,000 a year. London evidently exerted a tremendous pull on migrants from an early date.[28]

Among those who came in large numbers were apprentices. Their experience in the later seventeenth century is examined by Malcolm Kitch as a case study of one group of migrants to London.[29] He shows how apprentices were recruited from a reduced area of the country, yet the overall numbers of immigrants increased in proportion to its growth in population. People were pushed to London as well as pulled. A growing national population in the sixteenth and early seventeenth centuries was accompanied in many places by a falling standard of living, so that people left to seek livelihoods in the capital. In turn, London's growing demand for food encouraged agrarian improvements, which once again pushed surplus labour out of advanced farming regions to London.

Population trends in London therefore differed markedly from the rest of England. It is generally agreed that marriage was the key element in the demography of pre-industrial England: late marriage and large single populations enabled fertility to be kept below its maximum level. Since most raw materials were agrarian in origin and the capacity of the land for improvement was limited, production could only be slowly expanded, whereas the potential for population increase was infinitely greater. Population trends were consequently of major significance. Fortunately, late marriage held numbers in check and prevented the occurrence of subsistence crises, which persisted in France into the eighteenth century.[30] The London demographic pattern was a complete reversal of what occurred elsewhere in England, but both patterns were differing responses to the same underlying social framework. Mortality was the principal determinant in the case of London, whose growth depended on a steady flow of migrants.[31] Conversely, the capital's demand for migrants acted as a safety valve to counteract excess fertility in the provinces. But London's growth cannot be explained by reference to demographic factors alone. Above all, we must consider who migrants were and what brought them to the metropolis.

III

London's massive growth in the sixteenth and seventeenth centuries took place mainly because of two developments which encouraged migration: first, the centralization in London of the nation's political and economic life, which is discussed at some length in this section; and secondly, upheavals in the provincial economies, including the agrarian changes and urban crises mentioned above, which are briefly considered. In experiencing both changes simultaneously, England was peculiar. Political centralization in great capitals was a common feature of early modern urban life – Madrid and Paris are notable examples – and economic crises were frequent in the villages and towns of pre-industrial Europe. But in no other country were the two processes so potently and strikingly combined, apart possibly from Holland where protracted warfare created exceptional conditions. The result for London was extraordinary growth, which by 1650 may have put England near the head of the urbanized league in Europe.[32]

Is it possible to overemphasise the importance of political centralization in the growth of London? It would appear not, since generations of historians have connected the rise of the modern capital with its political role.[33] As early as 1527 the Government itself was aware of London's political significance, remarking in a proclamation that it 'is a populous city ... by reason of the laws there being ministered'.[34] Yet in spite of the unanimity of opinion, how centralization worked in practice and how important it was in the capital's expansion compared with, say, overseas trade are unexamined questions. We know that the landed upper classes increasingly resorted to London for business and pleasure, but the precise dimensions of the influx have not been documented, nor its economic consequences.

The direct influence of Government upon London's growth has probably been overstated. The sharpest increase in the capital's population came between 1580 and 1640, yet the size of the central Government appears to have altered little in this period. The number of Elizabethan officials of gentry rank and above has been worked out at just over 400, and the Government of Charles I had roughly the same numbers resident in Whitehall.[35] We have no figures for lesser clerks employed in the various departments under Elizabeth, but under Charles I they were not much more numerous than higher officials. Admittedly major officers of state like the Cecils kept private secretaries in their households, who also worked on Government business, but even if they raised the total by half as much again it would still not have involved more than 1,500 persons. The decisive period of expansion in the civil service came after 1650 and especially 1680; by 1725, it has been estimated, there were 2,700 career officials in London.[36] This increase undoubtedly helped sustain the capital's growth when others on the Continent were faltering. However, even using a multiplier of ten to allow for family and servants, the resulting total of 27,000 would only account for five and a half per cent of a total population of 490,000. The simple size of the Government, therefore, was insufficient to be considered a decisive factor in metropolitan growth.

Far more important numerically than full-time officials were those who followed in their wake. With royal government came the Court, which was considerably larger than the civil service for much of the period and which grew substantially. From about 1,000 in the reign of Elizabeth the monarch's household and entourage increased to 2,600 under Charles I, declining to just 950 by the early eighteenth century.[37] The numbers of peers living in London on a quasi-permanent basis rose by a similar margin from about 30 in the 1560s to 90 in the 1630s; by then, it is thought, the numbers of resident gentlemen ran to several hundred. Many of them attended the Inns of Court, which saw a five-fold rise in admissions between 1550 and 1650 and which housed perhaps 1,000 members in term time: 'a vast increase since Fortescue's day' in the mid-fifteenth century.[38] Finally, the numbers of MPs are estimated to have risen from 300 in the early sixteenth century to 500 by the mid-seventeenth. Even if Parliament met infrequently during most of the period, these gatherings were drawing rising numbers. After 1640, of course, meetings were more frequent and longer.[39] There was obviously some overlap between these groups of Government-related immigrants, but the total must still have involved several thousand people.

The origins of the landed classes' invasion of London were manifold. From Edward IV's reign the Court was almost permanently there or in the Home Counties, whereas in the High Middle Ages it had led a nomadic existence, tramping around the realm. To the Court came the peerage and upper gentry to seek favour and office.[40] Legal affairs also drew them; Westminster had long been the country's judicial centre, but the sixteenth and early seventeenth centuries witnessed a huge increase in legal business. The profits and prestige of land made it a precious commodity to be fought over when the national land market was vastly increased by the sale of church and crown lands between 1540 and 1660. In these matters, all roads led to London, where sales commonly took place and where the royal courts with ultimate jurisdiction in land disputes were located. The same desire for land drew the aristocracy to the monarch's Court, as did the possibility of a profitable office, patent, or monopoly.[41] The meetings of Parliament were now almost always at Westminster. This had been the case, too, in Edward III's reign, but the fifteenth century had seen something of a return to the earlier medieval practice of provincial assemblies. From Edward IV's reign, however, Parliament rarely met outside the metropolis.[42]

Political centralization had a number of important results for London. First, the influx of the landed classes boosted the city's population. At the beginning of the seventeenth century, a minimum of 750 upper-class young men were coming each year to be apprenticed and to frequent the Inns of Court; that was over a tenth of the annual immigration level necessary for the city's growth. In reality, upper-class movement into the capital, even though much of it was on a temporary basis, was probably two or three times higher. The peers alone, if they kept just 20 persons in their households (Gregory King reckoned on 40), might account for 1,800.[43] Secondly, this landed incursion inspired a great rebuilding in London. In Westminster the palace of Whitehall and its precincts, which Henry VIII took from Wolsey, were greatly extended from the latter part of the reign. Like the king, the nobility took over other bishops' palaces after the Reformation, which they transformed into personal residences. They also involved themselves in building for speculative and personal uses in the West End. The Inns of Court, too, were rebuilt and extended because of the gentry's demand for accommodation.[44] Thirdly, the centralization of Court and political life stimulated consumption. Historians have usually focused on conspicuous expenditure on expensive luxury goods and services, but it seems obvious that upper-class immigrants must also have generated considerable demand for the kinds of goods and services required by ordinary mortals. Seventeenth-century London was a huge consumer, as the chapter by John Chartres demonstrates, and the upper classes were undoubtedly significant spenders in this market.

The greatest difficulty is to estimate how much the centralization of political life meant to the metropolis in terms of cash. We shall probably never have a precise figure, but we can at least attempt to measure its order of magnitude and how much it was increasing. It has been shown that in the 1630s the crown was paying about £600,000 a year to the holders of high offices and privileges. Now this was a substantial sum, roughly equivalent to the official value of all London's exports handled by English merchants, shortcloths excepted, in 1640.[45] Admittedly the profits of office would not all have gone into the London economy, but a substantial part of them probably did, because the recipients were resident there for much of the year. In addition, the crown was spending a further £300,000 a year under Charles I for such items as household and wardrobe costs, much of which again flowed into the metropolitan economy. The government's contribution to the economy was therefore substantial, even if it did not outstrip the value of foreign trade, as has been claimed for a later date.[46] It also rose dramatically in the period, particularly in the case of office-holders. Towards the end of Henry VII's reign, the Exchequer was paying out about £10,000 a year in fees and annuities, not including those in the Household and Wardrobe. But even including all the expenses of those departments, annual expenditure did not surpass £25,000. Under Charles I, the cost of offices alone, leaving out the Household and Wardrobe, was £340,000 to £360,000 per annum or nearly 15 times more than in Henry VII's day and far surpassing the rate of price inflation. Most of it went to gentleman office-holders.[47]

It is doubtful whether political centralization alone accounts for London's growth in early modern times. Rather it was the combination of the political and mercantile roles that made the metropolis tick. It has been pertinently observed that London was almost unique in Europe in combining the role of capital city and great port. This combination in fact dated from the High Middle Ages, if not earlier, but it was intensified in the sixteenth and seventeenth centuries. London was able to play its dual role partly because the social climate was favourable. Although differences clearly existed between landed and monied interests in the capital, they were insignificant compared with many European cities and did not inhibit the developments of important links between merchant and gentry communities. In practice, the two shared the benches of the House of Commons, intermarried and because of primogeniture, younger sons went into trade. The landed classes also joined the merchants in supporting joint-stock trading schemes.[48]

The counterpart to political centralization was a remarkable increase of economic centralization. The crucial element in this development was London's domination of England's cloth export trade from the early sixteenth century. This change and the centralizing tendency in Government were the *sine qua non* in the making of the metropolis. As one authority has stated: 'London owed its economic ebullience and its aldermen their wealth to virtually one thing only – the English woollen cloth traffic'.[49] The rising metropolitan dominance in the cloth industry was of recent origin. When the export of woollen cloth supplanted the trade of raw wool to the Continent in the fifteenth century, Londoners came to the fore: in the early years of the sixteenth century, London's cloth exports accounted for 43 per cent of the country's total woollen exports; by the mid-1540s, its share had doubled to 86 per cent.[50]

The centralization of the English cloth trade in London had wide ramifications. It spelt difficulties for provincial outports such as Southampton and possibly exacerbated the malaise of inland towns such as Coventry because of Londoners' ready access to Low Countries' markets.[51] But more positively, it unquestionably stimulated London's economy and migration to the capital. As with the centralization of Government, the direct impact of the trade was limited, since it was in the hands of a small number of Merchant Adventurers – about 100 in the mid-sixteenth century – and involved limited numbers in actual production. But the spin-offs of London's quasi-monopoly were considerable. As this was a period of price inflation, merchants had to invest their money, which in turn, assuming intelligent investments, generated economic activity. More research is necessary to gauge precisely the channels into which the profits of trade flowed, but some of the directions are clear. Manufacturing was one outlet for capital. Thomas Myddleton began his career as an Elizabethan trader, but soon set up a sugar refinery in Mincing Lane. Similarly, Thomas Cullum, although a draper, was involved in financing a dyeing business in Jacobean London.[52]

Of course, not all great London entrepreneurs went in for manufacturing – Lionel Cranfield is a good case in point – but enough did to generate the expansion of a number of industries, as the chapter by Lee Beier on occupations demonstrates. This development is also reflected in the incorporation of a number of new craft gilds, increased membership in established ones, and the spread of production in the suburbs. These changes in turn attracted migrants. Thousands came to take up apprenticeships, and they came in increasing numbers. In the early 1550s the annual total was about 1,500; by 1600 it was between 4,000 and 5,000, a level that was maintained for most of the seventeenth century.[53] In addition, the population burgeoned and manufacturing flourished in the large northern and eastern extra-mural parishes, where apprenticeship was laxly enforced.

The profits of trade also flowed westwards to the landed élites and to Whitehall. The merchants were partly responsible for financing the conspicuous expenditure of the aristocracy through loans and pawnbroking.[54] But above all the great merchants involved themselves in Government finance. This liaison between merchant and monarch dates from the fourteenth century, if not earlier, but it became particularly close from the reign of Edward IV, who 'courted, honoured, flattered and rewarded leading London merchants more assiduously than any king before him', and cajoled them to invest in his Government.[55] Thereafter, with the possible exception of the war period of the 1540s, Governments relied substantially upon London merchants for loans, who in return received profitable jobs as revenue-farmers, patentees and monopolists. Even the revolutionary regimes of the 1640s and 1650s turned to city merchants to run the Excise and victual the Navy.[56]

The marriage was evidently a convenient one for both parties. Just how desperately each partner needed the other is suggested by the consequences when the two fell out under the early Stuarts: in 1642 the monarchy lost its power base in London and was eventually overthrown; while the great merchants, having lost their royal support, were soon overturned in city politics.[57] For a century or more, however, this connection had significantly augmented the centralization of political and economic life in London and undoubtedly contributed to the city's growth. The significance of the link between government and city is shown by how quickly it was restored after 1642 and how prominent it remained for centuries.

The trade of London evolved significantly in the seventeenth century, and its general buoyancy, despite numerous slumps, helped to sustain the city's growth when many European rivals were falling by the wayside. Paradoxically, as Brian Dietz argues in his essay, the contribution of overseas trade declined in relative significance as the metropolitan economy became more complex. Internal trade, as Chartres shows, gradually increased in importance to fuel London's continuing expansion. From the 1570s the Antwerp axis was broken, and merchants began to seek new markets in the Mediterranean and further afield. In the next century the gains in these areas made up for the almost permanent depression in the traditional cloth trade to northern Europe between 1614 and 1660.[58] Until 1690 there was what has been described as 'a great period of mercantile achievement', including significant expansion in the Mediterranean and the Americas, and the establishment of a foothold in India. The result at home was a diversification in the merchant community, in which gild membership ceased to be a prerequisite for success; and with respect to Government, the beginnings of 'Revolution Finance'.[59]

Diversification was also the pattern in metropolitan manufacturing. By the second half of the seventeenth century London had become the hub of the English economy, aided by improving transport facilities and by a high level of local demand. The London market had major repercussions throughout the economy, but also in the metropolis itself. In the chapter on occupations Beier argues that manufacturing came to assume major importance in London, particularly in the rapidly expanding suburbs. As the gilds failed to enforce their theoretical authority beyond the city walls, individual artisans set up there and hired journeymen. This far more laissez-faire system of labour gradually replaced the master and apprentice relationship as the dominant form of labour organization. Although the expansion of manufacturing involved the innovation of many new products, production processes were not mechanized in an 'industrial revolution'. The size and buoyancy of the London market arguably made cost-cutting of this kind unnecessary for the time being. More immediately, the extension of the capital's manufacturing base must have provided jobs for thousands of immigrants.

Migrants were also attracted to London by the wages there, which, as Chartres shows, were as much as 50 per cent higher than provincial ones in the seventeenth century. There are even signs of a popular belief that the city's streets were paved with gold for the immigrant.[60] But besides those who envisaged a move to London as a means of bettering themselves, there were others who were driven there by poverty. In the countryside the growth of capitalist agriculture and rising population levels caused migration. Towns, too, experienced increased numbers and had sluggish economies for much of the period. London itself, ironically, was partly to blame for the upheavals in the provinces, as Clement Armstrong observed in the 1530s. Her merchants, as successful traders of woollens, fostered sheep and wool production, and thus the engrossing and enclosure which led to depopulation. They also took trade from the outports, and themselves bought up land and attempted to maximize their returns in the manner of other improving landlords.[61] Nevertheless, despite Armstrong's strictures, London alone was not responsible for agrarian capitalism, for the process preceded the capital's major period of growth after 1580. It seems there was sufficient insecurity and poverty in provincial England to ensure a steady stream of migrants to London.

IV

Although London prospered in comparison with the rest of the country, the benefits of growth were inequitably distributed among Londoners. Immigration was so high that it had serious social consequences, which the municipality contained with great difficulty.

Unfortunately we are unlikely ever to be able to generalize about whether London as a whole was stable or unstable, growing richer or poorer. The city encompassed too many disparate communities and suitable evidence is too scarce to support such broad conclusions. At any rate, debates between optimists and pessimists, when not inconclusive, often prove to be irrelevant. In focusing upon such issues as the hypothetical 'wage-rates of hypothetical average workers', they provide only indirect evidence of poverty and ignore questions of the quality of people's lives and their perceptions of themselves.[62]

Such hard evidence of poverty as does survive suggests that it was a growing problem. An official survey in Edward VI's reign showed 650 city householders in need, while another census in 1598 had 2,196 in poverty. This was more than a three-fold increase in a period when the city's population rose by only a quarter. The local poor were extremely vulnerable to harvest failures. When bread prices rocketed in 1596, the number of households requiring relief jumped to 4,132 – more than six times the Edwardian total. These figures, it is worth noting, cover mainly well-off intra-mural parishes; had information for the suburbs been available, the totals would be even more depressing.[63] Vagrancy increased still faster, rising 12-fold from 1560 to 1625, a period in which metropolitan population only quadrupled.[64] On this evidence, it seems beyond dispute that poverty was growing faster than the population of London.

There is certainly massive evidence of concern about poverty in the capital among the learned and articulate, from the 'Commonwealth' writers and preachers of the early Tudor period through the Interregnum reformers such as Samuel Hartlib. The preoccupation of City and central governments with poverty seemed never to cease, as even a casual examination of the Journals of the Common Council and the Repertories of the Court of Aldermen will abundantly show. It is true that the poor never engineered major uprisings in London, but did they in any other early modern cities, apart from the exceptional cases of Münster in 1534 and Romans in 1580? Simply because the poor did not seize power or threaten to do so should not be taken to signify that the relief and control of the poor were not serious problems. Indeed, as will be shown, major cities such as London developed institutions precisely to ensure that poverty did not lead to unrest.

Destitution in London had many causes, which were aggravated by the city's growth. Naturally not all the thousands of immigrants found and kept secure niches. Some children were simply dumped by carriers who brought them to the capital after accepting fees from their home parishes. Those who found positions in service and apprenticeship were more secure, but even these situations were subject to a host of vicissitudes that resulted in vagrancy. The casual labour working in the expanding manufactures is poorly documented, but in all probability its livelihood was even more insecure. Fixed capital investment was nearly negligible in what was often domestic production, and entrepreneurs escaped the worst effects of trade slumps by employing less labour. Depressions were caused by poor harvests, foreign wars and monetary fluctuations, and of course plague epidemics. In fact epidemics probably caused greater social dislocation than economic crises; they especially affected the single population, many of whom were recent immigrants. The generally high mortality levels, which outstripped births in the first half of the seventeenth century *even ignoring plague epidemics*, in turn reflected appalling conditions of housing and sanitation.[65]

Many new strategies were developed to contain poverty. Perhaps the most important was the determination to maintain food supplies. That government intervention and municipal initiatives in this area were successful is suggested by the absence of major grain riots in the capital.[66] Another method of dealing with the poor was to incarcerate vagrants and to send them abroad to foreign wars and the colonies.[67] As the size of the conurbation increased, so did the relative significance of public rather than private provision. There are essentially two themes to the history of public assistance for the metropolitan poor. The first consisted of relief administered by the vestries, including a system whereby the wealthier central parishes assisted their poorer neighbours mainly located adjacent to the City Walls.[68] The second dated from the foundation of the five hospitals in the 1550s and involved institutionalizing the poor, an innovation that was revived a century later and yet again in the 1690s.[69] The immensity of the poverty problem and the inability of the municipality to extend its effective control over parochial affairs meant that the workhouse was never fully successful in the early modern metropolis. Stephen Macfarlane's chapter provides a detailed examination of the obstacles that would-be reformers met in this area in the later Stuart metropolis.

The character of charity evolved significantly in early modern London. In pre-Reformation times 'living in charity' was a social and religious ideal that affected many aspects of daily life. The level of giving to the poor increased substantially in the sixteenth century, although in time its impact diminished as poor rates rose. The extent of conflict between 'private' and 'public' relief has possibly been exaggerated.[70] The role of private benefactors was changing from a personal desire to be of assistance, often through bequests willed at death, to participating in the affairs of independent institutions. In reality, however, they also attempted to persuade the municipality to organize relief, and when this policy failed individual philanthropists provided greater support for their own schemes. As Macfarlane suggests in his essay on a later period, the major problems were over who should organize relief rather than how it should be done. The employment of the able-bodied poor, arguably the major innovation in thinking about relief, failed despite the foundation of Bridewell and later institutions for the purpose.

It is hard to decide how far new cultural forms were connected with the unique development of London, or alternatively the extent to which they were emerging features of pre-industrial England generally. It is also difficult to analyse individual reactions to conditions that are imperfectly understood. Certainly it should be stressed how greatly early modern London contrasted with its present-day counterpart. Nevertheless, it seems fair to think that many Londoners might have experienced feelings of alienation, a much over-worked but relevant concept. Almost everyone was a migrant; the operation of the labour market, together with child-care by nurses, meant that many people lacked family ties or any sense of belonging. Relatively poor communications made it very difficult to keep in touch with relatives; there was no Post Office until the later seventeenth century. In periods of peak alien immigration, language and dialect problems would also have been encountered. All this provided the conditions for a sense of isolation and insecurity with possible psychosocial effects.

In some measure civic and parochial institutions filled the vacuum. The systems of service and apprenticeship provided a stabilizing environment in which migrant youths received moral and religious guidance, as well as practical training. The gilds provided fellowship to the freeman during his working life and some security to him and his family in old age. In addition, there was the Church. In pre-Reformation London 'religious services and religious oaths marked the rites of passage in civic life', and religious fraternities proliferated.[71] However, whether the unity created by religion survived the Reformation appears doubtful. Civic pageantry developed from 1558 on an unprecedented scale, based on the principle that 'the public must be fed with shows'.[72] No doubt, civic office, the widely held freedom, and parochial and wardmote office all bolstered feelings of solidarity among those holding or aspiring to hold them. But it appears questionable whether these institutions alone could have stilled the anxieties of newcomers. As we have seen, service and apprenticeship were temporary, fragile relationships. In any case, by the early seventeenth century a minority of London's workers lived with masters, and the proportion fell as the century wore on. Moreover, if the freedom and office-holding were widespread in City parishes, what of the suburbs, those vast expanding places where, Graunt wrote, 'many vicious persons get liberty to live as they please, for want of some heedful eye'?[73] Office-holders and freemen were few in these lawless parts; the sense of community, at least in the City sense, sorely lacking and limited to the select vestries. Instead they were hot-beds of religious dissent and political radicalism by the time of the Civil Wars.[74] Whether the royal entrances and Lord Mayors' shows made much impact in these places seems doubtful.

If a sense of belonging existed in London it was more likely to have arisen through informal contacts and structures than from the formal ones just outlined. Kinship was one important means of keeping in touch: among single female migrants between 1565 and 1644 nearly two-fifths had relatives in the capital; more than a fifth were actually domiciled with kin.[75] Ethnic and provincial connections were also important. It is not wholly certain whether late medieval Dutch, German, and Italian traders lived in their own communities, but certainly the Huguenots, Irish, and Jews did so in the seventeenth century. It is also known that from the 1630s native immigrants hailing from the same shires formed clubs and met to feast and drink. How far one's regional origins affected residential patterns, as they demonstrably did in nineteenth-century Paris, is still unclear. Welshmen congregated in St Mary Somerset in the early seventeenth century, and some East End lodging houses were catering for particular regions and shires by the 1720s, but the extent of such affinities is difficult to determine.[76]

Youth was another ingredient in social solidarity in early modern London. We lack evidence for the exact age-structure of the population, but given the high level of immigration by young people and the importance of service and apprenticeship, adolescents were disproportionately numerous. There are in fact signs of a special youth culture geared to migrants and apprentices. The idealization of Dick Whittington in popular literature dates from Elizabethan times, which is unlikely to be coincidental, since it was then that London began bursting its seams with migrants.[77] Apprentices met regularly for meals and church services, and had their own holiday, Shrove Tuesday. The young men were also prominent in London street-life. Foreign visitors complained of gangs of itinerant youths mobbing them in the capital's thoroughfares, and Bridewell's Court Books show these remarks to be accurate: 70 per cent of those arrested were male, of whom 80 per cent were adolescents.[78]

The alehouse, the brothel and the theatre provided convenient venues for gatherings. It has been shown that the popular drinking house flourished in the late sixteenth and early seventeenth centuries, and nowhere was this truer than London. The alehouse was particularly useful to immigrants, who might find food, drink and shelter there; even loans, work in the house itself, or outside. The alehouse was particularly important in the poor extra-mural wards, where in the mid-seventeenth century one in every six houses might be a drinking establishment, compared to one in 30 or 40 in the wealthier central areas.[79] Brothels were large in number, although how large is unknown. Men had little difficulty finding prostitutes in Elizabethan London. There were high-class establishments like the Holland's Leaguer in Paris Garden, low-class ones in alehouses and private houses, where the mistress acted as bawd for her servants, and many ladies who worked the streets and alleys. Bawdy houses were again especially numerous in the suburbs, on the Bankside – despite their official suppression in 1546 – and on the northern fringes of the metropolis.[80] Like the alehouses, they provided a number of services. They chiefly catered for the sexual needs of a male population that significantly outnumbered females and many of whom, as apprentices, were forbidden to marry until their terms were completed, which usually meant their late 20s.[81] For the females involved there were some obvious purposes to prostitution. It offered shelter and wages in a period when opportunities were contracting for female labour and before demand grew again in domestic industries in the late seventeenth century. The life was probably also a way out to women who fell on hard times or were unmarried mothers. The Southwark authorities saw links between female paupers, unwed mothers, and prostitution, and females were exceptionally numerous among the poor of the borough. The classier type of brothel might provide meals and gambling as well as sex to customers.[82]

Lord Keynes reportedly said that Shakespeare was unthinkable without a commercial theatre, implying that without the London market his talent might not have flourished as it did.[83] Despite its reductionism, this remark makes some sense, for it seems that social life in London was becoming highly commercialized, as one might expect in the commercial centre of the country. Here, because of high immigration, was a considerable market for soothing feelings of *anomie*. The alehouse and the brothel were just two commercialized nexuses of social intercourse. Others included bowling-alleys and greens, tennis courts, taverns, gaming-houses, cockpits, beargardens, barber-shops, and of course theatres. In many of these places one might eat, drink, gamble, meet women, and be entertained.[84] The theatres have attracted most attention because of the fortuitous survival of many plays, but it is by no means clear that they were the most popular places for entertainment. It is unlikely they were serious competitors to alehouses, and in the early 1600s, when bust followed boom, a number were actually converted to such purposes as prize-fighting. It is even doubted whether the plebeian classes were likely to attend the theatres in very large numbers, considering the expense and that performances were usually matinees. The barriers were raised even higher in Charles I's reign with the advent of expensive admission charges in private playhouses.[85] But whether the populace were excluded or not, entertainment in the capital was now clearly on a commercial basis. Gone were the days of the mystery plays, financed by the gilds to teach morality and to glorify God. They survived only in civic pageantry, which glorified the monarchy and the City. Even Court performances largely ceased to coincide with traditional religious festivals in James I's reign.[86]

The effect of the commercialized London theatre upon provincial drama was serious, for the metropolis came to have a virtual monopoly on theatre, as in other things. Professional companies were established with royal and noble patronage, or under licence from the Master of the Revels, and they toured the provinces. Frozen out were unlicensed 'common players' and minstrels, who formerly dominated entertainment in the country and who were now legally vagrants.[87]

London had an impact upon other features of the scientific and literary life of the period. It has been argued that the capital, not the universities, was the centre of the new Baconian mathematical, scientific and medical discoveries. The new learning was propagated at Gresham College in Bishopsgate Street, in the halls of the City Companies, in the Inns of Court, and the Companies' schools. This efflorescence of ideas was probably not particularly élitist, since it was conducted chiefly in English and involved merchants and even artisans.[88] London was noted for its high level of educational achievement. The overall standard of literacy was the highest in the country, with about 70 per cent of men and 20 per cent of women able to sign their names. The great welter of printed sermons and pamphlets that appeared during the Revolution and the chapbooks of the late seventeenth century confirm the impression of exceptional literacy.[89]

Numeracy has received less attention, but the evidence points in the same direction as literacy. The general use of arabic rather than Roman numerals in merchants' accounts and double-entry bookkeeping were both features of the mid-sixteenth century. The accounts of churchwardens and overseers of the poor recorded relief payments in great detail. Literacy and numeracy were arguably the interface between commerce and the social structure: the rising number of small enterprises in the second half of the seventeenth century was mirrored by increasing literacy. Educational attainment was essential for the self-employed, but not for factory work, which is consistent with declining literacy during the industrial revolution.[90]

The potential for discord, which is perhaps intrinsic to education, was fully realized in early modern London. The populace on its own might not have seriously threatened the City and Westminster governments, but the same cannot be said of Londoners generally. First there was genuine controversy about the nature of religious faith and the pattern of worship, dating from the Reformation. The original split between Protestants and Catholics does not appear to have followed occupational or economic lines in London.[91] After the Elizabethan settlement many different kinds of opinion were incorporated within the framework of the established church. Controversies, if not always open, were expressed in the evolution of differences between parishes and were reflected by the hiring of lecturers to supplement incumbents imposed from outside, and in the development of totally separate churches.[92] The result in the mid-seventeenth century was bitter controversy and fragmentation.

Secondly, the precursors of popular political movements may be traced to seventeenth-century London. Contested Parliamentary elections were not uncommon. The City itself had a freeman franchise, meaning that almost half the adult male citizens voted, and scot and lot franchises in Southwark and Westminster were even wider.[93] The issues over which contests were fought in 1614 and 1628 were complex and illustrate the existence of political awareness well before 1640. In local affairs office-holding was a norm rather than an exception in the City itself.[94] Above all, the forging of links between merchants and citizens through the Puritan movement caused London to side with Parliament during the Civil War, a point of enormous significance for its outcome. The municipality's ruling groups were essentially Royalist in sympathy, if only because of their immense financial interest in maintaining the *status quo*. It is unlikely that the ideals of Pym, Hampden, Holles and the other early opponents of the Crown could have been successfully implemented without popular support in London.[95]

V

The significance of London in this period was so great that it is difficult to isolate the capital's history from that of the rest of the country. Scholars have understandably been inclined to examine the impact of metropolitan growth outside London: as a great market responsible for agrarian changes in the countryside; as a motor of national demographic change; as a centre for aristocratic expenditure and pursuit of Court favour, in the context of the 'gentry debate'; and as a factor in the complicated process that resulted in the industrial revolution. These aspects of London's development were undeniably important. By themselves, however, they do not provide a *raison d'être* for the study of metropolitan history unless it can be demonstrated that these processes would not have occurred anyway. As a result, London's significance has received limited recognition, and the impact of growth upon the city itself has not been thoroughly examined. The rise of the capital's population has been taken as given without examining the pace and incidence of the increase as it affected the different parts of the city. It is undeniably true that the outstanding fact of early modern London's history was its extraordinary growth, but we still know little about such major questions as who the migrants were who flocked there.

Similarly, the process of centralization is a relatively neglected, yet significant feature of metropolitan history. Perhaps the phenomenon is of such obvious importance in English history that it hardly merits discussion. But although centralizing tendencies were already striking in the Middle Ages, they appear to have accelerated greatly in the early modern period. The details of the concentration of state power in London require further study. Above all, since there is no reason to consider centralization a natural development, some explanations of the phenomenon are worth seeking. The gathering of economic power in the hands of Londoners was equally remarkable. It is, however, rather better understood, so that perhaps the most interesting questions for new work concern how and when London's near monopoly of foreign trade was broken. How metropolitan trade affected manufacturing in London and elsewhere, especially in questions of investment, is another subject deserving further investigation.

The concept of centralization also applies to the social and cultural spheres. Because of London's special political importance, as well as its extraordinary growth, the city's social problems demanded urgent solutions. Accordingly there were continued efforts to control them, and the city was something of a hot-house in which experiments and failures occurred with some frequency. A similar atmosphere pervaded the cultural life of the capital, because of the city's popularity with the landed upper-classes, and because it secured a quasi-monopoly in the budding entertainment industry.

It remains to consider what might be termed the 64,000 dollar question of seventeenth-century metropolitan history: why did London continue to grow when most of her continental rivals wavered? The question is particularly puzzling because England's rate of population growth did slow down noticeably between 1660 and 1710 in common with many European countries.[96] Detailed consideration of the development of other capitals would be premature, but at least some brief comparisons can be made. *Prima facie* there were good reasons for London's growth to slow down, as it did after 1650, and even to cease, which it did not. After all, its two major assets, the overseas cloth trade and the monarchy, risked disappearing from sight in the mid-century crises. Seen in long-term perspective, however, these threats to the metropolis were less serious than might be thought. While exports to northern and central Europe suffered, expansion was occurring to other areas as has been shown. After the Restoration trade recovered and flourished for much of the rest of the century. Based now more on imports of raw materials and re-exports, it was more likely to create employment opportunities in London.[97] The removal of the King's Court from the capital was obviously a blow, but on the other hand Parliament met more often, and the number of permanent Government officials was probably higher during the Interregnum than before 1642. During the Civil Wars London was never sacked or even subjected to a major siege, and its port was kept open to trade.[98]

Generally it seems that England fared better than many parts of Europe in the long and punishing wars of the seventeenth century. The country experienced civil wars and invasions by the Scots, and itself engaged in foreign adventures in France, Ireland, and the Low Countries. But the cost in money and men, were it precisely calculable, would probably be dwarfed by that paid by the Dutch, Germans, French, Irish, and Spanish.[99] These are important considerations for London, for as the country's wealthiest city it would undoubtedly have paid and paid heavily, as many continental cities did, for the expensive luxury of sustained warfare. But instead of extorting funds from her leading merchants, the English state from 1643 devised new and effective systems of national taxation, including the excise and later the land tax, to spread the burden.

Finally, London continued to grow because of fundamental economic changes that set it apart from many European capitals, including its nearest rival Paris. The City's gilds ceased from about the mid-seventeenth century to be able or willing to enforce their restrictions upon trading and manufacturing, which was a complete contrast to the situation in the French capital and to many Italian cities.[100] In addition, English agriculture was sufficiently productive to feed a growing capital city, which was not the case in France under Louis XIV, where 'Parisians still lived absolutely under the laws of Malthus'.[101] And because of the ongoing commercialization of agriculture in England, the involuntary departures from the land provided multitudes of migrants to London.

NOTES AND REFERENCES

1. H. Pirenne, *Medieval Cities. Their Origins and the Revival of Trade* (Princeton 1925), chapters on 'The Middle Class', 'Cities and European civilization'; J. Burckhardt, *The Civilization of the Renaissance in Italy* (London 1929 edn), Part 1, 'The State as a work of art'.
   We are most grateful to Mr P. Clark, Dr A. Grant, Professor T. K. Rabb, Professor Lawrence Stone, Dr K. Wrightson and Professor E. A. Wrigley for their comments on this Introduction. Any remaining imperfections are, of course, our responsibility. We must also acknowledge the support of the Nuffield Foundation for two conferences on London Economic and Social History, 1500–1700, in 1981 and 1983, and the interest shown in these meetings by Professor F. M. L. Thompson, Director of the Institute of Historical Research; and by Dr Caroline Barron, Mr Clark, Dr Valerie Pearl, and Professor Wrigley, who chaired sessions.
   This Introduction employs the term 'London' to refer to the metropolitan area generally, while the term 'City' means the parts under the authority of the aldermen and Lord Mayor.
2. J. Le Goff, 'The town as an agent of civilization', in C. M. Cipolla (ed.), *Fontana Economic History of Europe. The Middle Ages* (Glasgow 1972); Burckhardt, *Civilization of the Renaissance*; S. Ozment, *The Reformation in the Cities. The Appeal of Protestantism to Sixteenth-Century Germany and Switzerland* (London 1975), pp. 47ff.
3. R. Brenner, 'Agrarian class structure and economic development in pre-industrial Europe', *Past and Present*, 70 (1976), pp. 42–6; F. Braudel, *Capitalism and Material Life, 1400–1800* (London 1973), p. 440.
4. L. Martines, *Power and Imagination. City-States in Reniassance Italy* (New York 1980), Chs 7, 9; P. Clark and P. Slack, *English Towns in Transition* (London 1976), pp. 128–34.
5. F. Braudel, *The Mediterranean and the Mediterranean World in the Age of Philip II* (London 1973), ii, p. 725; J. Merrington, 'Town and country in the transition to capitalism', in P. Sweezy *et al.*, *The Transition from Feudalism to Capitalism* (London 1978), p. 180
6. Burckhardt, *Civilization of the Renaissance* pp. 356–7; Martines, op. cit., pp. 199, 212–13, 218–19, 229, 329–30.
7. Le Goff, 'The town as an agent', p. 90; Braudel, *Capitalism and Material Life*, pp. 48–9, 380–1, 399, 417.
8. P. Abrams, 'Towns and economic growth: some theories and problems', in P. Abrams and E. A. Wrigley (eds), *Towns in Societies* (Cambridge 1978), pp. 10ff.
9. Clark and Slack, *English Towns in Transition*, p. 83; further details in Ch. 1, *infra*.

10. J. Thirsk emphasizes the significance of change in the countryside in *Economic Policy and Projects: The Development of a Consumer Society in Early Modern England* (Oxford 1978).

11. Braudel, *Capitalism and Material Life*, p. 440; M. J. Daunton, 'Towns and economic growth in eighteenth-century England', in Abrams and Wrigley (eds), *Towns in Societies*, pp. 246–7.

12. See, for example, R. Ashton, *The Crown and the Money Market, 1603–1640* (Oxford 1960).

13. E. A. Wrigley, 'The process of modernization and the industrial revolution in England', repr. in T. K. Rabb and R. I. Rotberg (eds), *Industrialization and Urbanization* (Princeton 1981).

14. F. J. Fisher, 'The development of the London food market, 1540–1640', repr. in E. M. Carus-Wilson (ed.), *Essays in Economic History*, 1 (London 1954); 'London's export trade in the early seventeenth century', repr. in W. E. Minchinton (ed.), *The Growth of English Overseas Trade in the Seventeenth and Eighteenth Centuries* (London 1969); 'The development of London as a centre of conspicuous consumption in the sixteenth and seventeenth centuries', repr. in Carus-Wilson (ed.), *Essays in Economic History*, 2 (London 1962); 'Tawney's century', in Fisher (ed.), *Essays in the Economic and Social History of Tudor and Stuart England* (Cambridge 1961). On London and the industrial revolution, see E. A. Wrigley, 'A simple model of London's importance in changing English society and economy, 1650–1750', repr. in Abrams and Wrigley (eds), *Towns in Societies*. On topography, M. J. Power, 'The east and west in early-modern London', in E. W. Ives, R. J. Knecht and J. J. Scarisbrick (eds), *Wealth and Power in Tudor England* (London 1978); L. Stone, 'The residential development of the West End of London in the seventeenth century', in B. C. Malament (ed.), *After the Reformation* (Manchester 1980). On merchants, R. Brenner, 'The Civil War politics of London's merchant community', *Past and Present*, 58 (1973); D. W. Jones, 'London merchants and the crisis of the 1690s', in P. Clark and P. Slack (eds), *Crisis and Order in English Towns, 1500–1700* (London 1972). And on the capital's political role, V. Pearl, *London and the Outbreak of the Puritan Revolution* (London 1961).

15. Abrams, 'Towns and economic growth', pp. 10, 30.

16. Important works not referred to elsewhere in this Introduction include W. G. Bell, *The Great Plague of London in 1665* (London 1924); *The Great Fire of London in 1666* (London 1920); T. F. Reddaway, *The Rebuilding of London after the Great Fire* (London 1940); R. Grassby, 'Social mobility and business enterprise in seventeenth-century England', in D. Pennington and K. Thomas (eds), *Puritans and Revolutionaries. Essays in Seventeenth-Century History presented to Christopher Hill* (Oxford 1978); G. Unwin, *The Gilds and Companies of London* (4th edn, London 1963); D. C. Coleman, 'London scriveners and the estate market in the later seventeenth century', *Economic History Review*, 2nd ser., 4 (1951); M. P. Ashley, *Financial and Commercial Policies of the Cromwellian Protectorate* (London 1934).

17. Also of note are F. F. Foster, *The Politics of Stability* (London 1977); R. Ashton, *The City and the Court, 1603–1643* (Cambridge 1979).

18. Some of these questions are covered in J. Grant, 'The gentry of London in

the reign of Charles I', *University of Birmingham Historical Journal*, 8 (1962); M. G. Davies, 'Country gentry and payments to London, 1650–1714', *Economic History Review*, 2nd ser., 24 (1971); A. Clark, *Working Life of Women in the Seventeenth Century* (repr. New York 1968), Ch. 5; M. J. Power, 'East London housing in the seventeenth century', in Clark and Slack (eds), *Crisis and Order*; W. K. Jordan, *The Charities of London, 1480–1660* (London 1960); S. Brigden, 'Religion and social obligation in early sixteenth-century London', *Past and Present*, 103 (1984).

19. N. G. Brett-James, *The Growth of Stuart London* (London 1935).

20. Recent versions appear in Stone, 'Residential development'.

21. In particular, see M. Holmes, 'A source-book for Stow?', in A. E. J. Hollaender and W. Kellaway (eds), *Studies in London History* (London 1969); J. L. Howgego, *Printed Maps of the London Area circa 1553–1850* (2nd edn, Folkestone, 1978).

22. 'Introduction', in J. Stow, *A Survey of London*, ed. C. L. Kingsford (Oxford 1908), Vol. 1, p. xxix.

23. E. J. Davis, 'The transformation of London', in R. W. Seton-Watson (ed.), *Tudor Studies* (London 1924), is a valuable discussion.

24. Brett-James, *Growth of Stuart London*, Chs 3–4, 9–10, 12; T. G. Barnes, 'The prerogative and environmental control of building in the early seventeenth century: the lost opportunity', *California Law Review*, 58 (1970).

25. This neat phrase is taken from P. Clark and P. Slack, 'Introduction', in Clark and Slack (eds), *Crisis and Order*, p. 38.

26. Relevant demographic information is to be found in R. Finlay, *Population and Metropolis. The Demography of London, 1580–1650* (Cambridge 1981).

27. Wrigley, 'London's importance', p. 217; J. Graunt, *Natural and Political Observations . . ., Made upon the Bills of Mortality* (London 1662), pp. 43, 75–8, repr. in P. Laslett (ed.), *The Earliest Classics* (n.p., 1973).

28. Wrigley, 'London's importance', p. 218 for similar estimates. For births, E. A. Wrigley and R. S. Schofield, *The Population History of England, 1541–1871* (London 1981), p. 317.

29. Additional material on migration appears in S. R. Smith, 'The social and geographical origins of the London apprentices, 1630–1660', *Guildhall Miscellany*, 4 (1973); V. B. Elliott, 'Mobility and Marriage in Pre-Industrial England', (Unpublished Cambridge University Ph.D. thesis, (1978); J. Wareing, 'Changes in the geographical distribution of the recruitment of apprentices to the London companies, 1486–1750', *Journal of Historical Geography*, 6 (1980).

30. Wrigley and Schofield, *Population History of England*, Ch. 11.

31. This demographic pattern is suggested in Wrigley, 'London's importance'.

32. D. Ringrose, 'The impact of a new capital city: Madrid, Toledo and New Castile, 1560–1660', *Journal of Economic History*, 33 (1973); R. R. Harding, *Anatomy of a Power Elite. The Provincial Governors of Early Modern France* (London 1978), pp. 171–9 (reference kindly supplied by Dr A. Grant); H. A. Miskimin, *The Economy of Later Renaissance Europe, 1460–1600* (Cambridge 1977), p. 26.

33. W. Sombart, *Luxury and Capitalism* (Ann Arbor 1967; transl. of 1913

edn), pp. 31–5; above all, T. F. Tout, 'The beginnings of a modern capital. London and Westminster in the fourteenth century', *Proceedings of the British Academy*, 11 (London, n.d.); Braudel, *Capitalism and Material Life*, pp. 414–15.

34. P. L. Hughes and J. F. Larkin (eds), *Tudor Royal Proclamations* (London 1964–9), i, p. 173.

35. W. T. MacCaffrey, 'Place and patronage in Elizabethan politics', in S. T. Bindoff, J. Hurstfield and C. H. Williams (eds), *Elizabethan Government and Society* (London 1961), pp. 106–8; G. E. Aylmer, *The King's Servants. The Civil Service of Charles I, 1625–42* (London 1961), pp. 470–1, 476–87 (counting only asterisked positions, which total about 365 excluding the Privy Council and provincial councils).

36. A. G. R. Smith, *Servant of the Cecils: the Life of Sir Michael Hickes, 1543–1612* (London 1977); G. S. Holmes, *Augustan England. Professions, State and Society, 1680–1730* (London 1982), p. 256.

37. MacCaffrey, 'Place and patronage', pp. 106–8; Aylmer, *King's Servants*, pp. 472–5; Holmes, *Augustan England*, p. 256.

38. L. Stone, *The Crisis of the Aristocracy, 1558–1641* (Oxford 1965), pp. 397, 758; W. R. Prest, *The Inns of Court under Elizabeth I and the Early Stuarts, 1590–1640* (London 1972), pp. 6, 16.

39. L. Stone, *The Causes of the English Revolution, 1529–1642* (London 1972), p. 92.

40. B. P. Hindle, 'Seasonal variations in travel in medieval England', *Journal of Transport History*, new ser., 4 (1978), p. 173; C. Ross, *Edward IV* (London 1974), p. 271; G. P. V. Akrigg, *Jacobean Pageant* (London 1962), pp. 164–8.

41. Stone, *Crisis of the Aristocracy*, pp. 240–2, 386–7.

42. G. O. Sayles, *The King's Parliament of England* (London 1975), pp. 137–41; G. L. Harriss, 'The formation of Parliament, 1272–1377', in R. G. Davies and J. H. Denton (eds), *The English Parliament in the Middle Ages* (Manchester 1981), p. 37; A. L. Brown, 'Parliament, c.1377–1422', in ibid., p. 111; Ross, *Edward IV*, pp. 34, 133; S. B. Chrimes, *Henry VII* (London 1972), p. 146.

43. 500 of the 750 were apprentices, assuming 10 per cent of 5,000: G. D. Ramsay, 'The recruitment and fortunes of some London freemen in the mid-sixteenth century', *Economic History Review*, 2nd ser., 31 (1978), p. 530 (46 of 493 = 9.3 per cent). Cf. S. R. Smith, 'Origins of the London Apprentices', pp. 200, 205 (12.1 per cent). Further figures in Finlay, *Population and Metropolis*, p. 67. Numbers of peers in King's table, repr. in D. C. Coleman, *The Economy of England, 1450–1750* (London 1977), p. 6.

44. H. M. Colvin *et al.* (eds), *The History of the King's Works, 1485–1660* (London 1982), IV. ii, pp. 300ff.; Stone, *Crisis*, pp. 357–63, 395–6; Prest, *Inns of Court*, pp. 19–20.

45. Aylmer, *King's Servants*, pp. 248–9; F. J. Fisher, 'London's export trade', repr. in Minchinton (ed.), *English Overseas Trade*, p. 68.

46. Aylmer, *King's Servants*, loc. cit.; Sombart, *Luxury and Capitalism*, pp. 34–5.

47. F. C. Dietz, *English Public Finance, 1485–1641* (2nd edn, London 1964), ii, p. 81; Aylmer, *King's Servants*, pp. 249–51.

48. The point about London's two roles is made by G. D. Ramsay, *English Overseas Trade during the Centuries of Emergence* (London 1957), p. 10; for similar development in an earlier period, G. A. Williams, *Medieval London. From Commune to Capital* (London 1963), pp. 14-15. The points about the merchant-gentry relationship were made to us by Professor T. K. Rabb; see his *Enterprise and Empire: Merchant and Gentry Investment in the Expansion of England, 1575-1630* (Cambridge, Mass., 1967).

49. G. D. Ramsay, *The City of London in International Politics at the Accession of Elizabeth Tudor* (Manchester 1975), p. 37.

50. J. D. Gould, *The Great Debasement* (Oxford 1970), pp. 125-9; cf. H. S. Cobb, 'Cloth exports from London and Southampton in the later fifteenth and early sixteenth centuries: a revision', *Economic History Review*, 2nd ser., 31 (1978), pp. 607-8; J. L. Bolton, *The Medieval English Economy, 1150-1500* (London 1980), p. 195.

51. A. D. Dyer, 'Growth and decay in English towns, 1500-1700', *Urban History Yearbook*, (1979), p. 69.

52. Ramsay, *City of London*, pp. 48-9; A. H. Dodd, 'Mr Myddleton the merchant of Tower Street', in Bindoff *et al.* (eds), *Elizabethan Government and Society*, pp. 250-1; A. Simpson, *The Wealth of the Gentry, 1540-1660* (Chicago 1963), p. 118.

53. The figure of 1,500 is based on the assumption that if 1,088 became freemen in 22 months in 1551-3, then the figure for two years would be 1,187 (data from Ramsay, 'London freemen in the mid-sixteenth century', p. 532). Since only about two-fifths of apprentices completed their terms and took up the freedom (S. Rappaport, 'Social structure and mobility in sixteenth-century London: Part 1', *London Journal*, 9, 1983, pp. 116-17), the total annual entry would be 1,485. For 1600, see Finlay, *Population and Metropolis*, p. 67.

54. L. Stone, *An Elizabethan: Sir Horatio Palavicino* (Oxford 1956), p. 190; Dodd, 'Myddleton', pp. 261-2.

55. Ross, *Edward IV*, pp. 353-4.

56. Dodd, 'Myddleton', p. 254; Stone, *Palavicino*, p. 71; Simpson, *Wealth of the Gentry*, p. 128; D. C. Coleman, *Sir John Banks, Baronet and Businessman* (Oxford 1963), p. 9; R. H. Tawney, *Business and Politics under James I. Lionel Cranfield as Merchant and Minister* (Cambridge 1958), pp. 9ff.

57. R. Ashton, *The City and the Court*, pp. 2ff.; Pearl, *London and the Outbreak of the Puritan Revolution*, Ch. 4.

58. B. E. Supple, *Commercial Crisis and Change in England, 1600-1642* (Cambridge 1959), p. 258; R. Davis, 'England and the Mediterranean, 1570-1670', in Fisher (ed.), *Essays in the Economic and Social History of Tudor and Stuart England*.

59. D. W. Jones, 'London Merchants and the Crisis of the 1690s', in Clark and Slack (eds), *Crisis and Order*, pp. 312-15.

60. R. H. Tawney and E. Power (eds), *Tudor Economic Documents* (London 1924), iii, p. 96; Kent Archives Office QM/SB 213; Dorset County Record Office, Dorchester Borough Court Book, fol. 187a.

61. Dodd, 'Myddleton', pp. 260, 273; Stone, *Palavicino*, pp. 275-6; B. Winchester, *Tudor Family Portrait* (London 1955), pp. 172-3.

62. E. P. Thompson, *The Making of the English Working Class* (New York 1966 edn.), p. 314; cf. Rappaport, 'Social structure and mobility', pp. 125ff.

63. Tawney and Power (eds), *Tudor Economic Documents*, iii, p. 418; Corporation of London Records Office, Court of Aldermen, Repertory 23/479b–480a, Common Council Journal 24/322b–323a (the latter reference we owe to Mr Ian Archer). Even allowing that a further 350 'poor men overburdened with their children' in the Edwardian survey were householders, the new total of 1,000 still suggests that the problem increased two-fold by 1598.

64. A. L. Beier, 'Social problems in Elizabethan London', *Journal of Interdisciplinary History*, 9 (1978), pp. 204–5.

65. Finlay, *Population and Metropolis*, pp. 17, 131–2.

66. R. B. Outhwaite, 'Dearth and Government intervention in English grain markets, 1590–1700', *Economic History Review*, 2nd Ser., 34 (1981), is an important discussion.

67. Beier, 'Social problems', pp. 219–20.

68. R. W. Herlan, 'Poor relief in London during the English revolution', *Journal of British Studies*, 18 (1979).

69. P. Slack, 'Social policy and the constraints of Government, 1547–58', in J. Loach and R. Tittler (eds), *The Mid-Tudor Polity, c. 1540–1560* (London 1980), pp. 108–13; V. Pearl, 'Puritans and poor relief: the London Workhouse, 1649–1660', in Pennington and Thomas (eds), *Puritans and Revolutionaries*.

70. S. Brigden, 'Religion and social obligation', pp. 68–9; Herlan, 'Poor Relief'; cf. Jordan, *Charities of London, passim.*

71. Brigden, 'Religion', pp. 71, 94.

72. D. M. Bergeron, *English Civic Pageantry, 1558–1642* (London 1971), p. 2.

73. Graunt, *Natural and Political Observations*, p. 58.

74. Pearl, *London and the Outbreak of the Puritan Revolution*, pp. 38–42.

75. P. Clark, 'The reception of migrants in English towns in the early modern period', paper presented to International Urban History Conference, Göttingen, 1982 p. 4.

76. M. D. George, *London Life in the Eighteenth Century* (Harmondsworth, 1966 edn), pp. 117, 121–2, 132–6; Clark, 'Migrants', pp. 5, 12–13; cf. P. Ariès, *Histoire des populations françaises* (Paris 1971 edn), pp. 181–5; H. Le Bras and E. Todd, *L'invention de la France* (Paris 1981), pp. 243ff.

77. C. M. Barron, 'Richard Whittington: the man behind the myth', in Hollaender and Kellaway (eds), *Studies in London History*, pp. 197–8; P. Burke, 'Popular culture in seventeenth-century London', *London Journal*, 3 (1977), p. 159.

78. S. R. Smith, 'The London apprentices as seventeenth-century adolescents', *Past and Present*, 61 (1973), pp. 155–6; Beier, 'Social problems', p. 209; and for an earlier period, S. Brigden, 'Youth and the English Reformation', *Past and Present*, 95 (1982).

79. P. Clark, *The English Alehouse. A Social History, 1200–1830* (London 1983), p. 49.

80. Ibid., pp. 148–9; R. Ashton, 'Popular entertainment and social control in later Elizabethan and early Stuart London', *London Journal*, 9 (1983), pp. 13ff., to which this section as a whole is indebted; Guildhall Library,

Bridewell Hospital Court Books, Microfilms 510–515.

81. Finlay, *Population and Metropolis*, p. 19.

82. Greater London Record Office, P92/SAV/1422C, 1423F; Ashton, 'Popular entertainment', p. 14.

83. Cited by F. J. Fisher, 'The development of London as a centre of conspicuous consumption', repr. in Carus-Wilson (ed.), *Essays in Economic History*, 2, p. 205.

84. Ashton, 'Popular entertainment', pp. 4–9.

85. A. J. Cook, *The Privileged Playgoers of Shakespeare's London, 1576–1642* (Princeton 1981), esp. Ch. 6, although this study suffers from the same use of indirect evidence as those cited earlier of destitution. Cf. R. Ashton, 'Popular entertainment', pp. 4–5, 7.

86. Bergeron, *English Civic Pageantry*, pp. 7–8; R. C. Hassel, Jr., *Renaissance Drama and the English Church Year* (London 1979), p. 4.

87. This question is discussed in detail in Ch. 5 of A. L. Beier, *Masterless Men* (forthcoming, London 1985).

88. C. Hill, *Intellectual Origins of the English Revolution* (Oxford 1965), Ch. 2; also, C. Webster, *The Great Instauration* (London 1975).

89. D. Cressy, *Literacy and the Social Order. Reading and Writing in Tudor and Stuart England* (Cambridge 1980), Table 6.5, p. 121; M. Spufford, *Small Books and Pleasant Histories* (London 1981).

90. G. D. Ramsay, *The English Woollen Industry, 1500–1750* (London 1982), p. 56; B. S. Yamey, H. C. Edey and H. W. Thomson, *Accounting in England and Scotland, 1543–1800* (London 1963), pp. 155–70, 202–8; Cressy, *Literacy*, Tables 7.2 (p. 144), 7.3 (p. 146); cf. M. Sanderson, *Education, Economic Change and Society in England, 1780–1870* (London 1983), pp. 13–16.

91. S. Brigden, 'Popular disturbance and the fall of Thomas Cromwell and the reformers, 1539–1540', *Historical Journal*, 24 (1981).

92. Examples of these trends are provided respectively in P. S. Seaver, *The Puritan Lectureships* (Stanford, Calif., 1970); M. Tolmie, *The Triumph of the Saints* (Cambridge 1977).

93. D. Hirst, *The Representative of the People?* (Cambridge 1975), pp. 96, 215.

94. Ibid., pp. 142–3, 105; V. Pearl, 'Change and stability in seventeenth-century London', *London Journal*, 5 (1979).

95. Pearl, *London and the Outbreak of the Puritan Revolution*, esp. Chs. 6–7.

96. Detailed evidence in Wrigley and Schofield, *Population History of England*, pp. 208–9.

97. R. Davis, 'English foreign trade, 1660–1700', repr. in Carus-Wilson (ed.), *Essays in Economic History*, 2, pp. 257–8, 268–9.

98. G. E. Aylmer, *The State's Servants. The Civil Service of the English Republic* (London 1973), p. 172, which studies 1,175–1,180 officials over 12 years *versus* 900 in 17 years in Charles I's reign, and the latter figure also included persons in the Household: cf. Aylmer, *The King's Servants*, p. 254. We are most grateful to Professor A. H. Woolrych for information regarding London's military fate in the civil wars.

99. G. Parker, *Europe in Crisis, 1598–1648* (Glasgow 1979), esp. Ch. 7.

100. O. Ranum, *Paris in the Age of Absolutism* (London 1968), p. 294; C. M. Cipolla, 'The economic decline of Italy', repr. in B. Pullan (ed.), *Crisis and Change in the Venetian Economy in the Sixteenth and Seventeenth Centuries* (London 1968), pp. 136–8.

101. Ranum, *Paris*, p. 295.

PART ONE
Population and disease

CHAPTER ONE

Population growth and suburban expansion

Roger Finlay and Beatrice Shearer

The massive growth of London between the late sixteenth and early eighteenth centuries was one of the most important and strikingly visible changes in pre-industrial England. Many contemporaries felt the capital had become 'a head too big for the body', but not all considered its development detrimental.[1] The validity of their claims cannot yet be evaluated because the causes of the expansion of London, its impact on national economic development, and the social conditions it engendered are only patchily understood. London conformed to the general demographic pattern typical throughout Western Europe, which was characterized by late marriage and small family size, but its experience differed sharply from what is known about other areas. Very little research has been undertaken on the population of any of the larger cities.[2] This chapter outlines why London's population history is of signal importance; shows how its growth in size may be established; examines the associated demographic changes in fertility, nuptiality, mortality and migration; and provides an introductory viewpoint on some of their wider economic implications. The tentative findings comprise the first detailed investigation of the course of the fourfold expansion of London between 1550 and 1700 which transformed a compact capital city into a sprawling metropolis. No apology is therefore required for the empirical emphasis in this study.

I

An impression of the significance of the growth of population in London may be gained from comparison with the remainder of England

37

as shown in Table 1. The overall trends are so clear that the general pattern is not obscured by any uncertainties in the estimates, nor by the choice of dates for which figures have been presented. Whereas the population of England less than doubled from 3.0 million to 5.1 million between 1550 and 1700, London quadrupled from 120,000 to 490,000. This divergence in the rate of growth between the capital and the country as a whole was especially marked in both the first half of the seventeenth century, and also in the second half when the capital continued to increase rapidly while the national population declined slightly. In 1550 only about 4 per cent of the national population were Londoners, a figure which was slightly enlarged to nearly 5 per cent by 1600. The proportion then increased rapidly to over 7 per cent in 1650 and almost 10 per cent in 1700. By the second half of the eighteenth century the capital and the country as a whole were growing at about the same rate. The percentage increase in the population of London is even more accentuated when compared with the rate of expansion in England less the capital. The figures are given in parentheses in Table 1. In the first half of the seventeenth century London increased in size by 88 per cent compared with 24 per cent for the remainder of the country; and in the second half of the century it grew by 24 per cent whereas the rest of the country decreased by 6 per cent.

What happened in London was not simply a reflection of English urban history, because its growth contrasted very sharply with the experience of the other towns which contained over 5,000 inhabitants. Even the sketchy figures in Table 1 show that they did not grow much more rapidly than the remainder of the country before the end of the seventeenth century. However, the provincial towns were expanding rapidly in the eighteenth century, when the metropolis was more stable, so that one single city never again dominated national life to such a phenomenal extent.[3] In 1600 London contained nearly 5 per cent of the national population and 3 per cent inhabited the provincial towns. By 1700, 10 per cent of the national population were Londoners and only 5½ per cent lived in the other towns. London was almost twice as large as the combined populations of all other urban centres. By 1700 the latter were catching up quickly, and by 1800 they easily exceeded the metropolis, which itself maintained its position.

London's growth was also distinctive in comparison with Continental cities of over 100,000 inhabitants. It grew from a relatively small and unimportant European centre to its major city by 1700. Research on urbanization in early modern Europe is still at an early stage but preliminary findings suggest that larger cities expanded from 0.7 per cent of the population in 1500, to 1.5 per cent in 1600, 2.7 per cent by

Table 1. The population of London in comparative perspective, 1550–1800 (000s)

Date	Population of England[a]	Per cent increase	Population of London[b]	Per cent increase	Per cent population of England	Population of other towns over 5,000	Per cent increase	Per cent population of England
1550	3,010 (2,890)	—	120	—	4.0	—	—	—
1600	4,110 (3,910)	37 (35)	200	67	4.9	125[e]	—	3.0
1650	5,230 (4,855)	27 (24)	375	88	7.2	—	—	—
1700	5,060 (4,570)	-3 (-6)	490	24	9.7	275[d]	—	5.4
1750	5,780 (5,105)	14 (12)	675[c]	38	11.7	540[d]	96	9.3
1800	8,660 (7,710)	50 (51)	950[d]	41	11.0	1,430[f]	165	16.5

The figures in parentheses refer to the population of England excluding London.

Sources:

(a) E. A. Wrigley and R. S. Schofield, *The Population History of England 1541–1871* (London 1981), Table 7.8, pp. 208–9.
(b) Table 4 below, except where stated.
(c) E. A. Wrigley, 'A simple model of London's importance in changing English society and economy 1650–1750', repr. in P. Abrams and E. A. Wrigley (eds), *Towns in Societies* (Cambridge 1978), p. 215.
(d) P. J. Corfield, *The Impact of English Towns 1700–1800* (Oxford 1982), Table 1, p. 8.
(e) P. J. Corfield, 'Economic growth and change in seventeenth-century English towns', in P. Clark (ed.), *The Traditional Community under Stress* (Milton Keynes 1977), Table 1, p. 40.
(f) Corfield, *The Impact of English Towns*, Table 1, p. 8, less 15,000 for three towns in Wales shown on Fig. 3, p. 14.

1700 and 3.1 per cent in 1800. Other towns with over 5,000 people contained about 8 per cent of the population throughout the period, a considerably greater proportion than in England before the early eighteenth century.[4] Part of this difference must have been due to variations between Mediterranean, Central, and North-West Europe but data have not yet been published to permit numerical comparisons between the latter area and England. It is also possible that urbanization was so distinctive in England because the country was so much smaller in area than continental Europe, where the apparent uniformity of experience could have resulted from growth in some centres offsetting decline in others. However, it has been strongly argued that European urbanization was well-integrated, and three stages have been identified.[5] First, there was growth in all cities, especially those with over 40,000 inhabitants, which continued till around 1600 in the Mediterranean region and 1650 further northwards. Secondly, a period of stagnation occurred with production shifting to rural hinterlands except for capital cities and ports. Thirdly, renewed urbanization took place from 1750 to about 1850 with a great expansion of smaller cities due partly to increasing agrarian productivity prior to industrialization, which was itself associated with the concentration of the population into very large cities. The pattern of urbanization in England contradicts much of what happened elsewhere. Little evidence exists for the initial growth, deurbanization, and subsequent reconstitution of cities which occurred in the remainder of Europe.[6] By the mid-seventeenth century London contained a much higher proportion of the national population than other cities, even those like Paris which were the hub of very centralized states. Unlike other large European cities, London did not stagnate after 1650.

II

There has been some uncertainty about the absolute size of the metropolis and the general pattern of its expansion. 'London in 1600 was in many respects the London of 1400',[7] wrote Brett-James, 'and from that time its growth has been incessant.'[8] More recent findings on the development of the townscape require this chronology to be revised.[9] Wrigley considered that London's 'exact population at any time before the first census is a matter for argument but in round figures it appears to have grown from about 200,000 in 1600 to perhaps 400,000 in 1650, 575,000 by the end of the century, 675,000 in 1750 and 900,000 in 1800'.[10] These totals were obtained from an attempt to summarize the findings of all earlier writers and have probably been accepted as more authoritative than was intended. They suggest that the rate of population growth could have varied in London, but there is evidently a need for a more firmly based study.

The derivation of the demographic totals in Table 1 may now be examined. Estimates of the population of London have varied so considerably because they relate to different geographical areas. This confusion has partly arisen because the distinction has been blurred between the whole built-up area and that of the municipality's jurisdiction, which customarily existed only in the square mile of the City of London within and without the Walls north of the Thames and in Southwark on the south bank. Statistical totals must be based on known administrative areas, yet the municipality lacked both the will and perhaps the means to extend its authority throughout the whole metropolis. While at times it took some part in the affairs of the suburbs, this role was never consistent nor well defined.[11] However, it collected bills of mortality within the whole townscape to warn of the onset of plague. It is this area of the bills which defines the extent of London considered here.

Parish registers are the single most important source for deriving population estimates for London as well as for the remainder of England.[12] They contain much greater detail than the bills of mortality, also compiled by the parish clerks, which permits independent checks of the quality of the data. An ample number of good-quality registers are extant for the metropolitan area north of the Thames to enable totals of christenings and burials to be used for the full period between 1540 and 1700 for a sample of thirty parishes covering the City, suburban and rural areas. Full details of the sources used in this study are given in the Appendix (pp. 58–9). Monthly totals were collected which were subjected to a full range of computer test programs to pinpoint and correct for periods of under-registration.[13] Comparisons between the raw totals and the corrected data show few major discrepancies which would alter the general trends outlined below, so these tests are indicative of the veracity of the original data.

Population estimates for the area north of the river comprising the City within and without the Walls, the suburbs, and rural Middlesex are shown in Table 2. The method used to produce these estimates can be summarized as follows. Trends derived from annual baptism and burial totals for thirty sample parishes from the beginning of registration around 1538 through to 1700 were hung on two benchmark population estimates; the first calculated from the communicant figures in the 1548

Table 2. Population growth in London and Middlesex, 1560–1700 (000s)

Date	City within and without Walls	Suburbs north of river	Total north of river	Rural Middlesex
1560	80	20	100	25
1580	105	40	145	25
1600	100	55	155	30
1620	125	110	235	35
1640	135	175	310	40
1660	105	170	275	45
1680	105	265	370	50
1700	85	300	385	55

Sources: See text.

Chantry Certificates and the second from numbers of households in the 1664 Hearth Tax assessments.[14] Population totals could thus be estimated for every Middlesex parish for two fixed points in 1548 and 1664. The metropolitan sample parishes were grouped into the City, Eastern, Northern, and Western suburbs, and the remaining Middlesex sample parishes were designated Rural. It was then possible to consider separately the trends of each sample group, and to calculate their respective growth rates over 20-year periods. These rates were then applied to the population estimates for the total parishes in each group which had been made for the first fixed point in 1548, thus showing the estimated population size every twenty years throughout the period under investigation. The estimates for 1660 made by this procedure were compared with those for 1664 obtained from the hearth tax. Since there was very good agreement, the trends effectively fitted successfully on to each of the two sets of points, and these calculations made from three separate data sources consequently validate one another. The overall trends are very clear indeed, even allowing for imperfections in the statistics, which include the effects of short-term mortality crises, under-registrations of baptisms, and over-registration of burials due to high mortality among short-stay immigrants.

These figures introduce new perspectives to the pattern of London's expansion. They show that the area of the municipality was growing very rapidly up till 1640 and then declined, so that by 1700 the city within and without the Walls contained almost the same population as in 1560. The suburbs north of the river were expanding much more quickly. By 1630 they were as large as the city within and without, and their increase continued throughout the period until they numbered more than three times the population of the former area by 1700. The period before the outbreak of the Civil War thus witnessed an important transformation in the character of the metropolis with a change in emphasis from the municipality to the suburbs. The tremendous growth of the suburbs from the mid-seventeenth century may be considered as a second, complementary transformation. In essence, these were the changes which enabled the metropolis to quadruple in size during the period. Rural Middlesex was virtually unchanged in numbers during the second half of the sixteenth century, but from 1640 was growing at about the same rate as the metropolis as a whole.

Any discussion of the components of London demographic changes must also consider the position on the south bank of the Thames. This area consisted of four Southwark parishes in the liberties, extra-parochial areas, and the out-parish of St Mary Magdalen Bermondsey. In 1636 the distant parishes of Lambeth, Newington and Rotherhithe were added to the bills of mortality. More perfunctory population estimates have been made for the southern suburbs, due partly to the less extensive evidence in the parish registers. Southwark contained the parishes of St Thomas, St George, St Olave and St Saviour, of which only the latter has an unbroken series of registers. A fifth parish, Christchurch, was created from St Saviour's in 1671. The unsatisfactory nature of the registers means that any estimates of population size must be based on census-type sources compiled at specific dates, all of which are themselves incomplete, and are therefore very tentative.

The earliest fairly reliable data are the numbers of households given in the 1679 Hearth Tax provided by Gregory King. The figures are clearly rounded, and include Christchurch with St Thomas, but give a total of 7,586 households.[15] The number of persons per household is uncertain, but six would be a conservative estimate, enabling a population of 45,500 to be calculated.[16] This is a cautious estimate for the further reason that it fails to allow for omissions from the hearth tax, which might suggest numbers of around 50,000 in 1680. Data for the earlier period must rely on incomplete lists of communicants made in 1547, 1603, and 1631, supplemented by interpolation from the registers, when the numbers of communicants were estimated as 4,984, 11,451, and 15,409 respectively.[17] These figures may be converted into actual population totals by using back projection estimates of national population trends to suggest the assumptions required to multiply numbers of communicants into population totals which are as follows. In 1545 the age at first communion was 10 years, 25 per cent of the population was under that age and the figures should then be deflated by

10 per cent.[18] This gives a population total of 5,980 for Southwark in 1547. By 1602 the age of communion had risen to 15 years, 35 per cent of the population were too young to be enumerated, and 23 per cent of adults were missing.[19] On this basis, Southwark contained 21,700 inhabitants. Since both the age of communion and the age structure of the population were very similar in 1631,[20] the same method of inflation may be used to give a total for Southwark of 29,000. These estimation techniques suffer from the limitation that individual communities like Southwark did not necessarily conform to the national average, especially with respect to the effects on the age structure of higher mortality in urban areas and of migration of young adults into the area. The method used here is nevertheless sufficiently robust, especially as a more youthful age structure attributable to the former effect might be balanced by an older age structure resulting from the latter effect.

The southern suburbs were larger in area than Southwark itself. Their size has been estimated from 5-year mean burial totals given in the bills of mortality,[21] as a proportion of the new figures for the north bank which have been presented here in summary form. These calculations suggest totals of 50,000 in 1660, 65,000 in 1680 and 60,000 in 1700. Because of incomplete series it is questionable whether the bills may plausibly be used further back than this. In the second half of the seventeenth century Southwark contained two-thirds of the population of the south bank. Before then its proportion must have been greater, and estimates have consequently been interpolated on this assumption.

Summary population totals which present the situation in the suburbs in greater detail are given in Table 3. Between 1560 and 1680 the population of London increased fourfold whilst rural Middlesex only doubled in size. Whereas in 1560 the city within and without contained three-quarters of the population of the metropolis and the suburbs a quarter, by 1680 the situation was reversed with only a quarter of Londoners inhabiting the City and three-quarters in the suburbs. Thus the growth of the suburbs constituted a major part of the expansion of the metropolis. Table 3 has been designed to suggest that suburban growth was a more complicated process than is often thought, and encompassed the contrasting experience of many separate communities. There were marked variations in the pace of suburban expansion. The suburbs were growing most rapidly between 1560 and 1640. This was also the pattern of expansion in the largest suburbs to the east of the City which by 1680 easily exceeded the former area in numbers. A similar but slower rate of growth was evident in both the northern and southern suburbs. They expanded especially rapidly between 1560 and 1600 and subsequently increased in size at about the same rate as the

Table 3. Summary population growth in London and Middlesex, 1560–1800 (000s)

Date	City within and without Walls	Eastern suburbs	Northern suburbs	Western suburbs	Southern suburbs	Total suburbs	London	Rural Middlesex
1560	80	10	5	5	10	30	110	25
1600	100	30	20	10	25	85	185	30
1640	135	90	50	35	45	220	355	40
1680	105	140	60	65	65	330	435	50
Indexed to base 100								
1560	100	100	100	100	100	100	100	100
1600	125	300	400	200	250	285	170	120
1640	170	900	1,000	700	450	735	325	160
1680	130	1,400	1,200	1,300	650	1,100	395	200
Percentage of total London population								
1560	73	9	4.5	4.5	9	27	100	
1600	54	16	11	5.5	13.5	46	100	
1640	38	25	14	10	13	62	100	
1680	24	32	14	15	15	76	100	

Sources: See text.

metropolis. It was in the first half of the seventeenth century that the eastern suburbs increased very quickly compared with the other suburban areas. The western suburbs grew at the same pace as the conurbation before 1600, but thereafter expanded continuously so that they equalled the southern suburbs by 1680. These changes suggest that the growth of London was not uniform and happened in different areas at different times throughout the period.

The accuracy of the London population totals presented in Table 3 depends on how far the course of demographic trends in the metropolis may be captured by well-compiled parish registers. The relative magnitude of the figures certainly leaves less room for discussion than the absolute totals, but it may be valuable to consider some of the reasons leakage may occur. A major defining characteristic of pre-industrial urban populations is the presence of a high proportion of single adults, yet registers provide a better record of family events than of the demography of single people. Table 4 demonstrates that households were considerably larger in London around 1700 than in the provincial towns or rural areas for which data are available. This was entirely due to larger numbers of servants and lodgers per household than to significant differences in family composition. On average, families contained three to four persons in all kinds of settlements, while a mean of no more than one non-family member was present in each household outside London compared with three in the metropolis. The number of resident children was slightly smaller in the capital than elsewhere, due partly to its high rates of mortality, and also to the custom of nursing young children in the countryside.[22]

Another cause of omission from the registers was temporary mobility. People of all kinds stayed in the capital for short periods for a great variety of reasons. These included the marketing of goods; the conduct of business; consultation with lawyers, doctors, and members of the other nascent professions; a first step prior to emigration; for entertainment; to participate in the affairs of Parliament or the Court; or simply to visit friends and relatives.[23] The poor also found their way to London in large numbers, especially in times of economic distress. By 1700 one Englishman in ten was a Londoner, so that contacts with the remainder of the country were potentially very great. It is unlikely that visitors would have had much difficulty in finding somewhere to stay. Temporary mobility was also much easier when the labour market was typified by casual work and when residence and the ownership of property were not inextricably linked. Individuals temporarily staying in London would have been less likely than its permanent inhabitants to appear in parish registers, even though they would be enumerated in a

Table 4. Mean membership of households, c. 1700

Household membership	London	Provincial towns		Rural areas	
	7 parishes 1695	Southampton 5 parishes 1695–7	Shrewsbury 3 wards 1698	Kent 11 parishes 1705	Wiltshire 6 parishes 1700–05
Head (and spouse where present)	1.8	1.6	1.6	1.8	1.7
Offspring	1.2	1.6	1.7	2.0	1.7
Kin	0.1	0.1	0.2	0.1	0.1
Total family members	3.1	3.3	3.5	3.9	3.5
Servants and lodgers	3.0	0.7	1.0	0.8	0.4
Household size	6.1	4.0	4.5	4.7	3.9
Total households	771	435	1,112	455	292
Total persons	4,673	1,745	5,041	2,158	1,133

Source: Adapted from R. Wall, 'Regional and temporal variations in English household structure from 1650', in J. Hobcraft and P. Rees (eds), *Regional Demographic Development* (London 1979), Table 4.6, p. 103. The settlements studied are listed in the Appendix, p. 110, and the sampling methods are described on pp. 100–2.

modern census. Many vital events do not happen suddenly and some people at particular risk may consequently have postponed travel. Other events actually occurring in London would have been registered in the place of usual residence rather than in the capital itself.

It thus remains to estimate the extent to which population totals obtained primarily from the parish registers should be inflated to indicate the actual number of London residents. The corrections in Table 5 are made on the basis of the simplest solution, which is to inflate the totals by 10 per cent to allow for the floating population and by 20 per cent in 1650 because the quality of the registers was more variable during the Interregnum.[24] London may thus have increased in size from around 120,000 in 1550, to 200,000 in 1600, 375,000 in 1650, and 490,000 by 1700. It would be unwise to claim too much precision for these estimates, but they usefully amplify earlier notions about the size of London.[25]

III

It would be a mistake to conclude from these tables that the growth of London population was essentially a smooth process. Pre-industrial English society was characterized by its instability. Market shortages in country districts could often be supplemented by domestic food production but this was not possible in urban areas, so that fluctuations were much greater. The expansion of the metropolis was interrupted by continual crisis situations. Its economy was subject to marked vagaries in the harvest and to uncertain trading conditions mainly associated with its overseas markets.[26] They were exacerbated by crowding people together in an insanitary townscape, facilitating the diffusion of serious epidemic diseases, of which plague was the prime example. There were five major outbreaks in London during the century from 1563 to 1665, four of which claimed at least one-fifth of the total population as victims.[27] Each could accurately be described as a holocaust, so that the continuing ability of the metropolis to increase its size is especially remarkable.

Although the reasons for the disappearance of plague must remain a matter for discussion,[28] the absolute level of London mortality was probably rising towards the end of the seventeenth century. The pattern of population change became less fragile, aided by greater stability in the economy, but the implications of death for the social structure remained almost as prominent as before. The elimination of the worst epidemics means that endemic diseases correspondingly increased in importance. As mentioned above (pp. 37, 38, 40) London represented a special case of the West European demographic pattern. There is little doubt that small families resulting from late marriage were as characteristic of the metropolis as of provincial England.[29] However, mortality and the associated migration rather than nuptiality was the principal motor of demographic change and its significance increased in proportion to the size of the city. This caused widespread fluctuations in the composition of the population, which made demographic trends in other areas appear relatively stable by comparison.

Some bearing on the extent of these fluctuations is shown in Table 6, which gives summary demographic measures for four parishes for the

Table 5. Corrected summary London population totals (000s)

Date	North of river[a]	South of river[b]	Subtotal	Inflation ratio[b]	Estimated total
1550	100	10	110	1.1	120
1600	155	25	180	1.1	200
1650	290	50	340	1.2	375
1700	385	60	445	1.1	490

Sources: (a) Based on Table 2; (b) See text.

Table 6. Summary demographic measures for contrasting London parishes, 1580–1650

Parish	Proportion of substantial households 1638 (%)[a]	Survivors to age 15[b]	Crisis mortality ratios 1625[c]	Mean birth intervals 1–6 (months)[d]
St Peter Cornhill	60	631	4.40	23.0
St Michael Cornhill	35	596	5.65	22.7
St Mary Somerset	8	467	5.22	26.7
Allhallows London Wall	3	508	10.14	26.8

Sources:
(a) R. Finlay, *Population and Metropolis: the Demography of London 1580–1650* (Cambridge 1981), Table A3.1, pp. 168–72.
(b) Ibid., Table 5.15, p. 107.
(c) Ibid., Table 6.5, p. 120.
(d) Ibid., Table 7.1, p. 135; the figures for the poorest parish are for St Botolph Bishopsgate, adjacent to Allhallows London Wall.

period between 1580 and 1650. These are presented here only to illustrate how trends in fertility and mortality ensured that the composition of London's population was constantly changing; that its growth could not have been self-sustaining and that the fortunes of the metropolis were consequently dependent on the country as a whole. The sample parishes have been divided into two groups according to the percentage of substantial households, defined as those valued at over £20 in a rental of 1638. Noticeable differences are apparent between the two wealthier central Cornhill parishes and the two poorer parishes, of which St Mary Somerset had a riverside location and Allhallows London Wall and St Botolph Bishopsgate adjoined the wall in the north-eastern sector. However, all the parishes displayed urban demographic characteristics.

High mortality was the most evident of these. The number of survivors to age 15 exclude deaths occurring in plague years, an indication of the impact of which is given by the crisis mortality ratios for one of the epidemics. This measures the number of times deaths in a crisis year exceeds an average of the total for five years prior to the year before the crisis itself, in this case 1619–23. This evidence leaves little doubt that less than half London-born children survived to a marriageable age, especially as the wealthier parishes contained a smaller proportion of the total population than their poorer counterparts. Young adults who were new migrants to London were also particularly susceptible to plague, probably because they had not acquired resistance to the disease. The mean birth intervals shown in the last column are very short indeed, especially in the wealthier parishes, and are suggestive of exceptionally high marital fertility. In contrast, overall fertility was much lower and could not have offset the level of mortality. This situation was due to a number of factors: a relatively small proportion of the population that was married; similar levels of non-marital fertility to the remainder of the country; a distinct shortage of females in the first half of the seventeenth century; and the effect of migration in delaying marriage. Because mortality was so high and its level largely exogenous to the economic situation of the metropolis, migration was the principal cause of the growth of population in London.[30]

Migrants were predominantly single but comprised a very diverse group indeed. They included people from all social backgrounds and from all areas of the country, as well as aliens from religious persecution overseas. The composition of the migrant group varied at different times over the period. It is well known that migrants came from a reduced area in the second half of the seventeenth century; that a decreasing number were apprentices as the significance of this institution fell away; that there was an increasing proportion of female migrants; and that aliens came predominantly in two periods in the latter third of both the sixteenth and seventeenth centuries.[31] But it should also be emphasized that as London's population increased so must the absolute number of migrants, although the strength of the city's magnetism ceased to be directly measurable from those sources which depict their origins and destinations. The distinction between migration and temporary mobility outlined above is difficult to make in Tudor and Stuart times. The fluidity of society within the parameters set by the conventions for the formation of new families is well known, but must be included among the factors that contributed most to the increase of population in the metropolis.

Remarriage was another mechanism which facilitated a rapid recovery from crisis situations. Because the household was the basic economic as well as residential unit, marriage itself implied an economic as well as an emotional relationship. Remarriage intervals were often no longer than a few months,[32] as it was essential to maintain household and family life. This was a similar situation to the country as a whole, especially before 1640, when access to land or to a craft is thought to have been especially important.[33] The existence of a large single population was therefore absolutely essential for the reproduction of London society, especially in times of crisis. In such periods individuals were always available to take over an enterprise enabling output and services to be maintained, and creating time for new migrants to be recruited and for new children to appear. It was in this way that the structure of society persisted through largely exogenously determined fluctuations over which Londoners had little control. It did not cease with the decline of epidemic mortality, but continued for as long as high mortality meant that there was a good chance that any household would be prematurely broken.

The salient demographic features of the metropolis – including high mortality of both children and adults, wet-nursing, and massive migration and mobility – suggest that personal relationships may have been very tenuous. These comments provide a measure of historical perspective to the present concern about the nature of the family and the character of the welfare state. The insecurity of life in early modern London and the paramount need to maintain the functioning of its economy meant that instrumental rather than kin relations must have been at least equally important at this time, especially in view of the difficulty of maintaining contacts between relatives in different localities. Emphasis should be given to the massive contrasts between the metropolis in that period and its current counterpart.

IV

Developments in the national economy provided the general framework within which these demographic changes took place. London history diverged from that of other European cities in the sixteenth and seventeenth centuries, strongly suggesting that its actual course of growth and change was not inevitable. A fuller understanding of its expansion at this time may be achieved when the periods before 1560 and after 1700 have been better researched. However, the causes of its growth in the central period analyzed here can only be appreciated with general reference to the performance of the economy. As hinted above (see p. 43), London population history encompassed two separate phases. Before 1650 its expansion paralleled an increasing national population. Since numbers could in theory grow more rapidly than the means of subsistence, then migration to the metropolis may have helped prevent serious mortality crises elsewhere in the country. After 1650 London continued to grow when the national population was declining. This was in sharp contrast to the remainder of Europe, where urban demographic trends usually moved in step with non-urban trends. For example, in Holland, which was very heavily urbanized, the population of both sectors declined from the second half of the seventeenth century, the exact opposite of what happened in England.[34]

It seems fairly clear that in the period between 1560 and 1650 people were pushed out of the countryside into the towns, particularly London, which had already become the principal trading centre in England. This was due to a rising population resulting in a shortage of land and a need to use land more efficiently by enclosure and conversion to grassland in order to increase productivity. Opportunities were very limited, and the need to secure subsistence was one cause of migration. The general situation has been well documented for Kent but was not limited to one county.[35] In northern England conditions deteriorated so far as to result in famine,[36] and this is why migrants to London in this period may be traced from all parts of the country. The scale of migration meant that all the newcomers could not be accommodated within the City, and the suburbs took on their characteristic features at this time. It is often thought that they developed by movement out from the city centre. This is a misconception, as new migrants frequently settled first in the area outside the walls and may subsequently have moved into the centre. Table 3 gives a greatly simplified indication of the course of suburban development. In the late sixteenth century the eastern, northern and southern suburbs were taking the rural surplus into unskilled trades, labouring, the transport of goods and shipping. By the early seventeenth century the eastern and northern suburbs were developing most rapidly with a growing secondary sector based on artisan work and small industries. The western suburbs joined this fast increase from the mid-seventeenth century onwards, adding a tertiary sector of luxury items and services to the capital's growing manufacturing capacity. This brief sketch outlines how London had developed into a multicentred conurbation by around 1650.

Why metropolitan growth continued in the second half of the seventeenth century is harder to assess, despite London's unfavourably high mortality and when national conditions appeared less likely to promote large-scale urbanization. There is no doubt that the capital comprised the country's largest single market,[37] that high transport costs encouraged all forms of economic activity to be located as close as possible to the main centre of consumption; and that the existence of this market gave entrepreneurs an incentive to meet its demands. Indeed, this seems to have happened with remarkable efficiency. In manufacturing, a general freeing of the London economy facilitated the supply of an increasing variety of goods due to the inability of the gilds to extend their effective restrictive control into the suburbs. In agriculture, the adoption of mixed farming on the lighter soils of south-east England maintained their fertility by rotating fodder crops and cereals. This enabled food supplies to be secured, but a transition to arable farming was accompanied by slow changes in tenure, farm size and field arrangement in favour of large-scale production. These improvements caused by London's increased demand for food resulted in a new kind of push of population from the land into the metropolis. This is also shown by increased social differentiation in the south-east, which partly explains why migrants came from a much restricted area of the country by the later seventeenth century.[38]

Because London attained such significance, it is incontestable that its development was bound up with the general course of economic development, although the nature of these connections requires much further research.[39] This period also set the tone of metropolitan population trends for the succeeding two centuries. It was only in the mid-nineteenth century that a new phase of expansion began again when mortality ceased to be the principal characteristic of London demography.[40] The distinctive urban pattern disappeared and metropolitan population trends converged with the remainder of the country. Natural increase accompanied migration in heralding another period of rapid growth. New administrative structures reinforced by improved transportation gradually began to weld the conurbation into a single unitary city. While its growth resulted in movement out of the city into new kinds of suburbs, the essence of many of the features first established in the seventeenth century survived the passing of the Victorian age. These included its pre-eminent trade and service functions while the dominance of craft production centred around migrant workers in the local labour markets still existing in the inner suburbs.[41] In the longer run, as earlier, periods of rapid population growth were accompanied by immense changes throughout the metropolis.

V

This chapter has presented a general survey of the growth of London population from a fresh beginning after 1560 down to 1700, based on an analysis of the original parish registers. While more detailed investigations may improve the accuracy of the figures, the overall trends now lack the opacity which formerly clouded the subject. They suggest that the chronology of expansion should be revised to incorporate an especially rapid period of growth until the mid-seventeenth century, followed surprisingly by a further period of increase in the second half of the century. Newcomers could not be accommodated within the Walls, so the first period witnessed a massive expansion of the suburbs which established their own distinctiveness at this time. The evolution of a vast early modern conurbation was the principal feature of the second period, punctuated by extensive fire damage in the City in 1666 and in Southwark in 1676. These new figures further suggest the kinds of endeavours which could now profitably be pursued. They might include the detailed examination of a myriad of demographic, medical and topographic issues, together with a much fuller investigation of the broader economic linkage in which lies a more satisfactory explanation of the causes of the population changes described here. Some of these pursuits are begun in the other contributions to this collection in a less skimpy fashion than space here permits. Considered together, they amplify the central role of London history in this period as suggested by the population figures.

NOTES AND REFERENCES

1. For amplification, see F. J. Fisher, 'The sixteenth and seventeenth centuries: the Dark Ages in English economic history?', repr. in N. B. Harte (ed.), *The Study of Economic History* (London 1971), p. 192.

2. This point emerges from J. Hajnal, 'Two kinds of pre-industrial household formation system', in R. Wall, J. Robin and P. Laslett (eds), *Family Forms in Historic Europe* (Cambridge 1983), pp. 67–8; and the other chapters in this volume.

3. It would of course be a serious mistake to underestimate London's later significance. An example of its uniqueness is given in L. S. Sutherland, 'The City of London in eighteenth-century politics', in R. Pares and A. J. P. Taylor (eds), *Essays Presented to Sir Lewis Namier* (London 1956).

4. These figures have been calculated from J. de Vries, 'Patterns of urbanization in pre-industrial Europe 1500–1800', in H. Schmal (ed.), *Patterns of European Urbanisation Since 1500* (London 1981), Table 3.5, p. 87; and Table 3.6, p. 88.

5. Ibid., pp. 96–104.

6. This is partly admitted by de Vries, 'Patterns of urbanization', p. 104.

7. N. G. Brett-James, *The Growth of Stuart London* (London 1935), p. 27.

8. Ibid., p. 65.

9. For example, new cartographic evidence has suggested the possibility that Brett-James's reconstruction of London around 1600 based on Stow's *Survey* could possibly refer to an earlier date. M. Holmes, 'A source-book for Stow?', in A. E. J. Hollaender and W. Kellaway (eds), *Studies in London History* (London 1969), pp. 277–83.

10. E. A. Wrigley, 'A simple model of London's importance in changing English society and economy 1650–1750', repr. in P. Abrams and E. A. Wrigley (eds), *Towns in Societies* (Cambridge 1978), p. 215.

11. V. Pearl, *London and the Outbreak of the Puritan Revolution* (London 1961), pp. 31–7, 42–4.

12. The general reliability of the London registers is discussed in R. Finlay, *Population and Metropolis: the Demography of London 1580–1650* (Cambridge 1981), Ch. 2.

13. This was most kindly undertaken by Dr R. S. Schofield of the ESRC Cambridge Group for the History of Population and Social Structure. The methods are described in E. A. Wrigley and R. S. Schofield, *The Population History of England 1541–1871* (London 1981), pp. 23–32, 705–7.

14. C. J. Kitching (ed.), *London and Middlesex Chantry Certificates 1548*, London Record Society, 16 (1980); Greater London Record Office MR/TH/1–7. An extended discussion of the techniques described here is to be found in B. R. Shearer, 'Demographic Change in London and Middlesex 1550–1700', (unpublished Cambridge University Ph.D. thesis, forthcoming).

15. Gregory King, 'L. C. C. Burns Journal', in P. Laslett (ed.), *The Earliest Classics: John Graunt and Gregory King* (Farnborough 1973), p. 39.

16. In a study of seven contrasting London parishes in 1695, Wall found 4,673 persons in 771 households giving an average household size of 6.1 persons including servants and lodgers. R. Wall, 'Regional and temporal variations in English household structure from 1650', in J. Hobcraft and P. Rees (eds), *Regional Demographic Development* (London 1979), Table 4.6, p. 103. This represents approximately a 1 per cent sample of metropolitan inhabitants.

17. These figures have been derived from J. P. Boulton, 'The Social and Economic Structure of Early Seventeenth-Century Southwark', (unpub-

lished Cambridge University Ph.D. thesis, 1983), pp. 19–30. We are very grateful to Dr Boulton for providing us with his data, which form the basis for this discussion of Southwark.

18. Wrigley and Schofield, *Population History of England*, pp. 565–6.
19. Ibid., p. 569.
20. Ibid., p. 569; and Table A3.1, p. 528.
21. [T. Birch] *A Collection of the Yearly Bills of Mortality from 1657 to 1758 Inclusive* (London 1759).
22. Finlay, *Population and Metropolis*, pp. 146–8.
23. F. J. Fisher, 'The development of London as a centre of conspicuous consumption in the sixteenth and seventeenth centuries', repr. in E. M. Carus-Wilson (ed.), *Essays in Economic History*, 2 (London 1962), pp. 201–2.
24. Finlay, *Population and Metropolis*, pp. 40–3.
25. Ibid., Ch. 3.
26. An excellent study is B. E. Supple, *Commercial Crisis and Change in England 1600–1642* (Cambridge 1959).
27. I. Sutherland, 'When was the Great Plague? Mortality in London 1563 to 1665', in D. V. Glass and R. Revelle (eds), *Population and Social Change* (London 1972); Finlay, *Population and Metropolis*, Ch. 6.
28. Recent thinking is outlined in A. B. Appleby, 'The disappearance of plague: a continuing puzzle', *Economic History Review*, 2nd ser. 33 (1980); P. Slack, 'The disappearance of plague: an alternative view', *Economic History Review*, 2nd ser. 34 (1981).
29. This is suggested in Table 4 above, and in V. B. Elliott, 'Single women in the London marriage market: age, status and mobility, 1598–1619', in R. B. Outhwaite (ed.), *Marriage and Society* (London 1981).
30. See Finlay, *Population and Metropolis* for a fuller discussion of the evidence.
31. Ibid., pp. 64–9, 140–2.
32. Elliott, 'London marriage market', pp. 87–9.
33. Wrigley and Schofield, *Population History of England*, pp. 351–2; Table 8.16, p. 349, panel 2.
34. This is neatly shown in A. M. van der Woude, 'Population developments in the Northern Netherlands (1500–1800) and the validity of the urban graveyard effect', *Annales de Démographie Historique*, (1982), graph on p. 57.
35. P. Clark, 'The migrant in Kentish towns 1580–1640', in P. Clark and P. Slack (eds), *Crisis and Order in English Towns 1500–1700* (London 1972), pp. 138–51.
36. M. Drake, 'An elementary exercise in parish register demography', *Economic History Review*, 2nd ser. 14 (1962); A. B. Appleby, *Famine in Tudor and Stuart England* (Liverpool 1978), Chs 7 and 8.
37. For an interesting discussion, see N. McKendrick, J. Brewer and J. H. Plumb, *The Birth of a Consumer Society* (London 1982), especially pp. 9, 13, 21–2.
38. A. H. John, 'The course of agricultural change 1660–1760', repr. in W. E. Minchinton (ed.), *Essays in Agrarian History*, 1 (Newton Abbot 1968); E. L. Jones, *Agriculture and the Industrial Revolution* (Oxford 1974), pp. 90–5; K. Wrightson and D. Levine, *Poverty and Piety in an English Village: Terling, 1525–1700* (New York 1979), Ch. 7.

39. Many valuable suggestions are made in Wrigley, 'London's importance'.
40. J. T. Coppock, 'A general view of London and its environs', in J. T. Coppock and H. C. Prince (eds), *Greater London* (London 1964), p. 19; Table 1, p. 34.
41. For examples of survivals, see E. J. Hobsbawm, 'The nineteenth-century London labour market', in R. Glass (ed.), *London: Aspects of Change* (London 1964); P. G. Hall, *The Industries of London Since 1861* (London 1962); L. H. Lees *Exiles of Erin* (Manchester 1979).

Appendix. Thirty sample parishes

Parish	Area[a]	Sources Manuscript Location[b]	Reference	Transcript[c]
Allhallows Bread Street	C	GL	5031	H., vol. 43
Clerkenwell	N	GLRO	P76/JS 1	H., vol. 9, 17, 19
Cowley	R	GLRO	DRO 33	—
Cranford	R	GLRO	DRO 9	—
Edmonton	R	I	—	CG
Enfield	R	GLRO	—	CG
Hanwell	R	GLRO	DRO 6	—
Harrow	R	I	—	He
Heston	R	GLRO	DRO 26	—
Ickenham	R	GLRO	DRO 27	—
Isleworth	R	I	—	SG
Kensington	R	I	—	H., vol. 16
Littleton	R	I	—	SG
Northolt	R	I	—	CG
St Andrew Holborn	N	GL	6667/1-6, 6673/1-7	D
St Giles Cripplegate	N	GL	6418, 6419/1-12	H., vols 75, 76, 80/1
St Katharine by the Tower	E	GL	9659/1-3, 9660-9665	B; H., vols 64, 88, 89
St Margaret Westminster	W	WCL	—	—
St Martin in the Fields	W	WCL	—	H., vols 25, 66
St Mary Somerset	C	GL	5710/1-3	H., vols 59, 60
St Michael Cornhill	C	GL	4061, 4062, 4063/1	H., vol. 7
St Paul Covent Garden	W	WCL	—	H., vols 33, 36
Shadwell	E	I	—	P

South Mimms	R	GLRO	DRO 5	—
Stepney	E	GLRO	P93/DUN	P
Stratford Bow	E	GLRO	P88/MRY 1	—
Tottenham	R	GLRO	DRO 15	CG
Twickenham	R	I	—	SG
Wapping	E	I	—	P
Whitechapel	E	GLRO	P93/MRY 1	P

Notes:

(a) Areas
C   City
N   Northern suburbs
E   Eastern suburbs
W   Western suburbs
R   Rural Middlesex

(b) Location of manuscripts
GL   Guildhall Library
GLRO   Greater London Record Office
I   Incumbent
WCL   Westminster City Libraries, Buckingham Palace Road Branch

(c) Transcripts
B   A. M. Burke (ed.), *Memorials of St Margaret's Church Westminster: the Parish Registers 1539-1660* (London 1914).
CG   ESRC Cambridge Group for the History of Population and Social Structure. Monthly totals from completed aggregative analysis forms, by kind permission of the Group.
D   W. Denton (ed.), *Records of St Giles Cripplegate* (London 1883).
H   Harleian Society Publications, Register Section.
He   W. O. Hewlett (ed.), *Registers of St Mary's Church, Harrow on the Hill Vol. I, 1558-1653* (London 1899).
P   M. J. Power, 'The Urban Development of East London 1550-1700' (Unpublished London University Ph.D. thesis, 1971), by kind permission of the author.
SG   Society of Genealogists' collection.

CHAPTER TWO
Metropolitan government in crisis: the response to plague

Paul Slack

Plague has always provided rewarding material for the moralist, journalist, novelist and historian. Daniel Defoe successfully exploited all the possibilities in his *Journal of the Plague Year*, published in 1722; and that work had almost as many precursors as the epidemic of 1665 which it celebrated. From the beginning of the seventeenth century pamphleteers tried to make these crises intelligible and acceptable by combining fact, fiction and moral exhortation in a persuasive whole. In works with vividly expressive titles, they dwelt at length on the numbers of the sick and the dead who made *London like Ninivie in Sack-Cloth* and provided *London's Mourning Garment and Funerall Teares*. They urged Londoners to repent before further disaster struck: *London Look-Backe*. They wielded *A Rod for Run-awayes* against the richer citizens who fled in their thousands, and they noted the cruel welcome they received outside the city: *Londoners, their Entertainment in the Countrie*. Plague evidently offered ample opportunity for contemporary reflection on a variety of moral and social themes: the relations between God and sinful humanity, rich and poor, rulers and ruled, town and country, all contributing to *London's Miserie: the Countrye's Crueltie*.[1]

It would require a series of histories to do justice to all the manifold difficulties and dilemmas which plague presented. This essay will concentrate on the reactions of government, on the efforts made to enforce local and social control in wholly exceptional circumstances. But the exploration of this theme will also involve some discussion of the other stresses which plague brought to London and Londoners. For no picture of the capital during the two centuries in which it grew into a metropolis would be complete without some account of the crises which punctuated and temporarily impeded its economic and demographic growth, which regularly undermined the self-confidence of its citizens, and which reveal to the historian as they did to contemporaries the environmental, social and political problems which metropolitan growth necessarily involved.

I

Plague was a regular visitor to London throughout the three centuries from the Black Death of 1348 until the last outbreak of 1665–6, causing major epidemic disasters from time to time and persisting in some of the intervening years in a milder more endemic form. It is only from the mid-sixteenth century onwards, however, that we can observe the frequency and severity of its occurrence at all closely. By then it was certainly familiar. It has indeed become a truism that there was scarcely a year in the sixteenth and early seventeenth centuries when plague was absent from London. It is truism which requires some qualification. There were intervals when only a handful of plague cases was reported by the fallible searchers of the dead, and when London may in fact have been free from the disease, as from 1616 to 1624 and from 1650 to 1664; and there were possibly similar short intermissions earlier, in the 1550s, for example. But for the major part of our period, from the first great epidemic which we can measure, that of 1563, until the last, beginning in 1665, plague was present in one of two guises. Either it persisted in moderate form for years at a time, raising normal mortality levels by between 10 and 20 per cent, as from 1606 to 1610 and from 1640 to 1647; or it caused major mortality in a single summer and died away in the following year. The greatest epidemics of the period, which will particularly concern us in what follows, are listed in Table 7.[2] There were also two other years when plague threatened to take off and cause equal havoc, and when it necessitated precise government action: 1578, when 7,830 people died in the City and Liberties, 3,568 of them of plague; and 1630, when 7,509 people died in the same area, 793 of them of plague.[3]

The simple figures in Table 7 are eloquent. Nearly a quarter of the city's inhabitants died in 1563, the greatest mortality rate of the whole period. In 1665 more than 80,000 people died; that is equivalent to the total populations of contemporary Norwich, Bristol, Newcastle, York and Exeter – the next five towns in the kingdom – added together. Nothing in the modern world, short of nuclear catastrophe, could match that. Yet these figures to some degree understate the extent of

Table 7. Major epidemics in London, 1563–1665

Year	All burials	Plague burials	Estimated total population	Gross mortality, per cent
City and Liberties				
1563	20,372	17,404	85,000	24.0
1593	17,893	10,675	125,000	14.3
1603	31,861	25,045	141,000	22.6
1625	41,312	26,350	206,000	20.1
City, Liberties and Outparishes				
1636	23,359	10,400	313,000	7.5
1665	80,696	55,797	459,000	17.6

Sources: See note 2.

these disasters. Mortality was much more concentrated than the annual totals imply. Epidemics rarely got off the ground before June and the worst was over by November. In the three months from August to October 1665, for example, rather more than 70,000 people, nearly a sixth of the population, perished.[4] Moreover, we must add to the number of the dead the number of those who caught plague and subsequently recovered. Case-fatality rates for bubonic plague suggest that the latter might amount to as much as 40 per cent of all casualties.[5] It is probable, therefore, that more than one third of the population was incapacitated by plague in 1563, and scarcely less than a third in 1603, 1625, and 1665.

One further point needs to be made before we have finished with crude statistics. Plague was not only concentrated in time. It was concentrated socially and geographically. Since the disease was carried by rats and fleas, people in the most dilapidated overcrowded houses and with fewest changes of clothing were most vulnerable: the poor, in other words, who were 'pestered' together in those sheds, cellars and subdivided tenements which contemporaries recognized as the foci of infection.[6] The heavy incidence of pestilence in the alleys rather than the main streets of some of the inner city parishes can be plotted; and the same picture of social and hence topographical polarization in the incidence of plague can be seen in variations in mortality between parishes.[7] Differences between parishes were not particularly evident in 1563, partly because the city was still compact, and rich and poor rubbed shoulders in several neighbourhoods. But as the city grew, poverty and population density increased in the fringe parishes, bringing ever-increasing epidemic mortality rates with them. For comparative purposes we can measure the level of mortality in any parish by means of a ratio of burials in the epidemic year to burials in preceding years. The higher the ratio, the greater the mortality as compared with the norm. These ratios are shown for sample parishes or groups of parishes in selected parts of the metropolis in Table 8.[8]

Table 8. The distribution of epidemic mortality in metropolitan London: crisis mortality ratios

Epidemic Year	City Centre[a]	West[b]	North-East[c]	South[d]
1563	6.6	4.1	4.8	3.1
1593	3.2	3.4	6.0	3.8
1603	5.0	5.6	8.5	7.6
1625	3.8	3.7	6.6	6.7
1636	1.2	1.8	3.7	3.1
1665	3.4	4.9	7.0	7.9

Sources: See note 8. The parishes concerned are:
(a) Allhallows Bread St., Allhallows Honey Lane, SS. Antholin, Mary le Bow, Mary Woolnoth, Matthew Friday St., Michael Bassishaw, Mildred Poultry, Stephen Walbrook.
(b) SS. Margaret Westminster, Martin in the Fields, Clement Danes, Mary le Strand.
(c) SS. Botolph Aldgate, Botolph Bishopsgate.
(d) St Saviour Southwark.

After 1563 the rich parishes in the heart of the city were increasingly fortunate. By 1665 plague was half as severe there as in some of the suburbs, and half as severe as it had been in the same parishes in 1563. There was no similar improvement on the western edge of the city and in Westminster. The growth of the West End over this period brought new mansions for the gentry and the urban élite, but also blind alleys, sheds and penthouses around, behind and against them. Their inhabitants were ready fodder for plague in the seventeenth century. The most drastic deterioration in the environment and hence in health took place on the other fringes of the city, however: in Southwark, where the plague of 1665 was more than twice as severe as that of 1563, and to the north east, outside Bishopsgate and Aldgate, in what were acknowledged to be two of the poorest parishes in the city by the end of the sixteenth century.[9] As urban growth spread further north and east in the early seventeenth century, there was equally heavy plague mortality in St Giles Cripplegate and in Stepney and Whitechapel, in what was becoming the East End.[10] In short, plague slackened its grip on the inner city but tightened its hold on the suburbs. In 1593 half the reported plague burials still occurred within the City proper; by 1625, however, three-quarters were in the 'liberties' and 'outparishes', and in 1665 the proportion was five-sixths.

The problems caused by differential epidemic mortality were exacerbated by the fact that suburban parishes were much larger than those in the centre. Their churchyards were soon overflowing and their officials overwhelmed. As early as 1563 the clerk of St Botolph's Bishopsgate was reduced to noting the burial of 'two corpses' or 'three corpses' without further identification in his register. His colleague in St Saviour's Southwark in 1625 sometimes found 'twenty or thirty corpses left at the place of burial' and he 'knew not who brought them thither'.[11] By 1665 there were more deaths, and hence more bodies to be disposed of, in the two parishes of Stepney and Whitechapel than in all the 97 parishes within the Walls put together. On one day, September 11, 154 people had, somehow or other, to be buried in Stepney.[12] One can only speculate about what that meant as a psychological and administrative burden on the parish.

This is not to imply that the inner city ever escaped the effects of plague. The three-fold increase in mortality in 1665, which is indicated for the nine central parishes in Table 8, could not be shrugged off lightly. The city centre had graveyards literally piled high with corpses so that they 'began to smell and annoy the inhabitants', and bodies lying in the most fashionable of its streets.[13] There was also a particular cause of social dislocation here. For these streets were otherwise largely deserted. One reason for the relatively low mortality rates in the centre of town was the flight of the richer inhabitants, itself an epidemic phenomenon and one which was socially biased. Its extent cannot be measured precisely, but its existence is evident from falling numbers of baptisms in the richer parishes during epidemics; and its socially damaging effects were deplored by most contemporary writers. In the absence of employers and benefactors, those who remained in the City were said to be left impoverished and defenceless in the face of plague.

Nevertheless, the appreciation of a crisis is always relative, and it may have been some consolation for householders in the centre of the city to see how much worse things were elsewhere. In 1603 it was well known that plague flourished 'especially in the suburbs on every side', and by 1665 the newspapers were condescendingly noting the same fact and attributing it to the 'poverty and sluttishness' of the city's periphery.[14] Plague was a metropolitan problem, and not simply or even largely a city problem, in the seventeenth century.

II

Throughout the period, however, it was the government of the City which had to respond in the first instance to these crises, and it is perhaps remarkable that it never collapsed altogether under the strain. Although many of the ruling élite took to their heels with their social equals, and the Common Council met only rarely during epidemics, the mayor and a sufficient minority of aldermen always stayed behind to hold and preserve the reins of power. Usually they were among the most active of the City fathers, experienced men who in normal times controlled most of the City's affairs, and who often sat together on the governing body of one or other of the City Companies. The most energetic of them in the later sixteenth century was Rowland Heyward, a man who took an interest in every aspect of the corporation's activities, who regularly attended aldermanic meetings in the epidemic of 1563, who sat on a special committee appointed to consider plague policy in 1570, and who remained to be active again in the plague of 1593, when he was in his seventies.[15]

In 1563 such determined patricians already had precedents to guide them in the management of an infected city. Efforts had been made since 1518 to mark infected houses, and as far as possible to quarantine their inmates in order to prevent further contagion. The collection of vital statistics had begun in the first bills of mortality, and these provided regular information about the progress of disease.[16] It was possible to identify infected parishes and to watch the number of casualties increasing and then declining. The city also had, in the College of Physicians founded in 1518, a source of advice on matters of public health, and in the five London hospitals, founded or refounded between 1547 and 1553, exemplars of what might be achieved by urban initiative in social policy.[17] By 1583 an impressive set of plague regulations had been developed. They were printed in that year, and reissued with modifications in all later epidemics. Members of infected households, whether sick or healthy, should be isolated in their houses for a month, public assemblies at funerals and plays strictly controlled, the streets cleaned, and vagrants expelled from the city.[18] The materials were there for the sort of rigid police control of infected towns which was attempted by some urban patriciates on the continent.[19]

Yet the charge was made again and again by the central Government that the rulers of the City always did too little too late, and it was an accusation in which there was a good deal of truth. From the beginning, in 1518, new devices for the control of infection had been imposed on a reluctant corporation by the Privy Council, which wished both to safeguard the health of the Court and to see London demonstrate the same 'civility' in its social policies as other Renaissance cities.[20] In 1563, however, the aldermen adopted no firm policy until the crisis was almost over, understandably perhaps given the severity of the epidemic in the centre of town. Crosses were being attached to the doors of infected houses in June. There were collections for the sick in some parishes, and the Chamber distributed small sums of money to those most seriously affected. But when, in July, plague victims and their families were told to stay in their houses for a month, some were allowed out to collect food, and no arrangements were made to see the order enforced. It was only in February 1564, when the Privy Council signified its displeasure about the 'great negligence and remiss slackness of the citizens', that complete segregation of infected households was insisted on and that special officers were appointed to supply and guard them.[21] For the next decade the city experimented half-heartedly with varying degrees and periods of quarantine.[22]

In 1577 the Privy Council returned vigorously to the attack. It was then in the process of devising a uniform policy for public health for the whole kingdom, promulgated in the first book of national plague orders issued in 1578; and it regarded plague in London as one of the concomitants of that unbalanced metropolitan growth against which it waged a major, but unavailing, campaign from 1580 onwards.[23] There was hence little sympathy for the City in the printed articles which the Council circulated in 1577, asking with obvious irony 'what orders have been put in execution for the restraining of the infected of the plague within the City of London'. In 1578 the Council summoned representatives of the City to a conference on the subject, and threatened that if they did not act voluntarily it now had 'means and ordinances in readiness more chargeable and heavy'.[24] It further sent the mayor a draft set of regulations which survive with the City's comments.[25] They formed the basis for the printed orders of 1583, and they illuminate the standpoints of both sides: the ambitions of councillors, which the City thought hopelessly unrealistic, and the reservations of the City, which the Council thought the product of self-interested parochialism.

The differences arose over four items of policy. To begin with, the Council advocated a large corps of officials who would make the policy of household segregation enforceable in practice. In every parish there should be visitors and keepers of the sick, 'purveyors' of provisions with which to supply them, and overseers and treasurers, with their clerks, to arrange finance. The City replied that it could not afford so large a complement. The orders of 1583 reduced their number, and as a result had to allow that one member of each infected household might go out for food. Not until 1608 was complete isolation prescribed in the London orders, although it had been incorporated in the printed plague orders for the rest of the kingdom from their beginning in 1578.[26]

Secondly, the Council hoped for a team of physicians, apothecaries and surgeons to care for the sick. Here the city's difficulties stemmed from its equivocal relations with the College of Physicians. The College was a separate chartered corporation, not a subordinate organ of the City government, and although it consulted often with the aldermen about medical aid, it produced the necessary volunteers only slowly.[27] The city held out the hope of medical personnel in its orders of 1583, and planned for them in more detail in 1609, but it was not until 1625 that two doctors were certainly engaged and that large sums of money, nearly £300 in all, were paid for the expenses of members of the various branches of the medical profession.[28]

Associated with this was a third conciliar ambition: there should be a special hospital, a pesthouse, in which some of the infected might be isolated. With its usual combination of flattery and complaint, the Council noted in 1583 that pesthouses existed in other 'cities of less antiquity, fame, wealth, circuit and reputation' than London. Again, however, the City found itself short of funds and suitable property. A small pesthouse was finally begun in St Giles Cripplegate in 1594, financed partly by a levy on the City Companies which had made windfall profits from the seizure of a Spanish treasure ship.[29] Yet the building was still unfinished in 1603, and even in 1665, when there were five pesthouses in London, it is unlikely that they together housed as many as 600 people.[30]

Finally, at the root of all else lay the problem of finance. In its first article in 1578 the Council proposed that there should be a 'general taxation throughout the whole city' to cover the costs of quarantine, officials and pesthouses. This the corporation vehemently resisted. Church collections and charitable bequests would suffice, it argued. New impositions could only undermine the existing system of rates for the hospitals and parish poor relief, which was indeed coming under strain in the 1570s.[31] No mention was made of special plague rates in the orders of 1583, although some provincial towns had levied them decades earlier and almost all were to do so by 1610.[32] In 1608 the London orders provided in principle for an extra weekly rate, but it was only in 1636 that the aldermen, on their own initiative, raised such a levy throughout the city.[33]

The rulers of the City, therefore, scarcely showed themselves in the vanguard in instituting methods of controlling plague or its effects. But if there was justice in the Council's indictment, there was justice also in the City's response. It was not simply that the problem was much greater in size in London than in other towns. It was naturally much more difficult effectively to quarantine, supply, find physicians and provide pesthouses for thousands of infected than for a few hundred. More important was the paradoxical fact that London was hampered by its wealth and by its elaborate political structure, as compared with other English towns. Lavish donations from private citizens had supported the hospitals; they had contributed to the large poor stocks of many parishes; and the aldermen were used to regarding such philanthropy as a ready recourse in critical times. Just as they exploited the wealth and generosity of the livery companies in periods of dearth, so they preferred to do the same in years of plague – as in 1630 and 1636 – before they felt it necessary to turn to compulsory taxation.[34]

Politically, they were inhibited by the number of institutions which they had to supervise and whose interests they had to respect and to reconcile. Not only did they find it difficult to put pressure on the College of Physicians and, as they complained to the Council, on the bishop if they wished to use the city clergy to promulgate their orders and overawe their critics.[35] They also had to manage the representatives of their own citizens in wards and parishes which were both far more numerous than in any other English town and far more independent and politically active. It is significant that the centralization of parish poor relief, which was being established in other towns by 1600, proved impossible to achieve in London. The city had its rates in aid redistributing funds from one parish to another; it also had the hospitals and in the seventeenth century, the Corporations of the Poor.[36] But none of these effectively suppressed parish independence, and the latter institutions demanded deliberation and prolonged political effort which the aldermen were unable to undertake in the heat of an epidemic crisis. It has been shown that the citizens of the capital enjoyed an unusual degree of political participation in this period. The city suffered, it has been said, not from too little government but from too much.[37] That impeded any attempt at central direction.

Moreover, the growth of London and the spread of plague with it placed an increasing share of the burden outside the unfettered jurisdiction of the city corporation: either in the liberties where jurisdiction was mixed or in dispute, or on the edges of Southwark, in Westminster and the East End, in the counties of Surrey, Middlesex and Essex, where there were authorities which the City could only consult or influence, not browbeat or command.[38] As a result, the responsibilities of government in London during epidemics did not lie in practice with the corporation: they lay first with the parishes, whose autonomy the

City was reluctant to infringe too blatantly, and secondly with the central government, which alone could impose some measure of uniformity on the whole metropolis.

III

The parishes of the city seem to have been as overwhelmed by the epidemic of 1563 as the corporation. Their surviving records show that churchwardens had to make special arrangements for the burial of the dead, and several of them bought the new printed books of prayers for fasts against plague. But there is no evidence of any unusual expenditure on the poor or the sick.[39] In humiliating contrast, the congregation of the Dutch church in London was debating as early as July whether or not plague was contagious, and appointing surgeons and making provision for the care, as well as the isolation, of the infected members of its refugee community.[40] Here was an example of foreign 'civility' close to home.

After 1563, however, city parishes began to catch up, partly under pressure from the corporation. Not surprisingly, they were sometimes confused by the lengthy orders which came down to them. In 1584 the vestry of St Andrew Holborn minuted the need to choose 'viewers, searchers, keepers, watchers, surveyors, collectors, providers, deliverers, and such like officers of men and women to be attendant about the sick shut up of the plague'. The parish in the end appointed four women viewers to examine suspected cases, two female keepers of the sick, and two male overseers to keep an eye on them.[41] Other parishes had fewer officials, and several had to compel poor pensioners to take on the most essential and most dangerous jobs of searching and burying the infected by threatening to withdraw their dole.[42] But most parishes whose records survive did something. 'Surveyors' of plague orders and searchers of the dead were common from 1578 onwards, and there were watchmen and nurses for the sick in some of the richer parishes by 1608.[43] In 1603 infected households were receiving financial support in many, probably in the majority, of city parishes.[44]

The adequacy of that support depended, however, on the balance between needs and resources, and some parishes were very much better provided for than others. Before 1625, most of them relied on existing charitable funds and on casual gifts to finance additional household relief during epidemics. We know of only three vestries which imposed a special rate for the sick before then: St Margaret Lothbury and St Mary Aldermanbury in 1593 and St Martin in the Fields, in Westminster, in

1603.[45] The result was huge inequality between parishes. In the centre of the city benevolences no doubt often sufficed, at least after the great epidemic of 1563. But they cannot have done so in the suburbs: in St Botolph's Bishopsgate, for example, where expenditure on the poor in 1593 and 1603 only rose by the same proportion, around 50 per cent, as in some of the rich central parishes, despite enormously heavier mortality.[46] The mayor and aldermen made some effort to help, ordering charitable collections, persuading companies to give donations, and redistributing small sums to the parishes which were hardest hit, like St Saviour's Southwark.[47] But it was clear in 1603, as in 1593, that the parishes with the largest stocks for the poor and with the richest and most generous inhabitants, were those with least need.

Plainly, some fresh source of finance for the benefit of the suburbs was required. In 1625 it was provided by outside intervention: not, as might have been expected, directly from the Council, but exceptionally and uniquely from Parliament. In August the House of Lords, then sitting in Oxford, appointed a committee to consider the relief of plague-stricken London. No less a figure than the Duke of Buckingham was responsible for this move, and the two orders of the Lords which resulted were no doubt primarily inspired by the Council.[48] The first, a command that the poor rate in London and its suburbs be doubled for the benefit of the infected, had little immediate effect. The City continued to protest that existing resources were sufficient, several parishes did not impose an additional levy until 1626, and those which acted quickly, like St Martin's in the Fields, encountered resistance from ratepayers.[49]

The second of the Lords' prescriptions was more effective. Since the whole country would be threatened by the spread of infection if there was disorder in the capital, there was to be a general collection throughout the kingdom for the visited in London and Westminster. It was raised under a charitable brief, like those issued earlier by the Lord Keeper for towns suffering from fire. Until the money came in, the Chamber was to advance a loan to parishes. The City in fact paid out a little over £1,000, an unprecedented provision on its part.[50] This was not the end of Parliament's role. In 1626 the Lords returned to the task of supervising the collections, and inquired with some anxiety what steps had been taken in the city for the 'regulating of the visited persons'. In the Commons Dudley Carleton, another councillor, was also worried that new financial aid might not be matched by the *quid pro quo* of fresh rigour in police control. He proposed a select committee to draw up a bill for more sophisticated regulations like those which had provided good government in Paris, Venice and other great cities.[51]

Nothing came of this legislative initiative, however, and when plague again afflicted London in 1630, it was the Council which took up once more its admonitory and directing role. Inspired again by the example of 'Paris, Venice and Padua and many other cities' and influenced by the King's French physician, Theodore de Mayerne, the Council urged that as many of the infected as possible should be isolated in pesthouses. This was a 'better and more effectual course' than their quarantine in their own houses which had clearly failed. There should be new hospitals built on Parisian models. Above all, however, some novel 'political' remedy for the problem of plague was now to be sought. Mayerne wished for some magistrate with 'absolute power' to control both city and suburbs. He recommended a board of health, which should include two Privy Councillors and two bishops, as well as the mayor and selected aldermen. It would exercise jurisdiction over the whole metropolis from Richmond to Greenwich, and have authority in all matters of public health – defined to cover vagrancy, poor relief and public hygiene as well as plague. The College of Physicians concurred. What was needed was a 'commission or office of health' for the whole built-up area, like the bodies which had been 'found useful in Spain, Italy and other places'.[52]

Had it been created, the metropolitan board of health would have been a splendid plank in Charles I's claims to enlightened absolutist paternalism. But it was not. Partly no doubt for political reasons, but also because plague did not revive in 1631, it was never more than a pipe dream. Yet its advocates had accurately diagnosed the problem of government in the metropolis, and in practice the Council itself fulfilled the function of the board in the 1620s and 1630s, receiving reports from the parishes of Surrey and Middlesex, the burgesses of Westminster and the Lord Mayor, and even ordering the arrest of a recalcitrant alderman and his deputy.[53] As a result, there was some modest improvement in efficiency. The new policy of pesthouses proved impractical, but the old, of household segregation, was enforced more rigidly. In 1625 one observer had reported as early as July that 'it is not certain who is clean or foul at London, and they have given over the closing up of houses'.[54] In 1636, however, parishes were buying padlocks for doors and paying warders and nurses; and there were orders to open houses after long periods of quarantine as well as to shut them up.[55] In St Martin in the Fields more people were quarantined in 1636 than in the much worse epidemic 10 years earlier: over the year as a whole 388 families, comprising 1,328 people, were incarcerated and supported. Of course, the policy was never wholly effective, even in Westminster where the Council's influence was strongest. Complaints of infected paupers sitting openly at their doors and wandering the streets were still common.[56] But the strategy of household isolation was at last becoming something of a reality in London in the 1630s.

Thirty years later, in the last great outbreak of plague, the same story of grand plans and modest, but real, achievements was repeated. The Council again wished to replace household segregation with confinement in pesthouses, but the epidemic was largely over before its plans were completed.[57] Neither did it have time to consider the projects sent to it by Hugh Chamberlen, which commented, like Mayerne's, on the need for new forms of taxation and new political authority.[58] It appointed a special sub-committee to recommend action, but far from turning itself into a board of health, the committee fled from the city with the Court. Government was supervised by George Monck, now Duke of Albemarle, and in practice exercised under him by the Earl of Craven, one or two justices in the outparishes, and the mayor, Sir John Lawrence. The co-operation between Craven and Lawrence at least meant more coordination of policy over the metropolis than had been possible before.[59] There was also greater financial provision than before. Collections were organized throughout the kingdom, as in 1625, and the money paid to the bishop of London, who distributed it to infected parishes. The Chamber again made payments to parishes to help them until the collections came in, distributing £600 every week through the summer, sums quite without parallel in any earlier epidemic; and the aldermen ordered two extra years' poor rates as an additional means of relief.[60]

Unfortunately, no complete accounts of the money spent in 1665 survive to allow us to judge the scale of the contribution made. It seems clear, however, that the central parishes of the city were relatively well provided for. They were able to identify households as soon as they were infected, to transport some of the sick to pesthouses and isolate others in their houses, and even occasionally to provide nurses for them.[61] The insoluble problems lay, of course, in the suburbs. Westminster was relatively well off. The flight of its richer inhabitants vitiated any attempt to levy rates successfully, but the runaways had left generous gifts behind them. Of £1652 received in St Margaret's for expenditure on the infected, no less than £1117 came from donations from 'honourable persons'. As a result the parish was able to support 40 people at the pesthouse and another 1,500 in their own houses.[62] But other fringe parishes were wholly unable to cope. In St Giles Cripplegate it was reported in August 1665 that 'all have liberty lest the sick poor should be famished within doors, the parish not being able to relieve their necessity'.[63] Despite the endeavours of parishes, corporation and central government, gross inequalities in care and provision remained when plague ended in the capital.

IV

It is clearly inadequate to see the problems of plague in London solely through the eyes of government, however. The paper projects of Mayerne and Chamberlen look like blue-prints for a welfare state; the accounts of the parishes give an impression, in 1665 at any rate, of splendid effort. The historian is tempted to a Whiggish view of steadily advancing administrative sophistication, spearheaded by an informed and responsible Privy Council. It is only by looking more closely at the realities on the ground, at the reactions of the governed as well as of the governors, that we can fully appreciate the obstacles to the achievement of any such ambitions. For if plague tested the political structure of the metropolis, it also strained more fundamental ties of neighbourhood and community on which the stability of the city, as of any other local commonwealth, rested.

The reaction of many citizens to the regulations imposed on them from above was defiance. Not only was there general opposition to special rates for the infected. The infected themselves resisted the constraints of quarantine. They refused to keep their doors and windows shut in St Martin le Grand in 1593. They abused constables who tried to enforce household segregation and broke out of their houses in Westminster and Southwark in 1630. One widow got out and marched deliberately into Westminster Abbey, to the horror of the people there. In Holborn a watchman went round tearing padlocks off the doors of infected houses.[64] Later, in 1665, a weaver in St Giles Cripplegate, where the sick were not confined, went down into St Stephen Coleman Street and broke 'off the padlock off the door' of the house of a friend. There were disturbances of a similar kind in the same year in St Botolph's Aldersgate, in St Anne's Blackfriars, and in St Giles in the Fields. Four men even appear to have turned the tables on their rulers by shutting up the Lord Mayor's house in St Helen's.[65] A horrified observer of the disorders of 1665 thought that

> Death is now become so familiar and the people so insensible of danger, that they look upon such as provide for the public safety as tyrants and oppressors; whilst neither the richer sort will be brought to contribute, nor the meaner to submit, though to their own apparent good and preservation.[66]

What seemed to authority incomprehensible recklessness was, however, fully understandable. We can readily imagine the sufferings of those who were isolated, unable to see their friends, at the mercy of searchers who sometimes certified death before the fact and of nurses who mistreated or robbed their patients.[67] In 1593 the parish clerk of

Allhallows, London Wall, tersely recorded the burial of a man who 'died of grief, being now shut up in his house this sickness time'. The astrologer, Simon Forman, was shut up with the rest of his household when one of his servants caught plague in 1603, apparently from one of Forman's patients. Forman and his family were 'left destitute' and were 'much abused' by their fellow parishioners who locked them in: 'They would say to me that it was better that I and my household should starve and die than any of them should be put in danger'.[68]

The practice of household segregation was bound to be opposed, and it was not difficult to find grounds of principle for doing so. It was plausibly argued that shutting up the healthy with the sick increased mortality rather than reducing it: a case put forward by the aldermen as early as 1583 and one which lay behind the Council's shift towards the alternative of pesthouses from 1630 onwards.[69] More powerful and appealing, however, was the argument from Christian charity: that it was men's duty to visit and comfort their friends and neighbours when they were ill. It was popular appreciation of this imperative, with its potential for psychological reassurance and social cohesion, which lay behind much popular protest. When the poor of some London parishes in 1636 said that 'the Plague would not decrease till the infected had their liberty', it sounded like crude superstition. But it had behind it the view, also reported to be held by the London poor in the same epidemic, that it was 'a matter of conscience to visit their neighbours in any sickness, yea tho' they know it to be the infection'.[70]

It would be easy, but mistaken, to exaggerate this point. It would be wrong to think of all London citizens bravely defending communal norms which maintained some sort of social stability against destructive regulations imposed on them from above. For plague itself isolated people as much as the mechanisms devised by authority to control it. Fear of infection led to the shunning of the sick and of everything connected with them. There are many cases of masters turning out apprentices and servants into the streets 'all comfortless' when they caught infection.[71] Parish authorities paid to shift people 'out of the parish that had the sickness upon' them.[72] The infected were themselves no saints. Pepys was told that sick people shut up in Westminster 'would breathe in the faces (out of their windows) of well people going by'. Social antagonisms of all kinds were vented during epidemics. Pepys's doctor had to issue a public denial in the papers and on a notice at the Exchange when it was rumoured that he had murdered a servant who died of plague.[73] Even relations often proved wanting. In 1593 Richard Lane of St Mary Magdalen, New Fish Street, felt himself going down with plague. He staggered to the house of his aunt in St Botolph's

Aldersgate and appealed to her for help: 'Good aunt, stick to me now for I am very sick and my wife also is more sick and I know and am persuaded myself that not any of my friends or kindred or of hers will venture to come and visit us this time of infection.'[74]

In circumstances in which such appeals were necessary, however, people naturally clung to what fragments of normal social intercourse they could, whether in streets, in alehouses or in church. Orders restricting attendance at funerals to a few near relations were especially resented. In 1603 some London preachers led resistance, defending and leading public funerals despite the dangers of contagion; and the practice had irresistible popular support as an essential outlet for grief and stress. One writer noted with distaste how 'the poorer sort, yea women with young children, will flock to burials, and (which is worse) stand (of purpose) over open graves where sundry are buried together, that (forsooth) all the world may see that they fear not the Plague'.[75] In 1636 eleven trumpeters marched behind the corpse of a colleague, dead of the plague, 'with trumpets sounded and swords drawn'. Even in 1665, central and local government was unable to prevent such displays of social solidarity and collective defiance.[76]

The response of the Council was naturally to demand still greater administrative effort 'to the end that the people may be better governed'.[77] It was social control quite as much as disease control that they were concerned with. As plague became ever more serious over an ever larger area, it seemed to present a mounting threat both to the health and to the stability of the kingdom. The aldermen might well be more hesitant, however, and not only because the ravages of plague were diminishing over time within their own jurisdiction. They could not sanction popular disturbance. Their printed regulations against plague in 1583 had been significantly endorsed 'for repressing of disorders and relief of the poor'. Yet at the same time they were closer to the 'multitude' who 'are to be governed' and who 'will hardly conceive what is for their good provided', and they were aware that new kinds of social regulation were as likely to aggravate as to prevent disorder.[78] They were not averse, either, to turning a blind eye to their own regulations when it suited them. In September 1625 the mayor himself arranged a public funeral for a captain of the trained bands, with 244 troops in procession, watched by a crowd of thousands. Its purpose was to confute rumours in the country that the city was in total disarray in the face of plague.[79] The Council can scarcely have been pleased; but many citizens must have welcomed this demonstration that, for once, the city fathers felt as they did.

The rulers of the city were therefore caught in an impossible position.

On the one hand was popular suffering and distress, and the evident need for relief and reassurance. On the other was an interfering Council insistent upon radical action. The aldermen could not be expected to take the Council's view. They knew that government normally depended on open co-operation between various authorities, just as social stability depended on neighbourly collaboration with a minimum of interference from above. In the conditions of plague, of course, neither functioned normally. Ward inquests, parish vestries, gilds and companies, local communities and households were disrupted. But the rulers were reluctant in crisis circumstances to attempt methods of control which would cause further disturbance immediately and make government more burdensome and more difficult in the longer term. It was natural for them to put their trust in the benevolence of their richer citizens and in the existing resources of their parishes and companies, and to hope that the crisis would soon pass. They might well have echoed the prayer of the Merchant Tailors, that God would defend the city 'from grievous plagues and contagious sickness, that we may often in brotherly and true love assemble'.[80]

V

There were no right or wrong answers to the problems of government in London during epidemics of plague; there were only predicaments. Success, however defined, would have been impossible, even with all the bureaucratic instruments available in a modern city. We have only to imagine a similar disaster in twentieth-century London, and to visualize the burdens it would impose on central government, the Greater London Council, the boroughs and the neighbourhoods of the metropolis, to see that conflicts and controversies about power, resources, social responsibilities and moral obligations are inevitable in critical circumstances, in any age or place. The story of plague in London has its timeless quality, as Defoe appreciated. But it also tells us something about the nature of early modern London. Plague throws light not only on the environmental problems which came with urban growth, but on the problems of social and political control which growth and a metropolitan environment brought with them.

For the Privy Council, the answer to these problems was plainly more direction from the top: more government at an ever greater distance and less participation at the local level. The inescapable logic of metropolitan growth seemed to be greater anonymity on the ground.

Historians should beware of taking a similar view, however. Popular reactions to plague show that metropolitan life was not yet (if it ever became) anonymous; and when plague and government regulations conspired to make it so, they were often resisted. One London minister, clearly dismayed by current events, urged his congregation not to ignore the 'duties of humanity' both in their households and in their neighbourhoods in time of plague: 'For if we break these bonds, I see not how human societies may continue'.[81] London in the sixteenth and seventeenth centuries was not a single amorphous mass, ripe for strong magistracy, but a collection of functioning, if intractable, human societies.

NOTES AND REFERENCES

1. The authors and dates of publication of the titles mentioned were: T. Brewer (1625); W. Muggins (1603); A. H. (1630) in J. D., *Salomons Pest-House* (1630); T. Dekker (1625); R. Milton (1604); R. Milton (1625). All were published in London. For reactions to plague generally and for a more detailed account of its incidence in London, see Paul Slack, *The Impact of Plague in Tudor and Stuart England* (Routledge and Kegan Paul, forthcoming 1985).

2. All accounts of plague in London depend on the surviving bills of mortality, whose coverage and accuracy was variable. The burial totals in Table 7 have been taken from I. Sutherland, 'When was the Great Plague? Mortality in London, 1563–1665', in D. V. Glass and R. Revelle (eds), *Population and Social Change* (London 1972), p. 303, Table 4; and the population totals are Sutherland's middle estimates for the nearest appropriate dates, ibid., p. 310, Table 6. There are slightly different totals and calculations in R. Finlay, *Population and Metropolis. The Demography of London 1580–1650* (Cambridge 1981), pp. 118, 155–7, and full statistics from the bills in I. Sutherland, 'A summary tabulation of annual totals of burials, plague deaths and christenings in London prior to 1666' (typescript in Bodleian Library, Oxford).

3. Sutherland, 'When was the Great Plague?', p. 303; Sutherland, 'Summary tabulation'.

4. C. H. Hull (ed.), *The Economic Writings of Sir William Petty* (Cambridge 1899), ii, table opposite p. 426.

5. J-N. Biraben, *Les hommes et la peste en France et dans les pays européens et méditerranéens* (Paris 1975–6), i, pp. 10, 303; R. Pollitzer, *Plague* (Geneva 1954), p. 418.

6. For examples, see C. M. Clode, *The Early History of the Guild of Merchant Taylors* (London 1888), i, pp. 295–6; J. W. Sherwell, *A Descriptive and Historical Account of the Guild of Saddlers of the City of London* (London 1889), p. 74; Corporation of London Records Office (hereafter CLRO), Quarter Sessions File, Feb. 1665/6, 7 Aug. 1665.

7. E. Freshfield (ed.), *The Vestry Minute Books of the Parish of St Bartholomew Exchange* (London 1890), pp. xlv–xlix; *idem* (ed.), *The Vestry Minute Book of the Parish of St Margaret Lothbury 1571–1677* (London 1887), p. xxxiii. Cf. Finlay, *Population and Metropolis*, p. 121; P. Slack, 'Mortality crises and epidemic disease in England 1485–1610', in C. Webster (ed.), *Health, Medicine and Mortality in the Sixteenth Century* (Cambridge 1979), pp. 50–1.

8. The ratios in Table 8 for the epidemics of 1563, 1593 and 1603 are the number of aggregate burials in the named parish registers divided by the annual average for the previous decade in each case; and for 1625, 1636 and 1665 the number of burials in these parishes reported in the bills of mortality in Guildhall Library (hereafter GL) divided by annual averages for 1629–35 and 1655–64 from the same source. All the parishes named have registers published by the Harleian Soc., except for: SS. Mary Woolnoth and Mildred Poultry, originals in GL; St Saviour Southwark, original in the Greater London Council Record Office (hereafter GLRO); and the parishes mentioned in the following works which have all been used: A. M. Burke (ed.), *Memorials of St Margaret's Church, Westminster* (London 1914); A. W. C. Hallen (ed.), *The Registers of St Botolph Bishopsgate* (London 1889); T. R. Forbes, *Chronicle from Aldgate* (New Haven 1971).

9. Cf. R. W. Herlan, 'Social articulation and the configuration of parochial poverty in London on the eve of the Restoration', *Guildhall Studies in London History*, 2 (1976), pp. 43–53; D. J. Johnson, *Southwark and the City* (Oxford 1969), pp. 225, 324–6; M. J. Power, 'The east and west in early-modern London', in E. W. Ives, R. J. Knecht and J. J. Scarisbrick (eds), *Wealth and Power in Tudor England. Essays presented to S. T. Bindoff* (London 1978), pp. 167–85.

10. Cf. their parish registers in GL and GLRO.

11. *Register of St Botolph Bishopsgate*, i, p. 262; W. Caldin and H. Raine, 'The plague of 1625 and the story of John Boston, parish clerk of St Saviour's Southwark', *Transactions of the London and Middlesex Archaeological Society*, 23 (1971), p. 94.

12. W. G. Bell, *The Great Plague in London in 1665* (2nd edn., London 1951), p. 274.

13. GL, MSS. 4458/1, p. 295; 6836, fol. 146r; 12792/2, 1603–5 acct.

14. British Library (hereafter BL), Add. MS. 29597, fol. 13; *The Newes*, 20 July 1665, p. 616.

15. CLRO, Reps. 15 and 23, passim; 16, ff. 530v, 531r. Cf. F. F. Foster, *The Politics of Stability* (London 1977), pp. 73–4, 83.

16. F. P. Wilson, *The Plague in Shakespeare's London* (2nd edn, Oxford 1963), pp. vi, 56–7, 189–208.

17. C. Webster, 'Thomas Linacre and the foundation of the College of Physicians', in F. Maddison, M. Pelling and C. Webster (eds), *Linacre Studies* (Oxford 1977), pp. 206–8; P. Slack, 'Social policy and the constraints of government 1547–58', in J. Loach and R. Tittler (eds), *The Mid-Tudor Polity* (London 1980), pp. 108–13.

18. CLRO, Journal 21, ff. 284–6, 339r; Wilson, *Plague in London*, pp. 15–16. The 1583 orders are printed in C. F. Mullett, *The Bubonic Plague and England* (Lexington, Kentucky 1956), pp. 380–3.

19. Cf. Biraben, *Les hommes et la peste*, ii, pp. 114–43; C. M. Cipolla, *Public*

Health and the Medical Profession in the Renaissance (Cambridge 1976), pp. 11–66; B. Pullan, *Rich and Poor in Renaissance Venice* (Oxford 1971), Part II, Ch. 4.

20. CLRO, Journal 11, fol. 319r, 15, ff. 47v–48r; Rep. 9, ff. 187r, 190v.

21. Rep. 15, ff. 259v, 263r, 277v–279; Journal 18, ff. 123v, 136, 142r, 184, 189v–190r.

22. Rep. 16, ff. 2v, 70r; 19, ff. 229v, 395r; Journal 19, ff. 129r, 186r, 197v–198r, 216v, 219.

23. P. Slack, 'Books of orders: the making of English social policy 1577–1631', *Transactions of the Royal Historical Society*, 5th ser., 30 (1980), pp. 3, 6.

24. P. L. Hughes and J. F. Larkin (eds), *Tudor Royal Proclamations* (New Haven, 1964–9), ii, p. 420n; *Acts of the Privy Council 1577–8*, pp. 326, 387; CLRO, Journal 20 (ii), ff. 441v–442r, 450v, 451v, 455r; Rep. 19, fol. 395r, 20, ff. 136r, 137r.

25. Public Record Office (hereafter PRO), SP 12/98/38 (dated 1574 by the editors of the *Calendar*, but it certainly belongs to 1578).

26. Mullett, *Bubonic Plague*, p. 381; *Orders conceiued and thought fit, as well by the Lord Mayor . . .* (1608; *STC* 16723); *Orders thought meete by her Maiestie . . .* (n.d.; *STC* 9195). The latter is probably of 1578.

27. See, for example, Royal College of Physicians, Annals II, fol. 26; III, ff. lv, 63, 99.

28. Mullett, *Bubonic Plague*, p. 382; *Foure Statutes specially selected . . .* (1609; *STC* 9341), p. 86; Wilson, *Plague in London*, pp. 21–2. For the much more ambitious use of medical men in 1665, see Bell, *Great Plague*, pp. 86–8.

29. Wilson, *Plague in London*, pp. 76–80; CLRO, Rep. 20, ff. 136r, 414–15; Journal 21, ff. 278v, 283v; BL, Lansdowne MSS. 38, fol. 23; 74, fol. 75.

30. Bell, *Great Plague*, pp. 37–9, 47–8, 192–3.

31. PRO, SP 12/98/38, fol. 164r. Cf. CLRO, Rep. 16, fol. 112r, 17, ff. 109v–110r, 19, fol. 25v; Journal 20 (i), ff. 42, 119r, 20 (ii), ff. 323, 483r, 499v–503. The hospital funds in fact paid the £120 which the Chamber distributed to parishes in 1563: Rep. 15, fol. 304r.

32. Cf. A. Raine (ed.), *York Civic Records*, 5 (Yorkshire Archaeological Society, Record Series, 110, 1946), pp. 50–1; Lincolnshire RO, Lincoln Entries of Common Council 1541–64, fol. 69v; Exeter City Record Office, Act Book 3, pp. 244–5 (1570).

33. *Orders conceiued* (1608); CLRO, Journal 37, fol. 216. For parochial collections of this rate, see GL MSS. 9237, 1636; 9680, fol. 55r; 1423/4, 1636–7; 4415/1, fol. 76r; 4524/2, fol. 39.

34. N. S. B. Gras, *The Evolution of the English Corn Market* (Cambridge, Mass. 1926), pp. 82–9; CLRO, Rep. 44, fol. 320r; Cash Account Book 1/2, ff. 122v–123r; G. Parsloe (ed.), *Warden's Accounts of the Worshipful Company of Founders 1497–1681* (London 1964), p. 305. Cf. Wilson, *Plague in London*, p. 105.

35. PRO, SP 12/98/38, fol. 167r.

36. V. Pearl, 'Social policy in early modern London', in H. Lloyd-Jones, V. Pearl and B. Worden (eds), *History and Imagination. Essays in Honour of H. R. Trevor-Roper* (London 1981), p. 125; *idem*, 'Puritans and poor relief: the London Workhouse 1649–60', in D. Pennington and K. Thomas (eds), *Puritans and Revolutionaries. Essays in Seventeenth-Century History presented to Christopher Hill* (Oxford 1978), pp. 206–32.

Pearl, 'Social policy', pp. 116–7. Cf. V. Pearl, 'Change and stability in seventeenth-century London', *London Journal*, 5 (1979), pp. 14–25.

38. On the problems presented by liberties and outparishes, see V. Pearl, *London and the Outbreak of the Puritan Revolution* (London 1961), pp. 23–31; R. Somerville, *The Savoy* (London 1960), pp. 223, 259–60; Johnson, *Southwark and the City*, passim; BL, Egerton MS. 2623, fol. 30; CLRO, Rep. 16, ff. 530v–531r; PRO, SP 12/98/38, fol. 167r.

39. GL MSS. 4810/1, ff. 18v, 20v; 4956/1, fol. 93v; 9235/1, 1562–3; 645/1, fol. 67v; 4956/2, f. 93v; W. H. Overall (ed.), *Accounts of the Churchwardens of the Parish of St Michael Cornhill* (London 1871), p. 157. The only special payments to the sick I have discovered were in Southwark: GLRO, P92/SAV/1387.

40. A. A. Van Schelven (ed.), *Kerkeraads-Protocollen der Nederduitsche Vluchtelingen-Kerk te Londen 1560–3* (Historisch Genootschap, Utrecht, 3rd ser., 43, 1921), pp. 429–32.

41. GL MS. 4249, pp. 6, 12, 116.

42. GL MSS. 4249, p. 12; 1264/1, fol. 35v; 3570/1, fol. 61r.

43. GL MSS. 593/2, ff. 67r, 69r; 1016/1, fol. 91r; 1279/2, 1592–4; 1431/1, p. 33; 1432/3, fol. 45v; 2088/1, fol. 32v; 2593/1, fol. 63v; 3570/1, fol. 61r; 4165/1, p. 88; 4415/1, ff. 17r, 31v; 4810/1, fol. 137r; *Minute Book of St Bartholomew Exchange*, pp. x1ii–x1iii, 3, 5; *Minute Book of St Margaret Lothbury*, p. xxi; *Accounts of St Michael Cornhill*, pp. 196–7, 250.

44. Ibid., pp. 193, 255; E. Freshfield (ed.), *Accomptes of the Churchwardens of the Paryshe of St Christofer's* (London 1885), p. 40; GL MSS. 1176/1, 1603–4; 2968/1, fol. 482v; 4415/1, ff. 31v–32r; 4457/2, ff. 75v, 76r; 4810/1, fol. 137r; 4824, ff. 21–22r, 26v. Earlier instances in other parishes are: 1016/1, fol. 91v; 1432/3, fol. 45v; 3556/1, fol. 98r.

45. *Minute Book of St Margaret Lothbury*, pp. xxii–iv, 6–7; GL MS. 3570/1, 21 Jan. 1593; J. V. Kitto (ed.), *St Martin-in-the-Fields, The Accounts of the Churchwardens 1525–1603* (London 1901), p. 570.

46. GL MS 4524/1, 1592–3, 1602–3. Cf. *Martin-in-the-Fields Accounts*, p. 577. For examples of more fortunate parishes with adequate benevolences and large poor stocks, see GL MSS. 1432/3, fol. 45v; 2968/1, ff. 482–3; 4457/2, fol. 39v; 4824, fol. 20v.

47. Wilson, *Plague in London*, pp. 91–2, 105; E. B. Jupp and W. W. Pocock, *An Historical Account of the Worshipful Company of Carpenters* (London 1887), p. 68; J. J. Lambert (ed.), *Records of the Skinners of London* (London 1933), p. 288; GLRO, P92/SAV/450, p. 372.

48. *Lords Journals*, iii, pp. 473, 475, 486, 488; Historical Manuscripts Commission (hereafter 'Hist. MSS. Comm.'), *Buccleuch*, iii, p. 248; Essex Record Office, D/DMZ 10 (summary of Lords' orders).

49. GL MSS. 4813/1, fol. 27; 4165/1, p. 183; 1279/3, p. 8; Westminster City Library (hereafter WCL), MS 3354.

50. Wilson, *Plague in London*, pp. 166–7.

51. *Lords Journals*, iii, pp. 509, 526, 539–40, 572–3, 628; *Commons Journals*, i, p. 851; Hist. MSS. Comm., *Lonsdale*, p. 10.

52. Slack, 'Books of orders', pp. 8–9, 18.

53. BL, Add. MS. 46845D. Cf. PRO, PC 2/47, pp. 227, 232, 284, 331–2; SP 16/355/130. The Council's continuing interest in the suburbs can also be seen in the attempt to incorporate them: Pearl, *London*, pp. 31–7.

54. Hist. MSS. Comm., *Mar and Kellie*, ii, p. 230.
55. GL MSS. 942A, fol. 24v; 2088/1, 1636-7; 2593/1, fol. 364v; 4524/2, ff. 39, 41r, 48v; 4810/2, fol. 76; 9237, ff. 70v-71r; GLRO, P92/SAV/1405.
56. WCL, MSS. 4512, 4514, F4516, ff. 15v, 17; W. H. and H. C. Overall (eds), *Analytical Index to the Remembrancia 1579-1664* (London 1878), pp. 341, 346.
57. New orders were published only in May 1666: Bell, *Great Plague*, pp. 333-5.
58. PRO, SP 29/122/123, 131/12, 157/87.
59. PRO, PC 2/58, pp. 135, 178; Bell, *Great Plague*, pp. 69-70, 315-8.
60. Ibid., pp. 196-9; PRO, PC 2/58, pp. 199, 201, 207; CLRO, Rep. 70, ff. 156v-157r; Journal 46, fol. 98r; Sessions Minute Book 16, 9 Dec. 1665; *The Intelligencer*, 7 Sept. 1665, p. 842. There are incomplete accounts relating to the national collections in Lambeth Palace Library, Carte Misc. VI, nos. 4-45.
61. E.g., GL MSS. 4956/3, pp. 268-70; 877/1, p. 236; 2088/1, 1665-6; 1432/4, 1665-6; 3556/2, 1665-6; 593/4, 1665.
62. WCL, MS E47.
63. BL, Harl. MS. 3785, fol. 31. Cf. R. Latham and W. Matthews (eds), *The Diary of Samuel Pepys* (1970-6), vi, pp. 224, 297.
64. A. J. Kempe, *Historical Notices of the Collegiate Church of St Martin-le-Grand, London* (London 1825), pp. 169-70; PRO, SP 16/175/3, 22, 24.
65. CLRO, Sessions File Feb. 1665/6, 5 June, 2 Sept., 22 Aug. 1665; Lord Mayor's Waiting Book II, 22 Sept. 1665 (I owe this reference to the kindness of S. Macfarlane); PRO, PC 2/58, p. 118.
66. PRO, SP 29/134/31.
67. *Calendar of State Papers Domestic 1664-5*, p. 551; CLRO, Sessions File Feb. 1665/6, 23 Oct.
68. E. B. Jupp and R. Hovenden (eds), *The Registers of the Parish of Allhallows London Wall* (London 1878), p. 120; Bodleian Library, Ashmole MS. 1436, fol. 72.
69. BL, Lansdowne MS. 74, ff. 75-6; Slack, 'Books of orders', pp. 4-5.
70. J. Squire, *A Thankesgiving for the decreasing ... of the plague* (1637), p. 11; Hist. MSS. Comm., *Gawdy*, p. 163. Cf. Bell, *Great Plague*, pp. 114-6.
71. GL MS. 12806/2, 6 Nov. 1563, 29 April 1564; CLRO, Sessions File Feb. 1665/6, 29 July, 3 Aug.
72. GL MSS. 942A, ff. 24r, 15v; 593/2, fol. 149r; 1432/4, 1665-6; 1016/1, fol. 231r.
73. Pepys, *Diary*, vii, pp. 40-1; vi, p. 165 and note.
74. A. J. Jewers, 'The will of a plague-stricken Londoner', *Home Counties Magazine*, 3 (1901), pp. 109-10.
75. Hist. MSS. Comm., *Salisbury*, xv, p. 266; J. Balmford, *A Short Dialogue concerning the Plagues Infection* (London 1603), p. 32.
76. J. C. Jeaffreson (ed.), *Middlesex County Records* (London 1888), iii, pp. 62, 383; PRO, PC 2/59, pp. 123, 135.
77. PRO, PC 2/58, pp. 187, 207.
78. Mullett, *Bubonic Plague*, p. 383; Hist. MSS. Comm., *Salisbury*, ii, p. 224.
79. H. Petowe, *The Countrie Ague* (London 1626), pp. 20-1.
80. C. M. Clode, *Memorials of the Guild of Merchant Taylors* (London 1875), pp. 130-1.
81. H. Holland, *Spirituall Preseruatiues against the Pestilence* (London 1603), p. 173. Cf. Slack, *Impact of Plague*, Ch. 11.

CHAPTER THREE

Appearance and reality: barber-surgeons, the body and disease

Margaret Pelling

The later Tudor period saw an escalation in the problems of urban life. The decay of towns as a result of economic fluctuations was succeeded by epidemic disease and pressures caused by shifts of population. Population increase and the simultaneous loss of the real value of wages introduced a new dimension to the problem of poverty. All these adverse features of urbanization found their epitome in London. Many provincial centres showed an acute awareness of their difficulties, but the prodigious growth of London forced on contemporaries an appreciation of the city as a new phenomenon. Above all London represented mobility, change, and instability. It did not escape contemporary notice that for the city dweller this could represent degeneration or premature death. Urban living raised an already high level of anxiety about health to the point of obsession, and prompted an increasing resort to medical practitioners.

As a reflection of this the practitioners of the period were remarkable both in number and variety. It is not surprising that to some extent London practitioners were known for both the futility and extremity of their measures, but scepticism about certain incidents of practice did not reduce the level of demand for medical advice. Rather, it increased the level of lay interest in medical subjects, and strengthened resistance to the imposition of restrictions on the activities of unofficial practitioners. A high level of demand also cast doubt on the pretensions of small élite groups of practitioners, while at the same time increasing concern as to the maintenance of standards. Medical services became a major item of consumption for those classes which were becoming more prosperous by the late sixteenth century; at the same time medicine of a different kind and price provided an invaluable source of consolation for those most helpless in the face of change. These important trends are less obvious than some others in the London context at this time. Anxiety about health, awareness of the religious and economic implications of the demand for medical services, and conflicting attempts to regulate or monopolize practice, are all represented by institutional or administrative developments in the capital in the sixteenth and early seventeenth centuries. Of these the foundation of the College of Physicians, the introduction of the ecclesiastical licensing system, the amalgamation of the Barbers' and the Surgeons' Companies, the refoundation of a few of the hospitals, and the emergence of the Apothecaries' Society, are the best known. The significance of these events has often been exaggerated or misconstrued, but they are relevant to the sense of crisis in respect of health in this period.[1]

Of the groups active in medical practice in cities the best established, and the most numerous, were the barber-surgeons. For provincial centres, this has to be inferred from scattered evidence, but in London the occupation has left ample records of its corporate activities. As represented by their Company the London barber-surgeons were as well based in City administration as any other occupational group of middling rank, and constitute an important element in the comparatively neglected sector of craftsman-shopkeepers. As with other occupational groups, the hierarchy within the Company was in part a representation of the variation in estate from the rich craftsman to the very poor.[2] However, the position of the barber-surgeons in sixteenth-century London was not dependent merely upon their traditional role in city life. Many of them showed great initiative in rising to the challenges and changing circumstances characteristic of the period. This is evident in their prompt adoption of new remedies and in their creation of a body of medical literature, much of it in the vernacular; the academically qualified physicians of the London College lagged behind in both respects, and were not very productive even in Latin.[3] These more aggressive London barber-surgeons made a conscious virtue of the function generally adopted by barber-surgeons at this time, of practising physic as well as surgery, according to occasion. The urgency of such occasions, and the need for positive measures, were often cited in justification.

Where did London's multifarious medical personnel live, and under what circumstances? A quantitative survey of practitioners in London has been undertaken, and is proving a major task.[4] The numbers are considerable, and the distribution made arbitrarily uneven by the nature of the sources. However, it is possible to obtain some impression of the topographical distribution of freeman barber-surgeons in the 1640s, at the end of the period under discussion, and to make comparisons with the incidence of other types of practitioner over a longer timespan. The outcome of this exercise is highly suggestive, especially when taken together with evidence of the wide range of functions of barber-surgeons. It points ultimately towards features of the social competitiveness of early modern London, and to related aspects of contemporary sensibility, especially as expressed in the individual's own person. It also reveals the importance of an underestimated and highly emotive threat to health, in the shape of venereal disease, which came to symbolize current attitudes to life in the capital.

I

In turning first to the Barber-Surgeons' Company, it must be stressed that this collectively omits journeymen, apprentices, those who followed the occupation while remaining members of other companies, and those who simply remained outside company membership. Even so, in 1537, with a total of 185 freeman householders, the Barbers' Company was numerically the strongest of the City Companies, and held this position before overwhelming the tiny, self-styled Surgeons' Company in 1540. Runners-up were such occupations as the Skinners (151), Haberdashers (120), or the Leathersellers (113).[5] A hundred years later, in 1641, the strength of the Company had increased to 293, of whom about 30 could not be located or were then living overseas or in the provinces.[6] There were as many identified as surgeons as there were barbers. A quarter of the Company professed other trades, mostly in small numbers; most numerous were tailors (15) and dyers (15). Scattered or single bricklayers, potters, cutlers, upholsterers and bookbinders were probably, as was traditional, attached to the Company because they were regularly employed by it, particularly in relation to the maintenance of its property. The two chandlers and the single musician and distiller could also have made lights, music, and strong drink for company festivities, but these are in addition common diversifications for barber-surgeons.[7] It is notable that the remainder, headed by the tailors and the dyers, were all concerned in some way with costume, in which may be included the three perfumers. These other trades intermingled with the barber-surgeons proper in different parts of the city, the tailors and others especially in places of resort and to the west, and the dyers near the river and particularly in Southwark.

The distribution of freeman barber-surgeons in 1641 provides an apt reflection of the growth of the metropolis, its shift westward, and of the connection of barber-surgeons with areas of fashion, entertainment and ill-repute.[8] What is also striking, however, is the remarkably thorough distribution of barber-surgeons over the whole City within the Walls, indicating a role in providing services in the everyday life of most classes. This distribution contrasts with that of members of the Apothecaries' Society at the same date who, although sharing in the drift westward, were concentrated around the central commercial thoroughfares of the city, notably about Fenchurch Street, their traditional locality of Bucklersbury and Cheap, and St Paul's.[9] To the west the freeman apothecaries were again heavily concentrated along the thoroughfares (Fleet Street and Strand, and Holborn) and the routes connecting these, with a distinct preference for the vicinity of conduits.[10] The richest in this trade, distillers, apothecaries, and especially druggists, were still within the City Walls, around the Cheap-Fenchurch Street axis, reflecting the profitable growth in wholesale dealing in drugs, itself a measure of consumption of medical services.[11]

Not surprisingly, the military and naval service of the barber-surgeons, which did so much to distinguish them from the physicians and which so influenced their practice and writings, is also reflected in their distribution. In 1641 seven surgeons normally resident in London were 'in the King's service in the North'; only six were at sea, an indication of the extent to which ships were served by apprentice surgeons in their formative years, or by others who were not fully privileged members of the Company. Barber-surgeons also clustered in the growing suburbs near the river east of London Bridge, at Wapping, Ratcliffe (soon to be dominated by the activity of the East India Company), Greenwich, and as far down the Thames as Gravesend. Wapping, about a mile from the Tower, was known for brewhouses and executions, in both of which barber-surgeons may be said to have a vested interest. As well as their maritime connections, and partly as a result of them, all these centres had a reputation for immorality and especially for sexual licence.

Within the City Walls, the regular incidence of freeman barber-surgeons even extended to the crowded wharfside parishes south of Thames Street, where freeman apothecaries were fewest. The former were, however, comparatively scanty in some more prosperous northerly wards like Bishopsgate, which included Gresham College and which had a considerable complement of resident physicians. In addition, greater concentrations of freeman barber-surgeons can be detected around places of business and resort. In 1641 thirty-three can be located on a radius of 300 yards around the Royal Exchange in Cornhill, part of which had been designed in an unusual way to include an 'emporium' of different shops which featured articles of personal consumption, including haberdashery, apothecaries' wares, and small goods. Many of those making and selling goods were women, who became an attraction in themselves. Valentine Raseworme, a versatile empiric, was on one occasion arrested in the Royal Exchange, where he displayed his banners and wares.[12] To some extent the Royal Exchange had shifted the City's centre of gravity away from St Paul's and the Old Change, which ran north-south at its eastern end.[13] However, St Paul's, inside and out, although less a centre for commerce, was still a chief rendezvous for news, odd employments and hirings, fashionable display, and gull-catching. Twenty-eight barbers lived within 300 yards of its western door; St Paul's idlers were also served by the poets, painters, and the makers of pins, feathers, and looking-glasses who flourished nearby in Blackfriars. Barbers' shops have a continuous history as outlets of news, printed and verbal: Jonson satirically portrays as one of the clerks to an official newscollector, a barber 'bred' by the west door of Paul's.[14]

Barber-Surgeons' Hall was situated in Monkswell Street, directly under the most north-westerly section of the City Wall. It was thus within 500 yards of Paul's precinct and convenient for the western suburbs. In St Botolph Aldersgate, the parish lying outside the Wall between Barber-Surgeons' Hall and St Bartholomew's Hospital, there lived in 1641 four freeman barbers of the Company, and two liveryman surgeons, both of whom were at this time identified as among the richest inhabitants of Aldersgate ward. Three of the city's richest physicians also lived in St Botolph's parish; St Bartholomew's property was favoured accommodation among physicians.[15]

Freeman barber-surgeons participated fully in the westward shift of London life. By 1641, one third (88) of the total in the capital lived to the west of the City Walls, of which as many as 34 lived beyond the city boundaries in the suburbs and Westminster. By 1640 the western extramural wards were a mature mixture of grander newer buildings, main thoroughfares, small crowded or 'pestered' alleys, and liberties regarded as haunts of vice and vagrancy.[16] The numerous medical practitioners of the parish of St Dunstan in the West, the dubious pursuits of Ram Alley, the pawnbrokers and fortune-tellers of Fetter Lane, the prostitutes of the liberties, and the mercurial baths of Leather Lane across Holborn, were all adjacent and available to the Inns of Court. Both ends of Fetter Lane were used for public executions. More freeman barber-surgeons clustered around Fleet Bridge, where prodigies were sometimes shown. At the other end of the Old Bailey, a street found desirable by apothecaries as well as barber-surgeons, the many barber-surgeons of the crowded and disreputable parish of St Sepulchre were cheek by jowl with St Bartholomew's Hospital, the cunning men of Cow Lane, and the food and fairground amenities of Smithfield.

Further on towards Westminster, barber-surgeons were most numerous by 1641 in St Martin's in the Fields, one of only two parishes (the other, St Giles's in the Fields, being a suburb of Westminster) which John Graunt regarded as having submitted even partially honest returns for deaths from the French pox – his explanation of this being that the ill-repute of the neighbourhood made the concealment practised in other parishes futile.[17] Graunt had in mind such purlieus as 'the Bermudas', a complex of alleys at the bottom of St Martin's Lane at the west end of the Strand, where barber-surgeons had the opportunity of diversifying into alehouses, tobacco-selling, and the effects of prostitution. Like the apothecaries, the barber-surgeons had followed closely upon the newest building and were already established in such areas as Charing Cross and Drury Lane.

The topography of freeman barber-surgeons in London at the end of the period in question thus seems to suggest, firstly, that their services were required regularly, and secondly, that they had some degree of association with places of resort and even of vice. The latter suggestion may be taken further. It is unlikely that prostitution in London was ever confined to its traditional locality of the Bankside in Southwark; but after 1500 dispersal was encouraged by action on the part of the crown aimed at shutting down the stews, a policy apparently prompted by the frightening early years of the syphilis 'epidemic'. The Bankside stews were soon reopened, but the women established themselves in such localities at St Katherine's by the Tower, Shoreditch beyond Bishopsgate, Holborn, St Giles's in the Fields, and Westminster. Other sources identify, on the fringes of the extramural wards, Lambeth Marsh to the south; Hog Lane and Whitechapel to the east, outside Aldgate; 'Pickt-hatch' near the Charterhouse, beyond Aldersgate, in the north-west; Clerkenwell, especially Turnmill Street, just west of the Charterhouse; and localities in the western liberties such as Leather Lane and Whitefriars.[18] Prostitution cannot have been absent within the City Walls – there were brothels in Ave Maria Lane, near the west door of Paul's, and soliciting went on in Paul's itself – but the centripetal distribution of disorderly life outside City jurisdiction is clear, as is the connection between the location of social dangers and official concern over the physical expansion and condition of the capital. This connection was underlined at an early stage by a city ruling of 1552 that

St Bartholomew's Hospital should benefit from a 'second rent' paid by all the tenants of houses which had been turned into 'alleys' and taken over by rootless people.[19]

In 1641 very few of these mistrusted localities were without a resident member of the Barber-Surgeons' Company. An interesting outlying case is Hogsden or Hoxton, a countrified village north of Moorgate, to which Londoners resorted for such rural pleasures as open fields, cakes, cream, and wise women; this recreational locality also had its freeman barber-surgeon.[20] As might be expected, however, a much more marked centripetal distribution is shown by unlicensed practitioners, of all kinds.[21] Between 1550 and 1640 those prosecuted by the College of Physicians (including women and apothecaries) were almost never to be found near the central thoroughfares within the Walls, such as Cheap, but were common enough just within the walls, in the riverside wards, and in localities also favoured by freeman barber-surgeons like Newgate Market near St Paul's, or Wood Street near Barber-Surgeons' Hall. Six were detected in Bishopsgate within the Walls, which perhaps points both to the ubiquity of unlicensed practitioners and to the wish of physicians living there to remove competitors from their vicinity. To the west, the unlicensed practitioners were predictably numerous along Fleet Street, Holborn, and the connecting routes Fetter and Chancery Lanes, and around St Bartholomew's. They were not lacking in Cow Lane, which may be seen as an incidental testimony to the accuracy of contemporary satire.[22]

Obviously in many such instances of unlicensed practice the phenomenon may be that of the barber-surgeon pursued for practising physic, so that there is identity between the freeman barber-surgeon and the prosecuted practitioner. Nonetheless, unlicensed practitioners are noticeably more numerous than freeman barber-surgeons on the 'red-light' fringes already mentioned, such as St Katherine's, Shoreditch, Charterhouse, and Clerkenwell. Perhaps surprisingly, they are less present in Southwark. Other sources confirm this general impression. Essex people consulted cunning men, witches, and sorcerers on London Bridge, Bankside, Ratcliffe, and Whitechapel.[23]

Overall, then, topography seems to indicate that barber-surgeons and other practitioners of this period played an integral part in urban life in London, while being at the same time particularly desirable in certain social contexts. What was required of them? The services they provided were above all personal. Why were these important, and what was there for so many practitioners to do, even given the fact that barber-surgeons were apt to grasp at a range of other, often related, economic opportunities? To answer such questions it seems necessary to look, not at the sporadic crises of mortality of early modern London, in spite of their devastating effects, but rather at morbidity, deformity, and even the obstacles faced by the individual attempting to present a favourable image in an increasingly sophisticated – or degenerate – urban context.

II

In any period before antibiotics, scarring, and more importantly, chronic failure to heal, must greatly have prejudiced the individual's chances of appearing clear and unspotted before the world. It could be argued that the individual's response to this situation has varied little, being consistently negative, while the terms in which responses were cast, on the other hand, have varied greatly according to the beliefs of the society in which they were produced. An appearance of indifference can be given, in that scars and deformities, like such features as unusual height and hair colour, could provide important means of identifying individuals and even establishing credentials. In European folklore, however, the idealized protagonist typically combined a person entirely free of deformity with an identifying mark or feature which was small and hidden. In periods before the present day, medical practitioners and the laity alike placed great stress on disfiguring conditions, especially those affecting the face; modern medicine concentrates more exclusively on life-threatening conditions, although there is little evidence that the laity shares this comparative indifference.

It is notable that, while northern Renaissance portraiture shows a fascination with extremes of ugliness, it signally fails to depict the more minor defects which are so plentifully recorded in such sources as popular medical literature, satire, and private correspondence. The function of ugliness and blemish in witchcraft accusations and trials in the early modern period is another reminder of contemporary sensibility. The stress laid upon the devil's mark or nipple as a sign hidden by the clothing of the witch meant that a blemish could literally be a pointer to execution. This hidden blemish can be seen as symbolic of the less specific physical and emotional defects of the old women who bore the brunt of accusations of witchcraft.[24]

Such attitudes seem not to have been confined to any class or classes in society, whether rural or urban. Urban life, however, added new dimensions to attitudes to the body as the city became the main arena for competition among social aspirants. The pre-eminence of London was sealed by the increasing presence there of courts which were famous for their stress on personal good looks and accomplishments. Society still expected the individual to summarize his estate in his own person; now a new flamboyance and even fastidiousness was required.[25] It would be surprising if a climate of acute social competition were to foster indifference to personal appearance, death or decay. Early modern London produced infinite variations on the theme of false appearances; but this evidence of sophistication should be seen as based on relatively stable attitudes to physical life. It was still customary to seek the mind's construction in the face (and hands), even though one might, like Shakespeare's Duncan, despair of the attempt, or alternatively, look to more and more subtle means (physiognomy, chiromancy) of achieving the truth.[26] Dekker's rich lord, trying in vain to estimate the trustworthiness of his servants, was characteristic:

> He calls forth one by one, to note their graces,
> Whilst they make legs he copies out their faces,
> Examines their eye-brow, consters [construes] their beard,
> Singles their nose out, still he rests afeard ...[27]

Deformity of body was taken into account, and often assumed to represent quality of mind and moral nature, as it was by the surgeon Pickering with respect to a London empiric:

> ... a deformed and illfavoured body in proportion,
> is a lively representation of a vicious and ill-
> disposed nature, so that it is a necessary consequence,
> that as his body is crooked, crabtree like, and grown
> out of all order, so his mind is monstrous. He is
> deformed who sets hand to writing to defame the good
> artists and him whose good acts are manifest ...[28]

Such correspondences were still an effective part of political propaganda. The allegations as to his physical nature which Tudor historians used to discredit Richard III, which were given permanent currency by Shakespeare *c.*1593, are a notorious case in point.[29]

That Renaissance satire constantly made reference to the body seems incontestable, even if it may be doubted whether this emphasis is ever really displaced, for example, in the Enlightenment, by metaphors derived from mind. The satiric genre has been linked by Randolph with 'word-death' rituals, which were intended to threaten the health and even the life of the person attacked. Satire can also be seen as a particularly urban product, requiring a 'crowded society' for its generation. Awareness of the snares and limitations of the body, physical life as a rich source of terms of abuse, and the strength of the parallels between society and the human body, all achieve a high pitch of expression with the outburst of satirical writing which began in England at the end of the sixteenth century. In its attacks on the social aspirant and the luxurious rich, late Elizabethan and early Jacobean satire appears as a reflection of the anxieties caused by social mobility and urban excess. It was, of course, chiefly produced in London, and generated by experience of London life. Unlike the playwrights, English satirists paid little attention to setting the urban scene in specific detail, but a great deal to the defects and pretensions of the individual in his or her own person. Many writers signified their intention of adapting the fashionable bauble of the looking-glass to serious purposes: metaphorically, they held up a mirror to reflect deformity. There is abundant reference to contemporary disease conditions, particularly the more disfiguring, among which can be included the falling hair, collapsed nose, ulcerous teeth, boils, ulcers, scurf, and stink of venereal disease.[30]

Whatever the origins of the genre, the satirist emerges as having adopted some version of the medical role. The causes of the decline of civilized society were named and condemned in the same terms as disease was diagnosed and eradicated in the body.[31] In the satire of this period 'the satirist's most common metaphorical pose was that of the barber-surgeon', who 'burns, probes, cuts and purges'.[32] Thus the writer chose the *persona* of the practitioner who was seen at the time to be combatting the most extreme and visible conditions with the strongest and most effective forms of intervention. In frequently also using the metaphors of anatomy, satirists and other writers remained within the sphere of the barber-surgeon: cutting and revealing, but with less immediate reference to the hope of cure.[33]

The skeleton – called an 'anatomy' in the sixteenth and seventeenth centuries – served as a *memento mori* over a long period, reminding human beings of the greatest pretension of all, to immortality. Elizabethan satire, and the plays which followed the attempts to suppress satirical writing, pointed not only to rank corruption, but also to the vanity of pretension and the distance between appearances and reality. Reference was made not only to the worm beneath the surface of the skin, but also to the real body or character which hid behind cosmetics and pretentious clothing. The preoccupation with disguise obviously had a humorous and even positive side, just as the London playwrights and others were also prepared to make ribald or cynical use of every detail of physical frailty collected by the satirists. In the concealments and revelations which occur so often in plays of the period, enormous and significant stress is placed on clothing and accessories and their power to determine, in the eye of the beholder, the personality, occupation, rank, and sex of the wearer.[34] Inventories and wills which carefully identified and disposed of single garments, show clearly the high capital cost of outer clothing, its status as a durable, and the significance vested in it by the wearer. Protests against the rapidly changing fashions and frivolous assumption of styles of dress, which were typical of the urban setting and above all of London, had considerable social and economic justification.[35] At the same time, London fashion was acting as an engine of economic growth and change.[36]

Elizabethan and Jacobean clothing, although strong in outline and attractive in surface, played an important role in concealing the body from public view. Very little of the surface of the body was allowed to appear. Refinements introduced into the town dress of the wealthier classes pointed to the same desire to combine ostentation with concealment. It seems reasonable to connect this with a high incidence of, and even increased sensitivity to, defect or deformity caused by disease in the context of a crowded society. Beggars offended by baring their limbs and sores in public, as well as by breathing on passers-by. The few areas of the body normally left uncovered by clothing acquired, for the more prosperous, accessories which attempted to make a virtue of necessity. Decorative gloves were an important item and permanently perfumed gloves were especially prized. The pre-eminence of the face was stressed by many styles of the period, notably ruffs. Small looking-glasses were attached to the costume like fobs. It is not surprising to find that masks were also worn from about mid-century by both sexes, and that face-patches were adopted during the 1590s.[37] Cosmetics were also applied, particularly those calculated to improve the appearance of the skin. For most of the Elizabethan period, the hair of men was generally kept short, and women's hair was mostly covered; by a similar characteristic tension between desire and fulfilment, men's hair became longer and women's hair more visible just when it seemed that the likelihood of hair loss by disease was at its greatest. Wigs rapidly evolved to fill the gap. This expedient also solved the perennial problem of infestation by lice and other parasites, with its ugly *sequelae* caused by scratching and infection.[38]

Clothing at this time had other functions which were important for all classes, in both town and country. Parts of the body which were uncovered were also unprotected, a belief which has considerable justification in temperate climates and at a time when minor injuries could lead by unchecked infection to major disaster. This again points to the special sensitivity of the face and hands. Several reasons for the importance of clothing have already been given, but it would not be an exaggeration to suggest that, at this period, covering the body was thought to be necessary for survival. However, change, or 'shifting' of clothing was also essential, even for the poorest.[39]

It is usually assumed, on the basis of scanty evidence, that the Tudor and Stuart periods, coming after the communal and ritual bathing of the medieval period, and before the allegedly superior regard for cleanliness adopted by fashionable society in the eighteenth century, were distinguished by their dirtiness.[40] The question deserves much greater attention, but enough has been said to suggest that, at the least, there was no lack of sensitivity on matters relating to the body and its state of health. Stray comments by contemporaries on dirty habits are usually taken as incriminating, without also being considered as evidence of a kind of fastidiousness. It is also worth stressing that there are more ways than one of being clean. Even in the present day, in Western society, many people make a strong distinction between their persons and their surroundings with respect to cleanliness. Ritual bathing apart, regular and prolonged immersion of the whole naked body is, for good and obvious reasons, a very recent habit, and even now is probably more partially adopted than bathroom furniture might suggest.[41]

Similarly, it is only recently that it was thought acceptable for any major area of the outer clothing to be in contact with the skin. The main burden of absorbing dirt and vermin from the body, and protecting the outer garments which were often worn daily for long periods, fell on the intervening layers or underclothing. Very few items survive from the period under discussion, pointing to great wear and tear followed by the use of the material for other purposes, and it is not even certain what was worn.[42] It seems reasonable, however, to suggest that the layer next to the skin has been under, rather than overestimated. It is difficult otherwise to imagine (for instance) what work was carried out by the numerous washerwomen of the time. Washing has received little attention as an occupation yet, to take one example, it was the single most common occupation of poor women in Norwich in the 1570s if the textile-related occupations are left out of account, and was also commonly adopted as a second-string occupation.[43] Clothing was also cleaned by mechanical means, including brushing and beating, the latter being particularly important against vermin such as lice. Both the capital value of clothing and its relation to health and disease are further underlined by the frequent reference to clothes acting as fomites, or carriers of infection, with respect to contagious diseases like plague, or the French pox.

Although total immersion seems to have been rare, washing of the all-important face and hands, and even the whole head, may have been a regular and even daily occurrence. The persistently high incidence of death by drowning was in some cases at least due not to suicide, or the role of water in transport and industry, but (with the almost universal inability to swim) to the use of rivers and ditches for washing, either of clothes or bodies.[44] Self-medication was a universal habit in which forms of washing or bathing could play a vital and little-considered part. Like substances now commonly regarded merely as foods, water itself very often had a potent or medicinal role and there was widespread contemporary awareness of the properties of different waters. In addition a very broad range of health-giving, curative, or merely soothing procedures involved bathing part or even all of the body in water imbued with herbs and other substances. Causing the body to sweat was also a very common and related procedure. Thus Bullein recommended fennel, balm and bay for washing-water and 'barbers' baths', and fennel with endive as 'very good to wash one's feet to bedward'. Perfumed waters, although liable to perversion by 'light wanton people', had similar virtues; 'what is pleasanter in sweet water, to wash hands, head and beard, and good in apparel, and may be rightly used', was a gift of God. The potency of soap was not underestimated; it was used as an active ingredient combined with others (including heavy metals) to combat tetters, black morphew, ringworms, spots, melancholy infecting the skin, scalding, stinking scabs, and itch.[45] Although Bullein's prescriptions were not for the poor, it may be concluded that lack of personal hygiene in the modern sense (in which water is given a neutral role) was partly compensated for by the universal tendency to domestic self-help with respect to health. In the present context what is relevant is that the most important locality outside the home for washing, grooming, and every function relevant to hygiene and the presentation of the body to the outside world, was the barber-surgeon's shop.

The short hair and constantly changing beardstyles of earlier Elizabethan men obviously required regular attention. Beards were dyed as well as shaped; later, not surprisingly, barber-surgeons became involved in wigmaking as well as the shaving of heads so that wigs could be worn. However, there seem to have been few limits to the personal services offered by barber-surgeons. Among these, bloodletting and toothdrawing are well-known; but barber-surgeons also cleaned teeth by scraping them, pared nails, picked or syringed ears (which could involve the removal of worms or 'small beasts'), plucked with tweezers, and had a special role in the removal and mitigation of marks and blemishes. Soapballs were used for washing, and perfumes were applied with casting-bottles.[46] Even if the customer failed to follow the example of centuries, and did not confide in his attendant, the barber-surgeon was in an excellent position to acquire knowledge of state of health from skin, breath, odour, and even the state of the hair. In using such signs barber-surgeons could justifiably argue that they were following the best traditions of Hippocratic medicine. Even if he did not often practise the more extreme forms of surgery, the barber-surgeon was in a better position even than the tailor to know both the appearance and the reality of his clients. He was responsible for the crucial exposed areas of head and hands, but also dealt in what was hidden.

Barber-surgeons' shops in towns and cities emerge as places of resort for men, offering music, drink, gaming, conversation, and news, as well as the services already mentioned.[47] After 1600 many added to their attractions by selling tobacco, a contemporary obsession which first earned credit for curing diseases, including venereal disease.[48] Direct evidence is hard to find, but it seems plausible to propose that the barbershop also served as the first port of call for advice on sexual matters, being, unlike the brothel itself, primarily a male preserve. The later history of the barbershop suggests continuity in this as in other respects. It should be stressed that for the first half of the seventeenth century at least there was a 'marked surplus' of men – particularly younger men – in London's population.[49] It is unlikely that every barber-surgeon in London offered the full spectrum of attractions mentioned here, if only because of the number of competing outlets for such items as drink. Nonetheless, the range is sufficient to explain both the large numbers of this occupation in London, and the evennesses and concentrations of their distribution in the capital.

III

So far it has been suggested that the topographical distribution of barber-surgeons in London, and the services they provided, reflected not only the pattern of social activity in the urban setting, but also the state of contemporary sensibility with respect to the body and especially to its defects. As already implied, venereal disease was an element in all these concerns. This argument can be taken further, to suggest that by the end of the sixteenth century venereal disease, in particular the 'new' disease *morbus Gallicus* or the French pox, had become an essential element in the urban scene and subsequently in the crisis of mistrust of city and court.

Syphilis was apparently at its most virulent in England in the early sixteenth century. The humanist Bernard André described it as a new disease which, following the sweat of *c.*1485, was yet more detestable than the sweat, and as abhorrent as leprosy. High virulence gave probability to extragenital infection, and it was thought to spread with great rapidity. The disease immediately provided a literal meaning to more spiritual forms of corruption. For example, it was held against Wolsey that with the great pox 'broken out ... in divers places of his body', he daily sought the ear of the king, blowing upon him 'with his perilous and infective breath', and that when healed, he pretended he had merely suffered from an apostume of the head. Allegations as to infection with the pox were frequently an element in charges against the clergy during the Dissolution period; at the end of the century the same is true of scandal suits among the laity, with fornication similarly the sin implied. One mode of infectiveness did not preclude another. The association of the disease with venery was recognized in the earliest measures taken against it in Britain, although ideas about its mode of infection were never so specific as the modern explanation, and rapidly broadened to include a range of factors, including body heat, of which promiscuous sexual intercourse, and the genital region itself, were thought to provide the extreme examples.[50]

By 1540 the pox was affecting the organization of medicine in London. The Act of that year uniting the Barbers and Surgeons included the reservation that, in London, surgeons were not to practise barbery, nor barbers surgery, except for toothdrawing:

> ... forasmuch as such persons using the mystery or faculty of surgery, often times meddle and take into their cures, and houses, such sick and diseased persons as be infected with the pestilence, great pocks, and such other contagious infirmities, & do use and exercise barbery, as washing or shaving, & other feats thereunto belonging, which is very perilous for infecting the King's people resorting to their shops and houses, there being washed or shaven.[51]

This stipulation (for which no sanctions were specified) was undoubtedly a dead letter, but it does indicate that, as on the Continent, the barber-surgeons rapidly assumed the dominant role in the treatment of the disease. It is possible that the somewhat puzzling Act of 1542–3, the so-called Quacks' Charter, in which the licensed surgeons of London were condemned for venality and for harassing cunning men and women who ministered to the poor for nothing, may have been connected with attempts by surgeons to establish their ascendancy with respect to all venereal disease. This Act defended the right of humble practitioners to use 'herbs, roots and waters' to treat 'customable' diseases such as outward sores, 'apostemations', skin conditions, sore mouths, 'scaldings', and 'burnings'. Either of the last two could refer to gonorrhoea, a more 'customable' disease or symptom which was also thought to arise as a side effect of two more of the urino-genital conditions mentioned, strangury and the stone.[52] The majority of the conditions listed could, however, also be referred to syphilis, thus creating grounds for competition. Guaiacum, an imported wood derivative publicized in England in a translation of 1533, then rivalled mercury in the treatment of syphilis.[53] If the Act of 1542-3 reflects an anxiety that all available measures be used to halt the disease, and that treatment should be available to all classes, this is confirmed by its coincidence with further official attempts to suppress the Southwark brothels, made in 1535 and 1546.[54]

Disease incidence is usually measured in terms of mortality. It is part of the present argument that the event of death might say little about the experience of life itself, and that protracted, painful and disfiguring diseases which do not necessarily, or are not necessarily recorded as ending in death, may have as significant an effect upon contemporary experience and sensibility as more sudden disasters.[55] Some measure of the incidence of pox in mid-century may be gained from the records of St Bartholomew's Hospital. During twelve months in 1547-8, the Hospital's surgeons received gratuities for healing 87 patients. Of these about a quarter (21) had had the pox. The Hospital's administrators showed a significant tendency to record cases of pox rather than other diseases; only a few other conditions are specifically mentioned for this year (dogbite, amputation, gunpowder burns, scald head). In the 1550s the poor suffering from pox were segregated in a special ward of the Hospital (the Dorter) and provided with nurses, clothing, and mattresses exclusively to their use. A hot house or sweating ward was also instituted at this time. At one point twenty mattresses were urgently needed to prevent cross-infection; at this stage the Hospital was meant to hold 100 patients, although patients may have slept more than one to a bed.[56]

In addition to its ward space, the Hospital regularly overflowed into its own property, allowing rebates to tenants who accommodated the sick. One house where people were 'laid of the pox' was in Golden Lane, which ran north from Holborn Bridge. So customary did this practice become that a clause was introduced into some leases prohibiting letting 'to any butchers or any that shall lay any of the pox, etc.'.[57] The proportion of patients with pox taken into St Bartholomew's is more indicative than the absolute numbers involved. In any case the syphilitic poor were also placed elsewhere, in St Thomas's Hospital and in the lazarhouses or 'outhouses' of St Bartholomew's and Christ's Hospital, situated at a wider periphery of the city in Southwark, Mile End, Hackney, Highgate, Knightsbridge, and Hammersmith.[58]

It has commonly been assumed that syphilis declined towards the end of the sixteenth century.[59] There seems little reason to suppose even a diminution in virulence if the often-quoted claims of the London surgeon William Clowes have any validity. Clowes's classic monograph on *morbus Gallicus* (1579 and possibly earlier) was the first English study of the disease and one of the first vernacular English treatises on a single disease, although Bullein may have contemplated a separate treatise on pox in 1562, as John Woodall was to do rather later.[60] Clowes claimed that he and three other surgeons had cured over a thousand victims of the pox in five years at St Bartholomew's alone. He also asserted that of every twenty patients taken into the Hospital, it 'very often happened' that fifteen were found to have the pox. In a later edition of 1585, Clowes dropped his estimate slightly to conclude that over his full '9 or 10' years with the Hospital, the proportion infected (of 'diseased persons') was perhaps 10 in 20.[61]

Clowes's figures cannot be given greater precision, but there are good reasons for accepting his apocalyptic vision that the disease 'spreadeth it self throughout all England, and overfloweth as I think the whole world'. By the turn of the century syphilis had achieved an incidence such that it shared with scurvy (another condition which loomed large in the concerns of the London Hospitals) the distinction of being a regular constitutional factor affecting prognosis and the rate of healing of conditions in general.[62] From the 1590s evidence accumulates to show the importance given to the pox by local authorities investing in medical poor relief measures.[63] It is possible that some references which would conventionally be ascribed to the plague, should rather be taken to refer to syphilis; the two were often coupled together as contagious diseases.[64] The protean character of syphilis makes it difficult to set limits on the conditions caused or aggravated by it, especially scald head, ulcers, sores, and infections of the mouth. Similarly, Clowes and other advocates of the treatment of pox with mercury, found in Arabic and contemporary sources evidence of the successful use of mercurials in such conditions, including the sore heads of children.[65] By the early seventeenth century venereal disease had become another example of a condition identified differently according to the social class of the person affected. Among the upper or aspirant classes, syphilis – the 'bone-ache' – was euphemistically called gout, rheumatism, or even sciatica. These were conditions which traditionally emerged in later life as the price of a misspent youth. In the nineteenth century guaiacum was still recommended in the treatment of 'gouty and rheumatic pains, and some cutaneous diseases', and there are many other aspects of lingering overlap.[66]

The satire of the 1590s and the plays which followed provide no support for the view that venereal disease declined in incidence towards the end of the sixteenth century.[67] References to it are endless in number and variety, much capital being made out of the effects on the person, concealed and unmistakable. The pox, the gallows, and the devil were established as a retributive trio by the 1560s. Pox became the fitting end in satirical cautionary tales directed at all those who in some way deviated from the duty laid down for their place in life.[68] Whether taken seriously or cynically, the pox was a prominent aspect of comment upon the social mobility of the period. It lay in wait as the common punishment of peers who wasted their substance, foolish gentlefolk who left the country for the city, and city tradespeople with social aspirations. Felons and beggars were branded by the iron, or had their ears lopped; the physical effects of the pox served in like manner to punish other kinds of social transgression. When it emerged from its hiding places in the body, pox often betrayed the difference between appearance and reality, between bravado and pretended distinction and the common rottenness inside. For most, the scene of their sin and its punishment was set in London. London was praised, but also blamed, as the new Jerusalem; syphilis gave a new and literal meaning to the belief that the sins of the fathers were visited upon their children.[69] Syphilis, handed on to the next generation, could bring proud and overambitious families alike to an abrupt end. At the literal worst, an affected penis might slough off before a family could be founded.

In spite of its striking role in the perceived unity of spiritual and physical life, and the symmetry of crime and punishment, pox was also (like sedition and disorder) contagious and could therefore affect the innocent. For writers of a puritan bent like Clowes, pox became a very tangible reason for avoiding even the company of the godless. In condemning 'the pestilent infection of filthy lust', Clowes saw no cause as great as 'the licentious, and beastly disorder of a great number of rogues, and vagabonds: the filthy life of many lewd and idle persons, both men, and women, about the city of London'. Clowes testified to another current concern in pointing to 'the great number of lewd alehouses' which not only harboured the vagabond class but also provided the meeting ground where others 'of better disposition' could be infected, by 'unwary eating, or drinking, or keeping company, with those lewd beasts'. The disease had a 'flowing matter', which once it entered the body, went from part to part and especially to parts of apt disposition. Such eating and drinking could breed the disease in the mouth; other parts could be infected by wearing the clothes of infected persons, lying in bed with them or in their sheets, or 'sometimes it is said ... by sitting on the same stool of easement'.[70]

The use of wet-nurses, an important link between the growing city and its outlying suburbs and villages, led to further spread of infection. Clowes retold with feeling a case of 1583 from his own experience in which three children of one city parish were put to nurse, one in the country and two in the city; in less than six months all three were 'grievously infected with the pocks'. Being 'so miserably spoiled' the children could not be weaned, and the parents were forced ('as nature doth bind') to use other wet-nurses; by this means, five other 'good and honest nurses' were infected. All three babies as well as the nurses were treated; one baby died. Syphilis, congenital and contracted, is undoubtedly an underestimated factor not only in the deaths of adults but also in the urban crisis of infant mortality.[71]

Clowes, undoubtedly revolted and inspired by the loathsome sights and smells inevitably associated with his practice, warned that the whole land would shortly be poisoned, unless the Lord had mercy, magistrates punished vice, and the people speedily repented their ungodly life. There was only a certain time available for repentance; Clowes was publishing details of methods of cure not so that the sinful could cure themselves and continue to wallow in sin, but because God, in his mercy, provided a fit cure for all diseases inflicted. If there was no amendment of life, however, God's wrath might render the disease incurable, even by mercurials. In the later edition of 1585, Clowes's moral and religious severity was modified in favour of a more nationalistic strain. As with physical and moral life, the theme of nationalism was one on which venereal disease, especially as exploited by dramatists, provided endless more or less mocking variations.[72]

As one aspect of his conviction of the dignity of surgeons, Clowes asserted that surgery was more ancient than physic and had been practised by great men and spiritual leaders. This case drew strength from traditions and recent revivals of the royal touch, which brought spirituality and status to the surgeon's formal province of manual application to outward conditions. In a phrase also reminiscent of the medical metaphors of satire, Clowes urged all magistrates, as 'the second surgeons appointed by God', to seek out and punish fornicators. Although displaying conventional propriety in his references to physicians, Clowes made it clear that their role with respect to venereal disease and other serious conditions was a very minor one, and he gave himself the satisfaction of urging them to take a greater part.[73] His model of practice is the combination of expertise in barbery, surgery, and physic found in the competent and right-thinking sea-surgeon, rather than the strict divisions favoured by London physicians.

Physicians had been very rapidly left behind in the application of effective remedies in syphilis, just as they were to be in the later seventeenth century with respect to the use of cinchona bark against the ague. Continental as well as English writers commented on the failure of physicians to inspire confidence in the face of *morbus Gallicus*, their extreme caution, and their clinging to Galenic interpretations and treatments which had little relevance to the diseases characteristic of later ages of the world. This scorn was consonant with a climate of criticism of physicians, led by such figures as Paracelsus and Vesalius, who condemned them for having become divorced from real, and contemporary, experience.[74] It is thus misleading to suggest either that the treatment of syphilis was 'left to' the barber-surgeons as the disease became less epidemic, or that the involvement of barber-surgeons is evidence of the disease's decline.[75]

Mercurials were of course a strong remedy, but in the same way as the satirists justified the virulence of their vocabulary, Clowes maintained that the remedy matched the disease and that the skill of the operator made a great deal of difference in justifying the result. By another kind of symmetry which also suited the religious as well as the medical outlook of the time, the effects of mercurial treatment somewhat resembled the disease under cure. John Banister noted that 'barbers, and my servants', who applied mercurial ointments without understanding their effects, 'feared themselves to be catched with the same disease, because they were urged with the like accidents, as those patients whom they had anointed' – fluxes of the belly and mouth, 'eating of gums', stinking breath, ulcers, etc.[76]

As in leprosy, many of the diagnostic signs of pox were to be seen on the head and face; like leprosy, syphilis also affected the voice. In a particularly resonant incident, a woman accused in the 1580s of bewitching the vicar of her parish so that he lost his voice when he came to preach, deposed in her defence that the vicar was diseased of a hoarseness such that her neighbours thought he had the French pox, and refused to communicate with him until he obtained from London physicians a certificate stating that he had a disease of the lungs. Clowes urged his readers to take note of 'venomous pustules with a certain hardness sticking out in the head, forehead, brows, face, or beard, and in other parts ... especially the secret parts, or lowest part of the belly, or in the corners of the lips ... corns in the throat or mouth, pains in the head'.[77] Another effect of the disease, which was also characteristic of leprosy in its later stages, was alopecia, or hairlessness; hence Samuel Rowlands, in 1612:

> And some, because we have no beards, do think
> We are four panders, with our lousy locks,
> Whose naked chins are shaven with the pox.

Similarly, Dekker refers to 'the unwholesome breath of autumn, who is so full of diseases, that his very blowing upon trees, makes their leaves to fall off (as the French Razor shaves off the hair of many of thy *Suburbians*) ... '.[78] Lost or thinning hair, to the point of baldness, combined with the characteristic sores and pustules of the disease, was known as scalding, or scald head, a condition which may or may not be distinguishable from the scald head so common in children. The latter condition was of central concern to local authorities and the London hospitals, and has usually but rather inadequately been regarded as a minor parasitic condition caused by fungi or mites.[79] At a later period thin or brittle hair was regarded as a sign of overindulgence in lechery.[80]

Another sign by which the barber-surgeon could recognize the condition of his client, and which he might be expected to counteract, was that of odour. The driving out of bad by sweet odours was of course regarded as an effective, rather than merely palliative, measure. Contemporaries, from dramatists to local authorities, apparently recognized a characteristic odour or 'spice' of the pox which presumably preceded the stench of the more gross effects of the disease.[81] The barber-surgeon, led by these more outward signs, was inevitably prompted to offer all degrees of treatment. It is consistent with the role of barber-surgeons' shops that they offered remedies for affections of the sexual organs in general, many of which involved direct applications to or into the penis. Thus Woodall commented, in giving guidance in the use of surgical instruments, that it might seem pointless to do this in respect of the small syringe, 'for what barber's boy is not practised in the use of [it]?'. This instrument was used for a range of purposes, including applications to deep ulcers, but also for 'griefs of the yard', including gonorrhoea.[82] With the introduction of the sweating treatment for syphilis, as well as the more dangerous fumigation method, barber-surgeons naturally became the dominant figures in the setting up of 'baths' and 'bagnios' which offered mercurial as well as other kinds of bathing. Like the barber-surgeons' shops, these facilities were made as congenial as possible and were places of resort, but their connection with prostitution was more direct, as indicated by Jonson's Epigram of 1616 'On the New Hot-House':

> Where lately harboured many a famous whore,
> A purging bill, now fixed upon the door,
> Tells you it is a hot-house: so it may,
> And still be a whore-house. They are *synonima*.[83]

Sixteenth-century surgeons were notable for their adoption of Paracelsian medicine and for their use of the new metallic or alchemical remedies; this provided the intellectual underpinning of their effectual monopoly over the treatment of venereal disease. Clowes and his like-minded colleagues such as Banister and Baker count as the ornaments of their occupation in the period, and it is clear from their own publications that 'many others of their company' – that is, the London Company of Barber-Surgeons – were fully engaged in treating venereal disease. Clowes's intellectual, religious and moral premises, as well as his shrewdness and entrepreneurial instincts, allowed him to take the line that 'good things the more common they be, the better they are'; similarly William Pickering urged others to follow his friend's example and to make known hidden secrets, to banish idleness and sloth, 'to catch the plough by the hand ... and lustily lift up the mattock and the spade and fall a-delving'.[84] Having this outlook, freeman barber-surgeons were able to combine a vitriolic condemnation of intruders into medical practice (often from other trades), with a wider tolerance of certain types of practice and of practitioner than could consistently be adopted by academically qualified physicians. The London barber-surgeons of this period were thus able both to maintain intellectual respectability and to live and work where opportunities were greatest.

This is not to say that such a balance could be maintained indefinitely. Barber-surgeons continued to profit from the treatment of venereal disease by both land and sea, and continued also to be regarded as the especially useful branch of their profession. Many of them, however, were ill-served by the increasingly rigid social stratification of the later seventeenth century. Just as the drama lost its universality, became self-indulgent and more confined to certain social classes, so conceptions of the corruption of the flesh lost their sardonic and all-embracing brutality and became arch and class-related.[85] Barbers joined dairymaids as stock figures of sexual comedy in which the reality of their occupations seldom appeared. Many barbers joined the periwig-makers in social oblivion. In every real sense the concept of utility was discredited, and barber-surgeons consequently lost caste. Other practitioners were better able to benefit from the increased status of some trade and professional groups relative to the landowning classes.[86]

IV

This essay has been concerned to examine the distribution of one occupational group in early modern London and to stress certain aspects of its contribution to urban social life. On the one hand barber-surgeons can be seen as providing places of resort and as adding a further dimension to urban sophistication or vice. On the other, barber-surgeons had an important, more mundane role to play, not only in treating disease, but also in hygiene and in enabling the individual to present an acceptable face to the world. Medical practitioners, and especially barber-surgeons, provided means of fending off the threat, or appearance, of physical decay. Awareness of defect or deformity, and an obsession with personal health and appearance, were characteristics of the period which were greatly exaggerated by conditions of life in a 'crowded society' and by the contemporary sense of mutability in all things. Social mobility affected perceptions of city as opposed to country life, and created anxieties and conflicts which were expressed in terms of dress and appearance. The last refuge of Earle's younger son was the Low Countries, because there 'rags and lice are no scandal'.[87] However, there is little reason to believe that a preoccupation with the body and its coverings was confined to certain classes in London society, and there were, correspondingly, extremely poor barber-surgeons as well as those more familiar figures who appear as the personal servants and henchmen of their masters.

Venereal disease serves in the first place as a reminder of the importance from the contemporary point of view of long-term, painful, and often disfiguring conditions which do not necessarily reveal themselves in the bills of mortality. The demographic significance of syphilis, especially with respect to infant mortality, has yet to be estimated. In addition, however, syphilis had effects on contemporary social and even economic life which cannot be rivalled by other important chronic diseases such as the stone. Pox was the reality which undermined many of the pretensions of urban life and symbolized its vice and falsity. As a facet of disorderly life it sharpened contemporary attitudes to alehouses, vagrancy, poor relief, and the growth of London's suburbs. It must also be taken into account in analysing the 'increased sensitivity over plebeian sexuality' which is thought to be characteristic of the late sixteenth century.[88] At the same time venereal disease added depth and physical reality to the citizen's vision of a corrupt and wasteful court, which found expression before the Revolution in polarities of dress and behaviour.

The attitudes and activities of London barber-surgeons such as

Clowes are a reminder that a moral vision of the world as mortally decayed was not incompatible with a concern for physical as well as spiritual health.[89] The use of mercury and other heavy metals in venereal disease and seemingly related conditions exemplifies the intention of adopting strong remedies for strong disorders. However, it is also an example of the readiness of barber-surgeons to take advantage of new economic opportunities, some of which arose from the application of chemical processes. It is characteristic of the inextricable intermingling of the social and economic in the world of the barber-surgeon of this period that the mercury which he used with great profit against repellent and disfiguring diseases also created the looking-glasses which he held up to his customers. For their part, the satirists and playwrights who shared Clowes's sense of crisis held up another kind of mirror to society and used the strongest physical terms to warn of humanity's decay.

NOTES AND REFERENCES

1. See M. Pelling and C. Webster, 'Medical practitioners', in C. Webster (ed.), *Health, Medicine and Mortality in the Sixteenth Century* (Cambridge 1979), esp. pp. 167–92 (on London). I am grateful to Charles Webster for valuable suggestions with respect to this article and to him and to the editors for comments on the text. I should also like to thank the Royal Hospital of St Bartholomew's and their Archivist Janet Foster, for permission to quote from the archives of the Hospital; and Roger Holdsworth and Fenella Childs for bibliographical advice.
2. The main source on the London barber-surgeons is still S. Young, *The Annals of the Barber-Surgeons of London* (London 1890; repr. New York 1978). I hope to expand on some of the themes of this paper in a monograph-length study on London barber-surgeons.
3. Pelling and Webster, 'Medical practitioners', pp. 172, 176–7.
4. This survey exists in the form of an expanding biographical card index held by the Wellcome Unit for the History of Medicine, Oxford. It covers East Anglia as well as London. See M. Pelling, 'A survey of East Anglian medical practitioners, 1500–1640', *Local Population Studies*, 25 (1980), pp. 54–5.
5. Thomas Vicary, *The Anatomie of the Bodie of Man*, F. J. Furnivall and P. Furnivall (eds), Early English Text Society (London 1888), extra series, 53, pt. i pp. 202–8, 243–5. Young, *Annals*, pp. 78–80, 586–90, 94–6.
6. See the return for the Barber-Surgeons' Company made with others in 1641 by London livery companies for poll tax commissioners (Public Record Office [hereafter PRO] E.179/251/22 and E.179/272/36 and 49), and transcribed in T. C. Dale, 'The members of City Companies in 1641', 2 vols.

(London, Guildhall Library, bound typescript, Society of Genealogists, 1934), i, pp. 85–98. This return is particularly full in giving a street or parish for each name as well as occupation. R. R. James, 'A list of surgeons in practice in London and its suburbs in 1641', *Bulletin of the History of Medicine*, 19 (1946), pp. 282–90, extracts the surgeons and adds biographical information from Young, *Annals.*

7. See M. Pelling, 'Occupational diversity: Barber-Surgeons and the trades of Norwich, 1550–1640', *Bulletin of the History of Medicine*, 56 (1982), esp. pp. 504–5.

8. On topographical points in the following paragraphs see esp. E. H. Sugden, *A Topographical Dictionary to the Works of Shakespeare and his Fellow Dramatists* (Manchester 1925); F. C. Chalfant, *Ben Jonson's London* (Athens, Ga., 1978); John Stow, *A Survey of London*, C. L. Kingsford (ed.), repr., 2 vols. (Oxford 1971).

9. For the Apothecaries' return (PRO, SPD. 16/539, Pt. I, section 72); see transcription by T. C. Dale, 'Citizens of London 1641–1643 from the State Papers' (1936; bound typescript in the Guildhall Library, London), ff. 51–9. This return gives streets or places rather than parishes.

10. It would seem shrewd for apothecaries to locate themselves where people gathered to draw water, this being a daily rendezvous and a likely time for gossip about illness and health. I owe this point to Jonathan Barry.

11. R. S. Roberts, 'The early history of the import of drugs into England' in F. N. L. Poynter (ed.), *The Evolution of Pharmacy in Britain* (London 1965), pp. 165–86. For a transcription of SPD 16/453, section 75, ff. 117–71 (returns made by wards in 1640 of those thought ablest to lend to the crown) see Dale, 'Citizens of London', ff. 15–50.

12. Raseworme is denounced at length by William Clowes, *A Briefe and Necessarie Treatise, Touching the Cure of the Disease called Morbus Gallicus* (London 1585), ff. 9–13. As an immigrant 'spagyrist' Raseworme obtained letters of denization in 1574: C. Webster, 'Alchemical and Paracelsian medicine', in Webster (ed.), *Health, Medicine and Mortality*, pp. 305, 327.

13. On the Old Exchange see references in Stow, *Survey;* on the Royal (Gresham's) Exchange, and the 'New' (Cecil's) Exchange set up in the Strand in 1608, see Stow; Chalfant, *Ben Jonson's London*, pp. 72–5; M. R. Holmes, *Elizabethan London* (London 1969), esp. pp. 41–4, 86–7. The Royal Exchange was the most prominent centre in the period in question.

14. Pelling, 'Occupational diversity', p. 506; Ben Jonson, *The Staple of News*, ed. D. R. Kifer (London 1976), pp. 14, 26, 33.

15. Dale, 'Citizens of London'. Obviously medical practitioners are likely to have been the wealthiest inhabitants only in the less wealthy wards. It may be significant for these returns in general that the practitioners singled out to be taxed can often be identified as strangers.

16. On the westward shift see N. G. Brett-James, *The Growth of Stuart London* (London 1935), esp. Chs 5–6.

17. John Graunt, *Natural and Political Observations ... made upon the Bills of Mortality*, 5th edn. (London 1676), repr. in *Economic Writings of Sir William Petty*, C. H. Hull (ed.), repr., 2 vols. (New York 1963), ii, p. 356.

18. E. J. Burford, *Bawds and Lodgings: A History of the London Bankside Brothels* (London 1976), pp. 114–15; Chalfant, *Ben Jonson's London*, pp. 142–3, 198–9. A few decades later Pepys's *Diary* stresses the locations in the

western suburbs, and Moorfields: J. D. Rolleston, 'Venereal disease in Pepys's Diary', *British Journal of Venereal Diseases,* 19 (1943), p. 172.

19. Entry in City Journal, repr. in Vicary, *Anatomie,* Furnivall and Furnivall (eds), pp. 151–2.
20. See Chalfant, *Ben Jonson's London,* p. 96; Stow, *Survey,* ii, p. 363.
21. The following paragraphs are based on unpublished analyses of the 'Annals' of the London College of Physicians conducted by Charles Webster. I am most grateful to him for allowing the use of this information. Some of his findings were incorporated in a lecture delivered at the University of Adelaide, South Australia, in June 1979, under the title 'Physicians and magicians in London: 1550–1640'. See also *idem,* 'Medicine as social history: changing ideas on doctors and patients in the age of Shakespeare', in *A Celebration of Medical History,* L. G. Stevenson (ed.) (Baltimore and London 1982), p. 117.
22. See Chalfant, *Ben Jonson's London,* p. 61.
23. A. Macfarlane, *Witchcraft in Tudor and Stuart England* (London 1970), pp. 117, 280, 286, 302.
24. Reginald Scot, *The Discoverie of Witchcraft* (1584), B. Nicholson (ed.) (London 1886), pp. 5, 21. Cf. Macfarlane, *Witchcraft,* pp. 140, 158, 276. The implication of witchcraft presumably constitutes the defamatory element in alleging of a woman that she 'had a wart on her belly': J. A. Sharpe, *Defamation and Sexual Slander in Early Modern England: The Church Courts at York,* Borthwick Papers, 58 (York 1980), p. 15.
25. L. C. Knights, *Drama and Society in the Age of Jonson* (London 1937), pp. 118–19.
26. Shakespeare, *Macbeth,* I, iv, 11–12; A. Chapman, 'Astrological medicine', in Webster (ed.), *Health, Medicine and Mortality,* p. 292.
27. Thomas Dekker, *The Wonderfull Yeare* (1603), in *The Non-Dramatic Works,* A. B. Grosart (ed.), vol. I (Huth Library 1884), p. 91.
28. William Pickering, 'Epistle' in Clowes, *Morbus Gallicus* (1585), fol. 59.
29. Shakespeare, *Richard III,* I, i, 14–27, and *passim.*
30. See W. Haller, *The Rise of Puritanism* (New York 1957 edn); H. Smith, *Elizabethan Poetry* (Cambridge, Mass. 1952), Ch. 4; A. Kernan, *The Cankered Muse* (New Haven 1959); M. C. Randolph, 'The medical concept in English Renaissance satiric theory: its possible relationships and implications', *Studies in Philology,* 38 (1941), pp. 125–57.
31. See also P. Slack, 'Social policy and the constraints of government, 1547–58', in J. Loach and R. Tittler (eds), *The Mid-Tudor Polity c.1540–1560* (London and Basingstoke 1980), p. 96, who points out that concepts of disease and decay were 'more than metaphors' to describe social problems in mid-century.
32. Randolph, 'Medical concept in satiric theory', pp. 143–4; Smith, *Elizabethan Poetry,* p. 219; Kernan, *The Cankered Muse,* p. 93.
33. T. J. Arthur, 'Anatomies and the Anatomy Metaphor in Renaissance England', University of Wisconsin Ph.D. thesis, 1978, summarized in *Dissertation Abstracts International,* 39 (1979), 4263A–4A.
34. The Shakespearean instances are well known; for a fresher example see Thomas Dekker, *The Honest Whore,* Part I, Act IV.
35. In general see T. Veblen, *The Theory of the Leisure Class* (New York 1953 edn); Knights, *Drama and Society in the Age of Jonson;* R. König, *The*

Restless Image: A Sociology of Fashion, trans. F. Bradley (London 1973); M. E. Roach and J. B. Eicher (eds), *Dress, Adornment and the Social Order* (New York 1965).

36. See J. Thirsk, *Economic Policy and Projects* (Oxford 1978), and on dyeing see also C. Webster, *The Great Instauration: Science, Medicine and Reform 1626-1660* (London 1975), pp. 388-9.

37. One rationale for the type of mask which covered mainly the nose is directly suggested by Beaumont and Fletcher in 1630: "'He lay with his mother, and infected her, and now she begs in the hospital, with a patch of velvet, where her nose stood ... '": quoted by G. Williams, 'An Elizabethan disease', *Trivium*, 6 (1971), 50. For hospitals, see below.

38. C. W. Cunnington and P. Cunnington, *Handbook of English Costume in the Sixteenth Century* (London 1970 edn), pp. 144, 185, 182, 148, 179-80, 146-8, 141-2. See also M. C. Linthicum, *Costume in the Drama of Shakespeare and His Contemporaries* (Oxford 1936), esp. pp. 272-4. On the range of possible symbolic associations of hair, see C. R. Hallpike, 'Social hair', in T. Polhemus (ed.), *Social Aspects of the Human Body* (Harmondsworth 1978), pp. 134-46. On wig-wearing see also J. Woodforde, *The Strange Story of False Hair* (London 1971), who notes that historically wigs were often resorted to by prostitutes or to conceal hair loss through illness and over-use of remedies and cosmetics. For a City of London order of 1543 against long beards see Young, *Annals*, pp. 96-7. On the short hair and caps of citizens as originating demand leading to the foundation of barbers' companies see Thomas Dekker, *The Honest Whore*, Pt. II, Act I, iii.

39. See M. Pelling, 'Healing the sick poor: social policy and disability in Norwich 1550-1640', *Medical History*, 29 (1985).

40. See for example L. Wright, *Clean and Decent* (London 1980 edn), p. 53; R. Reynolds, *Cleanliness and Godliness, or the Further Metamorphosis* (London 1943 [*recte* 1946]), pp. 54-9.

41. On soap, and the new idea of cleanliness in the nineteenth century, see F. B. Smith, *The People's Health 1830-1910* (London 1979), pp. 218-19.

42. C. W. Cunnington and P. Cunnington, *The History of Underclothes*, (London and Boston 1981 edn). Scraps of linen were liable to destruction through a wide range of uses, e.g. as firelighters, napkins, lavatory paper, etc.

43. J. F. Pound (ed.), *The Norwich Census of the Poor 1570*, Norfolk Record Society, 40 (1971), p. 99. Women and girls described as helping or keeping wives or women may also have done washing and charring as well as nursing, etc.: for examples see *ibid.*, pp. 44-5. See also P. Slack (ed.), *Poverty in Early Stuart Salisbury*, Wiltshire Record Society, 31 (1976), pp. 114, 129 (for charwomen); A. Clark, *The Working Life of Women in the Seventeenth Century* (1919; repr., London 1982), p. 135. Laundresses working in Moorfields in the mid-sixteenth century are depicted in the so-called 'Copperplate Map': M. R. Holmes, *Moorfields in 1559* (London 1963), pp. 29-30. See in general C. Davidson, *A Woman's Work Is Never Done: A History of Housework in the British Isles, 1650-1950* (London 1982), esp. Ch. 7.

44. For an example see D. M. Palliser, 'Civic mentality and the environment in Tudor York', *Northern History*, 18 (1982), p. 93.

45. William Bullein, *Bulleins Bulwarke of Defence againste all Sicknes Sornes*

and Woundes (1562), facs. edn (Amsterdam 1971), Book of Simples, ff. vi recto, lix, lxxiv verso.

46. G. Lambert, 'Barbersurgeons', *London & Middlesex Archaeological Society Transactions*, 1st ser., 6 (1890), pp. 156–8, 153; Randolph, 'Medical concept in satiric theory', p. 146. Young, *Annals*, pp. 178, 181; John Woodall, *The Surgions Mate* (1617), facs. edn (Bath 1978), sig. A [i] – p. 39. For the barber's functions see also the curses laid upon his activities in Ben Jonson, *Epicoene*, III, v, 65–113. William Horman, *Vulgaria* (1519), M. R. James (ed.), Roxburghe Club (Oxford 1926), gives as a now mysterious item of common knowledge that combing hair backwards, forehead to crown – as was common in the sixteenth century – was 'medicinal' (p. 64).

47. On the other functions of barbers' shops see Pelling, 'Occupational diversity', esp. pp. 504–7.

48. See G. G. Stewart, 'A history of the medicinal use of tobacco, 1492–1860', *Medical History*, 11 (1967), pp. 228–68. Tobacco was generally sold as a sideline; see John Earle, *Microcosmography*, repr. of 1811 edn with addtns by S. T. Irwin (Bristol and London 1897), pp. 70–1: 'He is the piecing commonly of some other trade, which is bawd to his tobacco, and that to his wife, which is the flame that follows this smoke'. Inventories show that medical practitioners rapidly took advantage of this economic opportunity.

49. R. Finlay, *Population and Metropolis: The Demography of London 1580–1650* (Cambridge 1981), p. 19.

50. C. Creighton, *A History of Epidemics in Britain*, 2 vols (London 1965 edn), ii, pp. 420, 422; J. Y. Simpson, *Antiquarian Notices of Syphilis in Scotland in the 15th and 16th Centuries* (Edinburgh [1862]), pp. 31ff, 23–4, 4–14; Sharpe, *Defamation and Sexual Slander*, pp. 10–11; E. L. Zimmermann, 'The early pathology of syphilis especially as revealed by accounts of autopsies on syphilitic corpses (1497–1563)', *Janus*, 38 (1934), pp. 9–19, 57. Girolamo Fracastoro, *De contagione*, trans. W. C. Wright (New York and London 1930), p. 135.

51. Vicary, *Anatomie*, Furnivall and Furnivall (eds), App. VII, p. 206 (32 Hen. VIII, c.42).

52. Vicary, *Anatomie*, Furnivall and Furnivall (eds), App. VII, pp. 208–9 (34 and 35 Hen. VIII, c.8). R. Hooper, *Lexicon Medicum*, 8th edn, K. Grant (ed.) (London 1848), pp. 661, 669–70. See D'A. Power, 'Clap and the pox in English literature', *British Journal of Venereal Diseases*, 14 (1938), pp. 105–18. 'Gonorrhoea' referred particularly to any urino-genital discharge. The venereal disease proper, also called chaudepisse, became known as the clap in the late sixteenth century. After 1600 clap and the 'new' venereal disease, syphilis, were increasingly not distinguished. Strangury was a special degree of another common denominator and focus of attention, 'painful and difficult voidings'.

53. Girolamo Fracastoro, *Syphilis or the French Disease*, H. Wynne-Finch (ed.), intro. by J. J. Abraham (London 1935), pp. 23–7; Roberts, 'History of the import of drugs into Britain', pp. 169–70; Bullein, *Bulleins Bulwarke*, Book of Simples, ff. lx–lxii.

54. Burford, *Bawds and Lodgings*, pp. 122–7; Creighton, *Epidemics in Britain*, i, p. 420; F. Henriques, *Prostitution in Europe and the New World* (London 1963), p. 61.

55. See P. Slack, 'Mirrors of health and treasures of poor men: the uses of the vernacular medical literature of Tudor England', in Webster (ed.), *Health, Medicine and Mortality in the Sixteenth Century* (Cambridge 1979), pp. 237-73, esp. pp. 262-7; Webster, 'Medicine as social history', pp. 113-16; R. Sawyer, 'Ordinary medicine for ordinary people: illness and its treatment in the East Midlands, 1600-1630', *Bulletin of the Society for the Social History of Medicine*, 33 (1983), pp. 20-3.

56. London, St Bartholomew's Hospital, H 1/1, Ledger 1547-1561, ff. 23-9, 67; Ha 1/1, Journal 1549-1561, ff. 164, 4, 7, 121, 52; N. Moore, *The History of St Bartholomew's Hospital*, 2 vols. (London 1918), ii, p. 270.

57. Hb 1/1, Ledger 1547-1561, ff. 45, 58; Ha 1/2, Journal 1567-1586, fol. 165 [1581].

58. On the London lazarhouses see M. B. Honeybourne, 'The leper hospitals of the London area ... ', *London & Middlesex Archaeological Society Transactions*, 21 (1963), pp. 1-61. For the functions of similar institutions in a lesser urban centre, which included the treatment of venereal disease, see Pelling, 'Healing the sick poor'.

59. Creighton, *Epidemics in Britain*, i, p.425 (though cf. p. 428); A. Hirsch, *Handbook of Geographical and Historical Pathology*, trans. C. Creighton, vol. 2 (London, New Sydenham Society 1885), p. 64. Fracastoro claimed to have seen a decline during his lifetime, but this has been discounted: Fracastoro, *Syphilis*, p. 39.

60. Creighton, *Epidemics in Britain*, i, pp. 422-3; Slack, 'Uses of vernacular medical literature', p. 245; K. F. Russell, 'A check list of medical books published in English before 1600', *Bulletin of the History of Medicine*, 21 (1947), 922-58. Bullein, *Bulleins Bulwarke*, Book of Simples, ff. iiv-iiir, has been taken as evidence of such an intention but see *ibid.*, ff. lx-lxii. Woodall, *Surgions Mate*, p. 301.

61. William Clowes, *A Short and Profitable Treatise touching the Cure of the Disease called Morbus Gallicus by Unctions* (1579), facs. edn (Amsterdam and New York 1972), sig.Bii; *idem, Morbus Gallicus* (1585), fol. 2. Clowes's figures may be compared with the incidence of syphilis among admissions to nineteenth-century hospitals in Tunis (121 per 1000 over 20 years) and South America (485 out of 972 admissions in one year, 52 out of 912 deaths): Hirsch, *Handbook of Pathology*, ii, pp. 79, 83.

62. Clowes, *Morbus Gallicus* (1579), sig [Aiiiir]; Woodall, *Surgions Mate*, p. 149; Clowes, *A Profitable and Necessarie Booke of Observations* (1596), facs. edn (Amsterdam and New York 1971), p. 24.

63. Pelling, 'Healing the sick poor'.

64. See for example above, p.96; Creighton, *Epidemics in Britain*, i, p. 428.

65. See the description from John Read in Creighton, *Epidemics in Britain*, i, p. 425. Clowes, *Morbus Gallicus* (1585), fol. 25; George Baker, 'The nature and property of quick silver' in *ibid.* (1579). Mercurials were also used in scurvy, and quicksilver was employed to kill lice: Woodall, *Surgions Mate*, pp. 191, 114.

66. Williams, 'An Elizabethan disease', esp. pp. 43-4; Hooper, *Lexicon Medicum*, pp. 669-70.

67. The point is made by Williams, 'An Elizabethan disease', p. 52, and admitted by Creighton, *Epidemics in Britain*, i, p. 428.

68. Creighton quoting Bullein, *Epidemics in Britain*, i, p. 422; Kernan, *The Cankered Muse*, p. 85.

69. Kernan, *The Cankered Muse*, p. 99.
70. Clowes, *Morbus Gallicus* (1579), sigs. [Aiiiir], Biv, Biir, Biiir, Biiiiv–Bvr.
71. Clowes, *Morbus Gallicus* (1585), fol. 3. On wet-nurses in London see Finlay, *Population and Metropolis*, pp. 146–8. M.-F. Morel has pointed to the importance of urban syphilis among rural wet-nurses in France: 'Health and illness in traditional rural France in the 18th and 19th centuries ... ', *Bulletin of the Society for the Social History of Medicine*, 33 (1983), p. 25. For an Italian example involving a wet-nurse, see Hirsch, *Handbook of Pathology*, ii, p. 97. In some modern South African populations, up to 25 per cent of infant mortality has been ascribed to this cause: Shula Marks, personal communication.
72. Clowes, *Morbus Gallicus* (1579), sigs. Bii–Biiii; *ibid.* (1585), Sig. Aiiir; Williams, 'An Elizabethan disease', pp. 45–7.
73. Clowes, *Morbus Gallicus* (1585), ff. 8–9; *idem, A Right Frutefull and Approoved Treatise, for ... that Malady called in Latin Struma* (1602), facs. edn (Amsterdam and New York 1970), Epistle to the Reader; *idem, Morbus Gallicus* (1579), sigs. [Aiiir]; [Bviiir].
74. Fracastoro, *Syphilis*, App. to Bk II, p. 191. Webster, *The Great Instauration*, pp. 247–9.
75. Cf. for example J. J. Keevil, *Hamey the Stranger* (London 1952), pp. 92–3.
76. Clowes, *Morbus Gallicus* (1579), sigs. Diii–Diiii; *ibid.*, Epilogue by John Banister, sig. Gii.
77. Scot, *Discoverie of Witchcraft*, p. 5; Clowes, *Morbus Gallicus* (1579), sig. [Bviv].
78. C. H. Hoy, *Introductions, Notes, and Commentaries to Texts in The Dramatic Works of Thomas Dekker*, 4 vols. (Cambridge 1980), ii, pp. 25, 21. Women were similarly affected: Williams, 'An Elizabethan disease', p. 50.
79. See above, p. 97; Pelling, 'Healing the sick poor'; Hoy, *Introductions to Dekker*, ii, p. 21. There was also some association with 'leprosy': see 'scall', *OED*. In the sixteenth and seventeenth centuries St Bartholomew's employed highly paid women specialists to deal with scald head; around 1630 these were earning over £120 a year: Moore, *St Bartholomew's Hospital*, ii, pp. 732–3.
80. For example by Diderot: Woodforde, *False Hair*, p. 106.
81. Norfolk Record Office, Case 20, Shelf c, Mayor's Book of the Poor I (payment to Fysher, surgeon) *OED* gives slight touch, or trace, for spice used in this sense, but contemporary sources imply odour (as well as attempts at disguise by perfumes, or even, satirically, tobacco): John Webster, *The White Devil*, V, i, 157–63; Middleton, *Famelie of Love*, quoted by Williams, 'An Elizabethan disease', p. 44.
82. Woodall, *The Surgions Mate*, p. 21; Power, 'Clap and the pox', p. 107.
83. Ben Jonson, *The Complete Poems*, G. Parfitt (ed.) (Harmondsworth 1980), p. 36. Burford, *Bawds and Lodgings*, p. 173. French barbers were given a monopoly in hot bath-houses later in the seventeenth century: Woodforde, *False Hair*, p. 16. A close association of barbers and brothels was of course traditional. A supervisor of the London barbers was ordered to report on those keeping brothels *c.* 1308: Young, *Annals*, p. 24. On balneotherapy in the seventeenth century see Webster, *The Great Instauration*, pp. 298–9.
84. Webster, 'Alchemical and Paracelsian medicine', esp. pp. 319, 324–30; Baker, 'Nature of quick silver' in Clowes, *Morbus Gallicus* (1579), sig. Fii;

Young, *Annals*, pp. 398, 427; Clowes, *Morbus Gallicus* (1585), fol. [44]; Pickering in *ibid.*, fol. 60.

85. On changes in the drama see Knights, *Drama and Society in the Age of Jonson.*
86. See L. Stone, 'Social mobility in England, 1500–1700', *Past and Present*, 33 (1966), pp. 16–55.
87. Earle, *Microcosmography*, pp. 23–4.
88. Sharpe, *Defamation and Sexual Slander*, pp. 24–5.
89. On this point in general see Webster, *The Great Instauration*, section IV ('The prolongation of life').

PART TWO

Commerce and manufacture

CHAPTER FOUR
Overseas trade and metropolitan growth

Brian Dietz

If, as Braudel has observed of capital cities, 'their economy was only balanced by outside resources; others had to pay for their luxury',[1] London was no exception, and at no time, perhaps, was the rule more faithfully observed than in the sixteenth and seventeenth centuries when the parasitism of metropolitan growth was widely agreed and condemned. How outside resources were exploited to bridge the gap between London's limited capacity to produce and its immense propensity to consume was and remains less clear. Metropolitan history is not urban history writ large. Nor could London be considered a 'typical' metropolis. Consequently, studies of English provincial towns or of capital cities abroad cannot serve as prototypes. More pertinent are explanations of London's performance as an 'engine of growth' for the nation.[2] Because the relationship between capital and provinces was one of mutual reinforcement, studies of outputs indicate some of the returns of energy and resources. Flows were circular, outputs representing long-term investments in the external resource base. But in the short term, at least, they might constitute a loss of potential growth in the local economy. The use, for example, of outport shipping in metropolitan trade was a lost opportunity for local investment and employment. A reverse image of the 'engine of growth', would therefore display relationships between metropolis and provinces that are functionally different; and on the input-side only one, that of people, has been closely studied. Moreover, the assimilation of foreign migrants indicates the existence of a profitable overseas dimension to 'outside resources'.

London's demographic history illustrates the symbiosis of metropolis and province. By absorbing surplus population, the capital relieved pressure on the countryside. But there was a price to pay, and a model of

115

growth through exploitation would represent the mechanisms by which incomes were redistributed to support the high levels of immigration and population. Fundamental to the process was that quality of uniqueness which lay not in size, though 'circular and cumulative causation' may be argued for urban growth,[3] but in the range of diversity of functions, each providing a profitable contact with outside resources. The service economy comprised government, the professions and the facilities which made London a focus of social or cultural, as well as political, appetites and aspirations. There was also a basic sector of manufactures, much neglected by historians, while London was more recognizably the centre of an extensive distributive network. The relationship between the various sectors was of a dual nature. On the one hand it, too, was symbiotic. The bureaucratic element was vital for the development of the social function which, in turn, stimulated growth in the basic and distributive sectors, part of that growth being returned to government via taxation to maintain the flow. The variables were, on the other hand, competitive. Even those activities like transportation which were in a dependent 'service' relationship with overseas trade might develop into relatively discrete and competitive forms of investment and employment, while other variables that were largely autonomous, a category which would include building construction and non-exporting industries, were activities which Braudel had more in mind when he speculated that in urban economies 'one type ... can only develop to the detriment of others and not necessarily in harmony with them'.[4]

Because cities are open economies, growth models are difficult to build and test. Goods and money move almost as freely through their gates as people, leaving little trace of their passage. One of the few points where the flow was registered in London was when goods entered the stream of international exchange. Customs records are an imperfect guide, but they make estimates of growth and judgements on 'output' more feasible than for other activities. Partly for that reason overseas trade has attracted the most attention and there is a danger that accessibility might encourage exaggeration. There are obviously good grounds for believing that it was of prime importance in metropolitan growth, providing as it did a direct, extensive and highly visible link with outside resources. As well as serving the local market, the port was a junction for provincal and overseas markets and, through the re-export trade, for overseas producers and consumers. As entrepôt London occupied a strategic position in English trade, and as the domestic market became more national through regional integration, and overseas markets became global after the Discoveries, the scope for exploitation increased. Undoubtedly London fits better than most cities or towns the 'maritime' model of pre-industrial urbanization. But it also agrees well with the concept of the town as a 'multi-functional central point'; and as overseas trade increased, so did the scope and potential of other functions as alternative routes to development and growth.

If the mechanisms of income redistribution were complex, variable and problematical, the impact of foreign trade on economic growth is, as trade theory warns, 'indeterminate over a wide range'.[5] Nor are analysis and evaluation simplified when the scale of the economy is less than national. On the contrary, the openness of the urban economy generally and London's particular function as entrepôt make the task more complicated. London traded on two accounts, provincial and overseas. Gains from one could offset losses on the other. The question is what and how gains might be made. Income transfers in the form of mercantile wealth were clearly relevant to metropolitan growth, but even there the gains were qualified in various ways. One was the extent to which alien merchants diverted commercial profits from the city. This was, as will be seen, variable. A more constant factor, which could have the same effect, was the behaviour of native merchants as investors, employers and consumers. Although we need to know much more about London's merchant community, it is clear that there was no simple correlation between rising mercantile incomes and through-puts for the local economy.[6] A marked feature of metropolitan trade, though not unique to the city or to this period, was oligopoly, a tendency which had the effect of reducing the flow from mercantile incomes.[7] The mercantile élite invested in local shipping and manufactures, underwrote marine insurance policies and bought, or more commonly leased, town properties. On the other hand, it is a commonplace that the richest acquired rural estates for status and security and invested their money in other ways outside the local economy. As employers and consumers they were also less dynamic than their wealth allowed. 'Ostentation seems to have been the exception rather than the rule, great retinues not much in evidence, domestic expenditure was carefully related to income.'[8] With few exceptions even the most affluent inhabitants of the City eschewed the ostentatious life style of their aristocratic neighbours in the West End.[9]

The ways the merchants acquired their profits were, in any case, more important than the ways they disposed of them. Explanations of the impact of metropolitan trade on the national economy attach a particular set of values to the merchant's functions. His contribution is seen to be most limited and his role most passive when exports were the

117

leading sector. Nationally the dynamic factor was to be found in the exporting industries of the provinces. When imports led growth, the dynamic element was transferred from cloth producers to the merchants who 'scoured the world in search of desirable commodities to meet the English appetite for foreign wares'.[10] In the context of overseas trade and metropolitan growth, perspectives and evaluations are different. Exporters who channelled cloth shipments through London diverted incomes and employment from provincial outlets. Similarly, re-exports were a particularly 'pure' form of exploitation. What value is attached to the import merchant depends upon the location of his market. If the 'appetites' were provincial, the function was dynamic; if local, passive. In that part of the market he merely redistributed incomes within the city.

Sectoral analysis is not without its problems and limitations. Attempts to establish the chronology and extent of sectoral variations are bound to be hazardous, even though the data exist which make the exercise feasible. To try to distinguish further between local and provincial demand is an altogether more dubious undertaking, though inferences can be drawn about the marketing of imports from their composition. A further limitation is conceptual in that sectoral variations were largely irrelevant to the spin-off benefits which accrued from foreign trade. Gains by external factors, including shipping, marine insurance and manufacturing, were mediated through the commercial structure. The primary influences were the location and distribution of markets and the composition as well as value of the commodity exchange.

Structural changes and sectoral variations are thus the key factors in our explanation of the impact of overseas trade on the metropolitan economy. Although the model is essentially qualitative as well as informal and highly generalized, the Figure and Tables incorporate data which test its operation over three stages of growth. In the first, which begins with the revival of international commerce in the last quarter of the fifteenth century and ends in the mid-sixteenth-century recession, the distinctive features were concentration and specialization, the sale of one commodity, woollen cloths, by one company, the Merchant Adventurers, in a single market, securing most of the returns to the city. Towards the end, if not from the beginning, exports led growth. When the London-Antwerp axis was breached the search for alternative markets, which was geared to demand, produced a wider, more diverse commercial structure which after 1600 incorporated markets beyond Europe. This second stage also ends in a mid-century depression. In the final stage, which concludes in a brief interlude of peace at the end of the century, the dynamic element was transferred to the re-export trade and extra-European markets.

I

The recovery which marks the beginning of the first stage of growth was led by markets in the Netherlands and south Germany where the great centres of commercial exchange responded to increases in mineral production, especially of silver, in central and eastern Europe. As the system of exchange widened to incorporate Asian spices from Lisbon, overland traffic from Italy and the Mediterranean and silver from America, London was locked into the process of growth by the meteoric rise of Antwerp at its centre. For a half-century or so London became a satellite of Antwerp, a position of inferiority, but one which enhanced the capital's own position in the nation's trade. A market for cloth rather than wool concentration on Antwerp encouraged the switch from raw wool to manufacture, increasing the distributor's profits and, by reducing transport costs, extending the network of supply. The change in the composition of exports is recorded in Fig. 2. The near monopoly of the cloth trade which the Antwerp connection helped to create is a familiar fact of early Tudor commercial history. Before the upturn roughly half the trade passed through the port. At the turn of the century the share was 60 per cent, rising to nearly 90 fifty years later. London's cloth shipments had increased ten-fold compared with an actual decline at Bristol, the great centre of western trade, over the same period.[11]

The cloth monopoly was created so rapidly and is of such obvious importance that the demand-side of metropolitan commerce can be overlooked. For that reason a crude index of imports has been incorporated in the Fig. 2. Although the index will not bear any great weight of analysis, attention is drawn to imports, which appear to have led the recovery until the 1520s. This is plausible, given the elasticity of demand for imports, sterling's undervaluation before 1526, and the coincidence of export growth with the development of the Antwerp market. After 1543, when the index ends, conditions continued to favour exports. Wartime taxation and remittances abroad for military purposes, exchange depreciation and substantial grain imports in the 1550s kept the price of imports high, forcing the Adventurers to look for their profits from cloth sales.[12] In a disturbed market, exports, which achieved record highs before the slump in 1552, were some 10 per

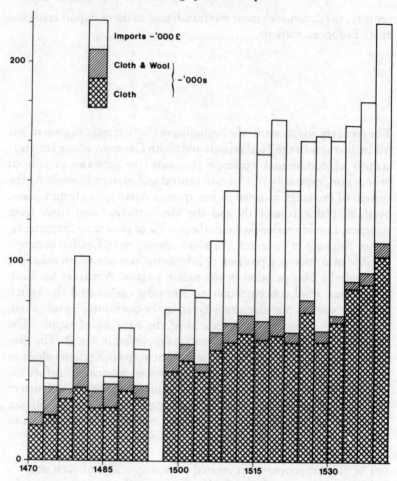

Fig. 2. Import and export trends, 1470–1542.
Sources: see Appendix. *Note:* no data available 1494–7.

cent lower in the 1560s than in 1539–45. But imports were down by more than a third.[13]

A particular difficulty facing importers was the competitiveness of alien merchants. During the upturn their strength had lain as much in the cloth trade as in the import sector. From a peak of 66 per cent in 1487/8, their share stabilized around 50 per cent at the turn of the century. With the recession it fell to a quarter or less, while imports remained high at around 40 per cent. Italians in particular were accused of draining specie out of the country by exchanging cheap kerseys for luxury textiles. Since Antwerp was the sluice, criticism of the Italians was extended to other harmful consequences of the high degree of concentration on the Flemish entrepôt. Logic was undoubtedly on the side of those who feared that the London-Antwerp axis had been damaging to the shipping industry. Short-haul exchanges of cargoes of high value-to-bulk made small demands on transportation. Judging from the record of incoming ships in 1567/8, the last full year of the Antwerp era, not more than 30 vessels of average size (around 50 tons) were required to carry the Merchant Adventurers' cargoes. Employment was secure, but remarkably unintensive.[14]

The axis had discouraged initiatives and investment elsewhere. A link was established between the flow of imports from Antwerp, where the range of manufactured goods was unique, and the decay of native industrial 'sciences and exercises'. London clothworkers in particular complained that Flemish demand for unfinished cloths had depressed their business.[15] Marine insurance was handicapped, firstly by dependence on Italian brokers and underwriters who were agents of Antwerp companies, and secondly by the lack of demand from high-risk native trades.[16] The port itself showed in its cramped, ill-equipped and decaying wharves and quays a disincentive to expand and rebuild.[17] The effects of the commercial structure were comprehensively negative. The main beneficiaries were undoubtedly the Merchant Adventurers. 'Their wealth had hitherto never been on such a scale ... [they] were the effective masters of London.'[18] The losers were the outports and most competing forms of investment and employment in the city.

II

Although the Antwerp axis was under strain in the 1550s and '60s, the breach was not made until 1569, when the Adventurers reluctantly moved their staple to Hamburg. The search for alternative markets, foreshadowed by the formation of the Muscovy Company and the return of English merchants to the Baltic in the '50s, began. As routes and markets were extended and diversified, growth was transferred to the import sector, which provided an alternative and profitable route to provincial incomes, more than offsetting a small reduction in the cloth monopoly. And the effect overall of the structural transformation was to remove the negative influences of the Antwerp axis. 'Spin-off' benefits were substantial and widely shared.

To the turn of the century routes and markets were developed within a structure which showed some continuity. As Table 9 shows, cloth

Table 9. Distribution by percentage of London's overseas markets

	Exports				Imports		
	English merchants 1565a	English merchants 1606	English merchants 1640	All merchants average of 1699–1701	English merchants 1567/8	English merchants 1633/4	All merchants average of 1699–1701
France	3	5	—	—	22	9	26
Netherlands	71	77	53	42	49	13	13
Germany	6	6	—	5	1	1	—
Baltic	4	—	—	—	5	2	9
Norway	—	—	—	—	—	—	—
Russia	1	2	—	—	2	20	—
Spain, Portugal and the Islands	12	2	47	33	11	31	30
Mediterranean	2	8	—	15	7	1	18
America and the West Indies	—	—	—	—	—	—	—
East Indies	—	—	—	3	—	16	16

Note: (a) Easter to Michaelmas
Source: see Appendix, p. 135

exports were in effect directed to the same markets along more extended routes. Traffic movements suggest the continuing importance of supplies from the same area of nearby and northern Europe. The decisive years came after 1600 in two distinct and equal stages. In the first the central event was the formation of the East India Company. Within twenty years of its foundation the company was responsible for 5 per cent of metropolitan imports.[19] From 1620 the growth areas were across the Atlantic, where the 'first American boom' produced a five-fold increase in tobacco imports between 1620 and 1640,[20] and southern Europe. Partly in response to changes in the fortunes of the Dutch, who were forced back on to northern markets by the renewal of war with Spain, there was a marked shift in London's trade from north to south. The redistribution of markets can be judged from the Tables. In southern Europe the main area of growth was the Levant. In the 1620s imports of currants, cotton, wool, raw silk and mixed fabrics rose by a quarter. By the early '30s, 21 per cent of imports originated in that region.[21]

A characteristic of the new trades was that they brought little or no increase in demand for domestic produce. Silver was shipped to the East, people to the West. In the expanding European markets there was probably a deficit on the commodity exchange through the Straits,[22] while 'new drapery exports to Spain were frequently subsidized by sales at or below cost price in order to command imports on which profits depended'.[23] After 1620 changes in the terms of trade in depressed northern markets reinforced the tendency for trade to be import-led. A feature of the commercial crisis of the early 1620s was the strength of sterling, after a long period of falling rates, on the Amsterdam exchange. The merchants' 'hope of gain is upon the commodities they return and not by the commodities they export', it was reported in 1623.[24] The change in northern markets was probably recent, but for the whole of metropolitan trade the evidence of the customs suggests that the transfer of growth to the import sector was made much earlier. Valuing shortcloths at prices current in 1606–14, shipments in the 1560s were worth in the region of £700,000. During the post-war boom years from 1606 to 1614, old and new drapery exports have been valued at £1,147,000 a year. In 1640 all domestic exports were worth £1,114,000. Imports at 1558 values rose from an annual average of £243,000 in 1561–7 to £585,000 in 1590–6, when conditions were far from favourable for the importer, increasing to an average of £834,000 in 1607–13. Wine imports had roughly doubled between the 1560s and the 1590s, doubling again over the next two decades. At the end of the second stage imports were five to six times higher than at the beginning.[25]

Table 10. The composition of London's import trade by value (£000) and percentage

	1559/60		Average of 1632/3, 1633/4 and 1639/40		Average of 1699, 1700 and 1701	
	Value	%	Value	%	Value	%
Linens	93	17.7	170	13.3	755	16.2
Silks etc.	60	11.5	110	8.6	208	4.5
Thread	18	3.4	35	2.7	74	2.6
Calicoes	—	—	21	1.6	367	7.9
Metalwares	15	2.9	11	0.9	55	1.2
Misc. manufactures	53	10.1	27	2.1	158	3.4
TOTAL MANUFACTURES	239	45.6	374	29.2	1617	35.8
Wine and brandy	10	1.9	82	6.4	467	10.0
Fruit	17	3.2	114	8.9	135	2.9
Pepper	9	1.7	38	3.0	103	2.2
Sugar and molasses	15	2.9	86	6.7	526	11.3
Tobacco	—	—	30	2.3	161	3.4
Misc. foodstuffs	56	10.7	105	8.2	191	4.1
TOTAL FOODSTUFFS	107	20.4	455	35.5	1583	33.9

Silk	6	1.1	100	7.8	344	7.4
Flax and hemp	16	3.1	33	2.6	116	2.5
Wool	4	0.8	28	2.2	67	1.4
Textile yarns	2	0.4	36	2.8	169	3.6
Dyes	39	7.4	128	10.0	203	4.3
Iron and steel	18	3.4	22	1.7	118	2.5
Timber	—	—	18	1.4	96	2.1
Oil	30	5.7	30	2.3	105	2.2
Misc. raw materials	23	4.4	55	4.3	249	5.3
TOTAL RAW MATERIALS	138	26.3	450	35.1	1467	31.3
TOTAL IMPORTS	524[a]		1279		4667	

Note: (a) Including £40 unallocated in the original
Sources: see Appendix, p. 135

125

The significance of import-led growth is obscured by the difficulty of distinguishing between local and provincial demand. However, the composition of imports, as displayed in Table 10, assists in locating demand socially and, by implication, geographically. A significant feature is the rise in luxury imports. Wines, silks – manufactured and raw – sugar, raisins, currants, pepper and tobacco alone accounted for 43 per cent of imports in the 1630s, which was twice the proportion early in Elizabeth's reign. An increase in upmarket demand of that magnitude cannot be attributed wholly or even largely to the local market. Rather it should be taken to reflect growth in the redistributive trade, which was at least as extensive in high value-to-bulk commodities as the areas which supplied cloths for export, together with the emergence of London as the 'inn of the kingdom', a centre of conspicuous provincial consumption for seasonal visitors and a small but affluent group of aristocratic residents. If the author of the *Discourse of the Common Weal* is to be believed, the diffusion of metropolitan styles and goods began in the 1530s.[26] The 'invasion of the city' by the aristocracy was, of course, a development of the late Elizabethan and early Stuart period.[27]

Even before the flow of imports turned into a flood, a provincial spokesman in the free trade debate in 1604 complained that 'merchants of London have all trades … [they] go around the world'.[28] The end of the export-oriented Antwerp axis had not been wholly to their advantage. Competition from east coast merchants trading in Yorkshire kerseys in northern markets helped to reduce London's share of the old drapery trade to 75 per cent.[29] A steady and perhaps increasing share of new drapery exports, mainly to the south, offset the loss;[30] but it was the search 'around the world' for imports for a national market which gave London 'all the trades' in the second stage. London, seemingly, had every advantage. The Flemish cloth market had favoured the city at the expense of the outports. When it failed, the new system of commercial exchange required access to markets, entrepreneurial skills and capital which only London could provide. The skills and investment were, moreover, English. A further consequence of the structural changes after 1569 was the retreat of alien merchants. The Italians abandoned the city soon after the disruption of their base at Antwerp; the few who remained were thoroughly anglicized.[31] By 1600, when alien exports were negligible, their share of imports had been reduced to a quarter. The post-war revival was impaired by a surge in imports, mostly of manufactured goods from Amsterdam, which restored the aliens' share to the levels of the 1560s. But the danger that London might become a satellite of another entrepôt in the Low Countries was averted by the transfer of growth from north to south. By the end of the second phase aliens were responsible for a mere 12 per cent of imports; and when they returned in some strength towards the end of the century, foreign firms represented not a threat but 'an important accession of strength to the London merchant community'.[32]

In transportation, as in trade, Londoners competed on two fronts: the dynamic effects of commercial expansion might be leaked to provincial as well as foreign shipping. Unfortunately our record of transportation is of small value in estimating gains from trade. For the years of modest growth prior to 1600 the data suggest that the increase in demand for English shipping was modest, although the gains before the outbreak of war with Spain disrupted southern trade, routes were more substantial.[33] (See Table 11, p. 128) In 1600, however, foreign competition was disconcertingly strong. Thereafter, as routes and markets were extended, the port books do not provide as full a view of traffic movements. Commercial developments were, however, favourable for English carriers. A 'warlike' reputation made them more competitive in the hazardous southern trades than in the secure bulk-carrying trades of the north. Consequently, the redirection of European trade routes from 1620, combined with the development of markets outside Europe, had a powerful effect on investment and employment in the English carrying trade. If the industry could not match the economical Dutch *fluit* in the North Sea and the Baltic, the Levanters and East Indiamen were sufficiently competitive to find intensive employment in the Mediterranean and around the Cape. On a typical Mediterranean voyage the *Dorothy* of London was at sea for a year and a half, earning £100 a month in freight. A companion vessel earned £1,312 on the outward voyage to Constantinople and almost as much again on the return leg.[34] Provincial carriers shared in the benefits from these developments, but probably not to the same extent as those that were London-based. Even in the Elizabethan period there are indications that London's employment of outport shipping was reduced;[35] thereafter the use of large ocean-going ships accentuated the trend. In view of the significance which we shall later attach to growth in domestic trade, it is worth noting that provincial carriers dominated coastwise traffic.[36]

The dynamic effects of trade on local transportation were relayed to a Thames-side shipbuilding industry which entered a period of unprecedented growth. Records of subsidy payments on ships of a hundred tons and above reveal that from 1558 to 1571, when the bounty was paid on approaching 5,000 tons of newly-built ships, none were 'of London'. Over the next two decades 23 vessels of 4,638 tons were so described. From 1591 to 1618, when payments ceased, 317 London

Table 11. Ships entering the Port of London ('000 tons burden)

	1567/8[a]				1599/1600				1686			
	English		Total		English		Total		English		Total	
	No.	Tons	No.	Tons	No.	Tons	No.	Tons	No.	Tons.	No.	Tons
North West Europe	197	9.9	612	23.7	238	18.9	864	36.4	674	56.4	809	65.9
Netherlands	55	2.9	373	12.6	4	0.3	467	10.8	—	—	252[b]	13.4
Germany	3	0.1	35	1.9	55	6.1	75	7.3	73	7.2	110	10.6
France	139	6.9	204	9.2	179	12.5	322	18.3	—	—	447[b]	41.9
Northern Europe	25	2.0	40	4.1	30	3.5	77	8.1	224	42.4	411	85.0
Norway	—	—	—	—	10	0.9	33	2.8	87	19.3	195	42.1
Russia	10	1.0	10	1.0	15	2.1	15	2.1	6	1.3	6	1.3
Baltic	15	1.0	30	3.1	5	0.5	29	3.2	130	21.7	208	41.1
Southern Europe	78	4.9	84	6.8	42	4.3	92	7.5	364	43.7	365	43.8
Spain, Portugal and the Islands	71	4.3	72	4.4	10	0.7	59	3.8	247	20.8	247	20.8
Mediterranean	7	0.6	12	2.4	32	3.6	33	3.7	117	22.9	118	23.0
Atlantic	—	—	—	—	4	0.3	4	0.3	314	52.0	335	54.6
East Indies	—	—	—	—	—	—	—	—	15	5.5	15	5.5
Total	300	16.8	736	34.6	314	27.0	1037	52.3	1591	200.0	1935	254.8

Notes: tonnages in 1686 are calculated from averages in 1715–17 or from Davis's estimates, as in Appendix, p. 135.

(a) Ships employed in carrying cargoes for English and Hanseatic merchants only.

(b) The original table does not allow us to distinguish between English and foreign ships *and* between Flanders and France. Of those listed by Davis as entering from Flanders and northern and mid-France 136 out of a total of 218 were English. All but 6 of 282 ships entering from southern France were English.

merchantmen totalling 90,155 tons were in receipt of the subsidy.[37] In the ten years following its decision in 1607 to build rather than charter, the East India Company alone constructed 15,000 tons of shipping in the company yards at Deptford and Blackwall. Fully-fitted, the ships represented an investment of not less than £100,000.[38] Private yards in Limehouse, Wapping and Ratcliffe, although smaller, nevertheless had the capacity to produce ships which were comparable with all but the largest East Indiamen.[39]

Historians by and large hesitate to associate London with manufacturing. An industrial image somehow seems inappropriate. Yet the existence of a substantial basic sector in a rapidly expanding market, with ample supplies of capital, labour and raw materials, would scarcely be surprising. If the labour-intensive shipyards could compete successfully with provincial and foreign builders, there were no obvious reasons why the whole sector should not be stimulated by the same influences and respond to the same incentives. Although no other industry was as closely and directly linked with foreign trade, the decline of imported manufactures as a proportion of the whole trade in the second phase and the corresponding increase in raw materials for manufacturing and processing is a noteworthy trend which is recorded in Table 10. The demonstration effect of imports, especially of upmarket wares, the difficulties import merchants found from the 1570s in their search for an alternative to the Antwerp emporium, together with a policy of import substitution which governments pursued from the mid-sixteenth century, made the environment more favourable for manufacturers. New industries, including silk-weaving, glass, pin and paper manufacture and sugar refineries extended the basic sector, while established trades like cloth dyeing and finishing enjoyed a revival in the aftermath of the end of the Antwerp era. In time, differential wage costs encouraged industry to migrate to the provinces. But it is possible to perceive, however dimly, the development in the late sixteenth and early seventeenth centuries of the basic sector as a significant variable in metropolitan growth: and it became so partly in response to the restructuring of overseas trade.[40]

III

The year 1648 is a better point at which to end the second phase than 1640, for although domestic crises were disruptive, the end of Spain's long war with the Dutch was in the short- and long-run more decisive in

129

altering the pattern of metropolitan trade. Peace brought abruptly to an end that particular period of growth and prosperity which had been generated by the politics of neutrality. The return of the Dutch in force to the Atlantic and the Mediterranean prepared the way for the Navigation Acts of 1651 and 1660, which provided a new protective framework for overseas trade. In the Book of Rates which accompanied the second act, import valuations were for the first time influenced by protectionist policies. Duties on manufactures were increased by as much as 100 per cent, while those on raw materials were reduced by upwards of three-quarters.[41] With the state accepting responsibilities hitherto delegated to monopoly companies, overseas trade recovered strongly from the mid-century recession until war in 1689 halted a general advance. The war's effects were selective. In a position similar to the Dutch in the 1620s and '30s, the English were driven back on to nearby and northern markets where business prospered. For the East India and Levant companies and colonial merchants the war was a disaster; and the effect of depression in import-led trades combined with wartime taxation and remittances abroad for military expenditure – the 'Jones effect' – was to transfer growth to exports. Peace in 1697 briefly restored a degree of confidence and normality in foreign trade.[42]

A half-century which contains major disturbances may seem too short a period to permit meaningful distinctions between short-run fluctuations caused by exogenous factors like war and secular developments within the commercial system. But with some adjustment of the bench marks the basic sectoral and structural trends emerge clearly enough from our Tables. Nearby and north European markets were relatively stable, but there was a marked decline in south European trades with compensatory growth in colonial markets and in the East. Evidence of the commodity exchange confirms that changes in the distribution of markets had made re-exports the leading sector in late seventeenth century commerce. Indeed, the growth rate of re-exports is seriously understated in Table 12 (p. 131). Approximately two-thirds of re-exports in 1640 originated in Europe; colonial products were worth in the region of £25,000 or a mere 2 to 3 per cent of all exports.[43] An increase to 38 per cent at the end of the century establishes even more firmly that London's function as entrepôt for Asian and plantation products was the key development of the later Stuart period. A near monopoly of re-exports – 84 per cent – offset a decline in the share of cloth exports to 68 per cent. Sales of 'other (domestic) manufactures', a miscellaneous group which included wrought silk and metalwares, improved, but from a narrow base. Import trends can only be judged, with some uncertainty, from Table 10, but if allowance is made for the

Table 12. The composition of London's export trade by value and percentage

	1640[a]			Average of 1663 & 1669			Average of 1699–1701		
	£(000)	%	%	£(000)	%		£(000)	%	%
Woollens	1150	94	88	1512	74		2013	73	45
Other manufactures	27	2	2	222	11		420	15	9
Raw materials	35	3	3	243	12		138	5	3
Foods	17	1	1	62	3		202	7	5
Total Exports	1229	100	94	2039	100		2773	100	62
Re-exports	76	—	6	—	—		1667	—	38
Total	1305		100				4440		100

Note: (a) By English merchants only. Alien exports totalled £89,160
Sources: see Appendix, p. 135

goods that were destined for re-export, price rises from 1604, when official valuations were unrealistically low,[44] and the element of exaggeration in the valuations after 1696, it is safe to conclude that domestic consumption of imports increased at a rate well below that of imports in the second stage or of re-exports in the third. None the less, London accounted for 80 per cent of England's imports in 1699–1701.

Although the composition of imports suggests that demand for articles of conspicuous consumption like wine and tobacco and for industrial raw materials remained firm, the appearance of continuity in both markets is deceptive. Rapid falls in some prices and a general increase in purchasing power had created a mass market for former luxuries. Tobacco and sugar led the trend.[45] The price of fine Dutch linens fell in response to the flood of cheap calicoes, which were themselves 'common wear' before their adoption by ladies of fashion.[46] Even brandy, despite its novelty and price, was drunk not by the masses, but by the urban 'pseudo-gentry', who were blamed for the 'more general affectation of Finery and Gawdry' and the proliferation of 'shop-keepers of all sorts' in later Stuart London.[47] As the market place was democratized it may have become more local: London certainly had lost its monopoly of the national market for tobacco.[48] At the same time the diffusion of manufacturing may have made the market for raw materials less local, reversing the proposed order for the second stage.

Neither trend in import marketing is offered as more than a possibility, logical perhaps, but not susceptible of proof. Overall, however, the gains from trade in the third stage were unquestionably more qualified and less extensive than in the second. Although the external resource base was extended by re-exports, the scope and potential for exploitation were limited and reduced in a number of ways. Contraction in south European markets was not attributable solely to foreign competition, Dutch and French. The East India Company acknowledged that it competed with the Levant Company, arguing in response to demands for controls on raw silk imports, which grew steadily from the 1670s, that one trade should not be 'interrupted because it worked upon another'.[49] The company's case was not improved by the fact that their trade encroached upon markets which were transport-intensive, while their own demands on shipping had been restrained by the change from bulky cargoes of pepper to raw silk and light textiles; calico accounted for 83 per cent of the company's imports in 1684.[50] In contrast, trade with the plantations did not 'work upon' other trades; and mass consumption of tobacco and sugar had, as the record of traffic movements shows, a powerful effect on transportation. Extra-European trades, however, had a common characteristic which on balance and in the longer-term reduced outputs from the commercial sector. Trade with the East and even more so with the plantations required a substantial overseas investment. Colonial profits, though among the highest of all trades,[51] flowed back to the plantations in the form of credits; and investment returns in the widest sense were shared with provincial competitors, who were beginning by 1700 to make inroads on this vital sector of metropolitan trade.[52]

A consequence of overseas commercial investment, as observed by Davis, was the diversion of capital from industry. If so, there were compensations. Sugar and tobacco continued to provide employment in processing plants in the East End and on the south bank, while metropolitan manufacturers took a share of the protected colonial market. On the other hand, in addition to the erosion of London's tobacco monopoly, since colonial demand was downmarket, trans-atlantic trade was a factor in the migration of 'coarse-ware' production to the provinces, where exports to the plantations were re-routed through western ports.[53] Proximity of the market and low labour costs relative to the finished product kept 'fine-ware' manufacturers in London. One, however, silk-weaving, faced competition instead from imported Asian textiles.[54] Shipbuilding was another manufacture which was unable to take full advantage of commercial growth after 1660. Such were the demands placed on the carrying trade by the Navigation Acts that an estimated third to a half of the merchant marine was foreign built, and the remainder was more likely to have been launched from provincial yards where low wage costs were important in a relatively labour-intensive industry.[55] Significantly, London builders looked to the government for naval contracts as private demand switched to the provinces.[56] For metropolitan manufacturers, if not for the country as a whole, gains from trade after the Restoration were mixed, as they were for the local economy generally.

IV

Although London had advanced over two centuries of massive growth from the periphery of a predominantly intra-European system of commercial exchange to the centre of one that was world wide, it is clear from our analysis that the gains from trade were not directly proportionate either to the increase in transactions or to growth in the commercial structure. A time profile would show not a simple linear progression, but a curve with a peak in output occurring in the second stage, when the combination of sectoral and structural developments was most effective in redistributing provincial incomes and generating local investment and employment. Our analysis also has implications for the performance of overseas trade in the total process of metropolitan growth, although, given our ignorance of many of the variables, even the most tentative working hypothesis might seem to be out of place. It might, however, be worthwhile to explore further the complex and changeable relationships of the variables, and in the process to warn against any assumption, however attractive, that overseas trade increased or even maintained its output as an 'engine of growth' in the multi-functional metropolis.

The full range of relationships and alternative competing routes to growth cannot be explored here. At most we might sketch in the outline of an explanatory model which incorporates the main features of commercial expansion in the context of competition. Thus the pattern of the early Tudor period lends some support to Braudel's speculation that one activity might develop to the detriment of others, the negative effects of the Antwerp axis accentuating the role of the overseas trader at the expense of transportation, manufacturing and other activities. When the axis was broken, the spin-off benefits of the more varied and rapidly expanding commercial system complicated and paradoxically diminished the status of the 'mere merchant'. By 1640 he could not assume the same right to control city government; nor did he display the same disproportionate wealth; nor were his contacts with government so productive as a group.[57]

The main competitors for power and wealth in the city were domestic merchants who supplied the huge local market with domestically produced food, fuel and clothing. After the Restoration their trade, in which the circulation of domestic manufactured goods was increasingly important, began to attract the attention and approval hitherto reserved for overseas trade. 'Foreign trade is a secondary help, home trade is our prime advantage' was a view that challenged conventional assumptions about the primacy of the former.[58] For London, however, if not for the nation as a whole, the order should be reversed. As a channel of income redistribution, the main flow from domestic trade and its carriage was out of the city. To redress the internal balance of payments, overseas trade made a significant contribution through the cloth trade in the first stage and import-marketing in the second. But from the Restoration the service sector may well have provided a more effective mechanism. Growth in metropolitan professional services and the increase in social appetites, which only the capital could satisfy, emptied provincial pockets at a remarkable rate.[59]

Voluntary transfers of provincial income were reinforced by compulsory redistribution via wartime taxation. How government income was circulated is a question of great complexity and well beyond the scope of this discussion, but the possibility that a disproportionately large amount was fed into the metropolitan economy is strong. The naval dockyards and government contracts for private shipyards illustrate the importance of public investment.[60] War and wartime government finance also had major consequences for the status and function of foreign trade in supporting central government. Until King William's War the customs had maintained their value overall as a source of public revenue. It has been written of the 1680s, not the 1630s, that the yield from a trade boom was 'a major factor in the financial solvency and political assertiveness of the Stuart monarchy'.[61] After 1689 the burden of taxation was transferred to land and, through the excise and such special taxes as those on salt and coal, to domestic trade and manufacturing.[62] Simultaneously, 'the remarkable transformation in the commercial and financial status of London, which began to take on that indefinable character conveyed by the later term "City"',[63] diminished the role of commercial capital in private as well as public credit and finance. Merchant money was prominent in the foundation of the Bank of England; overseas trade provided in the East India Company one of the stock-market leaders; and for marine insurance, which had become a considerable business by the end of the seventeenth century and a model for other forms of insurance, incomes from foreign trade were largely responsible for securing the risks.[64] Yet the wartime retreat of trading capital into the shelter of the Funds demonstrated that the old world of commerce and the new world of finance and banking were competitive as well as mutually reinforcing;[65] and they competed in an area which had long been vital for the dynamism of commerce. It was the merchants' ability 'to produce cash and generate credit which made the effective wealth and influence of the business world much greater than its net resources'.[66] By drawing upon and circulating money from non-commercial sources, the City challenged that role at a time when mercantile incomes were, as we have seen, committed as never before to investment overseas. The financial revolution thus added to the service sector a powerful engine of metropolitan growth; and it emerged at a time when the commercial revolution, which transferred growth to provincial ports, presented a unique challenge to the commercial hegemony of the metropolis.

APPENDIX

The import index in Fig. 2 is based on the record of payments of poundage on general merchandise and tonnage on wines in E. Power and M. M. Postan (eds), *Studies in English Trade in the Fifteenth Century* (London 1933), p. 346, G. Schanz, *Englische Handelspolitik gegen ende des Mittelalters* (Leipzig 1881), vol.ii, p. 73, and Professor Ramsey's generous communication of the annual figures which were the basis of the six-year averages in 'Overseas trade in the reign of Henry VII: the evidence of the customs accounts', *EcHR*, 2nd ser., 6 (1953), p. 79n. Some allowance has been made for payment of poundage on exports by deducting those on cloth, much the most important commodity. Before 1489 Spanish merchants were exempt from poundage on cloth. Their exports are listed in Childs, *Trade*, p. 90. In 1539–45 all aliens enjoyed denizen status. Wines are aggregated by valuing the tun at £2. The raw wool and cloth indices were compiled from the data in E. M. Carus-Wilson and O. Coleman (eds), *England's Export Trade 1275–1547* (London 1963). Cloth exports before 1495 have been reduced by 15 per cent following H. S. Cobb's recommendations in 'Cloth exports from London and Southampton in the late fifteenth and early sixteenth centuries: a revision', *EcHR*, 2nd ser., 31 (1973). The aggregate of cloth and wool values the sack at 2 short cloths. E. M. Carus-Wilson, *Medieval Merchant Venturers* (2nd edn, London 1967), p. xxiv. For cloth exports after 1547 see J. D. Gould, *The Great Debasement* (Oxford 1970) and Fisher, 'Trends'.

In Table 9 exports are of cloth only before 1640. In that year and thereafter the percentages are by value. The short cloth in 1640 has been valued at £8. W. B. Stephens, 'Further observations on English cloth exports, 1600–1640', *EcHR*, 2nd ser., 24 (1971). The sources for the Table are PRO E 190/2/1; 4/2 which is calendared in Dietz, *Port*; Friis, *Project*, p. 61; Fisher, 'Export trade'; Millard,

'Import Trade', and R. Davis, 'English foreign trade, 1660–1700', *EcHR*, 2nd ser., 6 (1954). In Table 10 the record for 1559/60 is from PRO SP 12/8 ff.63–9. Millard's and Davis's tabulations provide the data for the 1630s and 1699–1701. Table 11 presents traffic movements as recorded in PRO E 190/4/2; 11/1 and R. Davis, 'The Organization and Finance of the English Shipping Industry in the Late Seventeenth Century' (unpublished London University Ph.D. thesis 1955), Table VII. For Table 12 see Fisher, 'Export trade' and Davis, 'Foreign trade'.

In compiling the Table of Imports it has been necessary to allow for the differences in the basis of valuations before 1696, when the Books of Rates of 1558 and 1604 apparently valued goods at domestic wholesale prices, and after 1696 when the Inspector Generals adopted cost abroad as their basis. Willan, *Rates*, xxvii–xxxii; Dietz, 'Antwerp', pp. 187–8. To achieve conformity the domestic wholesale price has been reduced by 20 per cent, which was the allowance for customs, freight, insurance, merchant's profit and other charges that was made in early seventeenth century official trade statistics. Perhaps intentionally this represented a compromise between Thomas Mun's 25 and Edward Misselden's 15 per cent. J. Thirsk and J. P. Cooper (eds), *Seventeenth Century Economic Documents* (Oxford 1972), pp. 454–7, 473–4; Thomas Mun, 'England's treasure by forraign trade,' in J. R. McCulloch (ed.), *Early English Tracts on Commerce* (repr. Cambridge 1970), pp. 204–5. Wines and tobacco have been treated separately, following Davis's procedure of valuing them according to evidence of current prices. For 1559/60 the original valuation for wines, which at £68,000 was improbably high, has been discarded in favour of averaging three years' imports from 1560 at £2 the tun. PRO E 356/28; 122/88/13. Imports in 1633/4 have been calculated from data in Millard. Tobacco imports, in addition to being grossly overvalued by the 1630s, fluctuated sharply. The preferred figure is the annual average of imports from 1637–40 – 1,818,403 pounds – valued at 4d the pound in accordance with data in R. R. Menard, 'A note on Chesapeake tobacco prices, 1618–1640', *Virginia Magazine of History and Biography*, 84 (1976) and J. R. Pagan, 'Growth of the tobacco trade between London and Virginia, 1614–40', *Guildhall Studies in London History*, 5 (1979), pp. 248–62.

NOTES AND REFERENCES

1. F. Braudel, *Capitalism and Material Life 1400–1800* (London 1973), p. 414.
2. E. A. Wrigley, 'A simple model of London's importance in changing English society and economy, 1650–1750', *Past and Present*, 37 (1967); F. J. Fisher, 'London as an "engine of economic growth"', in J. S. Bromley and E. H. Kossmann (eds), *Britain and the Netherlands*, iv (The Hague 1971).
3. K. J. Button, *Urban Economics* (London 1976), pp. 82–3.
4. F. Braudel, *The Mediterranean and the Mediterranean World in the Age of Philip II* (London 1972), i, 323.
5. C. P. Kindelberger, *Foreign Trade and the National Economy* (New Haven 1962), p. 211. See also J. D. Gould, *Economic Growth in History* (London 1972), Ch. 4.

6. R. G. Lang, 'The Greater Merchants of London in the Early Seventeenth Century' (Unpublished Oxford University D. Phil. thesis, 1963). The author's main conclusions are to be found in 'London's aldermen in business 1600-25', *Guildhall Miscellany*, 3 (1971). See also R. Ashton, *The City and the Court 1603-43* (Cambridge 1979), Ch. 1; R. Grassby, 'English merchant capitalism in the late seventeenth century: the composition of business fortunes', *Past and Present*, 46 (1970).

7. In mid-Tudor London there were probably not more than a hundred well-off overseas merchants in a population of approaching 100,000. G. D. Ramsay, *The City of London in International Politics at the Accession of Elizabeth Tudor* (Manchester 1975), p. 74. For the early Stuart period see B. Dietz, 'England's overseas trade in the reign of James I', in A.G.R. Smith (ed.). *The Reign of James VI and I* (London 1973).

8. Grassby, 'Capitalism', p. 91.

9. L. Stone, 'The residential development of the West End of London in the seventeenth century', in B. C. Malament (ed.), *After the Reformation* (Manchester 1980), p. 188.

10. Fisher, '"Engine"'.

11. The standard work on Antwerp is H. van der Wee, *The Growth of the Antwerp Market and the European Economy*, 2 vols. (The Hague 1963). O. de Smedt, *De Engelse Natie te Antwerpen in de 16e Eeuw*, 2 vols. (Antwerp 1950-4) examines the English connection, as does Ramsay, *City*. A brief, more quantitative study of the London – Antwerp axis in its last years is B. Dietz, 'Antwerp and London: the structure and balance of trade in the 1560s', in E. W. Ives, R. J. Knecht and J. J. Scarisbrick (eds), *Wealth and Power in Tudor England* (London 1978).

12. F. J. Fisher, 'Commercial trends and policy in sixteenth century England', *Economic History Review* (hereafter *EcHR*), 10 (1940); C. E. Challis, 'The circulating medium and the movement of prices in mid-Tudor England', in P. Ramsey (ed.), *The Price Revolution in the Sixteenth Century* (London 1971), p. 128.

13. In 1561-7 the average annual value of imported general merchandise was £242,460. Public Record Office (hereafter PRO) E.356/28; 122/88/15. The figure is adjusted to allow for the upward revision of valuations in the 1558 Book of Rates. Taking a large sample of commodities T. S. Willan found this averaged 119 per cent: *A Tudor Book of Rates* (ed.) (Manchester 1962), pp. xxvii-xxxii. For wine imports see the Appendix.

14. Ships engaged in the Antwerp run rarely made more than one voyage to foreign ports, while none is recorded as making more than two.

15. Ramsay, *City*, 44-6, W. R. Childs, *Anglo-Castilian Trade in the Later Middle Ages* (Manchester 1978), pp. 82-4 provides convincing evidence of the earlier prosperity and sophistication of cloth finishing in London.

16. H. E. Raynes, *A History of British Insurance* (London 1948), Chs 2-4. W. J. Jones, 'Elizabethan marine insurance: the judicial undergrowth', *Business History*, 2 (1960).

17. B. Dietz (ed.), *The Port and Trade of Early Elizabethan London* (London Record Society, 8, 1971), pp. xii-xiii, App. IV.

18. Ramsay, *City*, p. 41.

19. K. N. Chaudhuri, *The English East India Company* (London 1965); A. M. Millard, 'The Import Trade of London, 1600-1640' (Unpublished London

University Ph.D thesis, 1956), Table VII.

20. E. S. Morgan, 'The first American boom: Virginia 1618 to 1630', *William and Mary Quarterly*, 3rd ser., 27 (1971). Cf. N. Williams, 'England's tobacco trade in the reign of Charles I', *Virginia Magazine of History and Biography*, 65 (1957).

21. Millard, 'Import Trade', Table VII.

22. R. Brenner, 'The Civil War politics of London's merchant community', *Past and Present*, 58 (1973); but compare R. Davis, 'England and the Mediterranean, 1570–1670', in F. J. Fisher (ed.), *Essays in the Economic and Social History of Tudor and Stuart England* (Cambridge 1961).

23. H. Taylor, 'Trade, neutrality and the "English road", 1630–1648', *EcHR*, 2nd ser., 25 (1972), p. 238.

24. J. J. McCusker and S. Hart, 'Rates of exchange in Amsterdam and London, 1590–1660', *Journal of European Economic History*, 8 (1979).

25. See the Appendix for the record of imports and exports in the 1560s; for the later period J. D. Gould, 'Cloth exports 1600–1640', *EcHR*, 2nd ser., 24 (1971), F. J. Fisher, 'London's export trade in the early seventeenth century', *EcHR*, 2nd ser., 3 (1950) and Millard's Tables.

26. E. Lamond (ed.), *A Discourse of the Common Weal of this Realm of England* (repr. Cambridge 1954), pp. 125–6.

27. F. J. Fisher, 'The development of London as a centre of conspicuous consumption in the 16th and 17th centuries', *Transactions of the Royal Historical Society*, 4th ser., 30 (1948); Stone, 'Residential development'.

28. *House of Commons Journals* 1547–1628, p. 987.

29. D. W. Jones, 'The "Hallage" receipts of the London cloth market, 1562– *c.* 1720', *EcHR*, 2nd ser., 25 (1972), p. 582n. For developments in northern markets A. Friis, *Alderman Cockayne's Project* (Copenhagen 1927) is still indispensable. B. E. Supple, *Commercial Crisis and Change in England, 1600–1642* (Cambridge 1959) is a masterly analysis of metropolitan trade, with special emphasis on traditional northern markets. Of these the Baltic has received the most attention in recent years. See H. Zins, *England and the Baltic in the Elizabethan Era* (Manchester 1972); J. K. Federowicz, *England's Baltic Trade in the Early Seventeenth Century* (Cambridge 1980); R. W. K. Hinton, *The Eastland Trade and the Common Weal in the Seventeenth Century* (Cambridge 1959).

30. Opinions on competition in the new drapery trade are divided. W. B. Stephens, 'The cloth exports of the provincial ports, 1600–1640', *EcHR*, 2nd ser., 12 (1969) was criticized by Gould, 'Cloth exports'. Stephens replied with 'Further observations on English cloth exports, 1600–1640', *EcHR*, 2nd ser., 24 (1971).

31. G. D. Ramsay, 'The undoing of the Italian merchant community in sixteenth century London', in N. B. Harte and K. G. Ponting (eds), *Textile History and Economic History* (Manchester 1973).

32. D. W. Jones, 'London merchants and the crisis of the 1690s', in P. Clark and P. Slack (eds), *Crisis and Order in English Towns 1500–1700* (London 1972), p. 326.

33. In 1580/1 488 English ships of 30,881 tons entered the port. PRO SP 12/148 ff. 123–9. In 1587/8 and 1589/90 the figures are 305–21,919 tons – and 340–26,941 tons. PRO E. 190/7/8;8/1; 122/178/26.

34. PRO HCA. 13/42 23rd Oct. 1613.

35. The percentage of London-based shipping engaged in the import trade rose from 56 in 1567/8 to 66 in 1599/1600. In the smaller export trade percentages were higher – in 1586/7, 88 and in 1596/7, 96 per cent. PRO E. 122/178/16 and 35.

36. Provincial carriers dominated the rapidly expanding north-east coal trade. In 1579/80, 79 per cent of the colliers were from the outports; in 1614/15 82 per cent. PRO E. 190/6/8; 18/1.

37. Payments are recorded in an almost continuous series in the privy seal books PRO E. 403.

38. On building costs see Chaudhuri, *East India*, pp. 97–8; S. M. Jack, *Trade and Industry in Tudor and Stuart England* (London 1977), p. 101.

39. Trinity House Certificates in the State Papers Domestic in the PRO throw some light on the Thames shipwrights. I am grateful to Mr Geoffrey Harris for making notes of the certificates available. They record, for example, that John Graves of Limehouse built on average a ship of between 250 and 300 tons yearly between 1625 and 1637, the largest being 500 tons.

40. References to London manufactures are to be found in J. Thirsk, *Economic Policy and Projects* (Oxford 1978) and Jack, *Industry*,. For the sugar refineries see K. R. Andrews, *Elizabethan Privateering* (Cambridge 1964), pp. 208–9.

41. C. D. Chandaman, *The English Public Revenue, 1660–1688* (Oxford 1975), pp. 12–13. Professor Chandaman kindly supplied details of the adjustments in the 1660 Book.

42. Jones, 'London merchants'.

43. Taylor, 'Neutrality', p. 251 n.2.

44. Willan found an average increase of only 13 per cent between the 1558 revision and the 1604 Book. *Rates*, p. xliii.

45. Compare price data in Menard, 'Chesapeake tobacco' with R. C. Nash, 'The English and Scottish tobacco trades in the seventeenth and eighteenth centuries: legal and illegal trade', *EcHR*, 2nd ser., 35 (1982), p. 369. For sugar prices see R. S. Dunn, *Sugar and Slaves* (Williamsburg, Va. 1972), pp. 202–5.

46. K. N. Chaudhuri, *The Trading World of Asia and the East India Company* (Cambridge 1978), pp. 282–3.

47. 'Britannia Languens, or a Discourse of Trade' (1680), in J. R. McCulloch (ed.), *Early English Tracts on Commerce* (repr. Cambridge 1970), pp. 421–6.

48. London's share of the tobacco trade fell from an average of 80 per cent before 1640 to 51 in 1685–8. J. M. Price, *France and the Chesapeake* (Ann Arbor, Mich. 1973), i,p. 589.

49. Chaudhuri, *Asia*, pp. 343–4, 346–7.

50. In the 1620s the company dispatched 3,000 tons and above of shipping annually to the East. Chaudhuri, *East India*, pp. 231–3.

51. M. Bogucka, 'The role of Baltic trade in European development from the XVIth the XVIIIth centuries', *Journal of European Economic History*, 9 (1980).

52. P. G. E. Clemens, 'The rise of Liverpool, 1650–1750', *EcHR*, 2nd ser., 29 (1976).

53. See especially Thirsk, *Projects*, pp. 92, 109–110, 128 for examples of the diffusion of manufactures; also J. Langton, 'Industry and towns 1500–1730', in R. A. Dodgshon and R. A. Butlin (eds), *An Historical*

Geography of England and Wales (London 1978), p. 175.
54. Chaudhuri, *Asia*, p. 277.
55. R. Davis, *The Rise of the English Shipping Industry* (repr. Newton Abbott 1972), p. 52.
56. Ibid. pp. 394–5; D. C. Coleman, 'Naval dockyards under the later Stuarts', *EcHR*, 2nd ser., 6 (1953), p. 152.
57. See above note 6.
58. Carew Reynel, *The True English Interest* (1674) quoted in Thirsk, *Projects*, p. 142.
59. M. G. Davies, 'Country gentry and payments to London', *EcHR*, 2nd ser., 24 (1971). On the growth of the professions, G. S. Holmes, *Augustan England* (London 1982).
60. Coleman, 'Dockyards'.
61. Chandaman, *Revenue*, p. 35.
62. P. G. M. Dickson, *The Financial Revolution in England* (London 1967), pp. 46–7.
63. Chaudhuri, *Asia*, p. 411.
64. Jones, 'Merchants', pp. 334ff; Rayne, *Insurance*; B. Supple, *The Royal Exchange Assurance* (Cambridge 1970), pp. 7–10; P. G. M. Dickson, *The Sun Assurance Office 1710–1960* (London 1966), Ch. 1.
65. G. S. Holmes, *British Politics in the Age of Anne* (London 1967), pp. 154–5.
66. Grassby, 'Capitalism', p. 106.

CHAPTER FIVE

Engine of manufacture: the trades of London

A. L. Beier

Considerable doubt surrounds the role of the metropolis in the emergence of industrial capitalism. One view is that early modern urban giants played a wholly negative part in the economy. They were parasites, themselves the victims of economic atrophy, who sucked dry the rest of the country. They underwent 'disproportionate growth', expanding by an 'eminently non-productive concentration of revenue' from government and rentier sources, and producing a 'swollen proletarian underworld of "non-work"'.[1] To Braudel the great capitals were destined to be spectators at the coming of the industrial revolution: 'not London, but Manchester, Birmingham, Leeds, Glasgow and innumerable small proletarian towns launched the new era'. Great cities were 'unbalanced worlds', consuming more than they produced, so that 'their economy was only balanced by outside resources'. Amsterdam, London, Naples, Paris and St Petersburg were all chiefly centres of government, which produced not goods but the modern state. They were centres of indolence and consumption, frequented by the very rich of their respective countries, but still parasites because 'others had to pay for their luxury'.[2]

A second school of thought takes a stage further the scepticism about the role of towns in the rise of capitalism, arguing that the critical developments occurred in the countryside. In this approach agrarian class structures and struggles were the keys to economic changes in pre-industrial Europe: commercialization, market forces, and urbanization are explicitly rejected as explanations.[3] Towns are said to have made little impact in the decline of serfdom in the West because of their small size and restrictive economies. In early modern England, furthermore, the success of industrialization arose from a highly productive rural sector. By contrast most towns of the period lagged behind in the

141

economic sweepstakes because of restrictive gilds and crippling social problems. Indeed, again, it was the countryside, especially forest and pastoral areas, that saw most development of new crafts and industries which left the towns for their greener and freer pastures.[4]

A third interpretation suggests that London was different from other European capitals and played a positive role in the industrial revolution. This view sees the English economy as essentially dualistic, with an advanced urban market sector and a relatively backward rural one. It stresses how London stimulated more efficient production in the provinces because of its gargantuan levels of consumption; how its markets prompted the improvement of transport facilities; and how its credit facilities greased the wheels of commerce. Demographically, moreover, the metropolis acted as a safety-valve for the rest of the country. By receiving thousands of immigrants each year, it helped to avert Malthusian crises and economic collapses that would have jeopardized progress in the countryside. Finally, London hastened the coming of the new order by breaking down traditional values, promoting social mobility and generating new patterns of consumption.[5]

The role of the metropolis in production is minimised in all three of the foregoing arguments. In the parasite and dual economy models its role is essentially as consumer; in the one that stresses the importance of rural capitalism, towns are of little significance in any respect. As regards London, however, all three interpretations are open to question. The capital was undoubtedly a great trading centre, possibly the greatest in the world by 1700, but it is argued in this paper that production was another, equally significant feature of its economy. It is true that the industrial revolution came late to London, but the teleology inherent in the term pre-industrial should not obscure the fact that the metropolis was actually the country's leading manufacturing centre in the early modern period and that it remained so well into Victorian times. Evidence of their occupations suggests that most Londoners were involved in some form of production in the seventeenth century and that the mode of production was changing in a capitalist direction. These developments in turn altered the social complexion of the burgeoning metropolis.

I

Patchy source materials create considerable difficulties for the student of the early modern London work-force. Most records provide no more than partial views of the numbers and types of trades practised in the capital. They rarely allow one to glimpse how the different crafts and professions were organized or how they evolved during the period. Records of apprenticeship and the freedom are valuable for studying migration and social mobility, but are of limited use when it comes to questions of occupations and the economy. Gild labels are imprecise and unrepresentative. Membership of the trading gilds did not always signify the actual practice of their trade because, by the 'custom of London', their members could take on any trade.[6] A further drawback to be noted is that a declining proportion of London workers entered the gilds and took up the freedom as the seventeenth century progressed. Already by 1650 their trades, whether fictitious or real, were probably unrepresentative of the capital's workers. Finally, formal apprenticeship and gild membership were relatively weak in the expanding suburbs which by the early seventeenth century had outstripped the municipality and its liberties in population, as Finlay and Shearer show elsewhere in this collection.[7] Thus from an early date gild titles ceased to bear much resemblance to economic realities.

London baptismal registers normally listed the occupations of fathers, but this source also has limitations. The studies so far published cover short periods, and long-term economic shifts cannot be gauged.[8] More seriously, these documents seldom listed females and dependent workers as parents. That was because of the importance attached to paternity in this male-dominated society, and because servants and apprentices were not permitted to marry and have children while in service. Similarly, probate wills and inventories are only of limited use for the study of Londoners' trades. Their survival is patchy and, as in the provinces, they are biased towards better-off workers. Moreover, the probate records arising from cases in the Court of Orphans are limited to the families of freemen who, as we have noted, are unrepresentative in economic terms.[9]

Further occupational evidence is contained in later Stuart taxation records. The Hearth, Poll, and Marriage Duty Act levies are probably the closest things to censuses in seventeenth-century England. All three sources listed householders' trades in London, and the Poll and Marriage taxes even took note of dependent workers. But the coverage of these records, too, is suspect. The hearth taxes did not, it seems, consistently list servants and apprentices. In addition, the Marriage Duty Act returns appear to survive only for City parishes, leaving the suburbs again in darkness. A final difficulty is the one-off quality of these records. They rarely concern more than a few years and hence provide no more than photographic stills of people's occupations, when ideally a series of pictures over several decades is needed to document long-term changes in the economy.[10]

Faced with such daunting problems of documentation, the student of the trades of London might be reduced to despair. Fortunately, however, London is blessed with other records that produce some reliable and meaningful results. The burial registers of London parishes constitute a first-rate source for the study of metropolitan trades. They provide details of the occupations and status of 26,737 persons buried in 15 parishes between *c.* 1540 and *c.* 1700 (see Appendix 1 for details). The present essay is largely based upon this information.

The evidence is first deployed to trace the broad outlines of London trades in the period. Here the various occupations are assigned to 13 categories ranging from building to victualling. Secondly, there is an attempt to distinguish those trades involved in production and those concentrating on exchanges, so that hypotheses about the-capital-as-market and as parasite can be tested. Thirdly, some of the changes associated with London's emergence as a centre of manufacturing are examined, including some effects upon metropolitan social topography. A major development in this context was the increased importance of free labour, that is workers outside traditional gild structures, a change paralleled by the rising significance of free traders in overseas, above all colonial, trade. All told, it is argued, these facts demonstrate that London, far from being a parasite in the rearguard of English economic advances, was actually in the vanguard by the early eighteenth century (that it did not enter the magic circle of the industrial revolution until a century after Manchester is beside the point). Finally, some of the reasons for the capital's evolution into a great manufacturing centre are considered. They are suggested to be political as well as economic; above all a willingness, thought to be the hallmark of the western city, to usurp authority.

How dependable are the burial registers as a source for this study? As with most records of the past, they have their strengths and their weaknesses. Generally, however, the first outweigh the second, making them perhaps the best single source for the study of occupations before the census of 1841. On the plus side the records are more comprehensive than most others, because everyone dies sooner or later. They also provide coverage over long periods, often a century and more, despite some hiatuses; therefore long-run economic shifts can be observed. Because the evidence is plentiful, moreover, one can attempt to select a representative group of parishes. Besides wealthy mercantile ones like St Michael Bassishaw near the hub of the City, there is evidence from busy industrial ones like St Olave's Southwark in the suburbs; and riverside places are represented as well as land-locked ones. Burial registers also list the occupations of females and adolescents employed as dependent workers, which are groups ignored by most other sources. Finally, these sources are likely to be accurate, because identification was the whole purpose of adding occupational and status titles. London parishes were becoming so large and their populations so mobile that these tags were required to identify the dead. Fortunately, however, the common form ascriptions like 'yeoman', 'gentleman' and 'labourer' found in many legal documents are not the rule in burial registers.[11]

The negative points against this source are fairly trivial. In theory variations in death-rates might distort the results, swelling the numbers of older, established persons while understating young apprentices and servants. But it is worth noticing that comparison of occupations in the census of 1841 and burial registers between 1812 and 1840 revealed negligible distortion.[12] Another problem about the evidence is that, while representativeness has been sought, the sample is not scientific; good evidence is simply too scarce for that. One result is that West End and Westminster parishes are comparatively poorly covered. Nevertheless, an effort has been made to show the special character of these western parts, based on fragmentary evidence. The parish of St Giles Cripplegate, by contrast, risks being over-represented in the second half of the seventeenth century, when we are fortunate to have Professor Forbes' tabulation of nearly 14,000 jobs there. To ensure that the results are representative two measures have been taken. First, all figures for London generally have been weighted to take account of the changing balance of population between intra- and extra-mural areas. Secondly, the St Giles Cripplegate evidence gathered by Forbes has been compared to early seventeenth-century figures for this and other extra-mural parishes and no significant deviations found.[13]

A further difficulty with the sources is that the work of women and children within the family is unrecorded. Status and company labels also present problems. The descriptions 'master' and 'servant' are guides to social positions, but tell us little about occupations, and have therefore been ignored when examining trades. One must additionally beware of misleading gild titles. A St Peter Cornhill man described as 'free of the Merchant Tailors' in 1601 was actually a clothworker, while another interred in St Lawrence Jewry in 1653 and listed as free of the Lorimars was in fact a tapster at the Bear.[14] Fortunately one has some control over such nominal titles. Company membership was regularly noted in five of the parishes and accounted for 16 per cent of occupational labels. Even if similar numbers were to slip through in other parishes, they would be unlikely greatly to affect the results.[15]

The reliability of burial registers for the study of occupations is confirmed by other sources. Thus in addition to appearing in the registers the drapers of St Michael Cornhill, the clothsellers of St Antholin Budge Row, merchants of St Michael Bassishaw and goldsmiths of St Vedast Foster Lane, are recorded in Stow's *Survey of London* of 1598.[16] Furthermore, quarter sessions and probate records confirm the importance of feltmakers and leatherdressers in St Olave Southwark's registers, the presence of large numbers of glovers and brewers in St Giles Cripplegate, and the importance of shipbuilders in St Dunstan's Stepney.[17]

Certain points are also worth raising regarding the methodology of this study. The aggregation of dozens of varied jobs into occupational categories inevitably involves anomalies and arbitrary decisions. Hence seamen and shipwrights have been included under 'Distribution and Transport', even though one built and the other sailed the ships. Similar difficulties arise with the many branches of cloth manufacture and trading. One alternative would be to list trades in a kind of seventeenth-century trade directory, but the result, while desirable in some respects, would be chaotic and indigestible. Some examples of the taxonomy used here are provided in Appendix 2.

The distinction between occupations involved in production versus exchange is admittedly somewhat artificial, since many producers themselves sold their products and many traders probably made the goods they sold. The decision about which they mainly engaged in will inevitably be arbitrary in some cases. In addition, it is unlikely that we shall ever know the *value* of production as against exchanges in the London economy. Producers might be far more numerous than traders, but the income of one great merchant might equal that of hundreds of backstreet tailors. Finally, production is broadly defined here to include the butchers, bakers and candlestick-makers of the nursery rhyme. This might seem odd to the modern economist, who sees mass production of consumer durables as the norm. But we should not forget that transforming raw materials into meat, bread and light were mainstream economic activities of this period. Certainly new monographic studies of manufacturers are to be welcomed; to date the merchants have received most of the attention.[18]

London is defined here as the metropolitan area included in the bills of mortality of 1636, that is the Greater London stretching from Stepney to Westminster.[19] The definition of suburban London employed here breaks with tradition, which normally treats such extramural parishes as St Giles Cripplegate as part of the City, because they came under its jurisdiction and that of its gilds.[20] But this is a political definition which ignores economic and social conditions. Instead intra- and extra-mural London are distinguished here, a simpler and actually more telling criterion than the constitutional one. The only awkwardness arises with the special development of the West End. Finally it is worth stating that non-Londoners dying during apparent visits to the capital have been excluded as far as possible. So have London women with the epithet 'mistress'. Their numbers grew enormously in the period, but the rise is illusory, because women of that rank were not labelled at all before 1600 or so.

II

Seventeenth-century London had an amazing array of traders, craftsmen and professions. If economic diversification, including proto-industrialization, characterized many parts of England in this period, London was no stranger to the process. The metropolis was undoubtedly the most diversified centre in Britain, and possibly Europe, by 1700. It is thought that in the late Middle Ages its trades and crafts numbered about 180; by the early seventeenth century the large extramural parishes of St Botolph Aldgate and St Giles Cripplegate had 130 different trades on their own.[21] Even such small parishes as St Thomas the Apostle and St Vedast might count two or three dozen different crafts; larger places had six dozen or so. Real increases were taking place in numbers of occupations. St Dionis Backchurch, St Mary Aldermary and St Michael Bassishaw all experienced rises of between 50 and 100 per cent in the seventeenth century. The giant St Giles Cripplegate alone added 260 new trades in the second half of the century.[22]

While the numbers of crafts were expanding, their distribution between various industries remained fairly stable. Clothing was the dominant industry right through the period, despite crises and depressions, accounting for over a fifth of the work-force (details in Table 13). Then there followed a number of lines of work, none of which surpassed a tenth or so of the total. The leader was victualling by the end of the period, clear testimony to the capital's growing need for food. Merchants of various types ('merchants' proper, merchant tailors, factors, grocers, mercers and brokers) were another important group, as one might expect considering London's traditional trading role. So for the same reason were the distributive and transport trades, which accounted for nearly a tenth of the total in the early seventeenth

Table 13. The trades of London, 1540–1700 (percentages)

Trades	All parishes^a			Intra-mural parishes			Extra-mural parishes		
	1540–1600^b	1601–40	1641–1700	1540–1600	1601–40	1641–1700	1540–1600	1601–40	1641–1700
Building^c	8.4	6.5	7.2	7.7	5.6	6.8	10.0	7.5	7.4
Clothing	22.4	23.3	22.7	22.9	21.1	21.2	21.2	25.5	23.3
Decorating/Furnishing	1.2	2.9	3.6	1.3	3.6	3.9	1.1	2.2	3.5
Distribution/Transport	6.4	9.2	7.5	3.0	4.8	4.5	13.5	13.7	8.7
Labouring	4.9	4.0	4.9	1.3	0.6	0.7	12.4	7.6	6.7
Leather	9.1	8.7	8.9	9.9	8.4	6.0	7.4	9.0	10.2
Merchants	12.8	10.9	7.0	17.5	19.4	20.0	2.9	2.2	1.5
Metal-work	9.1	9.1	8.9	10.1	9.7	7.5	7.1	8.4	9.5
Miscell. Services	5.5	6.2	5.4	5.5	6.6	5.1	5.5	5.8	5.5
Miscell. Production	2.1	2.3	3.6	1.1	1.0	2.1	4.1	3.6	4.2
Officials	3.6	2.8	1.9	5.0	5.0	4.4	0.7	0.4	0.8
Professions	5.6	4.0	2.5	7.0	7.0	5.6	2.7	0.9	1.2
Victualling	8.9	10.1	15.9	7.7	7.2	12.2	11.4	13.2	17.5
	100.0	100.0	100.0	100.0	100.0	100.0	100.0	100.0	100.0
	(n=2,388)	(n=3,620)	(n=12,259)	(n=984)	(n=976)	(n=1,243)	(n=1,404)	(n=2,644)	(n=11,016)

Sources: As in Appendix 1.

Notes:

(a) Percentages for 'all parishes' weighted to take account of population change in the sample area: for 1570 the ratio of intra-mural to extra-mural areas, (West End excepted) interpolated to be 2.13:1; for 1620, 1.04:1; and for 1670, 0.42:1. Based on population figures for extra-mural areas in Finlay and Shearer, Ch. 1, Table 3 *infra*; and on estimates of intra-mural population of 60,000 for 1560, 100,000 for 1600 and 80,000 for 1680: *ex info.* Dr R. A. P. Finlay.

(b) The 'fit' between dates and evidence is not always perfect. Thus St Michael Cornhill, 1628–58, has been included in 1641–1700. But such extreme cases were fortunately exceptional.

century. But industries also figured prominently among metropolitan occupations: besides clothing, the building, leather and metal trades together made up a quarter of the work-force. Officials and professionals together numbered nearly one tenth at one time and rarely fell below one twentieth. There were also decorators and furnishers to lighten and brighten the homes of the wealthy, as well as substantial miscellanies of service and production workers. 'Miscellaneous producers' included basketmakers, bowyers, boxmakers, fletchers, limners and watchmakers, while 'miscellaneous services' covered apothecaries, midwives, scriveners, soldiers, waterbearers and wood-mongers. A seventeenth-century London Trade Directory would be a substantial tome; certainly longer than the 215 occupations listed by Campbell's *London Tradesman* in 1747.[23]

The general profile of trades altered slightly, but not dramatically (Table 13, 'All parishes'). The major industries of building, clothing, leather- and metal-working changed no more than one or two per cent, while labouring, miscellaneous producers and service-workers remained roughly the same. The rise of victualling trades is perhaps most remarkable, amounting as it did to an 80 per cent increase from 9 to 16 per cent. Similarly sharp falls were recorded by officials, the professions and merchants, which are curious results for a period when these groups are supposed to have been rising in prominence. The answer lies partly in the sample, which excludes West End parishes where the first two groups were unquestionably numerous. But these results are accurate in reflecting the growth of extra-mural parts of the rest of London, where officials, professionals and merchants were exiguous in number.

The picture we have so far of London's economy already differs from the Braudel version. Victualling was certainly rising, but the metropolis was more than an overgrown parasite. Nor was the capital choked with office-holders and seekers. Merchants were numerous, but probably in decline. There were substantial industries, accounting for nearly half the work-force, and a diversified range of service workers. Production did not undergo great technological revolutions as in the following century, but trades were diversifying and growing in number, which was a more dynamic situation than the figures in Table 13 might allow.

Of course the broad taxonomy of trades in Table 13 ultimately tells us a limited amount about London's economy. We are none the wiser about working conditions, investment and production processes. We are also in the dark about the precise extent of production- versus exchange-based occupations and about where trades were practised in the capital, since their distribution was unlikely to be uniform in such a large city. London's great size and diversity, as well as the controversies surrounding its economic history, require us to probe beyond the figures in Table 13.

Reshuffling the evidence, we find that the metropolis was a centre for production as well as trade. Both in the sixteenth and the seventeenth centuries nearly three-fifths of London's occupations involved some form of production of goods, while those mainly in exchange-related positions formed just under a quarter, and others (mainly service and professional people) just below a fifth (see Table 14). These proportions did not change greatly over the period. Admittedly some of the producers in intramural parishes might have been traders in disguise, so to speak, because they were following the 'custom of London'. But even allowing, as before, that some 16 per cent were affected, producers of goods would still be left in the majority in both centuries, leaving aside the question whether some traders might not have been financing and organizing production. Inclusion of West End parishes might also have diminished the proportion of producers because of the large numbers of officials, gentlemen and hangers-on there. But judging by the example of St Dunstan's in the West this was not necessarily so: 52 per cent of occupations involved manufacturing, 15 per cent exchanges and the remainder a mixture of professionals and others.[24]

We should of course not be surprised at the extent of production in the metropolitan economy. The bulk of London's gilds were craft ones,

Table 14. Production and exchange in London, 1540–1700 (percentages)[a]

Dates	Activity	Intra-mural	Extra-mural	All Parishes[b]
1540–1600	Production	52.9	70.1	58.4
	Exchanges	28.2	7.5	21.6
	Other[c]	18.9	22.4	20.0
	Totals	100.0	100.0	100.0
		(n=1,277)	(n=1,472)	
1601–1700	Production	40.4	74.3	60.6
	Exchanges	35.9	12.6	22.0
	Other[c]	23.7	13.1	17.4
	Totals	100.0	100.0	100.0
		(n=2,660)	(n=12,742)	

Sources: As in Appendix 1.
Notes:
(a) Only masters and dependent workers with trades specified.
(b) Percentages for 'all parishes' weighted to take account of changing population levels, as in Table 13.
(c) Mainly trades involving distribution/transport of goods and people; services; professions and officials.

often founded when the cloth industry began to flourish in the later Middle Ages. Industries are also well-documented in that period in the eastern suburbs: water and corn mills on the rivers Lea and Thames; wharves and docks for repairing and fitting out ships between Shadwell and Limehouse; as well as lime-burning, brewing, bell-founding, brick and tile manufacture, wood- and metal-working.[25] Throughout the eighteenth century London remained the leading manufacturing centre in the country, particularly in silk weaving, brewing, shipbuilding, and many branches of metal-working and engineering. Its building industry was huge. In 1861 manufacturing still accounted for a third of the work-force, and London continued to dominate certain industries such as leather.[26]

Obviously London was not Manchester. Units of production were small well into the nineteenth century: in 1851 only seven firms employed more than 350 operatives. Employment was more seasonal and casual in character than in the mills of the industrial revolution.[27] Nevertheless, the evidence does suggest that the capital-as-market thesis is misleading where London is concerned. Even to associate London's economy chiefly with merchants and trade in the sixteenth and seventeenth centuries appears wrong-headed. That impression resulted partly from the fortuitous survival of evidence for this sector, including port books and collections of merchants' papers, and from the fact that the great merchants dominated the political and social life of early modern London. By comparison much less is known about the shipwrights of Poplar and Limehouse, the feltmakers of Southwark, the weavers and brewers of St Giles Cripplegate. Yet they and their ilk, of course, accounted for the majority of the city's work-force in the period.

III

If production flourished in early modern London, we still know precious little about where it was carried on, who was involved, and how it was organized. The why of the matter is superficially much more simple: once again the market provides an answer. Ever since Adam Smith's *Wealth of Nations* (1776) exposed the workings of the market economy, this model has been a powerful explanatory tool for understanding economic and social change. In our time it has provided the theoretical basis for overviews of Western development as different as Karl Polanyi's *Great Transformation* (1944) and Sir John Hicks's *Theory of Economic History* (1969). In the case of London the argument is no less potent, especially when allied with the findings of historical demographers. In sum, the sheer brute size of the place meant a huge market for locally produced or finished goods. Or, as more elegantly stated by Dr Corfield, London 'flourished as a manufacturing centre because it contained the largest single concentration of consumers in the country'.[28]

The market thesis receives considerable support, moreover, from other quarters. Professor Fisher showed in 1948 how London's growth as a centre of conspicuous consumption stimulated luxury and transport trades, as well as a nascent entertainment industry. His perspective was confined almost entirely to the demand generated by the landed upper classes.[29] More recently, Dr Thirsk has traced the beginnings of a larger, wider market for consumer goods to the first half of the sixteenth century. It was then that governments set out to revive home-based production with the twin aims of cutting imports and setting the poor to work. The policy worked, and by 1600 'goods that had been deemed rich men's luxuries in 1540 were being made in so many different qualities and at such varied prices that they came within the reach of everyman'. The trend continued after 1640, despite the levelling off in population and price levels, with agricultural and industrial output continuing to rise.[30] In the eighteenth century, *before* the industrial revolution, England is now thought to have experienced 'the birth of a consumer society'.[31]

London took part in this precocious consumer growth, as producer as well as consumer. The metropolitan market stimulated production locally as well as nationally, as the occupations of its work-force show. But to state that a lively market was responsible for large numbers of manufacturers in London is to state the obvious. It tells us nothing about who the consumers were – a question lying outside the scope of this paper. It also fails to tell us much about the circumstances in which production and trade in London were carried on: where, and in what social and political conditions. These questions, while deserving a monographic type of approach, are of more than parochial interest, for they show how production responded to the new consumer demand.

The most striking feature of London occupations is their great variation in topographical incidence. Broadly speaking, the sharpest contrasts were between intra- and extra-mural parishes, although the West End was a special case. In the walled city production declined in the period, while trading increased. Outside the walls production was vastly more important and exchanges less so (again with the exception of western parishes, where the landed and professional classes were increasingly significant). The split between central London and its periphery is clearest in the question of production- versus exchange-related jobs (see Table 14). Between 1540 and 1600 central parishes had just 53 per cent of their work-force in production, but 28 per cent in trade. In contrast extra-mural parishes had a huge 70 per cent occupied in production, but just 8 per cent in trading activities. The disparities between the two increased further after 1601. Production in intra-mural areas fell to 40 per cent of occupations and trading rose to 36 per cent, while parishes on the periphery were largely stable. Looked at from another angle, while the proportions of manual workers held steady or rose in extra-mural parishes – rising from 48 to 72 per cent of trades in the extreme case of St Botolph Aldgate – in eight out of 11 intra-mural ones it actually fell. In seven of the same 11, however, the proportion in exchange-related positions increased after 1601.

The divergence between intra- and extra-mural parishes went still further. As we might expect from their locations, the peripheral parishes had significantly more persons – as much as 10 per cent from 1540 to 1600 – in distributive and transport trades (see Table 13). In the east St Botolph Aldgate and St Dunstan's Stepney were heavily engaged in shipping and shipbuilding. In contrast St James Garlickhithe, a riverside parish within the Walls, had no trades indicating a maritime bias.[32] Merchants were roughly ten times more numerous within the Walls than without, accounting for as much as 20 per cent of the occupations there as opposed to just one or two per cent. And whereas about 10 per cent in central parishes involved an official or professional job, the share outside the Walls was again one or two per cent. Masters, gentlemen and dependent workers were also more plentiful in the centre. The abundance of merchants and masters there makes sense, of course, for this was the home of the City Companies. So for the same reason do numerous dependent workers, over a third of whom were apprentices (see Table 15 p. 154). Many masters and gentlemen were probably retired and living off investments.

In passing through the City's gates, one entered another world. The sights and smells of the busy, rambling extra-mural parts must have presented a sharp contrast to the well-ordered world of merchants and professional men within. To attempt detailed surveys of the fringe places would be premature, but a few examples are worth highlighting, for these were the workshops of the capital. St Botolph Aldgate had a maritime bent, as stated, but also increasing numbers of leatherworkers, smiths, cutlers, tailors and weavers. Bakers and butchers were also on the rise there. St Dunstan Stepney's many maritime-based trades included sailors, shipwrights, but also ships' carpenters and masters, anchorsmiths, sailmakers, lightermen, fishermen, ropemakers, caulkers,

Table 15. The decline of dependent labour, 1540–1700 (percentages)[a]

Dates		Intra-mural parishes	Extra-mural parishes	All parishes[b]
1540–1600	(n=5,579)	54.7	43.5	53.2
1601–40	(n=5,467)	47.5	30.7	39.1
1641–1700	(n=13,212)	33.1	18.5	22.8

Sources: As in Appendix 1.
Notes:
(a) Dependent labour defined as servants and apprentices.
(b) Percentages for 'all parishes' weighted to take account of changing population levels, as in Table 13.

pulleymakers, a teacher of navigation and a compass maker. Both it and St Botolph Aldgate had numerous labourers, presumably casual workers in the various trades. St Giles Cripplegate, for its part, was a great outfitter. Weavers more than doubled there between 1583 and 1637, cobblers more than trebled, and glovers rose six-fold. To transport the goods the numbers of porters nearly trebled. From 1654 to 1693 Forbes's list shows production running wild in the parish: 566 tailors, 996 weavers, 583 cordwainers, 371 glovers and 719 brewing workers and masters were buried there during the period, as well as 479 porters.[33] St Olave Southwark also concentrated heavily on garment production: feltmakers, tailors and weavers were all numerous there. This parish also had a sizeable stake in jobs in transport and distribution and, along with St Giles Cripplegate, in building trades.

It would be misleading to give the impression that production was limited to extra-mural London. Elsewhere in this collection Power shows how the yards and alleys within the Walls still contained craftsmen: silkweavers in Allhallows Honey Lane; coopers in St Michael Royal; and shoemakers in St Martin le Grand.[34] Moreover, St Dionis Backchurch saw the appearance of the new trades of calender, distiller and watchmaker. In St Mary Aldermary the cloth industry remained a stable source of work, while building and metal trades actually increased their share of the work-force. Nevertheless, there is no doubt that production was expanding most rapidly on the northern, eastern and southern edges of London. By sheer weight of numbers this was so, for these areas grew nearly 11-fold in population between 1560 and 1680 while central London increased its population by at most two-thirds.[35] The conclusion is inescapable that these parts of extra-mural London experienced a remarkable expansion of manufacturing.

The experience of West End parishes was rather different from the rest of London; already by 1600 they had a distinctive stamp to them.

For instance, St Dunstan's in the West had a clustering of professional men and ancillary trades unmatched by the other parishes studied. It also attracted great numbers of gentlemen. The main reason for the special configuration of the parish was the presence of two Inns of Court – Clifford's and Lincoln's – within its bounds. Besides four cursitors, an attorney, a butler at Clifford's and an undercook at Lincoln's, there were buried 110 gentlemen and 15 knights and esquires in St Dunstan's between 1591 and 1610; the latter groups included many leading legal figures. Allied trades in the parish included a dozen stationers and nearly as many scriveners. Moreover, professionals seem to have followed professionals into the place: four physicians and six surgeons were also interred in the period.[36] Further west in St Clement Danes a more extreme social pattern becomes clear from about 1570. Gentlemen and their servants abounded there to the virtual exclusion of other social and occupational groups, thus providing some justification for the later complaints of James I and Charles I about the gentry swarming to London.[37]

But the West End was not purely gentrified and professional in character. We have seen that over half of St Dunstan's occupations involved some form of manufacturing. The proportions in the various industries were about average for extra-mural parishes – building, 6 per cent; clothing 22 per cent; leather, 12 per cent; and metal, 10 per cent – with tailors, shoemakers and cutlers especially numerous. The western edge of London was indeed noted for skilled metal-work: goldsmiths in Holborn, Fleet Street and the Strand; the cutlers of St Martin le Grand; and the jewellers, engravers, gilders, and silversmiths of Westminster. Rich people naturally wish to remain rich, so lockmakers also proliferated in the West End.[38] If, as Professor Fisher argued, the gentry led the new trends towards conspicuous consumption, the producers of luxury goods were likely to be located close to this profitable market. This market clearly stimulated a large service sector. Even excluding servants *per se*, it accounted for ten per cent of positions in St Dunstan's in the West, including two musicians and a tombmaker, which was roughly twice the level for other parishes. Merchants, however, were largely absent from the West End. They made up just one in 20 occupations there, while in intra-mural parishes we have seen that the proportion was as high as one in five. So London's western parishes were a peculiar mixture of gentlemen and professional men, many no doubt temporary in residence, whose presence stimulated substantial service and manufacturing sectors.

Traditionally historians have seen two Londons emerging in the seventeenth-century metropolis: the old city, largely within the old walls and mainly mercantile in economic orientation; and the new aristocratic West End geared to big spending, the professions and Whitehall.[39] The analysis so far confirms the emergence of these two distinct communities, but also suggests the growing importance of a third London, that is the extra-mural parts on the northern, eastern and southern (mainly Southwark) edges of the old city. The economies of these places were mainly geared to manufacturing, as demonstrated above, and by 1680 their rapid growth meant that they formed the bulk of the city's population. In 1560 they accounted for just 23 per cent of the metropolitan population; in 1600 they made up 40 per cent; and in 1680, 61 per cent. If we assumed roughly equal family sizes in these areas, then persons dependent on manufacturing rose from 17,500 in 1560 to 196,100 in 1680. It now remains to attempt some explanation for the remarkable growth of production in this third London.[40]

IV

Since London's development had some striking topographical manifestations, it is tempting to seek the reasons for that development in the physical environment. Thus in the growth of the West End some essential factors were the upper-class demand for exclusive housing, greater salubriousness, and access to Westminster.[41] In the rest of London, however, other factors, especially economic ones, came into play. Outside the West End, housing was more than a question of residence; it was economic, since one's residence was usually also one's work-place, as Power shows in his essay on social topography.[42] Segregation by use certainly occurred in early modern London, but in economic and social formations that run counter to some modern theories of wealth-zoning.[43] Thus the great merchants remained within the City Walls instead of moving to the leafy suburbs to the west. For their part, the poor and industrious were not left stranded in a central ghetto and instead were located, as noticed, in a third London. For the great mass of the population the move to these other suburbs must have been the most natural of steps. The supply of housing in intra-mural London was contracting by 1600. Rents were lower outside the walls, a fact that drew leatherworkers and feltmakers to Southwark and St Katherine's by the Tower. Problems of space in which to work, as with the clothworker's need of tenter grounds, were further incentives to extra-mural moves.[44]

But the cost and availability of 'plant' were not the only, or the most important, factors behind extra-mural growth. There were also institutional ones, including the fact that the City authorities excluded or discouraged certain trades from working within the Walls. A number of manufacturing trades were affected – feltmakers, tallow-chandlers, many types of leatherworker, and manufacturers of alum, glass, oil, soap and starch – which must have helped to boost production outside the Walls.[45]

Official restraints on production went beyond a few noisome and hazardous industries. In addition, the City's 100 or so gilds (the numbers fluctuated) possessed great regulatory powers over trading and manufacturing. Most important perhaps was the requirement of a seven-year apprenticeship before one was granted the 'freedom' to ply one's trade. As Professor Pearl has shown, the gilds were far from defunct in the seventeenth century. Their areas of search were actually extended in many instances after 1600; to as much as 10 miles around the City. Up to mid-century and later the companies representing the manual trades continued to harass and prosecute violators of their monopolies. The gilds also still wielded great informal authority in the political and social life of the City, for the proportion of freemen among householders was as high as three-quarters. The small intra-mural parishes, which were just four and a half acres in size on average, were extremely tightly run ships in most respects.[46] To avoid such controls, particularly those of the gilds, probably inspired many to set up in the large extra-mural parishes where detection was more difficult.

Although many gilds remained influential forces in eighteenth-century London, the growth of production beyond the walls spelt their end as effective institutions of economic control so far as the mass of Londoners were concerned. Despite extended areas of search, significant increases in membership, and continued influence upon social and political life within the Walls, the gilds were quite unable to control the expanding manufactures outside them. This was true even of extra-mural parishes immediately adjacent, which were legally not suburban at all. The failure to exert economic controls in these places is not surprising. Parishes like St Giles Cripplegate, which had possibly 40,000 inhabitants *c.* 1700, were too large and populous to be run by the equivalent of a modern parish council.[47] Restricting entry into trades might have made some sense in the medieval period, when demand was limited, but once the metropolis started growing by leaps and bounds the system lost its *raison d'être*.

The figures in Table 15 show a secular decline in the employment of dependent workers, that is servants and apprentices, between 1540 and

1700. The drop was a sharp one: from 53 per cent of those with occupations and status listed *c.* 1570, to 39 per cent *c.* 1620, and on to 23 per cent *c.* 1670.

It is noticeable that extra-mural parishes generally employed less dependent labour; as much as 50 per cent less than intra-mural ones by the late seventeenth century. Apprentices and servants are rarely distinguished with any consistency in the records, but it seems a reasonable speculation that the difference mainly arose from apprenticeship being evaded in the outlying areas. This is a fair assumption because production-based trades usually employed large numbers of apprentices, and since production was booming in these parishes we should have large numbers of dependent workers there. The opposite was true, as we see from Table 15. Dependency was also declining in intra-mural parishes, even though they were the home of the City Companies. Again it is likely that the growth of extramural manufacturing was responsible, because the apprentice element in the work-force would decline as the manual trades left for peripheral parishes.

Fortunately we have more than speculations to suggest that apprentices were the main group involved in the falling numbers of dependent workers. When apprentices and domestic servants are distinctly labelled in the parish of St Antholin Budge Row, the fall in the apprentices' share of the dependent work-force is significant: from 44 per cent, 1538–48, to just 21 per cent, 1592–1624. In the suburbs the numbers were small, but clearly in decline: in St Dunstan's Stepney 8 per cent of dependent workers were apprentices, 1605–10, and the percentage dropped to just 3 per cent on the eve of the Civil War.[48] These isolated cases are confirmed by recent estimates for the whole of London, which suggest that apprentices formed as much as 15 per cent of the total population in 1600, but that their share fell to just four or five per cent by 1700.[49] The decline involved perhaps only 5,000 persons absolutely, but is still remarkable for two reasons. First, London's population was still growing, rising four-fold in the period. With growth of this magnitude one might have expected the apprentices' numbers to expand. Secondly, while diminishing in proportion to other occupational and status groups, nevertheless other dependent workers increased absolutely: a quarter of the cake in 1670 was much greater than half of it in 1570 because London had grown so much in the interim.

The serious difficulties faced by the gilds are well illustrated by the example of the Carpenters' Company. The company increased its membership significantly in the seventeenth century, but this was insufficient to maintain control of the trade. Already in 1600 only about

40 per cent of carpenters working in the City were members, and by 1640 the figure was down to 30 per cent.[50] Other companies were not so hard-pressed by interlopers, but even those such as the weavers who clung to the principle of monopoly into the next century virtually abandoned its enforcement by the 1730s.[51] In the *London Tradesman* (1747) Robert Campbell listed dozens of trades which did not take apprentices, including the ubiquitous brewers, 95 of whom employed over 600 men in St Giles Cripplegate between 1654 and 1693.[52]

The evidence suggests that seventeenth-century London saw major changes in the organization of its economy. The most striking shift was the decline of apprenticeship. Broadly speaking, this development involved a change in the mode of production from the regulated system of the medieval gilds to something like a free-market situation. Not all of London was affected, for the gilds remained vital institutions within the walled city. The mainspring of the shift was the growth of production outside the city Walls and outside the gild system. Gild exclusiveness and elitism, as Professor Pearl has observed, hardly came into the matter.[53] If the gilds became isolated, this was the result rather than the cause of growing non-gild production in the extra-mural parts. Far more significant than the gilds' exclusiveness was their inability to enforce their regulations in the outlying communities.

V

That London was a major and expanding centre of manufacturing in this period casts considerable doubt upon the view that it was a passive consumer. Consumers require producers, and it would be very odd if Londoners made none of the goods they purchased. Transport costs alone probably encouraged manufacturing in the metropolis, just as they no doubt quickened rural production in its hinterland.[54] The Keynesian preoccupation with the demand side of the economy should not blind us to shifts in the supply side, which were clearly happening in seventeenth-century London, however subject to crisis many industries remained.

The evidence of London's expanding manufacturing sector also raises questions about the role of the metropolis in the industrial revolution. If London was not just a consumer of goods, what was its role? We know that London was not the first off the mark, nor the first home in industrialization. But neither was the capital on a completely separate track from the future milltowns of the north. Contrary to the metaphor, the industrial revolution was not a race begun in 1780 and completed, by some, in 1830. Rather it was the terminus of a long-term process, the rise of capitalism, which had its origins in the Middle Ages, but which accelerated in the following centuries. Increased consumer demand and the growth of agricultural and industrial output formed part of the process; so did new value commensurate with these changes; and so did London's new and expanding manufactures.

London's example suggests that institutional factors should also be considered in the rise of capitalism. This is not a new idea – R. H. Tawney and George Unwin argued the case 70 years ago[55] – but it has lost ground to those who emphasize strictly economic and demographic factors. Only recently have students of urban history begun to re-examine the role of institutions in economic development and to assign them some significance. Thus Clark and Slack observed of towns between 1500 and 1700 that 'growth appears to have been encouraged by the absence of stringent community control ... or through economic initiative external to the traditional community'.[56] Moreover, Daunton found in eighteenth-century towns that the degree of gild and corporate control still influenced economic development.[57] In London we find manufacturers circumventing the gilds by setting up in places where detection was difficult. This was a political act, and it requires a political explanation.

The political dimension to the development of urban capitalism is well captured by Weber's concept of 'non-legitimate domination', that is the usurpation of legitimate authority. Weber considered this usurpation to be the salient feature of the western city and, in Philip Abrams's words, 'uniquely conducive' to the growth of capitalism.[58] Although the theory referred to the medieval town, it has relevance as well to early modern economic development. Setting oneself up to trade and manufacture in London without serving an apprenticeship was to usurp the authority of the gilds. Thousands did it, and thousands got away with the offence: usurpation was clearly central to the expansion of metropolitan production. The argument also applies to the London merchants who traded to the Americas in the seventeenth century, who were mainly new men. Few were members of the great monopoly companies, and they traded freely, unlike members of the regulated companies. Interestingly enough, they also invested in production in the colonies, again unlike the regulated companies, because colonial production was the basis of the trade. One wonders how far these free-trading interlopers might have involved themselves in London's extra-mural manufacturing boom, which ultimately encompassed the finishing and re-export of colonial goods.[59] Finally, it is worth recalling that usurpation figured prominently in the transition to capitalist agriculture: in the illegal engrossing of farms and enclosure of common land; in the setting of economic rents when they were supposed by custom to be 'reasonable'; and in seventeenth-century enclosures 'by agreement'.[60]

Who financed and organized London manufacturing outside the gild system remains a largely open question. In Maurice Dobb's schema there are two routes to capitalist production: first, by producers themselves accumulating capital and setting up; and secondly, by merchants taking over, providing capital but also goods on a putting-out basis.[61] Which pattern was dominant in London is uncertain, but there are some indications that the second development was taking place. Thus big City merchants, members of the Clothworkers', Drapers', Haberdashers' and Leatherworkers' Companies, are said to have organized craft production in the suburbs and countryside.[62] This was ironical but predictable, since the merchant élite were most likely to possess the requisite capital. But whether run by old or new groups of merchants, at the end of the day the producers were evidently not in charge. Eighteenth-century taxation records suggest that 90 per cent of London's male workers were employed by others; the 'Athens of the artisan' obviously involved a minority.[63] These figures are unlikely to be representative of London a century earlier, but they still suggest a remarkable evolution from the gild-based production of the sixteenth century towards a putting-out or domestic system. The two systems were not strikingly different in the size of units of production, but they were in respect of capital and control. In the old gilds the craftsman was in charge of production and capital, but in the new pattern he was dependent upon outside capital and lost control of production to the capitalist. This development had long-term consequences that led naturally to the industrial revolution because, as Dobb states,

> [T]he capitalist merchant-manufacturer had an increasingly close interest in promoting improvements in the instruments and methods of production: improvements which the craftsman's lack of capital as well as the force of gild custom would otherwise have frustrated. The very division of labour which is specially characteristic of the period prepared the ground from which mechanical invention could eventually spring.[64]

Of course the shift in the organization of production in London did not lead immediately to the industrial revolution. But then the factory system came late to many leading industrial centres, including Birmingham and Sheffield, where workshop production was retained. In any case many London industries – for example building, shipbuilding and tailoring – were unsuited to factory organization. Finally, to give the market thesis its due, the size of the London market probably made cost-cutting innovations like the factory less vital to ensure profits there.

Despite the economic gains, which clearly included jobs for thousands, the new system had social costs. Gone was the security of gild membership, which had included the defence of one's employment, a measure of community solidarity, and assistance in old age and other family crises. In its place grew up a system of casual labour in which security was minimal, giving rise to the horrors of 'outcast London', and in which solidarity was slow to develop because of the fragmentation of the work-force. Thus the making of the English metropolis involved a remarkable transformation of its social fabric as well as its economy.

Appendix 1. The data: occupational and status titles in parish burial registers

Parishes	Dates	No. Persons	Source[a]
Intra-mural			
St Antholin			
Budge Row	1538–75	156	Harl. Soc. VIII
	1592–1624	109	
	1625–48	62	
St Dionis			
Backchurch	1548–70	154	Harl. Soc. III
	1571–1603	213	
	1604–36	140	
	1643–75	158	
	1676–1708	202	
	1709–41	206	
St Helen's			
Bishopsgate	1575–1604	182	Harl. Soc. XXXI
	1605–34	240	
	1635–64	137	
	1665–94	157	
St James			
Garlickhithe	1563–71	129	Guildhall Ms. 9139
St Lawrence	1538–63	98	Harl. Soc. LXX
Jewry	1577–1609	242	
	1610–42	206	
	1650–76	200	
St Mary			
Aldermary	1558–82	217	Harl. Soc. V
	1583–1607	185	
	1608–43	196	
	1644–78	236	
	1679–1714	120	

St Michael Bassishaw	1554–77	196	Harl. Soc. LXXII–
	1578–1601	143	LXXIII
	1602–25	286	
	1626–49	179	
	1650–73	247	
St Michael Cornhill	1566–96	206	Harl. Soc. VII
	1597–1627	274	
	1628–58	201	
St Peter Cornhill	1563–97	169	Harl. Soc. I
	1598–1632	261	
	1633–66	287	
St Thomas Apostle	1558–97	252	Harl. Soc. VI
	1598–1637	235	
	1638–77	255	
St Vedast Foster Lane	1558–93	185	Harl. Soc. XX
	1594–1622	139	
	1632–63	163	
	Sub-total	7,623	
Extra-mural			
St Botolph Aldgate	1580–7	383	Guildhall Ms. 9222/1–2
	1630–7	852	
St Dunstan's Stepney	1605–10	455	GLRO Ms. P93/DUN
	1638–41	602	
St Giles Cripplegate	1583–93	1000	Guildhall Ms. 6419/1–3
	1633–7	1127	
	1654–93	13,783	T.R. Forbes[b]
St Olave Southwark	1583–88	353	GLRO Ms. P71/OLA/9
	1614–19	559	
	Subtotal	19,114	
	Grand total	26,737	

Notes:

(a) Abbreviations = Harl[eian] Soc[iety], Register Section; Guildhall [Library]; G[reater] L[ondon] R[ecord] O[ffice].

(b) 'Weaver and cordwainer: occupations in the parish of St Giles without Cripplegate, London, in 1654–93 and 1729–43', *Guildhall Studies in London History*, 4 (1980), pp. 120–9.

Appendix 2. Trades classified in Table 13 (examples)

Building: carpenter, bricklayer, brickmaker, glazier, joiner, mason, painter, paviour, plasterer, plumber.

Clothing: bodicemaker, buttonmaker, capper, cardmaker, clothworker, draper, dyer, embroiderer, feltmaker, girdler, haberdasher, hatbandmaker, hatmaker, hempdresser, hosier, milliner, orrisworker, packthreadmaker, silktwister, silkweaver, tailor, tapistryworker, weaver, woolwinder.

Decorating/furnishing: chandler, tallow and wax chandler, stationer, turner, upholder, upholsterer.

Distribution/transport: carman, carrier, coachman, farrier, ostler, packer, porter, postmaster, sailor, shipwright, waterman.

Labouring: labourers.

Leather: cobbler, cordwainer, glover, leatherseller, pursemaker, saddler, shoemaker, skinner, tanner.

Merchants: broker, factor, grocer, mercer, merchant, merchant tailor.

Metal-work: armourer, brazier, copper, coppersmith, goldsmith, goldwiredrawer, jeweller, locksmith, pump-maker, sheargrinder, sievemaker, silverspinner, smith, wiredrawer.

Miscellaneous services: apothecary, gardener, midwife, nurse, scrivener, soldier, waterbearer, woodmonger.

Miscellaneous production: basketmaker, boxmaker, bowyer, calender, cutter, drawer, fletcher, husbandman, hotpresser, limner, printer, watchmaker, whitster.

Officials: beadle, bellman, clerk, parish clerk, sergeant, sexton, singer (in St Paul's), warden (of City Companies).

Professions: attorney, barber-surgeon, bishop, doctor, lecturer, minister, parson, physician, schoolmaster, surgeon.

Victualling: baker, beerclerk, brewer, butcher, costermonger, cook, distiller, fenner, fishmonger, fruiterer, innkeeper, miller, oysterman, poulterer, tapster, tobacco-cutter, whitebaker.

NOTES AND REFERENCES

1. J. Merrington, 'Town and country in the transition to capitalism', in P. Sweezy *et al*, *The Transition from Feudalism to Capitalism* (London 1978),

p. 187. I wish to record my thanks to Roger Finlay, Ralph Gibson, Sandy Grant and John King for their advice in the preparation of this paper.

2. F. Braudel, *Capitalism and Material Life, 1400-1800* (London 1973), pp. 414-24, 440.

3. R. Brenner, 'Agrarian class structure and economic development in pre-industrial Europe', *Past and Present*, 70 (1976), pp. 30, 42-55; J. E. Martin, *Feudalism to Capitalism. Peasant and Landlord in English Agrarian Development* (London 1983), pp. 51-2, 97-8.

4. E. L. Jones, 'Agricultural origins of industry', *Past and Present*, 40 (1968), pp. 59-64; J. Thirsk, 'Seventeenth-century agriculture and social change', *Agricultural History Review*, 18 (Supplement, 1970), *Land, Church, and People*, J. Thirsk (ed.), pp. 174-6.

5. E. A. Wrigley, 'A simple model of London's importance in changing English society and economy 1650-1750', *Past and Present*, 37 (1967), pp. 62, 65-7.

6. V. Pearl, 'Change and stability in seventeenth-century London', *London Journal*, 5 (1979), p. 8.

7. *Infra*, pp. 44-6.

8. T. R. Forbes, *Chronicle from Aldgate. Life and Death in Shakespeare's London* (New Haven 1971), pp. 9-10; East London History Group, 'The population of Stepney in the early seventeenth century', *Local Population Studies*, 3 (1969), p. 50.

9. R. Grassby, 'English merchant capitalism in the late seventeenth century. The composition of business fortunes', *Past and Present*, 46 (1970), pp. 88-9.

10. Chapter 7, *infra*; P. E. Jones and A. V. Judges, 'London population in the late seventeenth century', *Economic History Review*, 6 (1935), p. 46; *info. ex* Mr N. P. Webb regarding late seventeenth-century poll taxes.

11. I owe the point about the importance of identification to Margaret Bowker.

12. *Info. ex* Professor E. A. Wrigley. For one attempt to take death rates into account, see P. H. Lindert, 'English occupations, 1670-1811', *Journal of Economic History*, 40 (1980), pp. 698-9.

13. T. R. Forbes, 'Weaver and cordwainer: occupations in the parish of St Giles without Cripplegate, London, in 1654-93 and 1729-43', *Guildhall Studies in London History*, 4 (1980), 120-9.

14. Harl. Soc., 1 (1877), p. 151; 7 pt. 1 (1940), p. 108 (full references in Appendix 1).

15. Detailed breakdown: St Dionis Backchurch, 1571-1603, six of 93 'free'; St Helen's Bishopsgate, 1635-64, seven of 100; St Michael Cornhill, 1597-1658, 32 of 264; St Peter Cornhill, 1598-1632, 56 of 281; and St Vedast Foster Lane, 1632-63, 31 of 81. Full references in Appendix 1.

16. J. Stow, *The Survey of London* (London 1956 edn), pp. 178, 224, 259, 272-4.

17. J. L. Archer, 'The Industrial History of London, 1603-1640', (unpublished London University M. A. thesis, 1934), pp. 10-11, 16-18, 232-4 (and Appendix F), 242ff.

18. E.g. L. Stone, *An Elizabethan. Sir Horatio Palavicino* (Oxford 1956); R. H. Tawney, *Business and Politics under James I. Lionel Cranfield as Merchant and Minister* (Cambridge 1958).

19. N. G. Brett-James, *The Growth of Stuart London* (London 1935), p. 253.
20. V. Pearl, *London and the Outbreak of the Puritan Revolution* (London 1961), pp. 30ff.
21. E. M. Veale, 'Craftsmen and the economy of London in the fourteenth century', in A. E. J. Hollaender and W. Kellaway (eds), *Studies in London History* (London 1969), p. 159.
22. Forbes, 'Weaver and cordwainer', pp. 120–9.
23. R. Campbell, *The London Tradesman* (London 1747; repr. Newton Abbot 1969); presumed to be the source cited by P. J. Corfield, *The Impact of English Towns, 1700–1800* (Oxford 1982), p. 73.
24. Guildhall Library, London, Ms.10342: 661 cases, 1591–1610.
25. K. McDonnell, *Medieval London Surburbs* (London 1978), pp. 77–81, 83–6, 91–100, 108–18.
26. J. Stevenson, 'London, 1660–1780', in J. Stevenson (ed.), *The Rise of the New Urban Society* (Milton Keynes 1977), pp. 18–19; Corfield, *English Towns*, pp. 73–4; F. Sheppard, *London 1808–1870: the Infernal Wen* (London 1971), pp. 158–61.
27. O. H. K. Spate, 'Geographical aspects of the industrial evolution of London till 1850', *Geographical Journal*, 92 (1938), p. 431 (reference supplied by Dr R. A. P. Finlay); G. Stedman Jones, *Outcast London* (London 1976).
28. P. J. Corfield, 'Urban development in England and Wales in the sixteenth and seventeenth centuries', in D. C. Coleman and A. H. John (eds), *Trade, Government and Economy in Pre-Industrial England* (London 1976), p. 218.
29. F. J. Fisher, 'The development of London as a centre of conspicuous consumption in the sixteenth and seventeenth centuries', repr. in E. M. Carus-Wilson (ed.), *Essays in Economic History* (London 1962), 2, pp. 197ff.
30. J. Thirsk, *Economic Policy and Projects: The Development of a Consumer Society in Early Modern England* (Oxford 1978), p. 179; A. H. John, 'Agricultural productivity and economic growth in England, 1700–1760', *Journal of Economic History*, 25 (1965), pp. 22–4.
31. N. McKendrick, J. Brewer and J. H. Plumb, *The Birth of a Consumer Society* (London 1982), *passim.*
32. In the 1660s as well as the 1560s: Guildhall Library Ms.9139.
33. Forbes, 'Weaver and cordwainer', loc. cit.
34. *Infra*, pp. 216–18.
35. *Infra*, Ch. 1, Table 3; and notes to Table 13 above.
36. Guildhall Library Ms. 10342.
37. Westminster City Libraries, Archives Department: St Clement Danes Burial Register, 1, 1558–1644.
38 Archer, 'Industrial History of London', pp. 13, 15; Thirsk, *Policy and Projects*, p. 128.
39. L. Stone, 'The residential development of the West End of London in the seventeenth century', in B. C. Malament (ed.), *After the Reformation* (Manchester 1980), pp. 186–8; M. J. Power, 'The east and west in early-modern London', in E. W. Ives, R. J. Knecht, and J. J. Scarisbrick (eds), *Wealth and Power in Tudor England* (London 1978), pp. 167ff., which refines the old view.

40. Figures from Chapter 1, *infra*, Table 3.
41. Stone, 'West End', pp. 173, 186–94; Power, 'East and west London', pp. 182–4.
42. *Infra*, Chapter 7, pp. 211–21.
43. J. E. Vance Jr., 'Land assignment in the precapitalist, capitalist and postcapitalist city', *Economic Geography*, 47 (1971), pp. 115–16.
44. Archer, 'Industrial History of London', pp. 61–2, 71, 73.
45. Ibid., pp. 87–8, 90–3.
46. Pearl, 'Change and stability', pp. 7–8, 13–15; J. R. Kellett, 'The breakdown of gild and corporation control over the handicraft and retail trade in London', *Economic History Review*, 2nd ser., 10 (1957–8), pp. 381–2.
47. Forbes, 'Weaver and cordwainer', p. 119; Pearl, 'Change and stability', p. 27.
48. These parishes' registers listed in Appendix 1, pp. 162–3.
49. R. Finlay, *Population and Metropolis: The Demography of London 1580–1650* (Cambridge 1981), pp. 66–7.
50. B. W. E. Alford and T. C. Barker, *A History of the Carpenters Company* (London 1968), pp. 32, 72–3.
51. A. Plummer, *The London Weavers' Company, 1600–1970* (London 1972), pp. 92–3, 354–5.
52. Campbell, *The London Tradesman, passim;* Forbes, 'Weaver and cordwainer', p. 121.
53. Pearl, 'Change and stability', pp. 8, 13–14.
54. F. J. Fisher, 'The development of the London food market, 1540–1640', repr. in Carus-Wilson (ed.), *Essays in Economic History*, 1, pp. 141–5.
55. Tawney, *The Agrarian Problem in the Sixteenth Century* (London 1912; repr. New York 1967); Unwin, *The Gilds and Companies of London* (London 1908).
56. P. Clark and P. Slack, 'Introduction', in P. Clark and P. Slack (eds), *Crisis and Order in English Towns 1500–1700* (London 1972), pp. 33–4.
57. M. J. Daunton, 'Towns and economic growth in eighteenth-century England', in P. Abrams and E. A. Wrigley (eds), *Towns in Societies* (Cambridge 1978), pp. 263–5.
58. P. Abrams, 'Towns and economic growth: some theories and problems', in ibid., pp. 28–9.
59. R. Brenner, 'The Civil War politics of London's merchant community', *Past and Present*, 58 (1973), pp. 65–9.
60. Martin, *Feudalism to Capitalism*, Chs. 7–8.
61. M. Dobb, *Studies in the Development of Capitalism* (London 1946; revised edn, 1963), pp. 123–4.
62. Ibid., p. 129.
63. L. D. Schwarz, 'Income distribution and social structure in London in the late eighteenth century', *Economic History Review*, 2nd ser., 32 (1979), pp. 257–8.
64. Dobb, *Capitalism*, p. 145.

CHAPTER SIX

Food consumption and internal trade

John Chartres

Urban history has recently entered a phase of uncertainty, attempts to define the threshold at which the town can be distinguished have produced no consensus. Other historians have denied the differentness of the town as a social organism. The tenor of many of the papers gathered together in Abrams and Wrigley's *Towns in Societies* was to propound a wholistic view of society in which the town, even the city, has little conceptual validity. Because in early modern England economic growth took place as much in the rural as the urban context, this analysis runs, towns may be further devalued as agents of economic change.[1]

This generalized critique of old assumptions on the economic and social functions of pre-modern towns was extended by Daunton who rejected the 'dual economy' model implicit in Wrigley's influential study of London. By the end of the seventeenth century, it was argued, and in England more than in the rest of Europe, differences in *per capita* real income between the town and the countryside were relatively small, at least in comparison with modern developing countries. For this reason capitalism cannot be seen as a novelty transmitted from an advanced urban sector to a retarded peasant countryside. Citing Saville's comment that England was 'a society in which the penetration of the capitalist ethos has reached into all important sectors of economic life', Daunton found no satisfactory evidence for regarding England as a dualistic economy.[2]

This links with the wider and more fashionable debate on rival models of the transition from feudal to capitalist society. In this the early modern period represents an extended battleground. From Brenner's class-oriented analysis, to the demographic preoccupations of Postan and Habakkuk, and the commercial model of North and Thomas, historians have sought to replace monocausal explanations of change with others and implicated London in the process. London's failure to dissolve away feudal ties served as one of the props to Postan's demographic analysis of the change; the capital's agency in extending free-market relationships is implicit in the commercial model; and it appeared as an element in sustaining the home market base of Robert Brenner's 'agrarian capitalism'. Depending upon the church one chooses for worship is the perception of the economic and social importance of the capital.[3]

Contemporaries troubled little with such abstracted notions and chose to regard the capital as no more nor less than a threat to the body politic. From the sixteenth century onwards, London was viewed very much as a parasite weakening or distorting the growth of the nation. Effectively, they saw the capital's role as one element in a dualistic economy but one in which the resource flows were in a single direction. Hence the paramount need in seventeenth-century terms was to limit its growth, by restricting new building, and gradually to undermine one of the further manifestations of its injurious dominance, monopoly.[4] Men saw commercial relationships as the expression of the excessive demands of this monster: 'All our creeks seek to one river, all our rivers run to one port, all our ports join to one town, all our towns make but one city, and all our cities and suburbs to one vast, unwieldy and disorderly babel of buildings, which the world calls London'.[5] To most other authors, Defoe's early-eighteenth-century pride about the extended provisioning network of the capital must have appeared as blinkered metropolitan prejudice. Lacking the benefits of reading Wrigley's classic article, or the nature of motion as propounded by the master of the Mint, people saw the drains of provisions as taxation.[6] Exploitation did not therefore end with purveyance.

Within this wide range of views on the nature of economic and social change after 1600, the capital and its domestic trade linkages represents an important case study. In both contemporary and modern assessments one can discern the perception of London as an engine of economic growth and as a simple form of exploitation; as an advanced commercial and commercializing sector in a relatively backward context; as an eater of people and therefore a powerful demographic force; and as a heightened example of mercantile capitalist relationships, a paradigm case of Brenner's model of transition. London's functions as consumer and purchaser, as agent and centre of domestic trade and as entrepôt, and as the focus of mercantile power, the transport and distributive networks thus relate to wider issues of the town's place in pre-modern society and the evolution of modern capitalism. On a more modest level, the following paper examines some aspects of London's power as a consumer, and the consequential impact on agrarian change, market structure, and the transport system.

I

As a first step it is important to test the differentness of London. In the context of the seventeenth and early eighteenth centuries did the capital in any way represent the advanced sector of a dual economy? If one concedes Daunton's case that the model is inapplicable to the eighteenth century as a whole, there is at least some case to be made with a longer time-scale. The linkages to be considered are essentially those of Wrigley's simple but for that reason comprehensive model. Fundamental to this analysis is the assessment of London's power to consume. To what extent did the earning and spending power of London's population distinguish it from the nation at large?

The question is not easy to answer, but can at least be approached through the analysis of incomes and of the tests of wealth and spending provided by various forms of taxation. To judge the extent of concentration in the capital of such personal economic power it is essential first to express its population relative to that of the country as a whole. Recent research on population trends has confirmed Wrigley's view that it was the seventeenth century which saw the decisive shift in the relative magnitude of London's population to 'modern' proportions. London grew from 5–6 per cent of England's population in 1600, to 7.7 per cent in 1650, 11.4 per cent in 1700, and 11.7 per cent in 1750, largely by sustaining growth during a period of stagnation.[7] Because its growth was largely through immigration, a motive for this shift in population is required. Thus, demographic change at once serves as the touchstone of London's consumer power and as a pointer to its distinctiveness.

The answer to at least part of the problem of immigration can be sought in a second area which can be roughly quantified, that of relative incomes. There is no space here to expand upon the notorious problems of wages in this period, but neither can they be assumed away. Before 1700, wage series must be drawn mostly from the work of Thorold Rogers, supplemented in a minor way by series taken from the Beveridge collection. After 1700, Gilboy provides most wage data, drawn from very similar institutional sources and relating principally to the building trade. Beyond the problem of the limited range and provenance of sources there is a further complication in their geographical coverage:

for the middle years of the period 1600–1750 evidence from London is predominant. London wages dominate Rogers's crude averages from 1672.[8] For this reason comparisons between the wage rates of the provinces and the capital must be based on fragmentary evidence. This comparison necessarily ignores the reality of income generation: no account can be taken of other sources of income which may have supplemented money wages in the provinces, nor of qualitative differences in labour, which Rogers thought may have inflated London rates.[9]

With these caveats in mind, figures of daily wage rates for craftsmen and labourers are presented in Table 16, together with an expression of the percentage differential in each observation. The figures represent an attempt to dovetail Rogers' series with five-year averages of median observations derived from Gilboy. Given the fragmentary nature and generally poor quality of the data, the results display a remarkable consistency. With the exception of the divergence of trend in craftsman's and labourer's rates in the last four observations, it is clear that the differential for similar work in London and southern England was always substantial. It was greater for most of the period than for the

Table 16. Wage rates of building craftsmen and labourers, 1590s–1750 (d. per day)

Years	Craftsmen			Labourers		
	London	Southern England	%	London	Southern England	%
1590s	18	12	+50	12	8	+50
1663–80	30	18	+67	18	12	+50
1681–9	30	18	+67	20	12	+67
1690–9	30	20	+50	20	14	+43
1700–2	30	18	+67	20	14	+43
1702–4	31	20	+55	21	14	+50
1705–9	32.5	20	+63	22	14	+57
1710–14	33	20	+65	22	14	+57
1715–19	33	20	+65	22	14	+57
1720–4	34.5	21	+64	22	14	+57
1725–9	34	21	+62	22	14	+57
1730–4	35	21	+67	23	14	+64
1735–9	35.5	24	+48	24	14	+71
1740–4	35.5	23	+54	23.5	13.6	+73
1745–9	35	23.6	+48	24	13.6	+77
1750–4	35.5	23	+54	24	13.8	+74

Sources: Notes 8 and 9.

first observation, for the 1590s, and may have represented a lure of sufficient attraction to explain at least part of the pronounced in-migration to the capital.

There are indications, too, that these money rates may not have been fully equalized by price differences. It is not possible to deflate London wages in a fully satisfactory manner, but some comparisons of the cost of living can be drawn from wheat prices and their equivalent. Lacking long-run data on wheat from London to compare with the standard Eton College series, the trend in prices in London has been represented in Table 17 by two series: that for the standard unit of bread retailed in the capital; and the same series converted to a wheat equivalent per quarter by reference to the provisions of the Assize of Bread. Even after making allowance for the baker's profit, the comparison explicitly overstates London price levels by contrasting a retail price with a near-wholesale supply price for Eton College.[10] As in Table 16, Table 17 contains a percentage expression of the differential.

Assessing the results of this exercise is hard. At some points the conversion factor of bread to wheat was altered, as in 1710 when the baker's allowance was raised in London from 8s. to 12s. per quarter.[11] But it is clear that grain prices in the capital were rarely strikingly above those at Eton. This view is confirmed by comparison of better price material, taken from Houghton, over the short period 1693–1701. Figures of annual averages of wheat prices for London and four southern markets are presented in Table 18. While the price of foodstuffs, as indicated by the principal southern bread grain, was generally higher in London, it was never so great as to offset the observed differences in wage-rates. Other things being equal, then, there is evidence of significantly greater purchasing power in the labouring population of London. This difference holds for the whole of the period, and may even have widened in the first half of the eighteenth century.

There is some evidence to suggest that this comparison may understate the extent of the difference. Fiscal and other related materials were collated by Charles Davenant in part to this end, *c*.1695, and these suggest that per capita wealth in the capital may have been at least double that of the rest of the country. His 'Essay on Ways and Means' discussed at some length the most appropriate basis for comparing London with the rest of the nation, defining 'London' in its broad sense as London, Westminster, and Middlesex. He suggested that excise and hearth tax materials were 'no ill measures to form a judgement by, of the trade, wealth and abilities of a country'.[12] Following his advice, some such materials are available to establish London's slice of the national cake.

Table 17. Wheat and bread prices in London and Eton, 1590s–1750–4 (wheat, s. per quarter; bread, d. per 4 lbs. loaf)

	Eton Wheat	London bread	London Wheat equivalent	Differential %
1590s	34.5	4.1	33.7	−2.3
1663–80	37.8	5.8	42.5	+12.4
1681–9	30.8	5.3	38.2	+24.0
1690–9	44.9	6.9	52.1	+16.0
1700–2	26.6	4.5	31.1	+16.9
1702–4	29.4	4.8	33.8	+15.0
1705–9	37.7	5.7	41.6	+10.3
1710–14	40.5	5.7	37.5	−7.4
1715–19	33.9	4.9	30.6	−9.7
1720–4	29.8	4.8	29.7	−0.3
1725–9	38.0	5.7	37.5	−1.3
1730–4	26.4	4.5	27.1	+2.7
1735–9	31.8	5.3	34.0	+6.9
1740–4	27.9	4.6	28.0	+0.4
1745–9	28.7	4.9	30.6	+6.6
1750–4	31.6	5.1	32.3	+2.2

Sources: Note 10.

Table 18. London wheat prices compared with those of four southern towns, harvest years, 1693–1700 (s. per bushel)

Harvest Year	London	Wycombe	St. Albans	Dunstable	Hitchin
1693–4	7.6	8.7	8.4	7.4	8.0
1694–5	4.5	4.8	4.5	4.0	4.1
1695–6	6.1	7.1	6.8	6.4	6.5
1696–7	5.9	6.2	6.3	5.7	5.9
1697–8	7.4	7.5	7.4	6.9	7.6
1698–9	7.1	7.9	7.8	7.1	6.8
1699–1700	5.1	5.9	5.3	5.0	5.0
1700–1701	3.9	3.7	3.8	3.6	3.6

Sources: See note 10.

These indicators do not present consistent evidence, but all point to the high levels of wealth, income, or consumption in the capital. The yield of the County Assessment of 1642 may appear disproportionately high, with over 14 per cent coming from London. But, throughout the seventeenth century, taxes of all kinds exhibited a bias against the south and east of England, a bias picked up and continued in the land tax of the eighteenth century. No doubt we can continue to explain these variations in terms of the differential enthusiasm of regions for the government, and the countervailing biases of parliamentary representation, but some element of real economic difference may have crept into the system as well. The most extreme case of such unevenness occurred in 1689, with the first of the William and Mary poll taxes. This tax was socially graduated, and perhaps therefore mildly progressive in impact, yielding a total of £288,310, of which London and Middlesex produced 28 per cent. Other taxes of the same era, such as the aids of 1689 and the Quarterly Poll, also point to a concentration of wealth in the City out of proportion to its share of population, providing respectively 17 per cent and 16 per cent of total revenue. Unfortunately, Davenant's recommended second-best test of wealth distribution, the hearth tax of 1690, produces no clear conclusions for the metropolitan region. London possessed fewer, more crowded houses than the country as a whole, and thus the share of hearths or hearths per house may best represent the contrast with England as a whole. London in 1690 had but 8 per cent of the housing stock as taxed, but 14 per cent of hearths, averaging over three (3.3) per house when the country as a whole averaged less than two (1.8). Davenant's combing of seventeenth-century tax data thus provides us with no certain confirmation of the differential indicated by wage and price materials, but is strongly supportive of the case.[13]

The point is made all the more clearly when one turns to the evidence of the consumption of luxuries. This offers further support to the conclusions drawn from the income and tax data discussed above. The earliest indications come from the taxation of tobacco, arguably in the first half of the seventeenth century still a good with a very high income elasticity of demand. Beresford's analysis of the licensing system of 1637 suggested that it seemed to lack the tightness of the later excise, but was still administered with sufficient enthusiasm to indicate the relative magnitude of consumption. While London held but 4.2 per cent of licences to retail, together with Middlesex it accounted for over 10 per cent, and the two together yielded over 16 per cent of total rents. If we follow Beresford in assuming that these rents bore some relationship to levels of consumption, this evidence clearly indicates London's 'concentration of fashion and wealth'.[14]

Statistics on the sale and consumption of drink suggest a still greater concentration of spending power in the metropolis. The excise returns from 1654–5 point very clearly to the uneven acceptance of the tax. Few secondary authorities have discussed them as evidence for the consumption of goods, rather than for the revenue flows of the Protectorate, and these figures find no discussion in Ashley's book.[15]

Even allowing for the natural differences in enthusiasm for Cromwellian taxation in various parts of the country, the figures are still telling. London produced nearly 40 per cent of the total yield from beer, and over half that from domestic and imported spirits. Later excise figures support these indications. Between 1684 and 1750, London's excised production of barrels of strong and small beer varied between a quarter and a third of the national total. Strong beer was often sent to a wider market, particularly after the beginning of porter in the 1720s, but small beer did not travel well, and may be taken as a fair indication of the capital's greater consumption.[16]

Similar materials yielding regional payments of excise do not seem to survive for the still more sensitive indicator of movements in real disposable income, spirits. Little in the contemporary or historical literature discourages the view that London's consumption of spirits was of a different order of magnitude from that of other towns. Even major centres like Bristol, Norwich, and Exeter seem to have displayed no serious symptoms of the mania for corn spirits before 1752. Making in these circumstances the fairly modest assumption that Londoners drank gin roughly in proportion to small beer, then radical differences in per capita levels of consumption emerge. These estimates are presented in Table 19.[17] Given the sensitive relationship between alcohol consumption and income levels, these figures powerfully reinforce our earlier conclusions on London's capacity to consume.

Some part of the estimated 'consumption' may be illusory, because of London's related function as the dominant importer of luxuries throughout the period. Not only did the capital consume luxury imports such as tobacco out of proportion to its population, but it also acted as the principal entrepôt for their supply. Wealth and commerce thus made London doubly synonymous with conspicuous consumption. Conclusions drawn earlier from the evidence of the consumption of

Table 19. Estimates of per capita consumption of beer and spirits, 1700 and 1750 (pints per annum)

	1700		1750	
	London	England	London	England
Strong beer	512.6	130.6	417.6	152.3
Small beer	307.2	78.9	207.4	87.0
Spirits	4.7	1.8	22.2	8.9

Sources: See note 17.

tobacco and brandy in the seventeenth century are fully supported by that of the new tastes of the eighteenth, coffee and tea. The distribution of licensed dealers in tea and coffee is presented in Table 20, and this strongly reinforces our earlier conclusions and the inferences drawn by Beresford from the similar material on tobacco. The consumption of exotic consumer goods was therefore at its greatest in London, but on the evidence of Table 20 the capital was also the point from which the contagion spread.[18]

Table 20. Dealers in coffee and tea in England and Wales 1736–7[a] (in rank order by Excise 'Collection')

	No.	*%*		*No.*	*%*
1. London	3415	69.8	11. Bedford	42	0.9
2. Rochester	134	2.7	12. Grantham	37	0.8
3. Suffolk	123	2.5	13. Hertford	36	0.7
4. Lynn	119	2.4	14. Northampton	33	0.7
5. Norwich	106	2.2	15. Lancaster	32	0.7
6. Essex	92	1.9	Surrey	32	0.7
7. Bristol	74	1.4	17. Buckingham	31	0.6
8. Durham	58	1.2	Derby	31	0.6
9. Cambridge	44	0.9	Oxford	31	0.6
10. Canterbury	43	0.9	20. Reading	30	0.6

The other 30 'Collections' of England and Wales, 349, 7.1%
Total of dealers 4,892.

Sources: See note 18
Note:
(a) The excise 'Collections' were units grouped around major towns as the base of the administrative unit. No exact correspondence existed with the boundaries of counties.

It seems clear, on the four tests applied here, that consumption patterns in the capital were radically different from that of the rest of England. A factor of two or even three may have been the order of that difference. There were no doubt factors offsetting this: levels of rent; regional variations in the administration of the excise and other taxes; and differing age compositions of the populations in the two groups represent some of these. There remains, on these terms, a strong case for regarding the capital as the advanced sector of a dual economy. For the purposes of the analysis of its contribution to economic change, it may therefore be taken as an independent 'engine of economic growth'. There seems little case, at least for the period 1600–1750, for regarding it as the product of other economic and social variables.

II

The most familar and best documented of these links is that with agriculture. The large and growing London market demanded foodstuffs, and from Fisher onward historians have identified this as a factor contributing to the process of agricultural improvement. Following Fisher, two aspects of this impact are considered here. By assessing the quantitative importance of London's demands for food in the period, and the sources of its supply, its contribution to general and regional innovation in agriculture can be evaluated. And second, by looking at the process of supply, its contribution to the advancement of commercial institutions can be analysed. Davenant, writing in 1695, perceived these same economic gains: 'On these grounds, and many others, some people are led to think the growth of London not hurtful to the nation; but, on the contrary, to believe there is not an acre of land in the country, be it never so distant, that is not in some degree bettered by the growth, trade, and riches of that city.'[19] Davenant clearly shared the views of Defoe, Fisher, and Wrigley that London was a stimulus to the countryside, and not a parasite preying upon it.

While agricultural change may prove to have been the most important of the interactions of the capital and the economy at large, the process of agricultural change is complex, and the degree of influence from London variable. To isolate that influence, it is necessary first to establish the broader context of agricultural change between 1600 and 1750. At the risk of presenting a crude summary of recent and forthcoming researches on the subject, this sketch can now be attempted. The period saw a decline in dearths of corn and the gradual development of a regular surplus. This was reflected in the cessation of inflation of grain prices from the mid-seventeenth century and the onset of a century of stagnation in the price level. While the primary livestock product, wool, continued to increase in value to the second half of the seventeenth century, it then stagnated before declining during the second quarter of the eighteenth century. Effectively, the terms of trade in agriculture turned in favour of the efficient producer of grain, the farmer growing fine long-staple wool, and the grazier and dairyman. The changing economic environment to which the growth of London contributed thus created conditions favourable to several superficially contradictory trends in agriculture.

The general pressure towards diversification of output may also have had cost-reducing effects. By spreading the peak of labour needs, greater productivity per worker may have been derived, thus permitting economies in an increasingly expensive input. Market changes may have favoured efficiency in grain production, and hence stimulated increasing scale and extended the comparative advantage of the south-eastern corner of England, but in other products there were increased opportunities for the small farmer. High value-added and extremely labour-intensive crops, such as tobacco, the dyestuffs, or even liquorice, offered economic viability to the smallest units. In such changes, which were fundamental elements of the proto-industrial economy, London was an important influence, and the extent of its contribution must now be assessed.

London's demand for bread represented one of two major factors tending to draw trade to the south and east of the country. The other influence was the export trade, which assumed growing importance after 1660, and which was based largely on sales of barley and malt to the Netherlands until around 1720, when wheat began to assume greater significance.[20] If, given the increasing and literal sophistication of its diet, the capital consumed grain at least in proportion to its share of population, then it represented a greater influence than exports under bounty. On average, exports of all grains never exceeded 5 per cent of total output, and at their peak in 1749–50 may have been no more than 12 per cent. To make the point rather more graphically, exports on average corresponded to the normal variation between harvests: London's demand may have approached the gap between dearth and glut.[21]

Fisher's analysis of the grain traffic into London naturally stressed the element which was roughly quantifiable, the coastwise import trade. But, as he also showed, for much of the period before 1640 overland and river supply routes predominated.[22] Following Gras's methods, some estimation of London's total grain supply is possible. The figures of Table 21 represent a simplified version of the Gras estimates, together

Table 21. Estimated consumption of corn in London, 1605–1750 (000 quarters)

Year	Bread and Drink		
1605	500		
1661	1,150		
1676	1,275		
1696	1.325		

	Bread	Drink	Total
1700	575.0	499.7	1,074.7
1750	675.0	600.7	1,275.7

Sources: See note 23.

with my own revisions for 1700 and 1750. In order to simplify the table, Gras's rather unconvincing columns representing fodder and exports have been excluded.[23]

Some explanation of the basis of compilation of the figures of Table 21 is required. Gras, whose figures have been used for 1605–96, simply took an estimate from the year 1528, that bread and drink requirements were 2½ quarters of corn per head per annum, and applied it to his own estimates of London's population. It seems probable that his population figures were rather low, while, by the dietary standards of the later seventeenth century, the allowance for cereal consumption may have been rather too high. For this reason the figures for 1700 and 1750 have been generated independently. The bread figures for both years are based upon Sir Charles Smith's estimate that in the South-east, including London, annual per capita consumption of corn was around one quarter and was largely of wheat (89 per cent wheat, 2 per cent barley, and 9 per cent rye).[24] The requirement of corn for drink has been estimated from excise figures, on the shares assumed in Table 20, and converting liquors to corn equivalents according to the highly impartial tract of 1726, *Distilled Spirituous Liquors the Bane of the Nation*.[25] These latter figures may well understate the inputs to distilling in the capital, but together with our bread figures are preferable to the anachronistic assumptions on diet which underlie Gras's estimates. While there is no doubt that London's grain consumption remained very high as a proportion of national output, for much of the period under consideration it may have stagnated or fallen as meat, dairy produce, and vegetables came to assume a greater contribution to the average diet.

These estimates allow a further assessment of the sources of supply. Coastwise imports to London, according to Fisher, rose from around 69,000 quarters in 1615 to 96,000 in 1638, and were running at 85,000 in 1649. By 1680 the trade had reached 192,000 quarters, but no comparable figures are available for the bulk of the eighteenth century. Despite this, it is clear that rather less of London's total consumption was imported by coastwise shipping than has often been thought. In the early seventeenth century the coasting trade brought 10–14 per cent of London's supplies, a figure which rose to perhaps 20 per cent by 1700.[26] The regional impact of this trade was clear: London's principal granary for these shipments was Kent, followed by Essex and the ports of East Anglia. Superimposed on these demands were those of the export trade, also supplied after 1700 from the same region. The implications for farming were clear: for virtually the whole period commercial demands for quality grains were able to support increased acreages, improved techniques, and perhaps structural changes in this south-eastern segment of the country. A large part of these commercial demands stemmed from the capital.[27]

Where did the bulky residue of London's supply come from? Large quantities came down the Thames to Queenhithe and Bear Quay, representing the output of the cornlands of Berkshire and Oxfordshire, exported through the great river ports of Reading, Henley, and Windsor. From the late sixteenth century grain also came down the navigable river Lea from Hertfordshire at whose mouth was located a great complex of water and tidal mills.[28] London's demands, and perhaps its reciprocating flows of manure, may therefore have transformed the rural economy of the home counties. If the introduction of the sheepfold during the seventeenth century represented the means to till the chalk downlands of Hertfordshire, Wiltshire, and Berkshire, the motive for its use may have been largely London's demand.[29]

However great these river-borne supplies were, it is clear that other sources had to make substantial contributions by overland transport. Ringing the capital were a large number of the country's principal corn markets, which seem to have been as important in 1750 as in the years before 1640. St Albans and Hitchin in the north; High Wycombe in the west; Reigate to the south; and Milton to the east were perhaps the most important of these, and many sent their corn overland. Some measure of the extent to which so many of the great corn markets of southern England supplied the capital may perhaps be found in the fact that in the years 1693-1700 London's wheat prices correlated significantly with those of eleven of the thirteen other markets sampled from Houghton's *Collection for Improvement of Husbandry and Trade*.[30] For the years 1723-62, Granger and Elliott's study confirms London's position as a dominant leader of price fluctuations in southern grain markets.[31] Its pull was being transmitted to increasingly distant satellite markets and through them to the farmer. If we treat Defoe's account of the 1100 teams of horses drawing waggons and carts loaded with grain into each Farnham market *c.* 1720 as an indication of the great distributed influence of the capital rather than as a precise estimate, then similar effects were felt by a dozen or so similar markets before 1640. By the 1750s places as distant from the capital as Retford, Stamford and Nottingham were falling under this influence.[32]

It was perhaps in the supply of dairy produce that the capital induced the greatest changes. Dairying was perhaps the sector of agriculture which displayed the most dramatic advances before 1750, as the white meats came to play a greater role in English diets. Shifting taste and real income created a new demand for dairy produce which the capital displayed in heightened form.[33] Unfortunately, while data on coastwise shipments of cheese and butter survive, reliable estimates of total consumption in the capital are lacking. Virtually all contemporaries, including both Defoe and Maitland, exaggerated the scale of the trade in the attempt to emphasise its size. As in the grain trade, then, one is left with material yielding only a part of the network of supply and, therefore, of the reciprocal flow of income.

Rather than repeat the guesses of Defoe and others, it may be preferable to provide new ones based on population figures. Such comments as were passed on the consumption of dairy produce indicated that roughly equal quantities of butter and cheese were consumed, but that neither may have been eaten as extensively in the city as in the countryside. Taking piecemeal evidences from Drummond and Wilbraham, per capita consumption for the later seventeenth and earlier eighteenth centuries may be taken as ranging between a minimum of eight ounces a week and Arthur Young's mid-eighteenth-century 'messes for a stout man' (which would rapidly have slimmed him) of twelve.[34] These fairly arbitrary assumptions permit an estimation of the total supply from which to assess the network of supply. These estimates appear in Table 22. If we take Maitland's figures for the year 1729–30 as a guide, then for at least the last two observations the upper of the two estimates may be the more appropriate.[35] However, for earlier years, there is no standard of reference with which to compare them.

Nonetheless, some general conclusions on the sources of supply can be drawn. Fisher's figures for shipments of dairy produce to London for the years 1579–1638 exclude those from the North-west. This represents no serious gap, because before the later seventeenth century,

Table 22. Estimated consumption of butter and cheese in London, 1600–1750 (tonnages of cheese, and firkins of butter)

Year	Lower Limit		Upper Limit	
	Cheese	Butter[a]	Cheese	Butter[a]
1600	2790	111,600	4353	174,120
1650	4464	178,560	6964	278,560
1700	6417	256,680	10,011	400,440
1750	7533	301,320	11,752	470,080

Sources: See note 34.
Note:
(a) Taking the firkin as containing 56 lb of butter, net of the cask.

coastwise shipments from the area were small,[36] much of the cheese produced in the region being carried to the capital by inland routes. Even as late as 1706–7 Cheshire farmers sought to break the stranglehold of local factors by carrying their cheese overland to London.[37] When clearer and more comprehensive figures for the coastwise imports are available for the year 1687–8, the coastal import of cheese represented between one quarter and one third of the total as estimated above. On the same basis, coastwise shipments of butter represented between 17 and 26 per cent of the total.[38] Butter and cheese thus came predominantly from the east coast ports, although the latter had its origin largely in the north-western counties of England. This leaves a very large gap to be filled and indicates the dairying specialisms developed by other shires: above all this was filled from Wiltshire, Gloucestershire, Somerset, Warwickshire, and Leicestershire. Butter for table uses probably came from rather nearer at hand, from the Chilterns and the vales on the fringe of the metropolis.

Our later and comparative evidence for the year 1729–30 drawn from Maitland makes it clear that supply routes were changing during the early eighteenth century. Stern has drawn attention to the pronounced shift towards bulk coastal shipment of cheese from the North-west and of butter from the North-east, and our estimates support this view: by 1729–30, three-quarters of our upper estimate for the consumption of cheese may have been supplied coastwise.[39] In the same year around half of London's butter arrived by sea. Maitland's figures as to the supplying ports pointed clearly to the extended contribution of the more distant producers. Three-fifths of the butter came from the Yorkshire ports, and another 30 per cent from Suffolk, while 70 per cent of all imported cheese was described as 'Cheshire'. In all but the relatively small fresh milk trade, which concentrated in the suburban villages, the radius of supply of dairy produce was significantly extended in our period, with very pronounced regional effects. The increase in London's demand was thus linked with developing markets and transport systems, and permitted the full expression of the comparative advantage in grazing possessed by such counties as Cheshire, Shropshire, Yorkshire, and Suffolk.

Two further aspects of food supply can be linked with agricultural change: meat and garden products. The main features of the meat trade are familiar and require no more than a brief recital here. London's requirements for beef expanded during the seventeenth century, reaching around 88,000 beeves per annum in the 1690s but perhaps stagnating thereafter as the taste for beef seems to have declined.[40] Sheep consumed as mutton assumed a correspondingly greater importance towards the end of the seventeenth century, and continued to do so to 1750. In addition, large numbers of pigs were fattened in the capital and on its fringes. Estimates of the quantities of these meat supplies are presented in Table 23.

As in our earlier estimates, these are fairly arbitrary figures, but they do allow some assessment of supply. Of the three, the figures for pigs probably understate total consumption, since for the year 1731 Middleton put total sales of hogs within the bills of mortality at 187,000.[41] The growth of demand for both beef and muttton provided an incentive for the expansion of grazing activity in the north and west of England, and increasingly drew Wales and Scotland into the droving trade. While one must take care not to overstate the direct link between the capital and the Celtic fringe, to some extent the 60,000 cattle crossing the Scottish border and the 100,000 cattle and sheep entering England from Wales around 1700 represented the ripples of London's influence.[42] Much as Davenant suggested, London was capable of commercializing even relatively backward regions.

Our final case study serves as a reminder that London's influence in food supply was broadly gravitational. If in the grain, meat, or dairy trades London came increasingly to generate specialization in more distant shires, within a radius of 20 or 30 miles its influence was several magnitudes greater. Fresh milk, pig fattening, and above all market-gardening demonstrated this power.[43] Fisher's account of the beginnings of this urban fringe farming needs no amplification, and it is clear that horticulture advanced still further to 1750. In the suburban villages of Middlesex, Surrey, Kent, and Essex the art of gardening flourished.[44] Two graphic examples show the extent of this advance. Seed for the Duke of Bedford's Streatham farm purchased in 1722–3 included the following items: 'Hotspur peas', London radish, Windsor

Table 23. Estimates of the growth in London's meat consumption, 1600–1750 (000s)

	Beeves	Muttons[a]	Hogs[a]
1600	38	–	–
1650	61	–	–
1700	88	600	150
1750	101	702	180

Sources: See note 41.
Note:
(a) No data on muttons and hogs are available for 1600 and 1650.

183

beans, marrow peas, dwarf peas, red beet, Italian celery, lettuce, parsley, and garlic.[45] The great storm which struck London in July 1750 proved still more revealing. Market-gardeners in Surrey suffered over £4,000 in damage to garden lights, bell glasses, and growing crops. Among these were such exotic growths as cucumbers and pickling cucumbers, savoys, French beans, fruit, vines, and artichokes.[46]

The metropolitan fringe thus demonstrated in heightened form the apparent benefits of supplying the capital's needs. Its requirements were rather different from those of the nation at large. Differences of work, of land endowment, of income and probably of the propensity to consume were the sources of important economic effects. Much as Wrigley suggested, these included agricultural specialization and productivity gains, and the further stimulus to transport improvement and the integration of the home market. Many of these benefits could and did accrue to relatively small farmers. Given the high profitability of so many garden crops, and their labour intensity, they were even adaptable to open-field farming. While stressing, therefore, the growth of London as a potent force in the commercialization of agriculture it was not a magic wand capable of creating overnight Robert Brenner's capitalist tenantry. The benefits ultimately derived by producers depended on the terms of exchange and the nature of market relationships.[47]

III

It is to the nature of London's position in home trade that we now turn. The assessment of this group of social and economic functions permits a more direct evaluation of the benefits derived by farmers through their trade with the capital, an analysis of the contribution of merchant factors to the efficiency of trade through which resources could be more efficiently employed, and some comment on the extent to which an integrated and modern market can be identified in England by 1750.

The first issue is fundamental to the findings of the previous section. Much of the articulation of the 'commercial' model of the transition from feudal to capitalist society assumes relatively equal exchange in such matters as food supply. Wrigley's argument that early modern towns were at once parasites and stimuli to the countryside upon which they depended can be tested in part by the analysis of such market relationships. If the effect of changing commercial structures was to increase the effective 'taxation' of the country by the capital, despite its observed creative effects, then it may be possible to see in home trade a mechanism transferring resources to more productive uses. This of course makes the perhaps reasonable assumption that capital employed in commerce, even in the era of the agricultural revolution, had a significantly greater marginal productivity than that employed on the farm. Demand from an advanced sector of the economy, in this case London, if translated through unequal exchange, may thus increase productivity by both direct and indirect means.

Was exchange then unequal? In the corn trade, which is probably the best documented, the evidence is unclear before the middle of the seventeenth century. Fisher, following Gras, noted the predominance of small men in the inward shipment of corn to London in the years up to 1640. To Fisher, 'the expansion of the corn trade was primarily the work of smaller men'. Indeed his evidence showed a trend towards a more competitive supply network between 1580 and 1638: rough estimates showed a decline from a five-firm concentration ratio of 50.3 per cent in 1580 (Herfindahl, 0.060), to 24.2 per cent in 1586 (H = 0.014), 11.5 per cent in 1615 (H = 0.005) and to a six-firm ratio of 13.4 per cent in 1638 (H = 0.005).[48] My own studies of the corn trade of Wiggins Key in the 1670s and 1680s suggest that there concentration was rather greater (six-firm concentration ratio, 1679–80, 26.2 per cent, H = 0.253) but still left a truly competitive market among the incoming hoys.[49]

This picture is misleading, for it represents an analysis of the wrong relationships, or rather looks at them from the wrong direction. While supplying merchant shippers in the grain trade were both small and numerous, at their home ports they were often oligopolists. Coleman's study of Kent and Burley's of Essex both point clearly to this fact: at its most extreme the concentration of shipments in the hands of the top six factors reached 93 per cent in 1699–1700 at Milton (H = 0.2395) and 84 per cent in 1700 at Maldon (H = 0.1196).[50] D. A. Baker's massive study of the Kentish marketing system up to 1760 presents no data for exact comparison, but implies a similar if less extreme degree of concentration.[51] While substantial quantities of grain no doubt remained to be traded locally, exports from the region were characterized by unequal exchange. No doubt similar patterns could be identified in the supply network of the international grain trade in East Anglia. Small farmers dealt therefore with millers and hoyman-factors on terms of inequality, and the net effect may have been to redistribute wealth towards mercantile capital.

At the London end, Fisher's analysis may be equally misleading, and certainly cannot be extended beyond 1640. As Gras indicated, the purchasers from these competitive suppliers of the London corn market were the cornfactors. In the years 1676–83, four cornfactors, Anthony

Sturt, Robert Buckle, George Moore, and William Russell purchased for a third of all grain shipments to the capital, and half of the total exported.[52] More formal analysis of their purchases confirms Gras's comments: the top six factors buying through Wiggins Key in 1679–80 held 84.2 per cent of total trade (H = 0.1937). Selling in runs or to single buyers was crucial to the economics of coastal shipping, because it allowed hoys to turn round most rapidly. But hoymen in this relationship became effectively the clients of the factors, and the economies in shipping cannot have entirely compensated for the losses through the market power of the greater dealers to whom they sold. Near-monopsony was evolving during the later seventeenth century, and had matured by 1750. By the end of the eighteenth century, according to Baker, the much greater volume of trade to London through the Mark Lane exchange was controlled by fourteen cornfactors.[53] The hierarchy of the corn trade thus represented an inverted pyramid, and tended to shift a substantial proportion of the gains from increased agricultural productivity towards urban merchant capital, above all in London. Thus, if the growth of London represented an important demand-side element in the expansion of the output of grain in Kent and East Anglia the relationship was not purely symbiotic: elements of parasitism remained.

The pattern of commercial relationships visible in the grain trade can be assessed further by brief reference to traffic in livestock and in dairy produce. Both may have exhibited a similar but less extreme case of exploitation of the supplier. Here, though, even the unsatisfactory quantitiative analysis of trade possible for corn cannot be attempted. To be brief, the extremes of the trades can be illustrated by a number of graphic but not unrepresentative cases. Primary production of store beasts and sheep in supplying regions such as north Wales tended to be relatively small in scale. Farmers were dependent upon the coming of the drovers building herds for England for a quick market. Some measure of the power of their purchasing can be gauged from the fact that in the year 1693 alone cattle to the value of over £4,000 were bought on behalf of one Denbighshire gentleman-grazier.[54] Not surprisingly, the farmers often suffered from the power of these purses, especially when, as in 1735 at Newborough (Anglesey), the drovers operated a ring.[55]

Like the hoymen of Kent, these Welsh drovers and graziers were often themselves vassals of Midland graziers and London cattle dealers. The latter were always held to be the cause of the high price of London's meat.[56] Jobbers, salesmen, and graziers in the metropolitan region clearly enjoyed considerable market power after 1650, but Westerfield's assessment of their strength was somewhat overstated. Relatively little of his evidence actually came from the period before 1760, the subject of his book. But these graziers and dealers were very powerful, as an example can illustrate. The extent of grazier/jobber power can be seen in the resources committed to feeding stocks of sheep on Essex pastures by William Cuxon. When he died in the late 1740s worth over £6,000, he had contracts outstanding for the feeding of over a thousand sheep and for the purchase of nearly 300 acres of turnips for their feed.[57] Maitland's comments on the extent of trade by leading salesmen in the London meat markets confirm this impression. Mr White, chief salesman at Newgate, had sold over 50,000 calves during 1725, and in 1731, the two leading dealers, Odell and Roberts, each claimed to have sold over 50,000 pigs, between them handling nearly 60 per cent of all trade.[58] While a case of exploitation through trade cannot be made with absolute certainty, the relative magnitudes of buyer and seller suggest a structure broadly similar to that of the corn trade. Small-scale producers were connected with the consumer through a pair of major middlemen, with a rather less powerful drover in between.

It is hard in such cases to separate the conspiratorial assessment of farmers from economic reality as they excuse failure today in terms of exploitation through the marketing board or the green pound.

Perhaps the most heightened form of such complaint occurred in the dairy trade, a trade which may be taken as the exemplar for the creative effects of the growing commercial population.[59] At the point of production in Cheshire there seems no reason to doubt the allegations of exploitation: local factors, acting on behalf of London cheesemongers, commanded the market and bought from the small dairy farmers whom they forced to grant very extended credit. By the beginning of the eighteenth century, farmers in the Wirral had co-operated in the attempt to break through the ring, but successes seem to have been only short-lived.[60] For most of the first half of the eighteenth century, the London cheesemongers were perhaps one of the most dominant groups of middlemen working in primary produce.[61]

While the evidence of the grain, livestock, and dairy trades may not be representative of producer-middleman relationships as a whole, and trade in such perishable commodities as fruit and vegetables seemed largely exempt from their machinations, they represented a sufficiently large part of London's linkage with the provinces to warrant further and more general assessment. Dr Ellis has shown the east coast coal trade at both ends to be an almost exact parallel case.[62] The principal economic functions of this growth in activity, number, and relative power of middlemen can be seen in the marked transition between 1600 and 1750 to a nationally integrated market, in transfers towards venture capital through unequal trade, and in the direct stimulus to the development of commercial infrastructure, principally transport change.

Of these three functions the first has already been alluded to in the discussion of London's price level. The evidence now does suggest that A. H. John's dating of an integrated market for cereal can be antedated by half a century, back to at least 1700. My own reworking of the Houghton price-currents pointed to this and Granger and Elliott's study confirmed the analysis. Thus the market for the most expensive grain had become modern and integrated before the era of the canal and the provincial press, the key communications factors stressed by John.[63] London, its middleman community, and its entrepôt function in the grain trade had induced this change by the end of the seventeenth century. Some appreciation of the importance of this last factor can be derived from the fact that London ranked very high among grain exporting ports by the 1740s. Between 1743 and 1751, London's share of total wheat exports averaged 32 per cent, or just under 148,000 quarters per annum. Thus, to the effects from middleman trade must be added gains from the export bounty which, as Adam Smith and most subsequent observers have agreed, accrued more to the merchant than the farmer.[64] If we take the logical step of assuming at least some of these redistributive effects in the other trades, we have evidence of both market integration and a substantial flow of resources into commerce.

IV

The third function of this middleman activity was in its contribution to the course of transport change. The first and most direct link was with investment and promotion. This new and growing community had, to employ Ward's term, clear economic rather than financial motivation for the improvement of transport.[65] Many, as we have seen, had passed beyond the stage of operating at margins and were engaging in very large trade activities. The notorious London cheesemongers were supporters of three of the most important river navigation schemes of the early eighteenth century, for the Weaver, the Derwent and the Don. In the last case, the cornfactors added their support.[66] Stern cited a further example of the cheesemongers' involvement in transport change when, in 1751, they opposed the bill before the Commons to further restrict the number of horses in draught on waggons. They argued the necessity for the speedy conveyance of new cheese from Gloucestershire, Wiltshire, and Berkshire to the London market.[67] While there is no case for making such influences any more than a marginal factor in the process of innovation, there can be no doubt that the possession of such powerful allies in London was a major asset to petitioners. London was therefore an influence on the provinces in promotional activity.

The second transport effect stemmed from London's demand for bulky raw materials and foodstuffs: and here we see its influence on coastal shipping. Wrigley has suggested that employment resultant upon London's growing needs for coal grew from 8,000 to 15,000 between 1650 and 1750.[68] The examples of the trades discussed above added similar effects. This led to the increase of the tonnage employed in coastal shipping, and helped to foster productivity change in the industry. On the evidence of Willan's work, gains in provincially-owned tonnage, much employed in the London trade, were smaller than those in the overseas trade but still averaged one per cent per annum, 1709–51.[69] Perhaps more important to the long-run development of the economy were the gains in productivity. Output of voyages per ship seems to have been rising in the century before 1750, and in the London coal trade was from four to perhaps six per year. Although Davis indicated that the gains in labour productivity observable by the middle of the eighteenth century accrued mainly to the larger ships engaged in the overseas trade, there are reasonable grounds for assuming some benefits in coasting. If, as seems probable, there was some increase in the size of shipping engaged in the coasting trade before 1750, then we may assume gains similar to the 20 per cent in tons per man which characterised the German trade.[70]

As we have seen, the coasting trade was a great source of supply to the capital but did not remove its large dependence on road transport. London's vital significance as a target for transport services is revealed by recent analysis of the improvement of England's roads. Albert's assessment of the turnpiking movement showed that by 1750 the greater part of the thirteen arterial routes to the capital had been thus improved. By 1730, 57 per cent of the mileage of these routes had been turnpiked and by 1750 the proportion reached 88 per cent.[71] Pawson's slightly more refined geographical analysis of the turnpike's temporal and spatial diffusion made it clear that in both senses London represented the key influence in the 'leading sector' of improvement.[72] In the physical improvement of English roads, the influence of the capital was fundamental. It represented in that sense an engine of economic growth.

London's mixed functions as the centre of an enormous and growing population, as a market, and as entrepôt, supplying the nation with imported luxuries, may explain a further development, that of land carrying services. In both goods and passenger carriage, London was a leading sector. Much of the relationship has already been outlined elsewhere, but the salient points can be restated. In goods carriage, the London route was the first to evolve public scheduled carrying on a large scale. It also showed early and extensive innovation in the means of carriage, much before the end of the seventeenth century being conducted by waggon rather than packhorse. It grew sufficiently fast between the 1630s and 1750s to suggest on some estimates that physical carrying capacity by 1750 in land transport to London was equal to that of coastal shipping. If this was so, then a further point, made in Turnbull's survey of provincial carrying, is that the London route absorbed a disproportionate quantum of resources, although it accounted for but a small share of the growing services.[73] This evidence supports that of the turnpiking of the arterial routes, and both point to the enormous premium being placed on communication with the capital. The effect was the creation between 1600 and 1750 of an extensive and relatively rapid system of land carriage, interlocking at the regional and local level with the lesser carriers, and thus advancing market structures.

In goods carriage both demand and the implications of expanded supply of services are clear, as is the fundamental role of London in creating the leading sector of improvement. This lead was even more striking in the case of passenger carriage. The century before 1750 saw the creation and maturation of a stagecoach system connecting the provinces to the capital. Even before 1700, the coach traveller going to London could discriminate between services in terms of price, hour of departure, and speed of travel. By 1750 the London route had a capacity of many thousands of passenger miles per week, and yet inter-provincial services had hardly begun.[74] The time lag between London and the provincial centres in the development of stagecoach services was of nearly a century's duration. The peculiar requirements for so many to reach London reinforces our earlier comments on its magnetic attraction, its differentness, and its consequent capacity for creative economic effects.

A specific example may help to specify some of these effects. Land carriage clearly aided the course of market integration through its contribution to both goods and information flows, and by easing the movement of factors and agents assisted their growth in scale and freedom. Equally, as in Wrigley's example of the coal trade, it had the power to create employment. Evidence from a dispute over the ownership of the Exeter to London stagecoach in the 1680s makes this point clearly. Innkeepers, smiths, ostlers, farriers, and wheelwrights all testified to the services they and their servants provided for the stage. In a single bundle of depositions, such testimony came from Honiton, Salisbury, Bridport, Dorchester, Sutton [Scotney?], Blandford, Fordington, and Axminster. Among the revenues derived from serving the four coaches performing the service were nearly £80 paid to Arthur Dassell, innkeeper of Bridport, between February 1687 and December 1688; over £230 in the same period to William Bennett of Sutton in Hampshire, innkeeper, for horsemeat; and £18 paid to George Tompson, of Bridport, blacksmith, for shoeing horses and making repairs to coaches and wheels.[75] If we multiply this example by hundreds or even thousands, and allow as much or more for the parallel relationships in goods carriage, then a major source of new employment, attributable largely to the capital, emerges. Thus London's generation of transport change had significant creative and multiplier effects. In the pre-industrial economy, in which the growth of services and commerce was arguably almost as important as that of agriculture or industry these effects were of great significance.

V

It is disappointing not to have made greater assaults on the metrocentric school of early modern history. London's influence was enormous while rarely expressed directly. The present paper has tended to support and confirm themes and relationships identified by Fisher and by Wrigley. But the linkages were not as simple in practice as in the form of Wrigley's flow-chart. Several of the elements of Wrigley's model – higher real incomes, agricultural change, new patterns of consumption, better transport, economic rationality, better commercial facilities, and the trend to a national market – have been touched on here, but it seems that the simplicity of Wrigley's model is illusory. The specified relationships are harder to sustain when examined in greater depth.

The present study has attempted to refine some of these linkages. In the attempt to examine whether the dual economy model was appropriate to early modern England, it became clear that the capital's power as a consumer was greater by a factor of at least two than that of the rest of the country. This led quite naturally to a range of agricultural effects which, together with the other major external influence after 1660, that of exports under bounty, generated productivity and structural changes. While these developments assisted in the commercialization of English agriculture, they did not automatically lead to the development of a large-scale capitalistic tenantry: many of the benefits of specialization accrued to the small farmer well-endowed with essential labour supplies.

It was for this reason perhaps that the net impact of many of these changes tended to be redistributive. Brenner's intuition was quite correct: in few cases was trade developed between equal partners. Trade in primary produce thus tended to transfer some part of the incremental gains from agricultural productivity into commercial capital. This prevented the development of complacency in the agricultural sector, and helped to stop farming in the protected conditions after 1689 from falling into a kind of welfare trap. London's influence thus offered the incentive of market opportunity while taxing some of the gains from specialization for future growth. Transport changes represented one of the main signs of this process, and contributed their own multiplier functions to it. Together these developments establish the place of London as a truly dynamic influence on economic and social change before 1750, and re-establish at least one city as a vital heuristic device.

NOTES AND REFERENCES

1. P. Abrams and E. A. Wrigley (eds), *Towns in Societies* (Cambridge 1978).
2. M. J. Daunton, 'Towns and economic growth in eighteenth century England', in Abrams and Wrigley (eds), *Towns in Societies*, p. 252.
3. The principal contributions alluded to here are: Robert Brenner, 'Agrarian class structure and economic development in pre-industrial Europe', *Past and Present*, 70 (1976); 'Symposium–Agrarian class structure and economic development in pre-industrial Europe', *Past and Present*, 78 (1978); *idem;* 79 (1978); *idem;* 80 (1978); *idem;* 85 (1979); *idem;* 97 (1982).
4. Daunton, 'Towns and economic growth', pp. 245–7.
5. Thomas Milles, Customer of Sandwich, 1604, quoted by E. G. R. Taylor, 'Camden's England', in H. C. Darby (ed.) *An Historical Geography of England before AD 1800* (Cambridge, repr. 1951), pp. 363–4.
6. E. A. Wrigley, 'A simple model of London's importance in changing English society and economy, 1650–1750', repr. in Abrams and Wrigley (eds), *Towns in Societies*, pp. 215ff.
7. Wrigley, 'Simple model', pp. 215–16; E. A. Wrigley and R. S. Schofield, *The Population History of England, 1541–1871* (London 1981), Table A3.1, pp. 528–9.
8. J. E. T. Rogers, *A History of Agriculture and Prices in England* (Oxford 1866–1900) Vol. 5, p. 634.
9. Ibid., Vol. 5, pp. 634–5. Rogers' figures are combined with those of E. W. Gilboy, as reworked by P. Deane and W. A. Cole, *British Economic Growth, 1688–1959* (Cambridge 1962), p. 19.

10. Eton College prices from B. R. Mitchell and P. Deane, *Abstract of British Historical Statistics* (Cambridge 1962), pp. 386-7; London bread, ibid., pp. 497-8; conversion factors from S. and B. Webb 'The assize of bread', *Economic Journal*, 14 (1904). Table 4 from J. Houghton, *A Collection for Improvement of Husbandry and Trade* (1692-1700). A more ambitious attempt to measure standards of living in the capital was made by R. F. Tucker, 'Real wages of artisans in London', 1729-1935, *Journal of the American Statistical Association*, 31 (1936), but the methods employed cannot be projected back to the sixteenth century with any certainty. In Tucker's study, London wage relativities appear strikingly different. Tucker's starting point from the perspective of the present study appears as a peak from which real wage levels decline.

11. Webbs, 'Assize of bread', p. 199.

12. J. Thirsk and J. P. Cooper (eds), *Seventeenth Century Economic Documents* (Oxford 1972), p. 804.

13. Ibid., pp. 802-3.

14. M. W. Beresford, 'The beginnings of retail tobacco licences', *Yorkshire Bulletin of Economic and Social Research*, 7 (1955), p. 139.

15. British Library (hereafter BL), Landsdowne MSS., 1215, fol. 7; M. P. Ashley, *Financial and Commercial Policy under the Cromwellian Protectorate* (London 1934), pp. 62-71.

16. Custom House Library, 'Quantities, rates & amounts of excise duties, 1684-1798', pp. 2-9, 24-6, 28-9.

17. Custom House Library, 'An account of the quantities of the several articles which have been charged with excise duties in each year', pp. 38-9. It may be worth noting modern comment on the nature of spirits consumption, as in S. Toland, 'Changes in living standards since the 1950s', *Social Trends*, 10 (1980), pp. 25-6. As a point of comparison, *per capita* consumption of beer in the United Kingdom was 4.1 pints per week in 1979, of spirits 0.11 pints per week, and of wine 0.24 pints per week. This may help to justify attribution of a 'drink problem' to London in our period. Central Statistical Office, *Annual Abstract of Statistics*, 117 (1981), Tables 2.1 and 8.81.

18. Public Record Office (hereafter PRO) Customs 48/13, p. 206, Excise Letterbook, 17 February 1738.

19. Thirsk and Cooper, op. cit., pp. 809-10.

20. Based on my chapter, 'The marketing of agricultural produce', in J. Thirsk (ed.), *The Agrarian History of England and Wales*, Vol. 5 (Cambridge 1985).

21. Ibid.

22. F. J. Fisher, 'The development of the London food market, 1540-1640', repr. in E. M. Carus-Wilson (ed.) *Essays in Economic History*, Vol. 1, (London 1954), p. 139.

23. N. S. B. Gras, *The Evolution of the English Corn Market* (Cambridge, Mass. 1926) pp. 76-7. W. Ashley, *The Bread of Our Forefathers* (Oxford 1926), pp. 24-5. Quantities of drink as in Table 20. On inputs to brewing and distilling, *Distilling Spirituous Liquors the Bane of the Nation* (1736), p. 19, suggests 3 bushels per barrel of strong beer, and p. 20, 1 quarter of corn to each 20 gallons of proof spirits.

24. Ashley, *Bread of Our Forefathers*, pp. 24-5.

25. *Distilled Spirituous Liquors the Bane of the Nation*, pp. 19–20.
26. Fisher, 'London food market', pp. 138–9; Gras, *English Corn Market*, p. 107 and Appendix D, pp. 297–323.
27. As argued by A. H. John, 'English agricultural improvement and grain exports, 1660–1765' in D. C. Coleman and A. H. John (eds). *Trade, Government and Economy in Pre-Industrial England* (London 1976), pp. 45–67; and Chartres, 'Marketing'.
28. Fisher, 'London food market'; Gras, *English Corn Market*.
29. E. Kerridge, *The Agricultural Revolution* (London 1967), pp. 42 ff.
30. Discussed at greater length in Chartres, 'Marketing', Section VI.
31. C. W. J. Granger and C. M. Elliott, 'A fresh look at wheat prices and markets in the eighteenth century', *Economic History Review*, 2nd series, 20 (1967).
32. Chartres, 'Marketing' section VI; D. Defoe, *A Tour Through England and Wales*, (London 1927 edn), Vol. 1, p. 142.
33. Ibid., and many of the other contributions to *Agrarian History*, Vol. 5.
34. J. C. Drummond and A. Wilbraham, *The Englishman's Food* (2nd edn, London 1957), pp. 206–210. Their survey has been used as the inspiration for these guesses from non-contemporaneous figures, allowing for probable differences in age-structure and observed income differentials.
35. W. Maitland, *The History of London* (1739), Book 3, pp. 553–4.
36. D. M. Woodward, *The Trade of Elizabethan Chester* (Hull 1970), pp. 66–72.
37. Cheshire Record Office, Aderne MSS., DAR/A/65/2.
38. As compared with the mid-point between the second and third observations of Table 22. Coastwise shipments have been taken from P. V. McGrath, 'The Marketing of Food, Fodder, and Livestock in the London Area in the Seventeenth Century, with Some Reference to the Sources of Supply' (unpublished London University M.A. thesis, 1948), p. 230, as converted in J. A. Chartres, *Internal Trade in England, 1500–1700* (1977), p. 29.
39. W. M. Stern, 'Cheese shipped coastwise to London towards the middle of the eighteenth century', *Guildhall Miscellany*, 4 (1973); *idem.*, 'Where, oh where, are the cheesemongers of London?', *London Journal*, 5 (1979); Maitland, *History of London*, Book 3, pp. 553–4.
40. Chartres, *Internal Trade*, pp. 23–4.
41. Maitland, *History of London*, Book 3, p. 553. In Table 23 beeves have been estimated at a constant level of consumption, 1600–1700, probably a slight underestimate, based on Houghton, at 0.152 per head per annum, and reduced for 1750 to 0.150; sheep estimated on the same basis, assuming constant per capita consumption, 1700–50; fat hogs estimated from the distillery records of Cook & Co., BL Add. Mss., 39683, 1767–8, assuming that all brewers' and distillers' grains were used for this purpose. Grain figures as in Table 21. These figures are significantly greater than those provided by Deane and Cole, *British Economic Growth*, p. 72, and may offer further substance to the plentiful contemporary comments on the erosion of inner London markets through the increasing use of satellite markets on its fringes, such as Barnet.
42. Chartres, *Internal Trade*, pp. 20–1.
43. References to urban pigkeeping abound, for example in the Surrey Sessions records of the 1660s: D. L. Powell and H. Jenkinson (eds), *Surrey Quarter*

Sessions Records, Surrey Record Society, 36 (1935), p. 265, and 39 (1938), pp. 110, 126, 198, 233.

44. Kerridge, *Agricultural Revolution*, pp. 173–80; R. Webber, *The Early Horticulturalists*, (Newton Abbot 1968), pp. 19–24.

45. Greater London Record Office, Lambeth Public Library, Bedford Papers, E/BER/S/E/7/4/12.

46. Surrey Record Office, Kingston, Quarter Sessions, Midsummer 1750, 6/2/62–106.

47. Brenner, 'Agrarian class structure', pp. 63ff.

48. Estimated from Fisher, 'London food market', p. 147, note 59. Of the two measures, the Herfindahl is generally to be preferred, since it allows for the size of the top shippers relative to that of the total number. Its reciprocal can be taken as the number of equal sized firms capable of supplying the entire market, i.e., 1580, 17, 1586, 77, 1615, 200 and 1638, 208.

49. J. A. Chartres, 'Trade and shipping in the Port of London: Wiggins Key in the later seventeenth century', *Journal of Transport History*, 3rd series, 1 (1980), pp. 29–47.

50. Chartres, 'Marketing', Table 11.

51. D. A. Baker, 'Agricultural Prices, Production, and Marketing, with Special Reference to the Hop Industry: North-East Kent, 1680–1760', (unpublished University of Kent, Ph.D. thesis, 1976).

52. Gras, *Corn Market*, p. 197.

53. Chartres, 'Marketing', Table 11.

54. PRO, E/126/17 ff. 16–17, 2 March 1697.

55. University College of North Wales Library, Bulkeley Diary, 15 September 1735, Henblas A 18.

56. For example, *Gentleman's Magazine*, 25 (1755), p. 294.

57. PRO, E/126/27 No. 8, 14 July 1750.

58. Maitland, *History of London*, Book 3, p. 553.

59. The theme of Westerfield's book, but surveyed rather critically by C. P. Kindleberger, 'Commercial expansion and the industrial revolution', *Journal of European Economic History*, 4 (1975).

60. Chartres, 'Marketing', based on Cheshire Record Office, DAR/A/65/2.

61. Stern, 'Cheesemongers of London'.

62. J. Ellis, 'The decline and fall of the Tyneside salt industry, 1660–1790: a re-examination', *Economic History Review*, 2nd series, 33 (1980). Further discussion of these restrictive practices will be found in P. Cromar, 'The coal industry on Tyneside,' *Northern History*, 14 (1978).

63. Chartres, 'Marketing'; Granger and Elliott, 'Wheat prices'; A. H. John, 'The course of agricultural change, 1660–1760' in L. S. Pressnell (ed.), *Studies in the Industrial Revolution* (London 1960), pp. 126–7.

64. A. Smith, *An Enquiry into the Nature and Causes of the Wealth of Nations*, (Oxford, 1976 edn), p. 514.

65. J. R. Ward, *The Finance of Canal Building in Eighteenth-Century England* (London 1974), pp. 126–42.

66. T. S. Willan, *River Navigation in England. 1600–1750* (London 1936), pp. 31, 137; Cheshire Record Office, Petition from Lancashire and Cheshire Dairymen, *c.* 1708, DAR/A/65/2.

67. Stern, 'Cheese shipped coastwise', p. 209.

68. Wrigley, 'Simple model', pp. 231–2.

69. T. S. Willan, *The English Coasting Trade, 1600–1750* (repr. Manchester 1967), p. 222.
70. R. Davis, *The Rise of the English Shipping Industry* (2nd edn., Newton Abbot 1972), p. 71.
71. W. Albert, *The Turnpike Road System in England, 1663–1840* (Cambridge 1972), p. 42.
72. E. Pawson, *Transport and Economy* (London 1977), Chs 5–6. Ch. 4 of this work removes any lingering doubts as to the position of the turnpike trust as a genuine innovation.
73. G. L. Turnbull, 'Provincial road carrying in England in the eighteenth century', *Journal of Transport History,* 2nd series, 4 (1977).
74. J. A. Chartres and G. L. Turnbull, 'Road transport', in D. H. Aldcroft and M. J. Freeman (eds), *Transport in the Industrial Revolution* (Manchester 1983).
75. PRO Exchequer Depositions, E/134/1 William and Mary, Michaelmas/23.

PART THREE
Society and change

CHAPTER SEVEN
The social topography of Restoration London

M. J. Power

I

The diversity of London neighbourhoods is often remarked upon as a feature that lends a particular character to the capital city. Distinct social and occupational groups, varying greatly in wealth, leave their imprint on parishes or quarters that they colonize. The resulting contrast in the physical environment of different areas, so obvious today, seems to have been equally evident in the past. John Stow, in his *Survey of London* of 1598, leaves no doubt that some quarters were as pleasant as others were miserable. In Aldermanbury he rejoiced in 'divers fair houses . . . meet for merchants or men of worship'. But outside Aldgate he lamented the 'filthy cottages, and . . . other purpressors, inclosures and laystalls . . . no small blemish to so famous a city'.[1] In distance Aldermanbury and Aldgate were not a mile apart; in character they were different worlds.

Such differences in the physical environment reflect wide variations in the wealth and character of London's inhabitants. Such contrasts were not peculiar to the capital city. Gideon Sjoberg has argued that social and occupational segregation is an inevitable part of any pre-industrial city, past or present: 'The . . . central area is notable as the chief residence of the élite . . . The disadvantaged members of the city fan out toward the periphery, with the very poorest and the outcastes living in the suburbs, the farthest removed from the centre.' Sjoberg's élite, who concentrate in the centre, are the natural leaders of society: landowners, those in political power, the controllers of religion and education. They are distinguished by their wealth and location. So are, by the same token, other groups, merchants, craftsmen and the unskilled, who congregate in a series of concentric circles outwards.[2]

It is with this pattern in mind that this investigation into London in the 1660s begins. It will attempt to establish where rich and poor lived and then, by adding to this a study of the location and wealth of occupation groups, it will seek to explain the social geography of the capital before the Great Fire. The major source for the study is the series of hearth taxes assessed in London, Middlesex and Surrey before the Great Fire. No one tax covers the whole City and suburbs. Of the 110 parishes in the City some 18 appear in the tax of Michaelmas 1662, and 69 in that of Ladyday 1666 (together 79 per cent of the parishes). The western and eastern suburbs are covered by a third tax, Ladyday 1664, and parishes south of the Thames by the tax of Michaelmas 1664.[3] What all these taxes have in common is a list of householders, arranged by street and parish, and beside each name the number of hearths in the dwelling. It is assumed in this paper that the average number of hearths per dwelling in each parish gives an indication of the relative wealth of its inhabitants. St Lawrence Jewry, with a mean of 6.17 hearths per dwelling, should be a parish with wealthier inhabitants, on the whole, than St Botolph Aldgate, with a mean of only 2.48.[4]

There is no doubt that the use of hearth taxes to indicate wealth is based on large assumptions. The first, that a large number of hearths equals wealth and a small number poverty, might seem crude. But it is suggestive that the Acts which imposed the tax worked on this assumption. In 1662 the Act establishing the tax exempted the householder 'who by reason of his poverty ... is exempted from the usual taxes and payments towards the church and poor'. And an amending Act of 1664 made the connection between the number of hearths and poverty explicit by allowing exemption only to those with two hearths or less: 'No person ... inhabiting any dwelling house (not being an alms house ...) ... which hath ... in it more than two chimneys ... shall be exempted from payment of the duties thereon imposed by colour of any exemption or pretext whatsoever'.[5]

The second assumption, that everybody was included in the hearth tax, even the very poorest, and that the average number of hearths per dwelling in each parish represents all strata of its society, poses greater problems. At first glance most of the hearth taxes seem to include this tail of poor. Although that of Michaelmas 1662 (18 City parishes in this analysis), based on an assessment of the summer of that year, listed only taxpayers and therefore excluded the poor, that of Ladyday 1666 (69 City parishes in this analysis), based on an assessment of summer 1666 made after the tax was due, includes those exempt as well as those liable.[6] Frequent entries of 'poor', 'pauper' and 'pensioner' occur, mixed in with the taxpayers.

It is, however, doubtful if this was done comprehensively. A study of vestry minutes and churchwardens' accounts of several City parishes in the 1660s brought to light some poor rate assessments and lists of poor relief recipients that suggest slightly larger numbers of inhabited dwellings than are included in the hearth tax. In St Lawrence Jewry, for example, 179 people were rated for poor relief and 4 pensioners were listed as recipients of relief in 1663. In the hearth tax of 1666 only 163 inhabitants were listed, and none was described as poor. In St Michael Wood Street in 1666 a total of 105 householders and 12 lodgers were listed on a poor rate assessment, 117 in all, and of these 11 had received a Christmas dole in 1663; in the 1666 hearth tax only 107 names are listed, and no poor. These examples suggests that the 1666 tax is deficient in listing inhabitants at the bottom end of the social scale. Other examples, in contrast, show the tax as equal or superior to poor rate lists. In St Stephen Walbrook a poor rate assessment of 1664 lists 69 names and no poor rate recipients; the 1666 hearth tax lists 68. And in St Margaret New Fish Street a poor rate of 1655 records 83 names and no poor recipients, whereas the 1666 hearth tax lists 110.[7] The figures do not, therefore, all point the same way, but that some suggest that the hearth tax omits the very poor leaves a question mark over the comprehensiveness of the 1662 and 1666 hearth taxes in the City.

The hearth tax used for the western and eastern suburbs, Ladyday 1664, was based upon an assessment of winter 1663-4 governed by an amending Act of 1663 which called for those exempted from tax to be listed separately from those liable. The poor should, therefore, be more systematically listed. It is certainly more comprehensive as a list of inhabitants than the 1666 tax. In the parishes which appear in both taxes the 1664 list is considerably longer: the Duchy of Lancaster Liberty has 522 names in the 1664 tax, to 427 in 1666; and in Shadwell the figures are 1,361 in 1664 against 991 in 1666. The same pattern of separate listing of exempt appears in the Michaelmas 1664 tax which covers parishes south of the Thames.

We would be wise to be cautious, therefore, in interpreting the pattern of wealth in London. The City parish data are derived from hearth taxes (1662 and 1666) which probably omit some poor; suburban parish data come from more comprehensive taxes (Ladyday and Michaelmas 1664) in which the poorest inhabitants seem more systematically listed. The average figures of hearths per dwelling in the City parishes will therefore be skewed upwards; those in the suburbs will probably be more correct. With this warning in mind we can move on to a consideration of the data.

II

'The central area is notable as the chief residence of the élite.' If
Sjoberg's thesis is valid, we should expect the wealthiest members of the
London community to cluster in the central parishes and, all other
things being equal, to be found living in larger than average dwellings.
Figure 3, which plots the average size of dwelling in each parish in the
City and suburbs, affords some support for the notion but, equally,
raises some doubts. Parishes favoured with large dwellings are indeed
found in the centre of the City and are surrounded by a ring of parishes
near the Wall and along the riverside with much smaller homes. The
concentric pattern is not perfect. The central 'wealthy' parishes are not
tightly clustered but straggle from east to west. There is a definable
cluster near the wall in the east, around St Helen's (36 on Fig. 3), with its
'fair and large built houses ... divers fair inns ... and houses for men of
worship', St Andrew Undershaft (14), with its 'fair and beautiful parish
church', and St Dionis Backchurch (28), which Pepys found remarkable
for its 'very great store of fine women'.[8] A second concentration occurs
in the centre of the City around St Lawrence Jewry (44), with its 'very
fine church', Allhallows Bread Street (2), 'wholly inhabited by rich
merchants', and St Stephen Walbrook (94), with its 'divers fair houses'.[9]
A third group is near the Wall in the west around St Faith's (32), the
stationers' church, and St Gregory's (35). Despite these three centres
the pattern is good enough, with some imagination, to be fitted into
Sjoberg's model.

A more intractable problem occurs as one moves out into the
suburbs. In the East End and in Southwark dwellings continue small in
size, a feature corroborated by other evidence.[10] But in the West End
the reverse is true. In this peripheral area, where 'the very poorest and
the outcastes' should live, there is another cluster of parishes with large
dwellings which apparently rivals the city centre in wealth and extent. It
begins with the legal quarter (St Andrew Holborn (98), St Dunstan in
the West (106), the Rolls Liberty, St Clement Danes), where there was
'a whole university, as it were, of students, practicers or pleaders, and
judges of the laws of this realm'. Further west, around the curve of the
river, the wealthy parishes continue (the Duchy of Lancaster Liberty, St
Paul Covent Garden, St Martin-in-the-Fields), graced with the
residences of 'gentlemen and men of honour'. The Strand, in particular
(running through the Duchy of Lancaster Liberty and St Clement
Danes), had long been the aristocratic centre of London. John Stow had
boasted in 1598 of the town palaces along its southern side: Essex
House, Arundel House, Somerset House, the Savoy, Russell House,

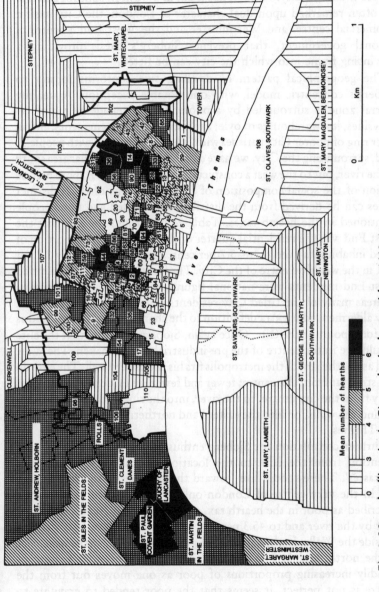

Fig. 3. Mean dwelling size in City and suburban parishes, 1662–66
Sources: see note 3.

Cecil House, Durham House and York House.[11] Their favoured inhabitants were precisely Sjoberg's élite: landowners, statesmen and higher clergy. Whereas he would have us place his élite in the centre of the pre-industrial city, London has them in a western suburb, and it is the often remarked upon dual character of London, the City itself a commercial centre, and Westminster and the West End a centre of national government, that prevents Sjoberg's thesis providing a convincing frame into which the city can be fitted.

The geographical pattern of dwelling size conforms loosely to Sjoberg's concentric model, with one notable exception. A wealthy central zone is surrounded by a poorer City riverside belt with its quaysides, its 'warehouses of oyle; and wines', and its tenements, and an inner ring of poorer City parishes with 'alleys ... pestered with people'.[12] And, surrounding the City, we have a poor East End, a similar area south of the river, but to the west a conspicuous area of wealth. A more precise notion of the social composition of the populations of these distinct zones can be derived from the distribution of titled and poor people mentioned in the hearth taxes. Table 24 underlines the fact that the West End was the residential quarter of the élite; a high proportion of titled inhabitants lived there, 3.7 per cent, compared with only 1.2 per cent in the wealthy centre of the City. The fact that many of these titled West-End residents were national figures, statesmen and aristocrats, whereas many of the titled City residents were but London notables, City aldermen, adds extra definition to the character of the West End as the focal point of the élite. Once again, Sjoberg's notion, that the élite should live in the centre of the pre-industrial city, is shaken. The West End aside, the rest of the metropolis fits his thesis very well. The élite do not stray far from the centre; fewer and fewer are evident as one moves away from the city centre, to the river, into the ring of the poor parishes around the walls, or into the eastern and northern suburbs, or south of the Thames.

Further consolation for Sjoberg enthusiasts is provided by turning attention from the élite to the location of 'the very poorest and outcastes'. These should live 'toward the periphery', and indeed they do. In the very centre of London only 1.5 per cent of residents are described as poor in the hearth tax, a figure which increases to 5.2 per cent by the river and to 45.3 per cent in the ring of poor City parishes outside the Walls. In the suburbs the percentage is 25.7 in the west, 49.1 in the north, and 51.9 in the east. Though a concentric pattern of steadily increasing proportions of poor as one moves out from the centre is not perfect, it seems that the poor tended to gravitate to peripheral areas.

Table 24. Elite and poor groups in different areas of London

	City			Suburbs				London total
	Centre	Parishes outside Walls	Riverside	West End	East End	North	South of river	
% titled[a]	1.2	0.2	0.6	3.7	0.1	0.6	0.2	1.1
% poor[b]	1.5	45.3	5.2	25.7	51.9	49.1	43.7	37.8
Mean hearths per dwelling	5.5	2.8	3.8	5.1	2.7	2.9	2.8	3.6

Sources: 1662 and 1666 hearth taxes for City and north suburbs; 1664 hearth taxes for suburbs except north (see note 3).
Notes:
(a) Described as sir, esquire, gentleman, alderman, bishop.
(b) Described as poor, pauper, pensioner, no distress, non-chargeable, shut.

The figures are dramatic enough to suggest that the pattern of centrifugal poverty existed, even though the evidence of the hearth tax is suspect. The fact that poor are more systematically listed in the hearth taxes which cover the suburbs than in the taxes for the City proper no doubt exaggerates the dichotomy between rich centre and poor periphery. But there can be little doubt that the difference existed. Within the City itself other sources indicate a similar pattern. R. W. Herlan, in examining poor rating and receipt in the City in the late 1650s, found that the poorest areas lay in the large city parishes outside the Walls, and in a few riverside parishes west of London Bridge.[13] Additional reassurance can be derived from analyses of two other London listings, the 1638 tithe rental, and the 1695 returns for the tax on marriages, births and burials. Finlay and Jones have independently studied the first and calculated the proportion of substantial households and the mean rent of property in each City parish in 1638 (perhaps more sensitive guides to the distribution of rich and poor than the size of dwelling suggested by the hearth tax). The results were encouragingly similar maps to that based on the hearth taxes. Although there are some differences in the ranking of the parishes the overall picture of a central straggling core of wealthy parishes, surrounded by poorer parishes along the Thames and around the Walls, is the same.[14]

The coincidence of results with the second list, the 1695 returns, is not quite so good. A map of 'surtax' or substantial householders in 1695 (a rather different kind of measurement from mean dwelling size, or mean rent) shows a similar central core of wealthy parishes, but this core extends southwards to border the river around and east of London Bridge. The rebuilding of the City after the Great Fire may help to explain the development, as the ancient and insalubrious Thames-side houses and warehouses were replaced. Despite this southern wealthy spur the map in 1695 still shows a recognizable if imperfect concentric pattern, of wealthy centre and poorer periphery.[15] The conclusion that the City of London had a wealthy core and poorer periphery seems to be firmly established.

III

If the wealthy congregated in particular parishes can they be shown to have gathered in particular streets? Figure 4 shows the result of analysing the average size of dwellings along the major streets in the city. No obvious pattern hits the eye. It might be argued that large dwellings are commonly situated along major thoroughfares. The major west-to-

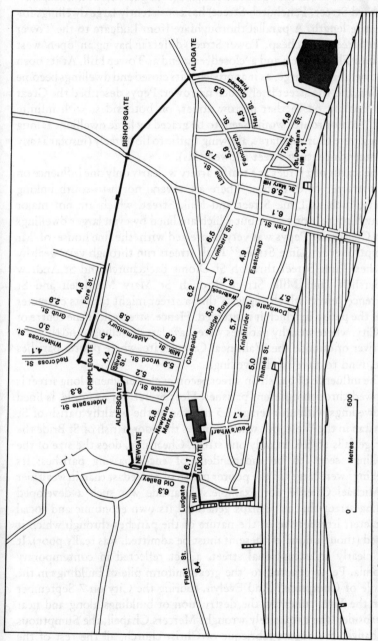

Fig. 4. Mean dwelling size in City streets, 1666
Sources: see note 3.

east route between Newgate and Aldgate (Newgate Market, Cheapside, Lombard Street, Fenchurch Street) has consistently large dwellings for its entire length. A parallel thoroughfare from Ludgate to the Tower (Fleet Street, Eastcheap, Tower Street) differs in having an 'open' west end into Fleet Street, and a 'closed' east end at Tower Hill. At its open end dwellings are large; as it approaches its closed end dwellings become smaller, and the street itself much narrower. Pepys described the Great Fire 'coming on in that narrow street, on both sides, with infinite fury'.[16] Major routes would seem to be graced by large dwellings as long as they were thoroughfares, allowing traffic to flow freely (insofar as any seventeenth-century street allowed this).

The status of a street as a traffic artery is clearly only one influence on the character of dwellings. There are several north-to-south linking streets, such as Lime Street and Milk Street, which are not major through routes for traffic but which are lined by even larger dwellings than Cheapside. Pepys was very impressed with 'the fine house' of 'Mr Comptroller' in Lime Street.[17] Both streets run through very wealthy parishes, Lime Street through St Dionis Backchurch and St Andrew Undershaft, and Milk Street through St Mary Magdalen and St Lawrence Jewry, which suggests that a street might take its character from the parish in which it is situated. Hence, streets near the centre of the City, where wealthy parishes were, have large dwellings, and those by the river or outside the Walls near Cripplegate, where poorer parishes were, tend to have small dwellings.

The influence of parish on street becomes clearer when a long street is followed through different parishes. Fleet Street, for example, is lined by dwellings with an average 7.5 hearths in the wealthy parish of St Dunstan in the West, but when it enters the poor parish of St Bride the average falls to 5.6. In only one street, Cheapside, does the size of the dwellings seem to be independent of encompassing parishes; its dwellings were larger in the poorer parish of St Vedast than in wealthier St Michael Querne, for example. Cheapside was such a developed trading street that it perhaps generated its own economic and social character, irrespective of the nature of the parishes through which it passed (though none of these, it must be admitted, was really poor). It was clearly an exceptional street, a fact reflected in contemporary encomia. Pepys referred to 'the great uniform pile of buildings in the middle of Cheapside'. And Evelyn, touring the City on 7 September after the Fire, lamented the destruction of buildings along and near Cheapside: 'the exquisitely wrought Mercers Chapell, the Sumptuous Exchange, the august fabricque of Christ church, all the rest of the Companies Halls, sumptuous buildings, Arches, Enteries, all in dust'.[18]

Not every Londoner could live in a street, however. Within the City perhaps a third of the inhabitants could boast such an address; about a third more lived along lanes; and the remaining third could be found in yards (or courts) and alleys. These four kinds of public way distinguished by the hearth taxes suggest distinct physical characteristics: a street was a major thoroughfare, wide and perhaps paved; a lane a narrow thoroughfare; a yard or court an enclosed space entered from a turning off the street or lane; and an alley a very narrow way between buildings. The four names suggest a progressive decline in space and physical graciousness, and this impression is reinforced by a survey of the dwellings and inhabitants of each. Table 25 (a), which analyses twenty City parishes for which the 1666 hearth tax gives the most detailed information, shows how much larger street dwellings were than those elsewhere, having on average 5.9 hearths compared with 4.5 in lanes, 4.1 in yards and 3.7 in alleys. Once one leaves the street the proportion of large dwellings falls away and that of small homes grows. The scale and character of houses and homes must have dramatically altered the moment one turned off a street into a side yard or alley. Within a few yards space and light gave way to confinement and gloom, a transition corroborated by even a cursory study of the distribution of buildings on Ogilby and Morgan's *Map of London* of 1676. It was a pattern that even the Great Fire and rebuilding did not eradicate.

Further light on the character of streets, lanes, yards and alleys is provided by hearth tax information on their inhabitants. Working on the assumption that a high incidence of titled residents and of institutions are positive signs of the desirability of a location, and that the existence of stoves or industrial hearths are a sign of industrial vitality, we can conclude from Table 25 (b) that the street enjoyed a unique combination of status and vitality; the lane shares only the industrial vitality; yards tend to share only social status. The propensity of titled people to live in yards seems odd, given the small dwellings which commonly surrounded them. Some yards were socially exclusive enclaves. Half Moon Court in St Botolph Aldersgate, for example, had six gentlemen and the bishop of London among its thirty-four residents, and the average size of their dwellings reached 7.8 hearths. At the other end of the scale, White Horse Court in St Mary Woolnoth, a haunt of porters and joiners, had no titled residents, and an average dwelling size of only 1.7 hearths. If, turning the coin, we look for signs of lack of status and economic vitality, the incidence of empty houses, the proportion of poor and widows, we find these most pronounced in yards and alleys, less obvious along lanes, and least noticeable in streets.

If it is difficult to put lanes, yards and alleys in a convincing pecking

Table 25. Dwellings in street, lane, yard and alley (20 City parishes)[a]

(a) *Size of dwellings*

	Number of dwellings	Mean hearths per dwelling	% small 1–3 hearths	% medium 4–6 hearths	% large 7+ hearths
Streets	791	5.90	19.8	47.5	32.7
Lanes	753	4.54	40.1	41.1	18.8
Yards	505	4.07	52.1	32.0	15.9
Alleys	368	3.73	58.9	30.7	10.4
20 parishes	2579[b]	4.77	38.7	39.9	20.9

(b) *Other characteristics of dwellings*

	% with titled resident	% used as institution	%with industrial hearth(s)	% empty	% with widow resident	% with poor resident
Streets	3.2	1.1	1.5	7.2	5.4	0.0
Lanes	0.4	0.4	1.7	9.4	10.2	0.5
Yards	3.4	0.8	0.6	13.1	11.5	2.6
Alleys	1.9	0.0	0.8	10.1	13.6	2.4
20 parishes	2.2	0.6	1.2	9.5	9.2	1.0

Sources: As in note 3.

Notes:

(a) 20 parishes (numbered to correspond with Fig. 3): Allhallows Honey Lane (4), Allhallows Steyning (8), Antholin (18), Benet Sherehog (24), Botolph Aldersgate (101), Katherine Coleman (42), Gabriel Fenchurch (33), John the Baptist (39), Magnus Fish Street (48), Margaret New Fish Street (51), Martin (16), Martin Ironmonger Lane (53), Martin-le-Grand (47), Mary Bothaw (61), Mary Bow (62), Mary Woolnoth (71), Michael Royal (78), Pancras (88), Stephen Walbrook (94), Swithen (95).

(b) Total includes 162 dwellings not listed under street or other heading.

order as a result of this analysis, there can be no doubt that the street was the place to be. On the street there was more air and light, more room, and, a crucial advantage, the world and its purse passed by. If a man was in business selling a commodity or service, street frontage was almost a necessity. The extent to which this was true can be gauged by analysing where different kinds of trader and craftsman chose to live. Table 26 sets out ten groups of occupations: three groups selling commodities or services, five craft groups making, and perhaps selling, commodities, and two semi-skilled groups who customarily worked away from their homes. More will be said shortly about the nature of these groups. For now, the clustering of these groups in streets, lanes, yards and alleys is

Table 26. Distribution of occupation groups in streets, lanes, yards and alleys (20 parishes)

| | Location quotients of | | | | | | | | | |
| | Selling groups | | | Craftsmen | | | | | Semi-skilled | |
	1 Dealers	2 Victuallers	3 Professions	1 Wood	2 Metal	3 Textiles	4 Leather	5 Miscellaneous	1 Builders	2 Carriers
Streets	1.5	1.5	1.5	0.8	0.9	0.8	0.6	0.8	0.5	0.4
Lanes	0.9	0.9	1.0	1.5	1.5	0.9	0.3	0.9	0.9	1.0
Yards	0.6	0.5	0.5	0.9	0.9	1.3	0.9	1.2	1.3	1.7
Alleys	0.6	0.9	0.4	0.4	0.4	1.2	1.5	1.3	1.9	1.4

Sources: see note 3.

indicated by location quotients (any figure above 1.0 showing a concentration of the group).

The advantage of street frontage for all three selling groups emerges very clearly indeed, for they congregate along streets, are much more reluctant to live in lanes, and shy away from yards and alleys. In contrast, craftsmen are not well represented on streets. Wood and metal craftsmen cluster along lanes; textile and leather workers tend to live in yards and alleys. This distinction is an interesting one which might reflect the nature of the different crafts at this time. Wood and metal craftsmen were commonly their own masters, making and selling a commodity. They would need to have access, via the open shutter at the front of their dwelling, to potential buyers. Ideally they would seek street frontage, but if high rents denied them this then a lane would afford a greater concourse of people than a yard or alley. In contrast, the textile and leather industries were highly developed, with various stages of manufacture, and entrepreneurs organizing the sale of the final product. A significant number of textile and leather workers were craftsmen engaged in the manufacturing process but not in selling the product to the public. They might sell to the next craftsman in the process of cloth or leather manufacture, or simply be employed by a textile or leather entrepreneur.[19] In either case direct access to the public would be unnecessary, and a workshop hidden away in a yard or alley would be no disadvantage. Finally, our semi-skilled groups, builders and carriers, are concentrated only in yards and alleys. These workers were exceptional in working away from their homes, the location of which had no commercial significance. Once again, to be hidden away in yards and alleys where the public did not penetrate would not have mattered.

I have interpreted Table 26 in terms of commercial interest dictating where occupation groups lived. An even more crucial determinant of location, and one which the hearth tax gives no guide to, is rent. If we assume that rents were high for street dwellings, and lower in yards and alleys, this would help explain why the wealthier selling groups monopolized the street, and the poorer craftsmen and semi-skilled workers had to make do with lanes, yards and alleys. Choice of residence was probably dictated by considerations of commercial advantage and rent, the two inextricably intertwined.

IV

The link between wealth and occupation, and which of these most influenced location, are the final problems which can be approached by using hearth tax evidence. In only twenty parishes does the hearth tax mention the occupation of householders, and all of these are the City itself, twelve in the very centre clustering around St Mary-le-Bow and St Stephen Walbrook, three inside Aldgate, three around Aldersgate, and two at the north end of London Bridge.[20] In consequence, this analysis can probe only the economic and social character of the central area of London.

Some 216 distinct occupations are listed in the hearth tax in these parishes in 1666. They are quite clearly real occupations rather than gild affiliations, containing many descriptions, such as merchant, which were not gild names. It is assumed that a person's stated occupation defines his economic role, but in fact it was common for individuals to pursue more than one avocation, and this analysis might be rather too cut and dried to reflect the reality of work in Restoration London. However, there is no easy way of solving this problem.[21] To make use of the information occupations have been divided into ten groups which seek to identify the type of work done: dealers, victuallers and professions are three groups in the business of primary selling of commodities or services. Craftsmen divide into five groups by the material they work on, wood, metal, textiles, leather and miscellaneous (often those working with more than one material). All are producers of commodities, and many would sell their product as well. Finally, two groups who can perhaps be categorized as semi-skilled and customarily travelled to work, builders and carriers, complete the list.[22]

Table 27 sets out all the significant occupations (occurring ten or more times) arranged in their groups. It is very clear that the selling groups live in the largest dwellings, craftsmen in much smaller homes, and semi-skilled workers in the smallest of all. The pattern fits in neatly with the general impression that people in trade or with some professional skill were the wealthiest groups in pre-industrial urban society; that skilled craftsmen were considerably less prosperous; and that semi-skilled or unskilled workers were poorer still. Within the general pattern interesting points stand out. Variation in dwelling size, and presumably wealth, is much more noticeable among the selling occupations than among the craft or semi-skilled groups: merchants and drapers stand above other members of their group, vintners dramatically above theirs, and doctors among the professions. Of the craft occupations only silkmen stand out as an aristocracy among the textile workers, and upholsterers among the miscellaneous group. Otherwise, craftsmen and semi-skilled workers were apparently homogeneous groups where wealth was concerned. Hazardous though comparisons between towns based on hearth tax evidence are, it seems

Table 27. Occupations and dwelling size in London in 1666 (20 parishes)

	Number in group	Mean hearths per dwelling		Number in group	Mean hearths per dwelling
Selling groups:			**Craftsmen:**		
1. Dealers:			**1. Wood:**		
Bookseller	25	4.5	Cooper	43	4.6
Broker	18	4.6	Joiner	26	3.8
Chandler	24	4.6			
Draper	21	6.8	Total	94	4.3
Grocer	18	5.4			
Haberdasher	43	5.3	**2. Metal:**		
Merchant	125	8.0			
Salesman	11	3.6	Goldsmith	79	4.3
Skinner	23	5.3	Pewterer	13	4.8
			Smith	22	3.4
Total[a]	381	6.4	Wiredrawer	19	4.8
2. Victuallers:			Total	194	4.2
Alehousekeeper	44	5.4			
Baker	18	5.4	**3. Textiles:**		
Cheesemonger	10	4.4			
Confectioner	11	5.4	Clothworker	22	4.5
Cook	18	5.8	Hosier	17	4.8
Fishmonger	23	3.9	Hot presser	18	4.7
Tobacconist	26	4.8	Milliner	15	4.7
Victualler	71	5.2	Sempster	12	4.2
Vintner	22	11.9	Silkman	48	5.1
			Tailor	113	3.7
Total	306	5.7	Total	286	4.2
3. Professions:			**4. Leather:**		
Apothecary	25	5.9	Shoemaker	58	3.2
Barber	24	3.8			
Doctor	12	8.3	Total	80	3.2
Druggist	27	6.4			
Rector	20	6.6	**5. Miscellaneous:**		
Scrivener	21	5.5			
			Jeweller	12	3.6
Total	176	5.7	Upholsterer	18	5.3
			Total	95	4.6

214

Semi-skilled:

1. Builders:			2. Carriers:		
Bricklayer	21	3.6	Porter	34	2.3
Carpenter	19	3.2	Total	64	3.2
Glazier	15	3.5			
Plasterer	18	3.9			
Total	89	3.5			

Sources: As in note 3.
Note:
(a) Totals include all those in a group. Individual occupations listed only
with 10 or more of that occupation.

that all our London occupation groups enjoyed larger dwellings than
their counterparts in at least one major provincial town. In Newcastle
dealers averaged 5.0 hearths per dwelling, in London 6.4; the figures for
victuallers were 2.9 and 5.7 respectively; craftsmen ranged from 1.5 to
2.6 in Newcastle against 3.2 to 4.3 in London; and builders averaged 1.8
against 3.5.[23]

Did occupation influence location? J. E. Vance has suggested that
'pre-capitalist' London was characterized by a spatial arrangement
where like occupations clustered together in neighbourhoods. All the
shoemakers, for example, would tend to congregate in one parish
around their gild hall. He goes on to argue that this system disintegrated
in the seventeenth century as the most economically aggressive
members of the community, the 'capitalists', began to use property for
profit. Initially they sub-let the upper floors of their houses to other
workers, while they plied their trade from the ground floor. Later they
let the whole house and moved out of the City to be with others in a
property owners' suburban estate, such as Covent Garden. Such
exploitation of City property, which involved steadily increasing rents,
forced poorer workers out too, into less salubrious suburbs, such as
Stepney and Southwark. Under the pressure of capitalist exploitation
the system of occupational zoning was thus broken up, to be replaced by
a system of wealth zoning; property owners pursuing a variety of
occupations gathered in wealthy suburbs, prosperous traders and
craftsmen of all kinds remained in the City centre, and poorer craftsmen
and workers of all kinds moved out into the poorer suburbs. 'Social
modernization' was taking place as people chose their houses in the city,
not to be close to fellow traders or craftsmen, but to be among others of
similar wealth. Location, which in the medieval city had been based on
occupation, was now becoming a function of wealth.[24]

We can agree with Vance's initial proposition that medieval London conformed to the pattern of occupational clustering. FitzStephen, in his description of London in the reign of Henry II, wrote: 'The artizans of the several crafts, the vendors of the various commodities, and the labourers of every kind, have each their separate station'. And although these stations had changed by the time that John Stow wrote, in 1598, the tradition had not: 'Men of trades and sellers of wares in this city have oftentimes since changed their places, as they have found their best advantage. For whereas mercers and haberdashers used to keep their shops in West Cheape, of later time they held them on London Bridge'. And he goes on: the goldsmiths have moved to West Cheap, the drapers to Candlewick Street and Watling Street, the skinners to Budge Row and Walbrook, and so on. Altogether he lists twenty-three occupations as peculiar to different parishes or streets, and in only five of these does he suggest that cohesion was being lost, as members dispersed: the mercers and haberdashers on London Bridge 'partly yet remain'; pepperers and grocers were becoming dispersed; pastelars were 'dispersed into divers parts'; and bowyers, 'almost worn out', were in 'divers places'.[25]

The hearth tax demonstrates that the tradition of occupational clustering was still very much alive in 1666. Table 28 sets out the location quotients of our ten occupation groups in twenty parishes. The parishes run from the wealthiest at the top of the table, to the poorest at the bottom (measured by mean hearths per dwelling). And the groups which cluster (with a location quotient of 1.3 or more) are underlined to make them emerge more clearly. Men of similar occupations clearly still found it advantageous to live close together. On the whole the selling groups cluster in wealthy and middling parishes, the craft and semi-skilled groups in middling and poor parishes. The few exceptions to this rule can in some cases be explained. The propensity of victuallers to cluster in the poorer parishes of St Magnus Fish Street, St Margaret New Fish Street and St Michael Royal, all close to the river, must stem from the nature of their trade. Their source of supply and much of their market lay on the Thames-side. The textile workers who figure so prominently in the wealthy parish of Allhallows Honey Lane were all silkweavers, a group which was notably wealthier than other textile workers (see Table 27). To some extent occupation clustering is part and parcel of wealth zoning. Parishes with high concentrations of wealthy selling groups are wealthy parishes, and vice versa.

More interesting conclusions flow from the intensity with which groups cluster. Of the selling groups only professions seem to concentrate intensely. In St Stephen Walbrook, for example, there are

Table 28. Concentration of occupation groups in 20 parishes in 1666 (location quotients)

Parish (No. on Fig. 3)	Mean hearths per dwelling	Selling groups			Craftsmen					Semi-skilled	
		1 Dealers	2 Victs.	3 Profs.	1 Wood	2 Metal	3 Textiles	4 Leather	5 Misc.	1 Builders	2 Carriers
Stephen Walbrook (94)	6.5	2.3	0.5	3.4	0.7	–	0.1	–	–	–	–
Mary Bothaw (61)	5.9	1.7	0.4	2.0	0.8	0.2	1.0	0.5	0.4	0.4	0.6
Antholin (18)	5.8	1.1	0.8	1.6	0.5	0.3	1.2	1.0	1.1	1.1	0.4
Allhallows Honey Lane (4)	5.7	1.1	1.2	0.8	–	–	3.1	–	–	–	–
Gabriel Fenchurch (33)	5.6	1.3	0.7	0.6	1.2	0.6	0.8	0.7	–	1.0	4.9
Pancras (88)	5.5	1.8	1.5	0.8	0.5	–	0.8	0.6	–	1.0	0.7
Martin Ironmonger L. (53)	5.5	1.5	0.7	2.6	1.6	0.5	0.9	–	–	1.1	–
Mary Woolnoth (71)	5.5	1.0	0.9	1.5	0.8	2.6	0.5	0.3	–	0.6	1.1
Mary Bow (62)	5.3	1.8	0.8	1.1	0.5	–	1.4	–	0.5	0.6	0.8
Swithen (95)	5.2	1.3	0.8	0.7	1.7	0.5	1.4	0.3	0.7	1.4	0.6
Botolph Aldersgate (101)	5.1	1.0	1.0	1.0	0.4	1.0	0.7	1.1	2.0	1.5	1.1
Benet Sherehog (24)	5.1	1.3	1.4	3.2	1.5	0.7	0.2	–	–	–	–
John the Baptist (39)	4.7	0.7	1.1	0.7	1.7	0.7	1.7	0.3	1.2	1.6	0.4
Magnus Fish St. (48)	4.6	1.3	2.0	0.6	0.4	0.5	1.2	0.7	0.4	0.4	0.6
Allhallows Steyning (8)	4.5	0.7	0.9	0.7	2.3	–	1.5	1.1	0.2	1.4	1.7
Martin (16)	4.4	0.5	0.8	0.7	0.5	3.7	0.2	–	1.7	1.1	–
Margaret New Fish St. (51)	4.4	0.6	1.5	1.2	1.9	0.9	0.5	0.6	0.3	1.3	2.2
Katherine Coleman (42)	4.2	0.7	1.1	0.8	2.6	0.5	1.1	0.9	0.4	1.0	3.0
Michael Royal (78)	3.6	0.8	1.5	0.3	3.2	0.3	1.2	–	–	1.7	0.8
Martin-le-Grand (47)	3.4	0.3	1.0	0.2	0.3	0.5	2.1	4.4	2.3	0.3	0.4

Sources: See note 3.

217

three-and-a-half times more professionals than one would expect, given their number in the twenty parishes as a whole. Similar intense concentration is found among all five craft groups in different parishes, and among carriers. It seems that craftsmen, in particular, found it economically useful, or socially convenient, to live with their own kind. Such concentration seems particularly marked among metal workers and leather workers whose crafts could cause industrial pollution, and who might therefore be even more inclined to cluster in a locality than other craftsmen. Metal workers are concentrated in only two parishes, St Mary Woolnoth and St Martin; leather workers are heavily represented in only one, St Martin-le-Grand. It is interesting that really obnoxious industrial processes, such as tanning or alum making, do not appear in these City parishes at all and were relegated to the suburbs.

What Table 28 does not show is how common it was for members of a single occupation to live as neighbours. The cluster of professionals in St Stephen Walbrook and St Benet Sherehog, contiguous parishes, were all druggists and apothecaries, for example. Stow had noted that 'this whole street called Bucklesbury on both the sides throughout is possessed of grocers and apothecaries'.[26] All but one of the wood craftsmen in St Michael Royal were coopers, perhaps serving the Thames-side brewers; of the 85 metal craftsmen in St Martin's, 51 were goldsmiths clustering around Goldsmith's Hall; all the textile workers in Allhallows Honey Lane were silkweavers; the leather workers in St Martin-le-Grand were all shoemakers. We find Pepys buying boots there in 1661.[27] And the heavy concentration of carriers in St Gabriel Fenchurch consisted of packers and porters. These are only the most obvious examples. Among dealers we find groups of merchants, skinners and haberdashers in St Stephen Walbrook and St Mary Bothaw, contiguous parishes; fishmongers and salters form the majority of the victuallers in St Magnus Fish Street, at the north end of London Bridge by Fishmongers' Hall, where Stow had noted 'fishmongers and fair taverns on Fish Street Hill'; and, among the miscellaneous craftsmen, printers and binders lived and worked together in St Botolph Aldersgate. At the beginning of the century Stow had noted there: 'one great house, commonly called Northumberland House ... is now a printing house'.[28] Such examples could be multiplied, but the general picture is clear enough. Merchant lived alongside merchant, goldsmith with goldsmith, shoemaker by shoemaker. The medieval tradition of occupation-based neighbourhoods was still strong.

Although occupational clustering is evident, it would be too much to claim that such concentration was an invariable rule. Most parishes contained a mixture of occupations, even though one or two groups were over-represented. Neighbourhoods were not exclusive to a group, and it may be that the process of occupations dispersing, which Stow noted in 1598, was continuing in the seventeenth century. Vance would claim that this process was symptomatic of the evolution of the City from its 'pre-capitalist' to its 'capitalist' form. Subjected to the stresses of an economic system stressing profit, and a social ethic emphasizing individualism, urban society was losing its cohesion as individuals sought to better themselves. In particular, the most wealthy City dwellers sought residence among people of similar wealth, an ambition which led the prosperous to leave their occupational ghettoes in favour of the uniform respectability of a 'better class' neighbourhood.[29]

It is difficult to test this hypothesis when analysing a source at one date. Had we an equivalent to the hearth tax in, say, 1600, we could much more fruitfully study the evolution of the social geography of London. It is, however, possible to approach the problem by establishing the level of wealth of each occupation group in each parish in 1666.[30] If it can be shown that a range of wealthy people from different occupation groups congregated in the more prosperous parishes we might conclude that wealth was as or more important than occupation in determining one's neighbourhood by that date. Table 29 shows exactly such a pattern. If we distinguish wealthy groups in each parish (say, those living in dwellings 20 per cent above average for the group, underlined in the table) we find that the wealthy members of almost all occupation groups tend to monopolize the prosperous parishes. Apart from dealers, the most wealthy of whom perversely seem to opt for poorer parishes, and leather craftsmen, who have wealthy representatives in both prosperous and poor parishes, the tendency for the prosperous to stick together seems overwhelming. By the same token, the poorer brethren from all occupation groups are left together in the poorer parishes.

I do not think that this contrast goes very far towards proving Vance's hypothesis about social modernization. While it is possible to argue that such a pattern could be the result of a seventeenth-century movement of the most aggressive and successful members of each occupations to wealthy parishes, analysis of the hearth tax gives no clue to whether this segregation by wealth was in fact new. The wealthier members of society may have always congregated in the most prosperous parishes, and the pattern in 1666 may have been a highly traditional one. Segregation may well have been encouraged by different levels of rent, which earlier was suggested as a determinant of who lived on the street, and in the yard or alley. High rents may have allowed only

Table 29. Average dwelling size of occupation groups in 20 parishes in 1666 (mean hearths per dwelling)

Parish (No. on Fig. 3)	Mean hearths per dwelling	Selling groups			Craftsmen					Semi-skilled	
		1 Dealers	2 Victs.	3 Profs.	1 Wood	2 Metal	3 Textiles	4 Leather	5 Misc.	1 Builders	2 Carriers
Stephen Walbrook (94)	6.5	6.6	9.0	6.6	4.0	—	3.0	—	—	—	—
Mary Bothaw (61)	5.9	8.0	7.0	6.2	6.0	5.0	4.6	4.0	3.0	4.0	3.0
Antholin (18)	5.8	7.0	7.2	6.4	6.5	5.0	4.7	2.7	5.5	4.5	1.0
Allhallows Honey Lane (4)	5.7	7.3	7.6	3.5	—	—	5.8	—	—	—	—
Gabriel Fenchurch (33)	5.6	7.3	4.9	5.8	7.3	5.8	5.5	2.5	—	3.0	5.4
Pancras (88)	5.5	6.9	5.8	4.7	4.0	—	5.2	4.0	—	3.5	2.0
Martin Ironmonger L. (53)	5.5	6.4	5.0	6.3	3.7	2.5	4.4	—	—	3.5	—
Mary Woolnoth (71)	5.5	5.3	9.2	6.1	3.3	5.0	4.3	3.0	—	4.5	2.0
Mary Bow (62)	5.3	5.5	7.3	5.5	5.5	—	4.6	—	6.0	2.0	3.5
Swithen (95)	5.2	6.5	5.3	5.3	3.9	5.2	5.0	4.0	5.0	—	3.5
Botolph Aldersgate (101)	5.1	5.5	5.5	6.4	5.3	4.5	3.7	3.6	5.7	—	2.4
Benet Sherehog (24)	5.1	6.7	6.2	4.8	4.0	2.5	3.0	—	—	—	—
John the Baptist (39)	4.7	5.6	6.0	5.8	4.0	4.8	4.3	5.0	3.8	2.7	3.0
Magnus Fish St. (48)	4.6	5.1	5.6	5.3	3.5	3.0	4.4	3.7	3.0	3.5	2.0
Allhallows Steyning (8)	4.5	7.7	5.1	4.7	4.1	4.2	3.7	3.8	3.0	—	3.5
Martin (16)	4.4	6.7	5.6	5.5	3.5	3.8	3.4	4.1	3.4	3.4	—
Margaret New Fish St. (51)	4.4	10.0	5.0	5.1	3.9	3.8	4.0	3.0	5.0	—	1.8
Katherine Coleman (42)	4.2	7.7	4.3	4.4	4.0	4.7	3.3	3.0	4.5	—	3.4
Michael Royal (78)	3.6	6.3	6.0	4.0	4.3	5.0	5.1	—	—	2.7	2.0
Martin-le-Grand (47)	3.4	4.1	4.4	1.7	3.0	3.6	3.5	2.7	3.6	2.0	3.5
20 parishes		6.4	5.7	5.7	4.3	4.2	4.2	3.2	4.6	3.5	3.2

Sources: See note 3.

the economically most active and successful into parishes such as St Stephen Walbrook and St Mary Bothaw, encouraging both a single wealthy occupation group to congregate there, and the infiltration of the wealthier members of less prosperous craft and semi-skilled groups. But differential rents were surely not a new development of the seventeenth century. Location must have been affected by rent from medieval times.[31]

If we cannot be sure of a seventeenth-century shift from location based on occupation to one based on wealth, it would be idle to pursue Vance's thesis further in speculating on whether such a change was the result of a conscious social aspiration of the wealthy to seek parishes where they could mix only with their own kind. To do this would require a source which revealed motivation, an insight which a mere fiscal list cannot give. Even if we could extend our scope to take in the suburbs, enabling us to discern an even more pronounced pattern of social segregation across the occupational spectrum, we could still not penetrate the process or the aspirations which created the pattern. But the fact that our focus is limited only to the City in this enquiry clearly hampers an attempt to probe a thesis which seeks to explain transition in an entire city, centre and suburbs. It is clear that some seventeenth-century suburbs did segregate society. The parish of Covent Garden established in 1635 allowed the rich to get away from the poor. It was 'well inhabited by a mixture of nobility, gentry and wealthy tradesmen ... scarce admitting of any poor, not being pestered with mean courts and alleys'.[32]

Given the limitations of hearth tax evidence it would be wise to proffer cautious conclusions. With regard to urban models, Sjoberg's concentric pattern of wealth seems to have some validity, but Vance's idea of an evolution from occupation-zoning to wealth-zoning as part of a process of social modernization is not provable. Moving away from the straitjackets these impose, it can be suggested that both occupation and wealth were strong determinants of location in 1666, both at street and parish level. If, among the welter of computerized data which attends systematic analysis of the hearth tax, an impression can be allowed to intrude, it would be of London as having a traditional rather than a modern urban society. As the eye runs down the long columns of tax assessments, seeing haberdashers living side-by-side with porters, lawyers beside pensioners, goldsmiths beside widows, all living in a random mix of large and small dwellings, the impression is gained of an urban scene where occupations and rich and poor are thoroughly jumbled. Evolution there no doubt was, but it had affected the City within the Walls to a limited extent. This central part of Restoration

London shows little evidence of the rigid class segregation so common in the modern city.

NOTES AND REFERENCES

1. John Stow, *A Survey of London* (Everyman edn, London 1956), pp. 262, 376. The questions addressed by this paper owe much to J. Langton, 'Residential patterns in pre-industrial cities: some case studies from seventeenth-century Britain', *Transactions of the Institute of British Geographers (TIBG)*, 65 (1975). I wish to thank Paul Laxton and Nicholas Alldridge for commenting on an earlier draft of this paper.
2. G. Sjoberg, *The Preindustrial City* (New York 1960), pp. 97–100, 118–23.
3. Public Record Office (PRO): E 179/252/27 (1662 tax, City); E 179/252/32 (1666 tax, City); E 179/188/506 and E 179/258/4 (1664 tax, south of Thames). Greater London Record Office (GLRO) (Middlesex): MR/TH 2; 4; 7 (1664 tax East and West Ends, and Westminster).
4. C. A. F. Meekings, *The Hearth Tax 1662–1689: Exhibition of Records* (PRO, 1962), p. l. Throughout this paper the domestic accommodation of a household is referred to as a 'dwelling', a unit not necessarily coincident with a house. Sub-division of houses was more common in some areas than others, especially in the parishes around the walls and the western suburbs: P. E. Jones and A. V. Judges, 'London population in the late-seventeenth century', *Economic History Review (EcHR)*, 6 (1935–6), p. 53; M. J. Power, 'East and west in early-modern London', in *Wealth and Power in Tudor England: Essays presented to S. T. Bindoff* (London 1978), E. W. Ives, R. J. Knecht and J. J. Scarisbrick (eds), p. 170.
5. *Statutes of the Realm*, 14 Charles II *c.* 10; 16 Charles II *c.* 3.
6. Meekings, pp. 3–5.
7. Guildhall Library: MS 9705; 525/1; Add. MS 243; MS 1175/1.
8. Stow, pp. 156, 130; *The Diary of Samuel Pepys*, R. Latham and W. Matthews (eds) (London, 1970–83), v, p. 356.
9. Pepys, vi, p. 34; Stow, pp. 309, 204.
10. The evidence of parliamentary surveys; Power, 'East and west in early-modern London', p. 170.
11. Stow, pp. 70, 393–401.
12. Pepys, vii, p. 270; *The Diary of John Evelyn*, E. S. de Beer (ed.) (1 volume edn Oxford 1959), p. 497; Stow, under Dowgate, Vintry, Queenhithe, Bishopsgate and Aldgate, *passim*.
13. R. W. Herlan, 'Social articulation and the configuration of parochial poverty in London on the eve of the Restoration', *Guildhall Studies in London History*, 2 (1976), p. 53.
14. T. C. Dale, *The Inhabitants of London in 1638* (1931), prints the tithe rental; R. Finlay, *Population and Metropolis* (1981), pp. 77–81; E. Jones, 'London in the early-seventeenth century: an ecological approach', *London Journal*, 6 (1980), pp. 123–7.
15. D. V. Glass, *London Inhabitants Within the Walls*, London Record Society, 2 (1966), p. xxiii; Jones and Judges, op. cit. pp. 45–63.

16. Pepys, vii, p. 274.
17. Pepys, i, p. 290.
18. Pepys, v, pp. 247–8; Evelyn, p. 498; see also Pepys at shops in Cheapside: i, p. 277; iv, pp. 68, 332.
19. G. Unwin, *Industrial Organization in the Sixteenth and Seventeenth Centuries* (Oxford 1904), pp. 19–24, 26–30, 95–6.
20. See list of parishes at bottom of Table 25.
21. I am grateful to Penelope Corfield for calling my attention to this problem.
22. In sorting occupations into generic groups I have been guided by A. J. and R. H. Tawney, 'An occupational census of the seventeenth century', *EcHR*, 5 (1934); W. G. Hoskins, 'An Elizabethan provincial town: Leicester', *Provincial England* (London 1965); G. Unwin, *The Gilds and Companies of London* (London 1908); J. Langton, 'Late-medieval Gloucester', *TIBG* n.s., 2 (1977), and 'Residential patterns in pre-industrial cities', *TIBG* 65 (1975); J. Patten, 'Urban occupations in pre-industrial England', *TIBG* n.s., 2 (1977).
23. Langton, 'Residential patterns,' p. 14.
24. J. E. Vance, 'Land assignment in pre-capitalist, capitalist and post-capitalist cities', *Economic Geography*, 47 (1971), pp. 101–20.
25. Stow, pp. 504, 74–5.
26. Stow, p. 233.
27. Pepys, ii, p. 132.
28. Stow, pp. 190, 276.
29. Vance, pp. 109–10.
30. Following the example of Langton in his study of Newcastle: 'Residential patterns', pp. 19–20.
31. Langton found that in fifteenth-century Gloucester rents were low near gates and tended to rise towards the business centre: 'Late-medieval Gloucester', p. 267.
32. J. Stow, *Survey of London*, J. Strype (ed.), (1754 edn), vi, p. 661. The character of suburban neighbourhoods is more closely examined in Power, 'East and west in early-modern London'.

CHAPTER EIGHT
Capital and kingdom: migration to later Stuart London

M. J. Kitch

I

In 1551 the Venetian ambassador accurately characterized both the extent of migration to London and the different motives of migrants when he observed to his masters that a great multitude of men and women flocked to London from all parts of England in pursuit of wealth, honour and matrimony.[1] He omitted the many continental immigrants – some 5,650 by 1583.[2] In the next century analysis of London's demography became increasingly sophisticated as first John Graunt, then Sir William Petty and finally Gregory King sought to explain and predict the dynamics of London's rapidly swelling population.[3] Graunt correctly contended 'that London is supplied with people from out of the country, whereby not only to repair the overplus difference of burials ... but likewise to increase its inhabitants.'[4] Recent studies of London's population endorse the existence of this excess of burials over baptisms (an excess which varied considerably between rich and poor parishes) and the need for an inflow of migrants to make up this shortfall and permit the population to expand.[5] Graunt and King attempted to calculate the requisite number of migrants. King also took into account out-migration to the colonies, although not to places in Great Britain. His most detailed calculation postulated the need for a gross total of 12,500 to 15,500 in-migrants each year, compared with Wrigley's modern estimate of c. 8,000 a year net.[6] King, however, exaggerated the rate at which London was increasing.

By the late seventeenth century the largest groups of male London migrants whose migration pattern can be examined are apprentices and freemen – almost all of whom were former apprentices. Consequently, this study is based on apprenticeship and freedom records. The deposition books of the Commissary and Consistory Courts of the Diocese of London also contain relevant material, but as most of the male deponents were freemen they overlap with apprenticeship and freedom records. Unlike freedom records, however, they contain information about female migrants.

In pre-industrial and modern societies migration is largely age-specific: most migrants are young adults. Since apprentices were usually bound in their mid, or late teens, in respect of age at least they were typical migrants. Too little is known about the characteristics of other types of migrants to London to know whether apprentices constituted a true sample, although a century earlier apprentices, servants and vagrants shared much the same geographical background. The recent hypothesis that in later Stuart England indentured servants who travelled to the New World via London were more representative is open to question: we know little about the geographical origins of migrants apart from apprentices, lawyers (a small and socially restricted profession) and indentured servants.[7] The last were clearly, at least in respect of their ultimate destination, a special group and fewer in number than apprentices. The fact that indentured servants demonstrated a slightly different migration pattern is not proof that this was more representative. The quest for the 'typical' migrant in such a large community composed of men and women from very different levels of society, who practised many different trades and occupations, is meaningless. It will, however, be seen that the majority of apprentices came from the lower to upper middling section of Stuart society and certainly in this respect they would have differed from vagrants and poor migrants and from some (but by no means all) servants. Quite apart from the problem of to what extent they were generally representative, apprentices were an important group in themselves: numerous and comprising a large proportion of the total number of migrants. From their ranks would come the next generation of London merchants, shopkeepers and skilled artisans. Apprenticeship remained not only the legal, but also the usual mode of entry to most male trades. Patten's comment that 'freemen and apprentice registers are not a bad surrogate for general patterns of immigration of one stratum of society, the more economically effective part of it'[8] is as valid for London as for provincial towns. The never-ending expansion of London meant that the area within the jurisdiction of the City became only a small part of the whole, but apprentices were bound throughout the capital, not only in the City proper and not only to freemen, many of whom lived outside the City. It has been argued that the proportion of apprentices in the London population fell from 13.6–17.0 per cent in 1600 to 4.0–4.8 per cent in 1700. Since the total population was increasing, the fall in the actual number of apprentices was less precipitate, from 32,000–40,000 in 1600 to 27,200–32,640 in 1700. The annual number of bindings dropped from 4,000–5,000 to 3,400–4,080. This estimate of the total number of apprentices in 1700 seems high in view of the fact that at this time most of them served only the legal minimum term of seven years and the drop-out rate was in the order of 50 per cent. In 1690, 1,590 males were freed, which would imply that approximately 2,450 youths had been apprenticed in 1682–3 – a third of Wrigley's net estimate of the annual number of migrants. Not all bindings to London freemen were, however, registered at the Guildhall (or even at the appropriate company hall), as the capital's laws required. Youths apprenticed to masters who were not freemen were not subject to these regulations and the numbers in this category increased, due both to the inability of the City to enforce its regulations within its jurisdiction and to the expansion of areas outside its authority.[9] Glass estimated from a sample of the 1692 Poll Tax data for 40 parishes that apprentices comprised 4.3 per cent of London's population, broadly in line with the figures given by Finlay.[10] Former apprentices (whether freemen or non-freemen) would have been far more numerous.

For the later seventeenth and early eighteenth centuries crude data exist for the population of England and Wales, for individual counties and for London itself. The principal sources employed here are the manuscript lists of freedoms for 1668 and 1683–4 (11 months only), the 1690 freedoms tabulated by Glass, and data relating to apprentices bound in 1711–13 derived from the first two years of the Stamp Duty records kept as a result of 8 Anne *c*.5. This Act required that a duty be levied on all apprenticeships for which a premium was paid. This source, unlike ordinary apprenticeship records, includes bindings to men who were not freemen. Premiums were customary but not universal. Most of them were small – three decades later they were generally in the range £5–10.[11] Apprenticeships legally omitted under the statute would presumably have involved youths from the poorest backgrounds, thus creating a biased sample in respect of the social background of apprentices listed in this source. Surviving freedom and apprenticeship records for the whole City have been used rather than data aggregated from individual company records. Unless considerable care is taken in selecting the companies there is a risk that they might not constitute a true sample.[12] Some companies, such as the Stationers,[13] had a typical migration fields and the social background of entrants varied enormously between them. Many of the City's freedom and apprenticeship records were lost by fire in 1786, so it is not possible to produce any long-run time-series.

In this study 'London' is taken to embrace the sprawling conurbation defined by Sir William Petty: not simply the City proper and its ancient out-parishes, but the whole area within the bills of mortality. These cover the built-up area clearly shown on the late-seventeenth century maps derived from the accurate survey made by William Morgan in 1682. These show the continuous riverside development from Limehouse to Whitehall north of the Thames, and a narrower development south of the river from Rotherhithe to Southwark, together with the extensive inland development of both the East and West Ends.[14] This conurbation, already the largest in Europe, comprised a single, if diversified, economic unit which transcended administrative and juridical boundaries. To list, like some studies, youths from suburbs such as Southwark as migrants makes little sense. If, as often happened, his master also lived in Southwark the youth would not have travelled at all, or he might have moved not to the City or one of its out-parishes, but beyond it to Stepney, Westminster or even some more distant part. Indentures seldom give the master's address, but company records show that freemen lived and worked throughout the conurbation, often beyond the jurisdiction of the corporation or the company.[15]

Estimates of the population of London around 1700 vary considerably. Gregory King's figures for London have proved pretty accurate (whatever the deficiencies in some of his other statistics) so his final total of 530,000 has been adopted rather than the 575,000 preferred by several recent writers.[16] Whether 530,000 or 575,000, London's clear primacy in the English urban system, where even the provincial capitals were small by European standards, is patent. Norwich, the next largest town, had only just under 30,000 inhabitants. Adopting the usual method of calculating a primacy index, $Pi/(Pii+ Piii+Piv+Pv)$, where Pi equals the capital and $Pii \ldots v$ represent the four next largest cities, London's primacy index is 6.7. Such a high level is commonly found in the modern under-developed world, where it is associated with a low level of economic development, a small country with a small population and a centralized cultural and political system: all characteristic of late Stuart England. Between 1690–9 and 1710–19, London baptisms rose by 11.7 per cent and burials by 5.4 per cent, although burials were about a quarter higher than baptisms. Substantial numbers of migrants, of whom apprentices comprised only a minority, were needed to sustain such increases. The capital's population expanded even when, as in the second half of the seventeenth century, the tempo of national population growth slackened or halted.[17]

This study confirms the accepted view that during the sixteenth and seventeenth centuries the proportion of London apprentices travelling long distances fell, although not uniformly from all directions: fewer migrants travelled from the highland zone, while the proportion from areas close to the capital rose. Nevertheless, London's migration field remained nationwide, and she continued to attract a far higher percentage of apprentice migrants from distances greater than 50 kilometres (30 miles) than did any provincial town. Detailed exploration of this trend would require investigation into the background of individual migrants which, even if extant source materials permitted, the large number of individual migrants would render impossible. Wrigley, followed by Wareing, suggested that differential regional birth rates may be one factor. 'In the Home Counties and the Midlands ... it may prove to be the case that a substantial surplus of births continued to be characteristic of these counties throughout the century 1650-1750',[18] a time when elsewhere the natural increase of earlier years was reduced or halted. Such purely demographic explanations are probably only part of the answer: individual motivation must have also been influenced by the divergent regional economic development of Stuart England.

II

The place of origin of migrants is usually tabulated by county. Apprenticeship indentures state the county and settlement from which the apprentice came. Counties are, however, unequal in area and population: they are administrative, not economic or social units, and when grouped into regions produce units which are economically and geographically arbitrary. Furthermore, aggregating data by counties or regions gives a misleading impression of sudden change, where in reality there may be a gradual spatial progression. Figure 5 is a computer-generated choropleth map which shows the spatial density of migrants in the early eighteenth century. It is derived from the Ordnance Survey coordinates of the places of origin of 1,206 London apprentices bound in 1711-13 who were born outside the capital. The number of points within a given distance of each place of origin have been averaged, giving a higher weighting to closer points in order to smooth out local irregularities.

This map depicts the spatial distribution of migrants more accurately

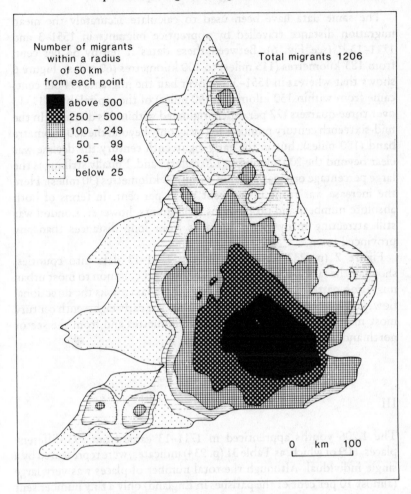

Fig. 5. Spatial distribution of migrant apprentices to London, 1711–13
Sources: see note 11 and text.

than aggregation by counties, the usual way such data are presented. The relative paucity of migrants from East Anglia, from west of Bristol and west Wales shows up very clearly. The large numbers originating in the Home Counties, in areas due west of London and from the Midlands south of Nottingham are also apparent. Few apprentices travelled from the sparsely populated upland regions including Wales, from the Kent and Sussex Weald or from the south coast. The sharp falling away in numbers originating from south of London is very striking.

229

The same data have been used to calculate accurately the mean migration distance travelled by apprentice migrants in 1551–3 and 1711–13,[19] (see Fig. 6). Between these dates it fell by 54 per cent, from 185 kilometres (115 miles) to 100 kilometres (60 miles). Figure 6 shows that whereas in 1551–3 just over half the migrants (54 per cent) came from within 150 kilometres (90 miles) of the capital, by 1711–13 over three-quarters (77 per cent) originated within this distance. In the mid-sixteenth century numbers fell away only beyond the 300 kilometre band (180 miles), but in the early eighteenth century the decline was clear beyond the 200 kilometre (120 miles) band. Equally striking is the large percentage originating from within 50 kilometres (30 miles). Here the increase was from 12 per cent to 33 per cent. In terms of both absolute numbers and proportions of migrants, however, London was still attracting many more migrants from long distances than any provincial town.

Figure 7 (p. 232) disaggregates the 1711–13 data into counties, showing the fairly regular distance-decay effect common to most urban migration patterns. This presentation of the data masks the directional flow which was clearly shown in Fig. 5. In the early eighteenth century most migrants came from within 150 kilometres and from the sector north and west of the capital.

III

The 1,206 youths apprenticed in 1711–13 came from 793 different places, 609 of which, as Table 31 (p. 234) indicates, were represented by a single individual. Although the total number of places was very large (almost 10 per cent of the parishes in England) only a tiny number sent more than three youths. Over a longer period many, if not most, of the towns and villages in England must have sent at least one youth to London as an apprentice – clear testimony of the extent and strength of the human links between the capital and the rest of the kingdom, and also the size and density of the national communications network. Even such a small settlement as the Shropshire village of Myddle, some 250 kilometres (160 miles) from London, had at least one member from 15 of the 91 families living there in 1672, mostly as apprentices.[20]

Neither this nor the earlier tables took any account of the population of the migrant's home settlement. One would expect towns and counties with large numbers of inhabitants to send more than those with few inhabitants. Some 10 per cent of the English population lived

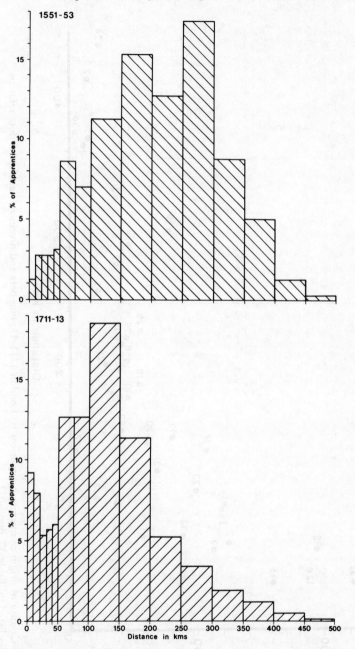

Fig. 6. Mean migration distances of migrant apprentices to London, 1551–53, 1711–13
Sources: see note 11 and text.

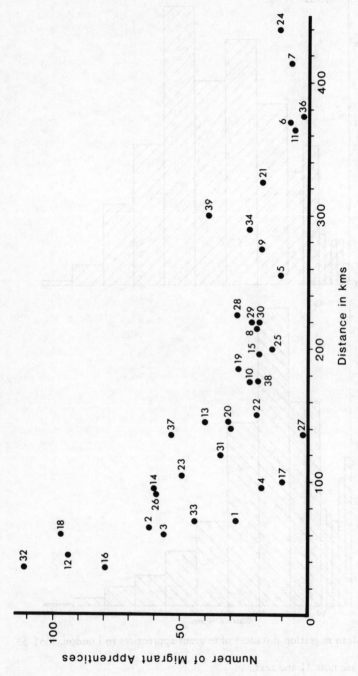

Fig. 7. County of origin of migrant apprentices to London 1711–13: numbers and distances (numbered dots refer to counties listed in Table 30, opposite).
Sources: see note 11 and text, p. 226.

M: Number of Migrant Apprentices   K: Kilometres

No.	County	M	K	No.	County	M	K	No.	County	M	K
1	BEDFORDSHIRE	28	70	14	HAMPSHIRE	60	95	27	RUTLAND	2	135
2	BERKSHIRE	62	65	15	HEREFORDSHIRE	19	195	28	SHROPSHIRE	28	225
3	BUCKINGHAMSHIRE	56	60	16	HERTFORDSHIRE	79	35	29	SOMERSET	22	210
4	CAMBRIDGESHIRE	18	95	17	HUNTINGDONSHIRE	10	100	30	STAFFORDSHIRE	19	210
5	CHESHIRE	11	255	18	KENT	97	60	31	SUFFOLK	34	120
6	CORNWALL	7	370	19	LINCOLNSHIRE	27	185	32	SURREY	111	35
7	CUMBERLAND	7	415	20	LEICESTERSHIRE	31	145	33	SUSSEX	44	70
8	DERBYSHIRE	20	215	21	LANCASHIRE	18	325	34	WALES	23	290
9	DEVON	8	275	22	NORFOLK	20	150	35	WARWICKSHIRE	30	140
10	DORSET	23	175	23	NORTHAMPTONSHIRE	49	105	36	WESTMORLAND	2	375
11	DURHAM	5	365	24	NORTHUMBERLAND	11	440	37	WILTSHIRE	53	135
12	ESSEX	94	45	25	NOTTINGHAMSHIRE	14	200	38	WORCESTERSHIRE	19	175
13	GLOUCESTERSHIRE	40	145	26	OXFORDSHIRE	69	90	39	YORKSHIRE	39	300

NOTE: MIDDLESEX EXCLUDED, SEE TEXT

Table 30. County of origin of migrant apprentices to London, 1711–13
Sources: see note 11 and text, p. 226

233

Table 31. Frequency distribution of places of origin of migrants, 1711-13

Number of migrants	Frequency of places	Number of migrants	Frequency of places
1	609	8	5
2	100	9	1
3	42	10	3
4	17	11	0
5	7	12	0
6	8	13	1
7	4		

Source: See note 11.

in the metropolis. A further 8 per cent were residents of towns with more than 2,000 inhabitants. Gregory King divided English towns into three categories: five 'great cities' (clearly Bristol, Exeter, Newcastle, Norwich and York); forty towns with more than 500 houses (the county towns and larger market towns) and some 800 smaller 'towns' with more than 150 houses. This last category includes many places we would rank as villages and has been omitted from this analysis. King's extant papers contain no listing of the forty towns in his second category, but recent research allows the identification of more than forty places with a population of over 2,000 in about 1700, thirty of which exceeded 5,000.[21] The total population of the five 'great cities', all of them much smaller than their continental counterparts, can be estimated at about 89,500. This was 1.7 per cent of the total population excluding London (or 1.9 per cent of the total population including London). The five great cities housed 1.75 per cent of the non-metropolitan population and produced 1.2 per cent of the migrants. The forty other large urban centres contained almost 400,000 inhabitants, about 6.4 per cent of the provincial population, and produced 8.1 per cent of the migrants. Thus, slightly fewer apprentices came from the provincial capitals and slightly more from towns in the second category than would be expected were the proportions of migrants and population equal. Sons of urban parents therefore showed no unusually strong propensity to migrate to London for employment, even though one might expect that the contacts between London and the rest of the kingdom would be greater for towns than rural settlements. The proportion of London apprentices from town and country thus roughly reflected the balance of the population between town and country. These calculations, however, take no account of distance from London.

A simple gravity model was used to compare the observed with the expected number of migrants from forty-three leading provincial towns calculated as a function of the population of the town of origin and the distance between London and each town. The best explanatory value accounted for only 24.7 per cent of the variance, although the combined effect of distance and population size was significant at the 0.05 level. Distance can be accurately measured, but the data for town populations are so often inexact that too much weight should not be given to these findings. Also, such significant elements in the linkages between London and provincial towns as ease and frequency of communications, as well as the nature and extent of local employment opportunities, cannot be quantified. Nevertheless, when the performance of individual towns is examined some interesting features emerge.

Eighteen towns sent more migrants than the model predicted, against twenty-five which sent fewer. Oxford and Reading, by no means the largest provincial towns, headed the list of towns which sent more than predicted. Chatham and Cambridge headed the towns sending fewer than predicted, as shown in Fig. 8 and Table 32. Of the provincial capitals (for which the population figures are more accurate) Bristol, Exeter and York sent almost exactly the number predicted, while Newcastle supplied more and Norwich fewer. The latter's position conforms closely to the general pattern of migration from East Anglia. Explanations which fit the results for other towns are not easy to identify, apart from a tendency for thriving towns to send fewer migrants than predicted and for less prosperous towns to send more. York still maintained a large population, but had declined from its earlier prosperity. On the other hand, Chatham had grown rapidly during the late seventeenth century, due to a shipbuilding boom which provided employment for 1,000 men in 1700. Yarmouth, another town with a large negative residual, was likewise prosperous and expanding, its economy based on herring fishing, overseas trade and an important share in the shipping of coal from Newcastle to London. East Anglia generally was wealthy and heavily urbanized with a thriving regional capital in Norwich, the largest town in England after London. Defoe noted that Norfolk possessed 'great and spacious market towns, more and larger than in any other part of England so far from London, except Devonshire, and the West Riding of Yorkshire'. All the East Anglian towns sent fewer migrants than predicted. Patten, writing of Norfolk and Suffolk, observed that 'East Anglia comprised a coherent area, undisturbed by the direct influence of London'.[22] An overstatement, given that London marketed much of its cloth, had swallowed much of its overseas trade and received a good deal of its food from this region,

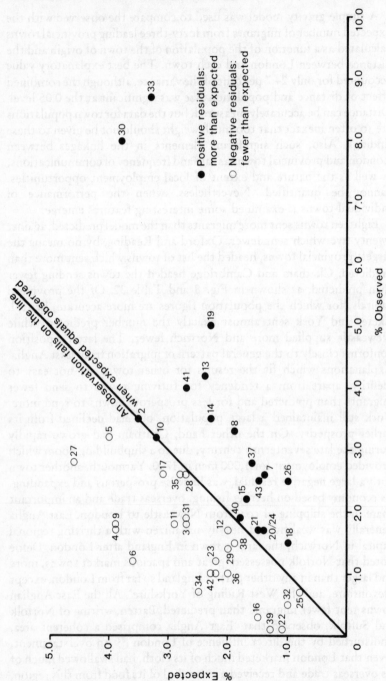

Fig. 8. Observed and expected numbers of migrant apprentices to London from 43 provincial towns, 1711–13 (numbered

No	Town	Observed %	Expected %	No	Town	Observed %	Expected %
1	BIRMINGHAM	1.0	2.2	23	KINGS LYNN	1.2	2.2
2	BRISTOL	3.5	3.5	24	MANCHESTER	1.7	1.4
3	BURY ST. EDMUNDS	1.8	2.7	25	MANSFIELD	0.7	0.8
4	CAMBRIDGE	1.7	3.9	26	NEWCASTLE	2.5	1.0
5	CANTERBURY	3.2	4.0	27	NORWICH	2.8	4.6
6	CHATHAM	1.2	3.6	28	NORTHAMPTON	2.6	2.7
7	CHESTER	2.6	1.4	29	NOTTINGHAM	1.4	2.0
8	CHICHESTER	3.3	1.9	30	OXFORD	8.0	3.8
9	COLCHESTER	1.8	3.9	31	PORTSMOUTH	1.9	2.7
10	COVENTRY	3.2	3.2	32	PLYMOUTH	0.5	1.0
11	DOVER	1.8	2.9	33	READING	8.7	3.3
12	EXETER	1.7	2.4	34	ROCHESTER	0.7	2.5
13	GLOUCESTER	4.2	2.4	35	SALISBURY	2.6	2.8
14	GUILDFORD	3.5	2.3	36	SEVENOAKS	1.0	2.0
15	HEREFORD	2.2	1.7	37	SHREWSBURY	2.8	1.6
16	HULL	0.3	1.5	38	SOUTHAMPTON	1.5	1.9
17	IPSWICH	2.6	3.1	39	TIVERTON	0.1	1.3
18	LEEDS	1.5	1.0	40	WARWICK	1.9	1.8
19	LEICESTER	5.0	2.3	41	WORCESTER	4.0	2.7
20	LICHFIELD	1.7	1.4	42	GREAT YARMOUTH	1.0	2.3
21	LINCOLN	1.7	1.5	43	YORK	2.5	1.5
22	LIVERPOOL	0.1	1.1				

Table 32. Observed and expected numbers of migrant apprentices to London from 43 provincial towns, 1711–13.
Sources: see note 11 and text.

but it does highlight the special nature of the area. However, the association between relatively large numbers of migrants and limited local economic opportunities is not universal. Nottingham, declared by Defoe to have no important industries, sent only ten apprentices, whereas Worcester, similar in size and distance from London, sent twenty-nine. The latter still enjoyed a booming urban economy based on its textile industry, and transported much of what it exported via London, while Nottingham, economically speaking, faced not towards London, but northwards along the Trent towards the Humber and the port of Hull.[23]

When the towns sending apprentices to London for the period 1676–1700 are ranked, Reading and Oxford continue to head the list. The highest placed provincial capital, Bristol, was down in fifteenth place, behind not only quite large towns, but even Berwick-on-Tweed and Chester, which were both smaller in size and farther from London than Bristol. These, along with Newcastle, were the only distant towns to send more migrants than predicted. Berwick was an ancient fortress town which had long since lost its military role without finding a new basis for its economy. It lacked a regular carrying service with London as late as 1715, but it did enjoy good sea communications with the capital. Chester had suffered serious economic misfortunes in the seventeenth century, including the silting of its port. Certain of the other towns to send unexpectedly large numbers of migrants, such as St Albans, Guildford and Maidstone, were close to London and had no nearer major competing urban centre. One group of towns did exhibit a special link with London: Abingdon, Henley, Kingston, Oxford, Reading and Windsor all stood high in the overall ranking and all sent unexpectedly large numbers of migrants. All were major towns on or close to the river Thames, a vital artery for goods travelling to and from London.

The poor information we possess about the urban economies of late Stuart England prevents any detailed examination of how far fluctuations in urban fortunes may have influenced the number of young men who decided to seek jobs in London. Also, proportions from individual towns and their ranking fluctuate over time in a sometimes unpredictable way, apart from the consistent Thames valley grouping.

IV

Migration in both modern and pre-industrial societies is often explained as a response to regional imbalances in population, wage levels and employment opportunities, and the migrants' perception of 'expected' benefits. Much migration was, and is, short-distance. Only a small proportion of early modern migrants who left any locality made their way to London. Chambers postulated that the decline in migrants to London from the north may well have been a function of the development of industry and thus jobs in this region, notably in the metallurgical and textile industries. It should be noted, however, that the migration trend is apparent before these regions began their eighteenth-century development. Some of these industries came into direct competition with London, for example framework-knitting. In 1669 it is estimated that 60 per cent of 660 framework-knitters lived and worked in London. By 1713, although numbers had risen appreciably to about 7,500 knitters, only 31 per cent worked in London.[24] Economic expansion was accompanied by the rise of urban centres in the north and Midlands: Birmingham, Derby, Hull, Leeds, Liverpool, Manchester, Newcastle, Nottingham, Sheffield and Sunderland, along with such lesser northern towns as Carlisle and Kendal. All expanded in the later seventeenth and early eighteenth centuries, although none was strictly speaking an industrial town, and none could rival London in its range of trades, crafts and professions. Much of this industrial activity, including the textile and metal industries, was still located in the countryside. An increase in by-employment was one of the factors which provided a greater prosperity for the less affluent peasant farmers and tradesmen in such a backward area as Cumbria.[25] The easing of population pressure after the 1650s might also have reduced the specifically economic incentives to migrate by improving the opportunities to acquire land whether by purchase or inheritance. Also of probable significance is the size of the 15–24 year age-group in the later seventeenth century, the age at which individuals were most likely to migrate.[26] After the Restoration many agricultural districts, too, were prospering, particularly in the hitherto less fortunate pastoral areas, including much of the north. Not all regions or classes benefitted, but this industrial, urban and agricultural expansion must have created both local and 'intervening' opportunities between London and potential migrants from the north and Midlands, and also reduced the local 'push' factor.[27]

Although real wages were generally edging upwards, they remained higher in London, an important inducement. Gilboy calculated that around 1700 annual wages for 300 days' work were £25 in London, £17 in the west and only £11 10s. 0d. in the north.[28] The wage-differential aspect of a rural 'supply push' on an urban 'demand pull' has been emphasized in many studies of rural-urban migration in the modern under-developed world, although it has reasonably been argued that other considerations may influence the would-be migrant so that the decision to migrate is never completely rational.[29] Also important are non-quantifiable, personal factors, of a kind rarely visible to the historian. The combination of the large number of migrants and places, on the one hand, and inadequate source material, on the other, prevents full examination of the economic background of migrants. The motives of individuals are very seldom explicit at this time. Data do not exist for such an important variable as employment opportunities. Even the population of individual towns and villages is seldom accurately known. The 1691 Land Tax assessments for London and the English and Welsh counties have been utilized as a crude surrogate for employment opportunities, although it is known that these assessments were not entirely reliable. County population totals have been derived from Deane and Cole's figures, modified by the 1690 Hearth Tax returns originally used by Gregory King.[30] From these a total population of 5.2 million for England (5.5 million for England and Wales) was obtained, close to the 5.1 million for England in 1701 recently calculated by Wrigley and Schofield.[31] Computed county totals have been used in a gravity model which takes into account distance from London and the differences in taxable wealth between London and each county: $N = e^{b^0} p^{b^i} w^{b^{ii}} d^{b^{iii}}$, where N is the expected number of migrants, p the population of each county, w the difference between the taxable wealth of London and each county, d the distance between London and the centre of each county (rounded to the nearest 5 miles) and $b^0 \ldots b^{iii}$ are fitted constants, estimated by multiple linear regression. The relationship was linearized by logarithmic transformation, with errors assumed to be normally distributed. By 1700 so much of Middlesex was either part of the London conurbation or very close to it that the county has been excluded from the model. One third of the population of Surrey and one third of its taxable wealth have been allocated to London. Data for men freed in the periods 1681–9 and 1690, and apprentices bound between 1711 and 1713, have been used. Analysis proceeds in the order distance, population and then wealth, it being hypothesized that distance has the greatest effect on migration, as illustrated in Fig. 7.

Distance, population and difference in wealth all prove to have statistically significant effects. The correlation between expected migrants and observed, that is actual, migrants was highest for 1711–13, when the coefficient of determination (r^2) was 0.56. In other words, 56 per cent of the variation in the number of migrants between counties is statistically explained by the effect of distance. The coefficient rises to 0.61 when population is taken into consideration and to an impressive

0.81 when difference in wealth is added. The F statistic in Table 31 is significant at the 0.001 level for each variable.

The effects of the variables population and distance on the number of migrants were subjected to a student's t test to assess the direct proportionality of the relationships. In the case of population the value obtained (1.603) is not significant and therefore we accept the null hypothesis $b = 1$, where b = population, and assume that migration was directly proportional to population. It is scarcely surprising that population would have a direct bearing on the number of apprentices from a county. Westmorland, for example, was not only farther from London than Nottingham but also had only a third of its population. In the case of wealth, however, the t test was significant at the 0.05 level, and it may therefore be concluded that migration was not directly proportional to differences between the wealth of London and of individual counties, although its effect was significant in terms of variance.

For the two earlier periods the predictive value of the model was weaker. For 1681–9 the coefficient of determination was 0.56 and for 1690, 0.55, although both were significant at the 0.05 level. The t test confirms that migration in these two periods was directly proportional to both population and wealth. The reason for the lower correlation coefficient is that in these periods more migrants were travelling long-distances than in 1711–13. Although the time between these two periods and 1711–13 is relatively short, it may be argued that by the early eighteenth century, the economic and demographic trends noted above were increasingly exercizing an influence on potential migrants to London. Men freed in 1681–9 would have left their homes 7 or 8 years earlier (even longer in some cases), at a time when these trends had barely begun to have an impact.

Table 33. Analysis of variance for multiple regression of log migrants on distance, log population and log wealth, 1711–13

Source of variation	Sum of squares	df	Mean squares	F statistic	Level of significance
Distance	17.18	1	17.18	89.57	0.001
Population	8.93	1	17.18	46.56	0.001
Wealth	2.33	1	2.33	12.15	0.001
Error	6.61	35	0.192	—	—
Total	35.05	38	—	—	—

Source and method: See text and note 11.

This model has certain limitations, and like all gravity models it is predictive, not explanatory. It makes no provision for any changes in the population and wealth of counties between 1681 and 1713, though both were increasing; it does not allow for differing economic conditions within counties; and does not distinguish between migrants travelling similar distances but from different directions, although it has already been noted that the direction of the migration stream changed over time.

Why should some counties have sent appreciably more or fewer migrants than predicted? How far were these divergences due to deficiencies in the data or the model; how far attributable to economic and demographic changes? In order to simplify analysis only counties appearing in the upper and lower quartiles, when ranked by magnitude of residuals have been examined (see Table 34). In the case of counties in the lower quartile, where the numbers of migrants were small, relatively small changes in the number of migrants can produce considerable changes in the rank order, although the effect on the size of the residuals will be less.

The effect of distance produces some changes in rank order, mostly minor readjustments, apart from the elevation of Yorkshire (the largest and most populous of the northern counties) into the leading ten. It slides just out of this group when population is taken into account, but reappears in the final column after the wealth factor has been included. It is the only northern county to appear in this quartile in any column. No other county in this top quartile was more than 150 kilometres (90 miles) from London. Wiltshire and Gloucestershire, the two most distant counties in this group, were linked with London by the Thames, which has already been noted to have created a special relationship between the capital and the towns which lay on the river. The Thames also connected London with three other counties in the top ten, Berkshire, Buckinghamshire and Oxfordshire, while the other four in this group, Essex, Hertfordshire, Kent and Surrey, were all situated very close to London. There is, then, nothing very notable about the composition of the upper quartile, apart from the appearance of Yorkshire and the block of Thames counties to the west of London.

The composition of the lower quartile is, however, more interesting. In terms of absolute numbers of migrants the four most northerly counties (Cumberland, Durham, Northumberland and Westmorland), along with the two most westerly (Cornwall and Devon), occupy six of the bottom ten places, together with diminutive Huntingdonshire and Rutland, before distance is taken into account. But Cornwall and the most northerly counties, except for Westmorland, are eliminated from

Table 34. Upper and lower quartiles of migrants by county of origin in rank order, 1711–13

Rank order	Total		Distance (log residual)		Distance and population (log residual)		Distance and wealth (log residual)		Distance, population and wealth (log residual)	
Upper quartile:										
1	Surrey	111	Surrey	55.0			Surrey	51.9	Essex	41.2
2	Kent	97	Kent	48.8			Herts	35.4	Kent	40.7
3	Essex	94	Essex	43.4			Oxford	32.7	Herts	30.2
4	Herts	79	Oxford	27.8			Berks	26.8	Oxford	24.7
5	Oxford	69	Yorks	26.6			Kent	20.3	Surrey	22.2
6	Berks	62	Herts	25.7			Wilts	16.0	Berks	21.1
7	Hants	60	Wilts	22.3			Bucks	15.4	Gloucs	15.4
8	Bucks	56	Hants	18.6			Essex	15.2	Wilts	13.8
9	Wilts	53	Berks	18.4			Hants	13.6	Bucks	9.9
10	N'hants	49	N'hants	11.5			Salop	10.2	Yorks	9.7
Lower quartile:										
30	Notts	14	Cheshire	-3.4			Rutland	-4.1	Cheshire	-4.7
31	Cheshire	11	West'land	-4.8			Lincs	-5.1	Derbys	-4.8
32	N'land	11	Devon	-5.7			Worcs	-5.3	Rutland	-4.8
33	Hunts	10	Worcs	-6.1			Hunts	-6.3	Lancs	-8.9
34	Devon	8	Notts	-7.6			Wales	-8.2	Devon	-10.5
35	Cumb'land	7	Norfolk	-9.2			Somerset	-8.9	Worcs	-10.6
36	Cornwall	7	Beds	-16.4			Cambs	-15.2	Staffs	-12.2
37	Durham	5	Cambs	-21.4			Suffolk	-18.7	Wales	-14.2
38	West'land	2	Hunts	-27.5			Devon	-18.8	Norfolk	-17.5
39	Rutland	2	Rutland	-28.7			Norfolk	-35.2	Cambs	-17.9

Sources and method: see text and note 11.

this group when distance is included. More interesting is the emergence of an East Anglian grouping consisting of Cambridge, Suffolk and Norfolk. The inclusion of population brings into this quartile a collection of north and west Midlands counties, Cheshire, Derbyshire, Lancashire, Staffordshire and Worcestershire, together with Wales. Remoteness (but not isolation) from London in both distance and economic contacts probably had a strong effect on most counties in this group, apart from Worcestershire. Thirsk has drawn attention to the diversified economic expansion of Staffordshire.[32] The presence of Devon in this quartile is notable. It consistently sent fewer migrants than expected; it possessed in Exeter a large and thriving regional capital, and its economy was soundly based on agriculture, fishing and a textile industry which exported much of its product via Exeter. The county was in no sense isolated from London; indeed communications with it were good. It is interesting that, although Exeter sent approximately the predicted number of migrants to London, the county in which it was situated sent far fewer. It would seem that rural expectations could be met locally, but ambitious town youths had to look to London.

Detailed interpretation of the ranking of individual counties requires hard economic and demographic evidence which does not exist. The same problems also seriously impede any systematic analysis of changes in the rank order over time. There are some interesting differences in the ranking of counties in 1711–13 compared with the period 1681–90, for example in the earlier period the consistent appearance of Sussex in the lower quartile once distance, population and wealth are included. In general, however, the composition of the quartiles is similar, even though the rank order is not identical.

How far did differential population growth account for these changes? The surplus population in the Midlands and Home Counties has already been noted. The size of England and its geography meant that communications with London were seldom a significant problem. It had long enjoyed economic ties with every corner of the land and had attracted migrants from all parts of England since the Middle Ages.[33] Its economic hinterland, usually an important element in determining the extent of an urban migration field, was the whole country. Even the notorious Sussex Weald with its heavy, wet clays, which made travelling in winter extremely difficult as late as the eighteenth century, scarcely acted as a total barrier to migration or cut off the county from regular access to London. It is usually argued that improvements in communications permit an increase in long-distance migration, but in the case of seventeenth- and eighteenth-century England improvements in roads and canals and the expansion of regular carrying services were accompanied by a contraction in London's migration field.[34] It is not easy to identify, in the absence of statistics for internal trade, the strength and nature of economic contacts except in rather general and descriptive terms. A comparison of the geographical origins of London migrants plotted in Fig. 5 and the distribution of the cloth industry shows no clear spatial association, even though London and Londoners played an important role in the marketing and export of the finished product.[35] Classification of the counties of early eighteenth-century England simply as 'agricultural' or 'industrial' is anachronistic, although industry, chiefly the textile industry, was more extensive in some counties than others. With the exception of Wiltshire and Yorkshire the counties sending more migrants than expected were predominantly agricultural and supplied food for the London market. Gloucestershire, high in the upper quartile, was noted by Defoe as sending both food and raw materials to London up the Thames, via Lechlade or Cricklade. Alternatively, some agricultural counties, notably in East Anglia, which also supplied London with food, appear in the bottom quartile.

V

Studies of migration in modern industrialized countries show that better educated migrants and migrants from higher status occupations tend to travel longer distances than unskilled or semi-skilled workers. It is not, however, possible to equate exactly apprentices with modern professional or skilled workers. There were high status London companies, such as the Mercers, which contained a high proportion both of wealthy members and of apprentices from gentle backgrounds, and low status companies, such as the Carpenters, most of whose members were at best of modest wealth and from humble backgrounds. But one cannot determine either a man's occupation or his wealth by the company he belonged to. The custom of the City allowed freemen to take up any trade or occupation, so that most companies contained members practising different occupations as well as members of very different levels of wealth. Cressy's study of the geography of literacy shows some association between areas where literacy levels were low and low levels of migration to London, although he noted that low literacy areas did not exactly coincide with the highland economic zone. Literacy levels may stand as a crude surrogate for levels of education among occupational or status groups. The stated occupation or social

245

status of the father of each apprentice has been used to investigate whether in the early eighteenth century sons of gentlemen travelled, on average, longer distances than sons of husbandmen. Sons of the former were much more likely to be literate than sons of the latter.[36] The social background of London apprentices did not accurately mirror provincial society at large; at least one third of the adult male population were labourers or paupers, yet boys from such backgrounds comprised only a small proportion of apprentices even in the low status companies. Advancement from such a background was difficult. In the seventeenth-century Essex village of Terling no family rose from the ranks of labourers, although Terling may be an extreme case.[37] Advancement by migration to a town was also less easy in practice than one might suppose. By 1691–1700 and 1711–13 sons of labourers ranked seventh and eighth amongst parental occupations, but comprised only 1.7 and 1.8 per cent of the total apprentices. The majority of apprentices were sons of yeomen, husbandmen and gentlemen. Between 1691–1700 and 1711–13 the proportion of yeomen's children fell from 18.6 to 11.5 per cent (slipping from first to second place); husbandmen's sons declined from 7.7 to 3.3 per cent (third place in each period); while the proportion of apprentices from a privileged background as sons of gentlemen and esquires rose from 14.9 to 17.9 per cent (from third to first place). In terms of the overall social structure the last were clearly over-represented. Even in this short period the trends then are clear: more sons of the gentry, fewer sons of yeomen and husbandmen. The real change may be less dramatic. Status labels were never exact, especially in the case of families on the borderline between status groups, while by the later seventeenth century usage of the labels gentleman and esquire became less strict and more families placed themselves in these social categories.[38] Regional variations in usage further complicate the problem. For instance, in Northumberland and Cumberland the term husbandman was apparently rarely employed.[39] Economic advance, too, may have increased the numbers of families properly entitled to be called gentlemen and yeomen. But since the proportion of sons of yeomen fell more than the proportion of sons of gentlemen and esquires rose, change in usage alone cannot explain the upward shift in social background. The proportion of sons of labourers remained constant, but at a low level. In spite of some anomalies, social and occupational labels reflected real, if not universally consistent differences in wealth and literacy: most husbandmen were poorer and less literate than most yeomen, and most gentlemen were wealthier and more literate than most yeomen.

The total numbers of freemen remained relatively stable, even though by the later seventeenth century freedom of the City was increasingly taken up for political and social rather than commercial reasons.[40] The City corporation became even less able to force all shopkeepers, artisans and traders to become freemen, and an ever increasing majority of London's inhabitants lived outside the jurisdiction of the City. London continued to attract as apprentices some, but progressively fewer, boys from humble backgrounds – sons of provincial artisans and labourers. Few of those who did secure a London apprenticeship would ever make more than a modest living, but even at this level of expectation prospects for the sons of the mass of the English and Welsh population were poor. Most people lacked both the necessary contacts and the resources to apprentice their sons in London. The only realistic avenue open to the sons of the mass of the population, if they wished to work in London, was employment as a domestic servant or labourer. For such people the likelihood of any significant social or economic advancement, even in London, was remote. For the issue of slightly better-off families the option was usually restricted to apprenticeship with a less prosperous master, but with some prospect of at least modest success with hard work and a modicum of good fortune.

Table 35 shows the mean migration distances travelled by migrants from the three most frequent social groups – gentlemen plus esquires, yeomen and husbandmen. Sons of labourers are too few to permit a proper statistical breakdown by distance bands. The usual distance-decay effect is visible for each social group. A Kendall's tau test

Table 35. Mean migration distances of migrants by parental occupation, 1691–1700 and 1711–13

Distance (km)	1691–1700			1711–13		
	Gentlemen & esquires	Yeomen	Husband-men	Gentlemen & esquires	Yeomen	Husband-men
<80	180	249	99	105	80	23
81–159	160	200	78	68	42	11
160–239	123	121	55	42	20	7
240–319	53	65	33	24	13	3
320–399	10	20	3	4	0	1
>400	7	10	7	7	2	2
Total	533	665	275	250	157	47

Sources: See note 11.

established that there was no significant difference between the mean migration distances of each group. The values were 0.004 for the earlier period and 0.020 for the later. A value of +1.0 would mean that the higher status groups travelled longer distances than the others, and 0.0 that there was no difference. The actual values were extremely close to the latter. Thus it clearly emerges that sons of the more literate and wealthier inhabitants of later Stuart England did not migrate longer distances than the offspring of the less literate and less prosperous, an unexpected finding.

VI

In later Stuart England the capital's migration field was still nation-wide, although mean migration distances had fallen considerably since the mid-sixteenth century. The decline was not uniform in all directions: certain regions, notably East Anglia, the South-West and the north-west Midlands sent fewer apprentices than expected, when allowance is made for distance from London, the population of the counties and taxable wealth. Towns and counties on or close to the Thames sent more. In the years 1711–13 apprentices originated from every shire and from almost 800 places, but showed no clear propensity to migrate from other urban centres. Their social background did not reflect provincial society at large, but over-represented its middling and upper ranks. Thus the prospects of social advancement which apprenticeship offered for sons of the rural and urban labourers were poor. London was an important engine for the economic growth of the economy as a whole, but its role in promoting significant upward social mobility by entry to its trading and commercial classes was restricted. Access to all but the most menial occupations in London was in practice beyond the reach of the sons of the mass of the population of later Stuart England.

NOTES AND REFERENCES

1. *Calendar of State Papers, Venetian*, ed. R. Brown (London 1873), Vol. 5, p. 344. My thanks for the unstinting help given and the understanding shown by the staff of the Research Data Analysis Unit of the University of Sussex over many years and in particular to David Hitchin and Mervyn Thomas who have written the programs used here and provided statistical advice. Any errors in interpretation are my own.
2. D. Ormrod, *The Dutch in London* (London 1973), no pagination.

3. John Graunt, *Natural and Political Observations Made upon the Bills of Mortality* (London 1662) repr. in P. Laslett (ed.), *The Earliest Classics: John Graunt and Gregory King* (Farnborough 1973); C. H. Hull (ed.), *The Economic Writings of Sir William Petty*, 2 vols. (Cambridge 1899); Gregory King, *Natural and Political Observations and Conclusions upon the State and Condition of England 1696* (London 1802), repr. in Laslett (ed.), *The Earliest Classics*.

4. Graunt, *Natural and Political Observations*, pp. 41-2. The spelling has been modernized in all quotations.

5. R. Finlay, *Population and Metropolis: the Demography of London 1580-1650* (Cambridge 1981); D. V. Glass, 'Introduction', in *London Inhabitants within the Walls 1695*. London Record Society, 2 (1966); *idem*, 'Notes on the demography of London at the end of the seventeenth century', repr. in D. V. Glass and R. Revelle (eds), *Population and Social Change* (London 1972).

6. Graunt, *Natural and Political Observations*, p. 43; Gregory King, 'L. C. C. Burns Journal', in Laslett (ed), *The Earliest Classics*, p. 29; E. A. Wrigley, 'A simple model of London's importance in changing English society and economy 1650-1750', repr. in P. Abrams and E. A. Wrigley (eds), *Towns in Societies* (Cambridge 1978), p. 217.

7. J. Wareing, 'Migration to London and transatlantic emigration of indentured servants 1683-1775', *Journal of Historical Geography*, 7 (1981). For summaries of research on the origins of migrants, see J. Wareing, 'Changes in the geographical distribution of apprentices to the London Companies 1486-1750', *Journal of Historical Geography*, 6 (1980); Finlay, *Population and Metropolis*, pp. 64-6.

8. J. Patten, *English Towns 1500-1700* (Folkestone 1978), p. 128.

9. Finlay, *Population and Metropolis*, Table 3.7, p. 67. Calculations of drop-out rates and average length of indentures are from my own unpublished research into manuscript and printed livery company records in the Guildhall Library and Company halls. Also see *Privilegia Londinensis* (London 1702), pp. 302-4 for masters, who were not freemen, taking apprentices.

10. Calculated from D. V. Glass, 'Socio-economic status and occupations in the City of London at the end of the seventeenth century', repr. in P. Clark (ed.), *The Early Modern Town* (London 1976), Table 10.6, p. 223.

11. Public Record Office, Apprenticeship books, Inland Revenue 1/1-2; Corporation of London Record Office, Chamberlain's records; Glass, 'Socio-economic status', pp. 228-9. The freedom registers are described by M. T. Medlycott, 'The City of London freedom registers', *Genealogists' Magazine*, 19 (1977), pp. 45-7, together with a Comment by G. Thompson. Examples of premium levels in the 1740s are given in R. Campbell, *The London Tradesman* (London 1747, repr. Newton Abbot 1969), pp. 331-40.

12. The valuable studies by S. R. Smith, 'The social and geographical origins of the London apprentices 1630-1660', *Guildhall Miscellany*, 4 (1973) and Wareing, 'Changes in the geographical distribution of apprentices' both rather haphazardly aggregate data from different companies.

13. D. F. McKenzie, 'Apprenticeship in the Stationers' Company 1555-1640', *The Library*, 5th ser. 13 (1958); [G. E. Briscoe-Eyre (ed)], *A Transcript of the*

Registers of the Worshipful Company of Stationers from 1640–1708 A.D.]1709], 3 vols. (London 1913–14).

14. P. Glanville, 'The topography of seventeenth-century London', *Urban History Yearbook*, (1980). Studies of the development of London include N. G. Brett-James, *The Growth of Stuart London* (London 1935); L. Stone, 'The residential development of the West End of London in the seventeenth century', in B. C. Malament (ed.), *After the Reformation* (Manchester 1980).

15. For example, a 1676 list of residences of Merchant Taylors' freemen is found in Merchant Taylors' Hall, MS L4; or for 1673 Fruiterers in A. W. Gould, *History of the Worshipful Company of Fruiterers in the City of London* (privately printed, Exeter 1912); or for 1641–2 and 1661 lists in J. E. Oxley, *The Fletchers and Longbowstringmakers of London* (London 1968), pp. 21, 40.

16. King, *Natural and Political Observations*, p. 36. Recent authorities include P. Corfield, 'Urban development in England and Wales in the sixteenth and seventeenth centuries', in D. C. Coleman and A. H. John (eds), *Trade, Government and Economy in Pre-Industrial England* (London 1976), p. 223; Patten, *English Towns*, p. 88.

17. E. A. Wrigley and R. S. Schofield, *The Population History of England 1541–1871* (London 1981), Table 6.4, p. 167; pp. 168, 207–12.

18. Wrigley, 'London's importance', p. 219; Wareing, 'Changes in the geographical distribution of apprentices', p. 248.

19. The 1551–3 data were independently derived from the Guildhall Library manuscript of the list of freemen used in G. D. Ramsay, 'The recruitment and fortunes of some London freemen in the mid-sixteenth century', *Economic History Review*, 2nd ser. 31 (1978).

20. D. G. Hey, *An English Rural Community: Myddle Under the Tudors and Stuarts* (Leicester 1974), pp. 192–4.

21. Figures for town populations are given in Corfield, 'Urban development in England and Wales', p. 223; C. W. Chalklin, *The Provincial Towns of Georgian England* (London 1974), pp. 4–25; Patten, *English Towns*, pp. 107–20.

22. Daniel Defoe, *A Tour through the Whole Island of Great Britain* (London 1724–6, repr. Harmondsworth 1971), p. 85; Patten, *English Towns*, p. 245.

23. Defoe, *Tour*, p. 454.

24. J. D. Chambers, *Population, Economy, and Society in Pre-Industrial England* (London 1972), pp. 136–7; *idem*, 'The worshipful Company of Framework Knitters (1657–1758)', *Economica*, 27 (1929).

25. For examples, see D. G. Hey, *The Rural Metalworkers of the Sheffield Region* (Leicester 1972); J. D. Marshall, 'Agrarian wealth and social structure in pre-industrial Cumbria', *Economic History Review*, 2nd ser. 33 (1980).

26. A. S. Kussmaul, *Servants in Husbandry in Early Modern England* (Cambridge 1981), pp. 99–100; Wrigley and Schofield, *Population History of England*, Figure 7.4, p. 216.

27. S. A. Stouffer, 'Intervening opportunities: a theory relating to mobility and distance', *American Sociological Review*, 5 (1940).

28. E. W. Gilboy, *Wages in Eighteenth-Century England* (Cambridge, Mass. 1934), p. 20.

29. A valuable analysis is contained in E. S. Lee, 'A theory of migration', *Demography*, 3 (1966).

30 P. Deane and W. A. Cole, *British Economic Growth 1688-1959* (2nd edn, Cambridge 1967), p. 103. Data from the hearth tax and the land tax were taken from C. Davenant, 'An essay upon ways and means' (London 1771), repr. in J. Thirsk and J. P. Cooper (eds), *Seventeenth-Century Economic Documents* (Oxford 1972), pp. 802-3.

31. Wrigley and Schofield, *Population History of England*, Table 7.8, pp. 208-9.

32. J. Thirsk, *Economic Policy and Projects* (Oxford 1978), p. 168.

33. E. Ekwall, *Studies on the Population of Medieval London* (Lund 1956), pp. xlii-xliii.

34. J. A. Chartres, 'Road carrying in England in the seventeenth century', *Economic History Review*, 2nd ser. 30 (1977). For relevant maps, see E. J. Pawson, *Transport and Economy: the Turnpike Roads of Eighteenth-Century England* (London 1977).

35. See the map of the distribution of textile areas around 1700 in P. J. Bowden, *The Wool Trade in Tudor and Stuart England* (London 1962), p. 49.

36. D. Cressy, *Literacy and the Social Order: Reading and Writing in Tudor and Stuart England* (Cambridge 1980), Ch. 6. Also see R. A. Houston, 'The development of literacy: northern England, 1640-1750', *Economic History Review*, 2nd ser. 35 (1982).

37. K. Wrightson and D. Levine, *Poverty and Piety in an English Village: Terling, 1525-1700* (New York 1979), p. 108.

38. The less restrictive usage of the term 'gentleman' is noted in L. Stone, 'The size and composition of the Oxford student body 1580-1910', in L. Stone (ed.), *The University in Society* (Princeton 1975), Vol. 1, p. 14.

39. Houston, 'Development of literacy', p. 205.

40. J. R. Kellett, 'The breakdown of gild and corporation control over the handicraft and retail trades in London', *Economic History Review*, 2nd ser. 10 (1958).

CHAPTER NINE

Social policy and the poor in the later seventeenth century

Stephen Macfarlane

A widely-expressed concern over the state of the poor has long been recognized as a central feature of the contemporary literature on trade in seventeenth-century England. Indeed, Charles Wilson has characterized this aspect of the many tracts and pamphlets which flowed from the presses between 1640 and 1700 as 'the great debate on the poor'.[1] Much less attention has been paid, however, to local attempts to put ideas into practice.[2] Between 1696 and 1715, fourteen provincial towns and cities attempted to overcome the limitations of parish-based poor relief by founding municipally-administered workhouse corporations to employ the able-bodied poor and supervise the indigent, of which the Bristol workhouse, associated with the writer and merchant John Cary, is the best known example.[3] This local activity under the later Stuarts was matched in Parliament by a series of attempts to legislate wholesale reform of the poor laws in accordance with the proposals of reformers. Parliament considered poor law reform at least thirteen times between 1694 and 1704, and in 1705 nearly enacted a codifying measure sponsored by Sir Humphrey Mackworth.[4]

The City of London was very much a part of this movement for reform, yet the contribution of its citizens has largely gone unnoticed by historians. Between 1698 and 1713, the citizens of London founded and financed an ambitious municipal project to employ the poor which, its proponents hoped, would provide a better government for the poor than could be found in the City's parishes. This essay will examine that institution – the London Corporation of the Poor – in the light of contemporary attitudes to poverty and the operation of poor relief at the parish level. The independence and discretion of parish officers and vestrymen formed precisely those aspects of poor relief which proponents of this institution wished to curtail. Yet the goals of the

London Corporation of the Poor were undermined within a few years of its foundation, thereby reaffirming the control of the City's 111 parishes and extra-parochial precincts over the poor and the sources for their relief.[5] The conflict engendered by the London Corporation of the Poor shows how local interests and party conflict could frustrate attempts to carry out social policies. The essay that follows suggests that late Stuart debates on the poor were thus as much about *who* ought to govern indigent or able-bodied paupers as *how* they should be governed.

I

'There is no Nation I ever read of' [complained Sir Francis Brewster in 1695] 'who by a Compulsory Law, raiseth so much Money for the Poor as *England* doth: That of *Holland* is Voluntary, and turns to a Revenue to the Common-Wealth, as they manage it; but our Charity is become a Nusance, and may be thought the greatest Mistake of that Blessed Reign, in which that Law passed, which is the Idle and Improvident Mans Charter.'[6]

That 'Idle and Improvident Mans Charter' to which Brewster referred was, of course, the Elizabethan poor law of 1601.[7] His view was by no means a cry in the wilderness. During the second half of the seventeenth century, concern over the state of agriculture and trade and alarm over the size of the kingdom's poor rates turned the minds of many would-be social reformers and improvers of trade to the reform of the poor laws.[8] Men like Brewster, Sir Matthew Hale, Sir Josiah Child, and Thomas Firmin proposed more effective ways of implementing those provisions of the 1601 statute which enabled parishes to set their able-bodied poor to work; or they advocated the replacement of the poor laws with new measures in which employment provisions were prominently featured.[9]

While specific remedies for unemployment varied from author to author, a common theme in many reports, tracts, and legislation was the belief that the failure of parish authorities to employ the poor encouraged idleness and vice among them. 'Wee atribute the increase of the Poor', reported the Board of Trade in 1697, 'to the relaxation of discipline, corruption of Manners and ill Education of the Poorer sort and more particularly to a Neglect of the Execution or rather a pervertion of the intention and end of those most Excellent Laws made ... for the relief and Imployment of the Poor, apprehending of Vagabonds and prevention of Beggars and Idle Persons.'[10] The Gloucestershire M.P. Sir Richard Cockes saw the answer to the problem of poverty in the outright repeal of the poor laws and their replacement with harsher methods 'to affright [the poor] from their idle and negligent practices and behaviour, and force them to be as willing to work as we [are] to employ them'.[11] One should not exaggerate the degree of uniformity in attitudes to poverty at the end of the century. Other writers, echoing the optimism of reformers of the 1640s and 1650s, still contended that poverty was not necessarily the fault of the poor.[12] Nevertheless, opinions such as Cockes's were not uncommon: the origin of poverty lay in moral defects encouraged by bad laws for which the only cure lay in measures to compel the poor to work.

Critics of the poor laws expressed special alarm at the failure of parochially-administered relief to prevent what they perceived as an increase in unemployment, and therefore in begging and idleness, in large towns, especially London.[13] Indeed, the writings of Sir Josiah Child and Thomas Firmin in particular were concerned with poverty in London and can be read as responses to the growth of casual labour and industry in the metropolis in the decades after the Fire of 1666. Child proposed doing away with parochially-administered relief entirely in London and replacing it with a system of employment and relief which would encompass the entire area within the bills of mortality, and which would be administered by a select group of 'Fathers of the Poor'.[14] His proposal was never taken up, but concerned citizens did attempt to overcome the limitations of parish poor relief in the City of London at the end of the seventeenth century.

II

The parish formed the backbone of poor relief in post-Fire London. Professor Pearl has rightly called attention to the wide range of assistance which many of the City's 111 parishes and extra-parochial precincts provided for their poorer inhabitants before the Fire; her account generally applies to the later seventeenth century as well.[15] Indeed, the administration of poor relief comprised a significant portion of what local government actually did in some parishes. Even a well-to-do parish, like St Dionis Backchurch, spent between 54 and 64 per cent of its yearly revenue on about 3 per cent of its population. For the poor intra-mural parish of St Katherine Coleman, annual expenditure on the poor varied from 60 to 80 per cent of total expenditure.[16] These sums went to support children and adult pensioners, who together comprised between 2.8 and 4.4 per cent of its population of around 1100 in the 1690s, and to provide occasional grants of relief to a larger group, mainly poor families, ranging in size from 4 to 23 per cent (in 1693–94) of the parish.[17] Indeed, the vestry minutes of St Katherine Coleman record few entries which do not concern the poor. Nearly all of this revenue was raised from poor rates assessed on householders. Aggregate figures for the size of the poor rates in London cannot be derived directly from parish records, but the most reliable contemporary estimate suggests that City ratepayers in 1695 contributed at least 36 per cent of an aggregate poor rate for metropolitan London of £40,847, whereas the City's population at that time comprised only about 21 per cent of the metropolis.[18]

Churchwardens, overseers of the poor, and parish vestries had a well-established tradition of autonomy in the collection and distribution of these funds by the late seventeenth century. In 1686 a provincial writer might claim that 'Justices of the Peace are emphatically, or more eminently, the Overseers of the Poor in the county (all others being their substitutes and acting by their orders)', but the situation in the City of London was different.[19] Although each alderman could exercise within his ward the powers of a justice of the peace as defined in the poor law statutes of 1598 and 1601, parish records show that churchwardens and vestrymen administered relief in the 1680s and 1690s with considerable independence from higher authorities.[20] No examples of individual aldermen directly supervising parish relief have come to light, such as occurred in Middlesex and Westminster early in the eighteenth century.[21] The City sessions of the peace did revive rates-in-aid after the Fire of London, whereby wealthier parishes subsidized parishes unable to relieve their own poor. Otherwise, the activities of the City's justices, as far as poor relief was concerned, were confined largely to hearing appeals in settlement disputes and bastardy cases. The Lord Mayor heard more poor law business at his daily sittings as a magistrate, and settled much of it without further recourse to the courts. Even here, however, his Lordship did not initiate intervention in a parish's affairs, but only issued an order after hearing a complaint which arose either from the parish officers or from the poor themselves.[22]

Whom to relieve and how much to give were, therefore, decisions usually left to the discretion of the churchwardens, although in smaller parishes the entire vestry might hear requests for relief or adjust the size of individual pensions.[23] In St Dionis Backchurch, for example, the general vestry of ratepaying male householders – certainly no restricted oligarchy – annually set the size of individual pensions by vote.[24] Pearl found that a basic pension of £2.3s.4d per annum might, with supplementary aid, amount to as much as £7.2s.6d. By the 1690s, annual pensions in a wealthy parish like St Michael Cornhill could average over

£11 per pensioner, which covered rent but not clothing or gifts from other charities. At the other extreme, the poor intramural parish of St Andrew by the Wardrobe paid only one to four shillings per month to each of its pensioners.[25] The detailed accounts of St Katherine Coleman show that parish to have spent £6.5s. annually to support each of its foundling children, and between 19s.6d. and £5.4s. on adults.[26] The churchwardens set the latter sums according to their perception of the pensioner's need. The ability to perform some form of work was certainly one criterion observed here, although the parish itself did not attempt to provide stocks of raw materials with which to employ its poor as required by statute.[27] The parish did take special circumstances into account. One Ellinor Elliston, pregnant and accompanied by 'A young Childe', was passed on St Katherine in late 1694 in accordance with settlement legislation. She received 'present Releife' from the churchwardens, and the parish subsequently paid for a midwife, baptism of her baby, and the services of a nurse for two months. Thereafter the vestry set her pension at 2s.6d. per week 'for Maintenance of hirselfe, & hir two Children, House Rent, & Clotheing', which she continued to receive up to 1701.[28] The parish's occasional recipients of relief – usually unemployed artisans and their families – were given smaller sums of money for particular purposes, such as buying food or burying a member of the family.

Perceptions of need, of course, worked two ways, and the vestry of St Katherine Coleman imposed certain conditions on the receipt of relief. The pension of one woman was reduced after her husband died. The widow Turner was given a yearly rent of 30s. 'according to hir good behaviour'. If a pensioner changed her accommodation without the approval of the vestry, she could find herself removed to cheaper lodgings. The parish often made grants of pensions or rent conditional on the wearing of a badge.[29] Thus, while the discretionary powers of parish officers were often limited by the extent of parish resources, individual need and the forms of relief customarily doled out in City parishes gave churchwardens and vestries considerable authority over their poor.[30]

Although contemporary concerns about poor relief focused largely on the failure of parish administration, poor citizens of London were not confined to seeking aid solely from their parishes, and it is important to note the wide range of institutions in the City which supplemented incomes or assisted the poor when times got bad. Wardmotes, livery companies, and the Court of Aldermen all continued to dispense aid to the poor in various forms after the Fire.[31] John Strype, in his edition of the *Survey of the Cities of London and Westminster*, listed over fifty almshouses and hospitals in the London area, many of which were administered by livery companies for aged freemen, their wives, or their widows.[32] While Christ's Hospital had completed its transition from an orphanage to a school by the 1670s, St Thomas's and St Bartholomew's Hospitals expanded their capacities in caring for the sick poor: the combined bed capacity of the two hospitals rose from approximately 470 in 1676 to approximately 820 in 1711, and continued to grow into the 1720s.[33] The number of charity schools in the metropolis expanded from the 1680s; and, while these institutions were primarily concerned with the moral welfare of their charges, they frequently provided clothing and meals as well.[34] Finally, there were the informal sources of relief, loans, or credit about which we know all too little. Loans at extortionate rates of interest from pawnbrokers or innkeepers were notorious; but they could be contrasted to voluntary groups of tradesmen who formed their own clubs, like the box clubs of the eighteenth century or friendly societies, designed to assist their members. One group of curriers operated such a club in the City, whose members paid four pence each month towards the relief of poor curriers and their families.[35]

Although few generalizations about parochial charity are possible for a city whose parishes differed so widely in wealth and size, it is clear that assistance to the indigent, unemployed or casually-employed in London did not include the handing out of stocks of materials for the able-bodied poor to work on. Some parishes did employ a few of their poor in the machinery of poor relief, as parish nurses for example, while other parishes gave recipients of charity occasional jobs as labourers around the churchyard or as pallbearers. Poor relief consisted primarily of doles of money, supplemented occasionally by payments of rent, nursing, or funeral expenses, apprenticeship premiums, gifts of bread or fuel, and a range of miscellaneous payments for specific purposes, such as the recovery of one's tools or clothes from a pawnbroker or a small payment to get a sick person into one of the London hospitals. The doles made few demands upon the time of the poor, nor did they provide the possibility of regular supplements to income as rural by-employments might. These were among the aspects of parochial relief which alarmed critics and reformers of the poor laws most.

III

The move to centralize the treatment of the poor which the citizens of London made in 1698 should be seen as a culmination of efforts to provide a more effective means of governing the able-bodied pauper, adult and child alike. These efforts stretched back well before the Revolution of 1688 to mid-century attempts to supplement parish poor relief in the City, and were kept alive in the intervening decades by a small group of citizens centred around the Socinian yarn-dealer and philanthropist Thomas Firmin, his kinsman through marriage, the scrivener and Whig alderman Sir Robert Clayton, and their associates.[36] Yet the decision to found a municipal Corporation of the Poor in 1698 also reflected more pressing and immediate problems: unemployment in London during the Nine Years War, growing concern – manifested in part in the Reformation of Manners movement – over the moral state of the labouring classes, and the failure of parliamentary efforts in early 1698 to enact a national reform of the poor laws in which provision of employment, especially in cities, was a prominent feature.

The City's earlier experiment with a municipal workhouse corporation during the 1650s was significant for the later institution not only because it provided a precedent for employing the poor, but because the confirmation of its legal existence in 1662 provided the basis on which the citizens of London proceeded when parliamentary efforts at national reform collapsed in 1698.[37] The earlier Corporation of the Poor was founded by parliamentary ordinances in 1647 and 1649, in response to agitation from concerned citizens and social reformers like Samuel Hartlib, Gabriel Plattes, Henry Robinson, and Rice Bush.[38] During the 1650s, the two workhouses operated by the Corporation gave out stocks of hemp and flax to poor Londoners to spin in their own houses, and they took in poor children who were taught to read and were given vocational training in spinning, weaving, knitting, lacemaking, buttonmaking, and silkwinding.[39] The poor law statute of 13 and 14 Charles II, c. 12 (1662) subsequently included provisions enabling the citizens to erect workhouse corporations in the City and liberties, yet the Corporation of the Poor was abandoned shortly after the Restoration. The City did not actively turn its sights to another municipal employment project until 1698, perhaps because of the disruptions of the plague and the Fire, and the City's worsening financial condition. More importantly, the 1662 statute itself contained a critical flaw. While it allowed for the existence of a Corporation of the Poor in law, it neglected to vest in it the sole authority for the relief and employment of the poor; for by the Elizabethan poor law each City parish was still legally obliged to rate its inhabitants and relieve its own poor. Thus loomed the prospect of a double poor rate on City householders: one to their parish, and one to a Corporation of the Poor.[40]

While publicly-funded employment projects were not established in the City until the 1690s, privately-organized schemes did appear earlier, in response to the migration of labour to London after the Fire, to economic dislocation at the time of the Dutch Wars, and to the expansion of the City's market and port facilities. In March 1677, the Six Weeks Meeting of London Quakers began a flax-spinning project to employ poor Friends; the merchant and social reformer John Bellers became the treasurer of this project in 1680.[41] More influential was the project which Thomas Firmin began in the parish of St Botolph Aldersgate around 1677. Like the provincial gentlemen-employers about whom Dr Thirsk has written, Firmin gave out stocks of hemp and flax to poor people to spin in their own houses, and he subsequently purchased the yarn. He also took poor children from the age of five into his workhouse in Little Britain Street, and provided them with instruction in spinning and, for two hours each day, had them taught to read.[42] His employment project was designed to show what should be done to aid the casually employed and to prevent poor children from acquiring habits of vice and idleness; yet during his lifetime he was unsuccessful in persuading the Court of Aldermen to adopt his methods for the entire City.[43] Firmin's project lost money during the 1680s, despite financial help from Sir Robert Clayton and other wealthy citizens; and, although he continued to employ poor spinners up to his death in 1697, his project never was self-supporting.[44] Nevertheless, it provided a working model for what might be done to reform parish poor relief, and a method of organizing the employment of the poor which appeared to some influential citizens appropriate in the hard times after 1688.

The political events surrounding the Revolution of 1688, followed by the outbreak of war against France the following spring, shook London's economy and ushered in nearly a decade of distress for the poor of the metropolis. Depressions in the City's cloth markets in 1689, 1693–4, and 1696–7; arrears in pay to seamen and their families; a major shortage of coal in 1691; high bread prices in 1693–4 and from 1696 to 1698; and shortages of coin: all these contributed to unemployment among the London poor and strained the resources of many parishes in the City as well as in the suburbs.[45] As early as 3 December 1688, a group of concerned citizens and supporters of the Prince of Orange, including Thomas Firmin and Sir Robert Clayton, organized voluntary, house-to-house collections for the poor in City parishes, to which William contributed £2,000.[46] The money was then distributed to poor parishes throughout the metropolis, and subsequently became an annual collection known as 'The King's Letter', although royal contributions after 1689 were reduced to £1,000 yearly. Because supplements from rates-in-aid and the King's Letter proved inadequate, however, poorer parishes in London fell into debt during the decade; St Botolph Bishopsgate had to sell some of its property in 1694, for example.[47] Some parishes which had been assessed for rates-in-aid before the 1690s came to petition the City justices of the peace that they were no longer able to collect the additional assessments: they had difficulties enough relieving their own poor.[48]

The response of the aldermen to economic dislocation was a series of *ad hoc* measures familiar to students of social policy in early modern England. The Court tried to ensure that supplies of fuel and grain were brought to market, that stocks of coal or corn were maintained for the poor, that forestallers and engrossers were prosecuted, and that the assizes of bread and fuel were kept.[49] These remedies proved inadequate. By July 1693, the Grand Jury found it necessary to present 'the neglect of the poor, & their being suffered to begg in great numbers up & downe the streets of this City, to be a dishonour to the City, & an injury to the Inhabitants of the same'.[50] Following the poor harvest that autumn, scores of hawkers and pedlars roamed the streets, prompting Common Council to enact a measure to restrain them, which had little effect.[51]

Contemporary fears about petty crime and disorderly conduct extended to the moral state of the labouring classes. If the Reformation of Manners movement never attracted unqualified support from the government, clergy, or substantial inhabitants of London, it did underscore the limitations of parochially-administered relief in the capital during a period of widespread unemployment and unrest. The movement for a reformation of manners gained momentum after a royal proclamation in October 1690 for the apprehension of robbers and highwaymen and the suppression of bawdy houses thought to shelter them, and a letter from Queen Mary to the Middlesex bench in early July 1691.[52] These expressions of royal alarm at the manners of the poor provoked sympathetic responses from the Court of Aldermen. The Court issued orders following the Queen's letter to curtail popular entertainments at Bartholomew Fair that August and for the strict enforcement of laws against sabbath-breaking, tippling, drunkenness, gaming, and disorderly alehouses throughout the City.[53] These measures were followed in the autumn of 1693 with a campaign against 'nightwalkers' and disorderly behaviour by women.[54] The need to do more than simply relieve the able-bodied poor was also reflected in popular appeals for action. In February 1694, Common Council received a petition from 'diverse Cittizens and others Inhabitants within the Citty of London and Weekly bills of Mortality', which expressed alarm over the level of theft and the absence of workhouses.[55] Common Council responded by appointing a committee of aldermen and common councilmen to consider the matter, but nothing more was heard from it. The City fathers may not have been simply dragging their feet, however, for six days after the appointment of the committee a bill was presented in the House of Commons 'for the better Relief of the Poor, and setting them on Work', which may have included separate provisions to establish workhouses within the bills of mortality. As with much social and economic legislation of the period, however, the bill failed to complete its progress and was not enacted.[56]

In the autumn of 1696, the focus of poor law reform shifted to the newly-established Board of Trade. The Board had been given instructions to inquire into ways of employing the poor among its other duties, and that mandate was taken seriously by the commissioners in light of conditions in London and elsewhere in the kingdom. While the impact of the recoinage crisis on the poor is difficult to assess, French smuggling of silk and the East India Company's importation of cheap calicoes brought protests and unemployment among weavers and their families from September 1696 into the next year.[57] The Commissioners of Trade and Plantations, who included John Locke, heard testimony on ways to employ the poor, conducted a survey of poor rates around the kingdom, and drafted proposals for legislation.[58] Among those who advised the Board on employment projects were Thomas Firmin and the Bristol merchant John Cary, whose own project was in its early stages, while petitions and correspondence (including a letter from Clayton) related the extent of unemployment among London silkweavers.[59] Supporters of an employment project in London had reason to hope that new legislation might be forthcoming: some of the Commissioners' early drafts included special provisions for London within the bills of mortality.[60] Yet the recommendations which the Board of Trade finally sent to the lords justices in December 1697 made no mention of the City or the suburbs. For reasons which remain unclear, the Commissioners did not recommend wholesale reform of the poor laws, but devoted their proposals instead to ways in which existing provisions to employ the poor could be more strictly enforced. When the employment of the poor was again introduced in the House of Commons the following February, it failed to make progress.[61]

The failure of this effort to enact a comprehensive reform of the poor laws, with provisions for London in which the relief and employment of the poor would be vested in the municipality instead of the parishes, finally compelled the City to take the initiative. A little over a month after the introduction of the bill in the Commons, Lord Mayor Sir

Humphrey Edwin recommended to Common Council that it take steps to revive its Corporation of the Poor, using the 1662 statute as a basis.[62] By October 1698, fifty-two assistants had been selected, who in turn had 'voluntarily' chosen Sir Robert Clayton as the Corporation's vice-president and its effective head (the Lord Mayor was *ex officio* president).[63] Clayton submitted proposals for the employment of the poor to Common Council, which in November ordered a half-year's poor rate on the City's parishes to raise £5,101 for the project.[64] Clayton's proposals, which were put into effect early in 1699, called for the creation of an employment scheme organized along lines similar to Thomas Firmin's. Indeed, Firmin's nephew and business partner Jonathan James had been selected as one of the Corporation's assistants for Langbourn Ward.[65] The only major difference, aside from the scope of the new project, was that the poor were now to spin wool, which commanded higher wages, instead of flax. Two 'undertakers' were hired to teach the poor to spin in workhouses for a training period of six weeks, whereupon the poor would return to their parishes with wheels, reels, and other implements with which the undertakers had provided them. The similarity with rural domestic manufacture was underscored by an agreement that the undertakers would continue to supply the poor with 'such work as women & Children in the Contrey use to do att which any willing industrious & capeable person may earn from two shillings to four shillings per weeke & some five or six shillings per weeke'.[66] The parishes would then be responsible for keeping the poor spinners at work. Some 400 people, mostly children, were trained by the undertakers, yet the employment scheme collapsed during the summer of 1699.[67]

The reasons for this collapse were several. Sir Robert Clayton himself thought that the Lord Mayor who had succeeded Edwin in October 1698, Sir Francis Child, had sabotaged the project by discouraging parish authorities from collecting the assessments ordered by Common Council.[68] Difficulties also arose in persuading constables to enforce the laws against begging and vagrancy with vigour, and the assistants felt compelled both to request that Child issue a mayoral precept ordering strict enforcement of those laws and to publish their own admonition to City constables.[69] The greatest difficulty, however, lay in the failure of churchwardens and overseers to employ those poor people whom the undertakers trained. According to the assistants, parish officers had simply continued to pay those poor people their pensions instead of keeping them at work, and so those who had been trained ceased to spin.[70]

The failure of this project led the assistants to shift their approach to the use of a workhouse, where the labour of the poor could be directly supervised and disciplined work habits more readily imposed. Moreover, the assistants turned their attention now to the employment of poor children. These children were taken primarily from City parishes, and later from benefactors who exchanged the privilege of placing a poor child in the workhouse for a cash donation.

The reason for this shift is not clear; it may be, however, that the initial contact with poor parishes early in 1699 convinced the assistants of the need to train poor children from the age when they were capable of regular work. Accordingly, the Corporation took a house in Half-Moon Alley, off Bishopsgate Street, in August of 1699, and in December the first group of 100 children was admitted to the 'steward's side'.[71] By-laws governing the workhouse were approved at the City sessions of the peace, which allowed the Corporation of the Poor to charge parishes an additional 12d. weekly for every child of theirs maintained in the workhouse. Vagrants – probably vagrant children known as the 'Black Guard' – were first admitted in November 1700, and a 'keeper's side' of the workhouse was subsequently opened where 'grown *Vagrants*, sturdy *Beggars*, and other *Idle* and *Disorderly Persons*' apprehended by the City constables or workhouse beadles were set to work.[72] By Easter 1703, the workhouse in Bishopsgate Street maintained 427 children, and had corrected some 430 vagrants and disorderly persons during the preceding year.[73]

The presence of both groups within the walls of the London Workhouse reflected the assistants' belief that poverty was a moral as well as a social condition. The discipline of regular work was thus a moral, not merely economic, necessity which had to be taught to human beings when they were young, before they could acquire habits of idleness and vice. As one defender of the workhouse put it in 1713, suppose that poor children

> had been otherwise kept from perishing for Want, yet great would have been the Loss of their honest Labour and Industry, at least to themselves; and greater would have been the Evil, if they had follow'd the wicked Practices their miserable Condition expos'd them to: So that the real Truth of the Matter seems to be this, *That if the poor are not taken in to one side of the House, when they are Young, it's great odds but they will deserve to be sent to the other when they are grown up.*[74]

Thomas Firmin had said as much in 1681, as had other critics and would-be reformers of the poor laws at the end of the seventeenth century.

The daily routine within the workhouse was designed 'to inure [the children] betimes to honest *Labour* and *Industry*'.[75] Children under the age of seven were not admitted from parishes or benefactors, and they were not usually kept beyond the age of fourteen. They were awakened by a bell at 6 each morning, and at the sound of another bell at 6:30 they went to prayers and breakfast. They were set to work from 7 a.m. until noon and again from 1 until 6 p.m. Another bell rang at 6 p.m. and the children went to prayers and supper. During the day they were sent twenty at a time for two hours' instruction in reading, writing, and arithmetic. They were allowed to play after their midday meal until 1 p.m. and between supper and bedtime. By 1703 fifteen teachers were employed to instruct and supervise the children in spinning wool, hemp and flax, shoemaking, tailoring, and knitting, although the majority of children spun wool. The assistants made special mention in their annual printed reports that the children made their own clothes, and in 1704 a silkthrowster was hired to teach a few girls silkwinding.[76] The Corporation of the Poor advertised the availability of its children as apprentices in City newspapers and claimed that 'great Care is taken in putting them out *Apprentices* to *honest* and *sober People*'.[77] Most of them in reality were apprenticed into the ranks of casual labour or the poorer trades. During a thirty-two month period from 1703 to 1705, 314 children were discharged from the 'steward's side': of the 240 for which information survives, 104 were returned to the parishes from which they had been sent to be apprenticed by parish officers. For the remaining 136, thirty-six were sent into maritime-related trades, with twelve apprenticed directly to shipmasters; while another thirty entered the textile trades, with sixteen apprenticed to weavers; clothing manufacture took another twenty, with seven apprenticed to fanmakers; while eight were apprenticed as household or domestic servants; the remaining children were apprenticed across a broad spectrum of London's petty trades, including gardeners, chimney sweeps, bricklayers, market women, a painter, pinmaker, basketmaker, and a hayman.[78]

Despite the emphasis on labour-discipline, however, it would be misleading to portray the Bishopsgate workhouse in Dickensian terms: there is little evidence to suggest that the assistants or the workhouse officers treated their charges with cruelty or neglect. Two recent authors are probably correct in saying that the clothing and food provided in the workhouse were better than the children might otherwise have received. Nor can there be any doubt about the care the assistants displayed in seeing that physicians, apothecaries, and surgeons attended ailing children, or in acquiring houses away from London where the sick could recuperate.[79] The steward's side of the workhouse had more in common with earlier workhouses in this respect than with later institutions designed to terrorize or punish the poor.

Clearing the streets of vagrants, beggars, and other disorderly persons such as nightwalkers or ballad singers continued to be a regular part of the Corporation of the Poor's activities. The keeper's side presented a contrast to the treatment afforded poor children, and the descriptions of those committed are identical to those of people committed to Bridewell Hospital. Inmates on the keeper's side were set to work beating hemp and picking oakum, and the punitive nature of this labour is made more apparent by the short length of time offenders usually remained in the workhouse: seldom more than a week, usually only a few days. The short length of stay also explains why the yearly number of vagrants maintained in the workhouse exceeded that of children.[80] Yet the assistants employed only two beadles to apprehend beggars and vagrants, a number inadequate to the task. The Corporation did exhort City marshals and ward constables to attend to their duties more diligently, but with little success.[81] By 1704 the Corporation had turned to offering bounties of a shilling per beggar to every overseer, constable, beadle, marshal's man, warder or other person who apprehended beggars and brought them before an alderman or justice for committal. The response was such that the keeper was subsequently ordered to stop payment 'for such Whores and other Idle & Disorderly Persons that are comitted to the Workhouse ... and only pay for the future 12 pence per Head for Beggars'.[82] The response of poor people to these policies is indicated by reports of 'Mobbs and Tumults' among the almspeople dwelling in Half-Moon Alley each time an offender was committed, or by the remarks of a former workhouse nurse, who was committed for accusing the assistants of being 'Presbyterian Dogs & Rogues that Cheat the Poor'.[83]

IV

Resistance to the Corporation of the Poor in certain parishes appeared almost from its refoundation. Two aspects of the institution attracted opposition: it was expensive, and it was clearly linked to Whig and dissenting interests in the City.

The first of these problems can be dealt with briefly. As the London Workhouse expanded early in the eighteenth century, the assistants had to return to Common Council for further assessments from the City's parishes. In all, seven such assessments were granted by Common Council between 1698 and 1713, authorizing the collection of a total of £34,644.6s.7d. from parish ratepayers.[84] Although no charges of corruption have come to light – Common Council audited the accounts and never found anything suspicious – parish rates formed the most important source of Corporation revenue; gifts from benefactors rarely exceeded 30 per cent of yearly income between 1700 and 1713, while the sale of goods manufactured in the workhouse amounted on average to only 14 per cent.[85] The problem went back to the 1662 Poor Law. In the absence of further statutory reform, the revival of the Corporation of the Poor brought the prospect of a double poor rate into reality in a period when City ratepayers were heavily taxed to refund the orphans' debt and to support the war effort after 1702.

As to the second objection, the original fifty-two assistants were recruited from among the mercantile and trading élite of the City, and twelve of the twenty merchants among them were associated with the leading institutions of Whig finance – the Bank of England and the New East India Company – as investors or directors.[86] The distinctly whiggish complexion of this group was thus apparent from the start. Fifteen of the assistants can be identified as dissenters, and another five may have been as well.[87] Only one assistant, George Newland of Farringdon Ward Without, was a Tory, and he used his position to discourage parishes in that ward from paying their original assessments to the Corporation.[88] The assistants included men with established philanthropic interests: John Bellers, the Quaker social reformer; Jonathan James; Clayton himself, president of St Thomas's Hospital; and ten governors of Christ's Hospital.[89] Not all of these assistants were equally active in the Corporation's affairs, and it has not been possible to trace the backgrounds of men who became assistants after 1698.

Initially, opposition to the Corporation of the Poor was concentrated in the populous and mainly poor extramural wards of Farringdon Without and Cripplegate Without. The first signs of resistance came in the refusal of the vestries of St Giles Cripplegate and St Sepulchre Holborn to co-operate fully with a survey of the poor which had been ordered in April 1698. An audit of the accounts of St Sepulchre had revealed that money from the rates was still due from an overseer of the poor, and the vestry was reluctant to expose its books to further scrutiny.[90] During the next two years, thirteen parishes refused to collect assessments for the Corporation of the Poor, all but two of which were clustered on the western edge of the City, primarily in the predominantly Tory wards of Aldersgate and Farringdon Without.[91] The churchwardens of St Sepulchre were among those threatened with indictment at the City's sessions if they continued to refuse to collect assessments, while others were bound over for putting collected assessments to other uses. Resistance continued, however, and by

December 1700 only £3,758 had been collected, an impressive amount, but still short of the £5,101 which was due to the Corporation of the Poor.[92]

As a result, the assistants sought more effective ways of forcing recalcitrant parishes to co-operate. Early in March 1700, a bill was introduced in the House of Commons to augment the legal authority of the Corporation of the Poor beyond what had been established in 1662. It included provisions authorizing the assistants to order parishes to pay pensions to their indigent poor and allowing the assistants to set the amount of those pensions; it gave them authority to supervise voluntary collections on behalf of the Corporation in churches and meeting houses in the City; and it gave them the authority to enforce the settlement laws. Finally, it granted the assistants immunity from the penalties under the Test Act and, by extending to anyone who had given the Corporation £50 or more full voting rights under the title of 'honorary governour', opened the Corporation to any substantial tradesman, including dissenters.[93] Together with the authority the assistants already possessed to employ the poor, the bill would have effectively deprived churchwardens, overseers, and vestrymen of the disposition of much of the money they regularly collected.

The reaction to the bill was swift. Two days after its introduction the Commons received a petition against it from the predominantly Tory parishes of St Sepulchre, St Andrew Holborn, St Bride, and St Martin Ludgate in Farringdon Ward Without. Protesting the creation of 'a new Magistracy', the petitioners claimed that parish officers, not Corporation assistants, were 'the best Judges of the Necessities of their Poor'. They went on to claim, in effect, that the employment of the poor was too much of a burden on parish ratepayers and too great a responsibility to give dissenters, who could buy their way on to the Corporation's governing body.[94] The petitioners concluded with an appeal to be allowed to establish their own workhouse in the ward of Farringdon Without, an inconsistency in their argument which the Corporation seized on in its reply. The assistants protested their own public-mindedness and philanthropic dispositions, and asked what had these parishes got to hide?[95] Nevertheless, the assistants' reply was generally an evasive one, and the bill failed. The dispute, however, was clear. No longer was the question in the City simply whether to employ the poor, but *who* would control the funds raised for their relief and employment: the parishes, or the Corporation of the Poor?

Having failed to obtain legislation enlarging its powers, the Corporation of the Poor turned to the City's law courts. At the sessions of the peace in April 1700, the justices in attendance, including Sir

Robert Clayton, cited parishes in the ward of Farringdon Without for failing to bring their poor rate assessment books to the bench for inspection, pursuant to provisions in 43 Elizabeth, *c*.2.[96] This was the first time since the Fire that the London justices had issued such an order or even enforced that section of the statute. Its intention, to compel parishes to pay their assessments to the Corporation of the Poor, was obvious. Churchwardens from St Bride and St Martin Vintry in Vintry Ward were subsequently bound over to sessions, and Clayton sought indictments against them, but at the August sessions the men were discharged after appearing on their recognizances.[97]

The tactic of threatening churchwardens with indictment worked in the short term. By 1703 the records of the Corporation of the Poor show that even the recalcitrant parishes in Farringdon Ward Without were grudgingly collecting and turning in assessments.[98]

In the long run, however, the expense of the Corporation of the Poor proved more than many parishes could bear. New assessments of nearly £5,000 apiece were voted by Common Council in 1702, 1704, 1706, 1710, and 1713 in response to requests from the assistants, and parishes slowed in their payment of these additional quotas. By 1711 arrears from parishes to the Corporation stood at over £3,000, while the workhouse had slid into debt to the amount of £3,293.[99] In 1708 a committee of Common Council began to search for ways to reduce the expense of the workhouse and even challenged the legality of maintaining children there from the City's parishes. The committee argued that, in fact, the workhouse 'was intended as a place of Punishment for Rogues Vagrants & Sturdy Beggars & other Idle & Disorderly Persons thereto be set to Worke'.[100] Common Council sought legal counsel from the City Recorder, Sir Peter King, who replied with an opinion supporting the present function of the workhouse, especially in its employment of children. If parishes objected to the admission of parish children, asked King, why had it taken so long for them to question its legality?[101]

Nevertheless, opinion in Common Council was moving away from the view that the Corporation of the Poor had any authority over parish children. The cost of the London Workhouse had come to weigh more heavily than the need to impose work discipline. Reports that children had been brought to London by country carriers and waggoners and dropped in the streets so that they might be admitted to the workhouse prompted one committee of Common Council to urge that Lord Mayors be denied the power to place children in the workhouse by their warrants alone. Continual pressure on the assistants led them to drop the 12d. charge in 1710, although parish children continued to be taken in.[102] The request for another assessment in 1712, however, proved to be the last straw. The committee appointed to investigate the workhouse submitted unanimous opinions from the Attorney General, Solicitor General, and the Common Serjeant, that Common Council could not compel parishes to pay assessments for the maintenance of children in the workhouse since, *pace* Recorder King's earlier opinion, the 1662 statute *was* intended for the correction of vagrants only. But the committee also reported that the assistants had at last agreed to alter the by-laws of the workhouse to prevent the admission of children as had been practised since 1700.[103] This alteration of the by-laws occurred in July 1713. Henceforth, no parish children could be maintained in the workhouse, although benefactors might still place a City child there for £50 or a child from elsewhere for £70. Otherwise, the London Corporation of the Poor was to confine itself to the correction of 'Rogues, Vagrants, Sturdy Beggars, or other idle or disorderly Persons within this City and Liberties thereof'. Having waited until the change in by-laws before agreeing to a new assessment, Common Council voted an assessment of £887 on the parishes in October 1713.[104]

The alteration of the workhouse's by-laws had its intended effect. Although the London Workhouse survived into the nineteenth century, it did so in reduced circumstances and remained essentially a house of correction, as the figures in Table 36 show.

Table 36. Children and vagrants apprenticed or discharged from the Bishopsgate Workhouse, 1700–44

	Dates	No.	Yearly Av.	No. Years
Children	Easter 1700 to Easter 1713	1243	96	13
	Easter 1713 to Easter 1744	1504	48	31
Vagrants	Easter 1700 to Easter 1713	5555	427	13
	Easter 1713 to Easter 1744	14,487	467	31

Sources: An Account of the Corporation of the Poor of London (London 1713), p. 9; *An Account of the Corporation of the Poor of London* (London 1744), pp. 19–20.

Were these continual attacks on the scope of the Corporation of the Poor politically motivated? The cost of the workhouse and the number of assessments passed in its support alone may have gained it opposition from a wider spectrum of London ratepayers than from merely one party or another. Nevertheless, many of the men who sat on the Common Council committees which advocated reduction in the scope of the London Workhouse can be identified as Tories on the basis of their votes in the divisive parliamentary election of 1710, and the committees included some earlier opponents of the Corporation of the Poor from Farringdon Ward Without. Sir Francis Child himself sat on a majority of those committees and in 1710 was joined by Sir George Newland, the former assistant of the Corporation from Farringdon Ward Without and soon to be elected Tory M.P. for the City.[105] The expense of the London Workhouse together with the patronage it received from dissenters and interests connected with the Bank of England made the Corporation of the Poor an easy target for City Tories later in Anne's reign, who opposed dissent, high taxes, and the Bank and its close connection to the War of the Spanish Succession.

In some respects the London Workhouse was an anachronism anyway by 1713. The charity schools which proliferated throughout the metropolis after 1698, funded through voluntary subscriptions, provided a cheaper means of inculcating the children of the poor with habits of deference and diligence, while remaining firmly under the control of parish élites. In contrast, the London Workhouse had expanded too rapidly and had provided a level of supervision which, if laudable by the standards of Samuel Hartlib's – or Thomas Firmin's – day, was too costly for the first decade of the eighteenth century.

The ultimate success of the Corporation of the Poor would have required a thorough reform of poor relief practices in London involving fundamental changes in the location of authority over the disposal of poor rates in the interests of a more rigorous regulation of the poor. As it developed, the question of authority over the parishes pushed aside the question of authority over the poor. Indeed, that the whiggish governing body of the Corporation of the Poor collected taxes from burdened householders, claimed authority to inspect parish accounts, and attempted to increase its authority over the parishes well beyond what the 1662 statute specified helps to explain why *voluntary* and parochially-controlled charity schools received such enthusiastic support from London Tories and high churchmen. The reforms which would have centralized poor relief in the hands of the London Corporation of the Poor did not occur, and the last bill to enact a comprehensive national reform of the poor laws for decades failed in Parliament in 1706. The Corporation of the Poor ran afoul of the parochially-administered system it was intended to eclipse; and, as long as vestrymen, churchwardens, or overseers of the poor were obliged to rate parish householders and to administer poor relief, the assistants could bend the system but not break it. As for the London Workhouse in Bishopsgate Street, its site is now occupied by a part of Liverpool Street Station.

NOTES AND REFERENCES

1. C. Wilson, 'The other face of mercantilism', *Revisions in Mercantilism* D. C. Coleman (ed.) (London 1969), pp. 125, and 118–39 *passim*; see also E. S. Furniss, *The Position of the Laborer in a System of Nationalism* (New York 1920); T. E. Gregory, 'The economics of employment in England, 1660–1713' *Economica*, 1 (1921), 37–51; W. D. Grampp, 'The liberal elements in English mercantilism' *Quarterly Journal of Economics*, 66 (1952), 465–501; J. O. Appleby, *Economic Thought and Ideology in Seventeenth-Century England* (Princeton 1976), pp. 129–57.
   I am grateful to Mark Benbow, Marcia Carlisle, Hether Macfarlane, Paul Slack, and the editors of this volume for their comments on earlier drafts of this essay; I alone am responsible for what remains.
2. But see E. M. Hampson, *The Treatment of Poverty in Cambridgeshire, 1597–1834* (Cambridge 1934), pp. 51–65; J. Thirsk, *Economic Policy and Projects: The Development of a Consumer Society in Early Modern England* (London 1978), pp. 133–48; V. Pearl, 'Puritans and poor relief: The London workhouse, 1649–1660', *Puritans and Revolutionaries: Essays in Seventeenth-Century History Presented to Christopher Hill,* D. Pennington & K. Thomas (eds) (Oxford 1978), pp. 206–32.
3. S. & B. Webb, *English Poor Law History, Part 1: The Old Poor Law* (London 1927), p. 120; E. E. Butcher (ed.) *Bristol Corporation of the Poor. Selected Records 1696–1834*, Bristol Record Society, vol. 3 (Bristol 1932); *A Bill for Erecting a Work-House in the City and County of the City of Norwich* (n.p. 1711); W. G. Hoskins, *Industry, Trade and People in Exeter, 1688–1800* (Manchester 1935), pp. 142–4.
4. *Commons Journals* (hereafter *C.J.*), vol. 11, pp. 96, 172, 573; vol. 12, pp. 99, 360, 493ff., 621; vol. 13, pp. 4–5, 366, 655ff.; vol. 14, pp. 11ff., 231ff., 392ff.; *Lords Journals*, vol. 17, pp. 665ff.; the text of Mackworth's bill is printed in HMC, *House of Lords MSS*, n.s., vol. 6 (1704–6), pp. 273–87; for an example of a proposal for poor law reform as suggested legislation, see C. Davenant, *An Essay Upon the Probable Methods of Making a People Gainers in a Balance of Trade* (1699), *The Political and Commercial Works of ... Charles D'Avenant,* C. Whitworth (ed.) (London 1771), vol. 2, pp. 205–15: the proposal on pp. 207–15 had been submitted to the House of Commons and forwarded to the Board of Trade in Feb. 1698, Public Record Office (hereafter PRO), Colonial Office 388/5/309–11, 391/10/16.
5. I have used the terms 'City' and 'City of London' to refer only to the area under the jurisdiction of the Lord Mayor and aldermen; 'London' without further qualifications refers to the metropolis generally.
6. F. Brewster, *Essays on Trade and Navigation* (London 1695), p. 58.
7. *Statutes of the Realm* (London 1819), vol. 4, pt. 2, pp. 962–3: 43 Eliz., *c.2.*
8. See Roger Coke, *A Discourse of Trade* (London 1670), pp. 14–16; *The Grand Concern of England Explained* (London 1673); 'Sir William Coventry on the decay of rents, 1670', *Seventeenth-Century Economic Documents*, J. Thirsk & J. P. Cooper (eds) (Oxford 1972), pp. 80–1; F. M. Eden, *The State of the Poor* (London 1797), vol. 1, pp. 188–9, 196–8, 229–30.
9. Matthew Hale, *A Discourse Touching Provision for the Poor* (London

1683); Josiah Child, *A New Discourse of Trade* (London 1693), pp. 47, 55–79; Thomas Firmin, *Some Proposals for the Imployment of the Poor* (London 1681).

10. PRO, CO 389/14/129; cf. Child, *New Discourse of Trade*, p. 56; John Pollexfen, *A Discourse of Trade and Coyn* (London 1697), pp. 50–1; Furniss, *Position of the Laborer*, pp. 96–116.

11. Bodleian Library, MS Eng. Hist. b. 209, fol. 81.

12. Wilson, 'The other face of mercantilism', pp. 124–8.

13. Dudley North, 'Some notes concerning ye laws for the poor', British Library (hereafter BL), Add. MS. 32512, fol. 125.

14. Firmin, *Some Proposals*, pp. 13, 16; Child, *New Discourse of Trade*, pp. 47, 61–3, 64, 75–79.

15. Valerie Pearl, 'Social policy in early modern London', *History and Imagination. Essays in Honour of H. R. Trevor-Roper*, Hugh Lloyd-Jones, Valerie Pearl & Blair Worden (eds) (London 1981), pp. 123–31.

16. Guildhall Library (hereafter GL) MS 4215/1 (St Dionis Backchurch, Churchwarden Accounts); 1124/1 (St Katherine Coleman, CAs); 1123/1 (St Katherine Coleman, Vestry Minutes); see also MS 4525/6–31 (St Botolph Bishopsgate, CAs).

17. GL MS 1145/2, *passim.* (St Katherine Coleman, poor rate assessment books, 1678–1708); Corporation of London Records Office (hereafter CLRO), Assessments on Marriages, Burials, and Baptisms, 1695, no. 42.

18. For poor rate returns see the results of the Board of Trade's survey, conducted in 1696–7: PRO, CO 389/14/128–9; the proportion of poor rates for London are taken from commissioner Abraham Hill's MS notes on the returns, in BL Sloane MS. 2902, fol. 238; for population estimates, see P. E. Jones & A. V. Judges, 'London population in the late seventeenth century', *Econ. H.R.*, 6 (1935–6), p. 54; E. A. Wrigley, 'A simple model of London's importance in changing English society and economy, 1650–1750', *Past and Present*, 37 (1967), p. 44, n. 1.

19. Richard Dunning, *A Plain and Easy Method Showing How the Office of Overseer of the Poor May be Managed* (1686), quoted in S. and B. Webb, *English Local Government from the Revolution to the Municipal Corporations Act: The Parish and the County* (London 1906), pp. 390–1.

20. S. and B. Webb, *English Local Government: The Manor and the Borough* (London 1908), vol. 2, p. 662, n. 2.

21. *At the Court House in Bloomsbury, in the Parish of St Giles's in the Fields, in the County of Middlesex* (London 1712), in BL, 816 m. 9 (74); S. and B. Webb, *The Parish and the County*, pp. 403–5.

22. CLRO, Lord Mayors Waiting Bks., vols. 12–16; Mansion House Justice Room Charge Bks, vols. 1–4; for a further discussion of the Lord Mayor's activities as a magistrate, see S. M. Macfarlane, 'Studies in Poverty and Poor Relief in London at the End of the Seventeenth Century' (unpublished D.Phil. thesis, Oxford, 1983), pp. 195–233.

23. Overseers of the poor were seldom more than collectors of poor rates, while effective decision-making was left to churchwardens; see William Maitland, *The History of London* (London 1756), vol. 2, p. 1188; GL MS 1123/11/118, 135, 184, 197.

24. See, e.g., GL MS 4216/2, pp. 142, 143, 154, 171, 181, 203, 216, 245, 252.

25. Pearl, 'Social policy in early modern London', p. 124; GL MS 4072/1, pt.

2, fol. 336 (St Michael Cornhill, CAs); 4215/1, no fol., *passim*. (St Dionis Backchurch, CAs); 2092/2, no fol. (St Andrew by the Wardrobe, CAs); cf. 3149/3, fols. 198–201 (St Sepulchre Holborn, CAs, 1695).

26. GL MS 1145/2, *passim*.
27. GL MS 1123/1/77, 16 Apr. 1692.
28. GL MS 1124/2/67; 1123/1/102, 7 Feb. 1694/5; 1145/2.
29. GL MS 1123/1/59, 145, 161, 186, 207; for badging of the poor before the Act of 8 & 9 Wm. III, *c.* 30 (1697), see GL MS 1453/3, no fol., 4 May 1680 (St Botolph Aldersgate, VMs); 1311/1/265, 19 June 1693, fol. 274, 14 Feb. 1694/5 (St Martin Ludgate, VMs); Pearl, 'Social policy in early modern London', p. 128.
30. For a further discussion of the exercise of this authority, see Macfarlane 'Studies in Poverty and Poor Relief', pp. 140–94.
31. William F. Kahl, *The Development of London Livery Companies: An Historical Essay and a Select Bibliography*, The Kress Library of Business and Economics, Pub. no. 15 (Boston, Mass. 1960), pp. 21–4; CLRO, Repertories of the Aldermanic Bench (hereafter Rep.), vols. 85–118, *passim*, for appointments to Emmanuel Hospital (an almshouse) in Westminster.
32. John Stow, *A Survey of the Cities of London and Westminster*, John Strype (ed.) (London, 1720), 2 vols., *passim*.
33. GL MS 12806/6/611–2; CLRO, Sessions Papers, Settlement Papers, 1697 (undated petition, Christ Church parish); *Calendar of State Papers Domestic 1676–7*, p. 43; Strype (ed.), *Survey*, vol. 1, bk. 1, Ch. 23, pp. 187–8; Greater London Council Record Office, HI/ST/A41.
34. *An Account of the General Nursery or Colledg of Infants* (London 1686); BL, Add. MS 34510, fol. 115v; *An Account of the Charity-Schools in Great Britain and Ireland* (London 1713), pp. 11–14; J. Simon, 'Was there a Charity School Movement? The Leicestershire evidence', *Education in Leicestershire 1540–1940* B. Simon (ed.) (Leicester 1968), pp. 63–4.
35. On the Houndsditch pawnshops, see Strype (ed.) *Survey*, vol. 2, bk. 2, pp. 23–4; CLRO, Lord Mayors Waiting Bk, vol. 13, fol. 137; Maitland, *History of London*, vol. 2, p. 1326.
36. For descriptions of Firmin's philanthropic activities and his workhouse project see [Stephen Nye], *The Life of Mr Thomas Firmin, Late Citizen of London* (London 1698), p. 31 and *passim*.; Firmin, *Some Proposals, passim*.; for Firmin's occupation see GL MS 82, fol. 12; for his relationship to Sir Robert Clayton and circle of associates see *D.N.B.*, 'Thomas Firmin'; Macfarlane, 'Studies in Poverty and Poor Relief', pp. 246–9; H. W. Stephenson, 'Thomas Firmin 1632–1697' (unpublished D.Phil. thesis, Oxford, n.d.), 3 vols.
37. CLRO, Journals of the Court of Common Council (hereafter Jor.), vol. 52, fols. 177v–8; *Statutes of the Realm*, vol. 5, pp. 401–2: 13 & 14 Chas. II, *c.* 12, sec. 4–14.
38. Pearl, 'Puritans and poor relief', pp. 207–10, 215–17; C. Webster, *The Great Instauration: Medicine, Science and Reform 1626–1660* (London 1975), pp. 361–3.
39. Pearl, 'Puritans and poor relief', pp. 219, 225–6; Bodl. Libr. MS Carte 74, fol. 501.
40. Parish resistance contributed to the failure of a Corporation of the Poor

in Middlesex and Westminster by the early 1670s, which had been established in accordance with the 1662 statute and had erected workhouses in Clerkenwell and Tothill Fields: see HMC, *8th Report*, p. 126b; A. Grey, *Debates of the House of Commons* (London 1769), vol. 1, pp. 403–5.

41. I. Grubb, *Quakerism and Industry* (London 1930), pp. 136–7; A. Raistrick, *Quakers in Science and Industry* (London 1950), p. 84; A. R. Fry, *John Bellers* (London 1935), pp. 6–7.

42. [Nye], *Life of Mr Thomas Firmin*, pp. 29–38; Firmin, *Some Proposals*, pp. 2–3, 11, 13, 36, 61; Thirsk, *Economic Policy and Projects*, pp. 102–5, 110–11, 136–9.

43. [Nye], *Life of Mr Thomas Firmin*, p. 33; Firmin, *Some Proposals, passim.*

44. Early subscribers to Firmin's workhouse included, in addition to Clayton and his business partner John Morris, alderman and merchant Sir John Frederick, and merchants Joseph Hearne, Jeremy Sambrooke, Thomas Frederick, and Thomas Westerne: see GL MS 5286/1, no fol. (I am grateful to Professor Frank Melton for this reference and for his help with the Clayton Papers); J. R. Woodhead, *The Rulers of London 1660–1689* (London 1965), pp. 73, 88–9, 143–4, 174; [Nye], *Life of Mr Thomas Firmin*, pp. 35–6.

45. D. W. Jones, 'London Overseas-Merchants Groups at the End of the Seventeenth Century and the Moves Against the East India Company' (unpublished D.Phil. thesis, Oxford, 1970), pp. 94–5, 111–19, 129–30; CLRO, Jor. 51, fols. 284–4v; *The Sea-Martyrs; or, The Seamen's Sad Lamentation for their Faithful Service, Bad Pay, and Cruel Usage* (n.p. 169–); CLRO, Jor. 51, fol. 77v; HMC, *5th Report, Pine Coffin MSS*, p. 381; B. R. Mitchell & Phyllis Deane, *Abstract of British Historical Statistics* (Cambridge 1971), pp. 497–8; HMC, *12th Report, Le Fleming MSS*, p. 339; Gloucestershire Records Office, D3459/Box 77a/Bundle L/21, L. C. J. Holt to Archbishop Sharp of York, 16 July 1696 (I am grateful to Mr Andrew Federer for this reference); *A Proposal for Relieving Such Families, As are Render'd Poor by Want of Imployment in their Lawful Callings* (n.p. 169–).

46. CLRO, Distributions on the King's Letter, Bundle 1688, 434C; CLRO, London Poor from 1690 to 1703, 35B.

47. PRO, SP 44/162, *passim.*; 44/163, *passim.*; GL MS 4526/2/27v (St Botolph Bishopsgate, VMs); see also, for example, CLRO, Sessions Papers, July 1690 (Audit of Churchwardens' Accounts, St Bride Fleet Street, 11 July 1690).

48. For example, CLRO, Sessions Papers, undated 1689 (St Faith, petition); Sessions Papers, undated 1690 (St Mildred Poultry, petition); Sessions Papers, settlement orders, 1694 (St Gregory by St Paul, petition).

49. PRO, PC 2/74/59v, 60v, 67v, 71–1v, 73v, 82–2v, 132–3v, 141v; Narcissus Luttrell, *A Brief Relation of State Affairs* (Oxford 1857), vol. 2, pp. 187, 191–2; CLRO, Rep. 95, fols. 270, 275v–6; Rep. 96, fols. 3, 70–2, 73; Rep. 97, fols. 416–7; Rep. 98, fols. 273–4.

50. CLRO, Sessions Papers, July & Sept. 1693.

51. Maitland, *History of London*, vol. 1, pp. 497–9; CLRO, Rep. 98, fols. 213–14, 324.

52. Richard Lapthorne, *The Portledge Papers* R. J. Kerr & I. C. Duncan (eds)

(London 1928), p. 95; HMC, *12th Report, Le Fleming MSS*, p. 315; PRO, PC 2/74/23–4v ('A proclamation for apprehending of robbers on the highway and for a reward to the discoverers', 30 Oct. 1690); PC 2/74/66v; for the beginnings of the Reformation of Manners movement in London see D. W. R. Bahlman, *The Moral Revolution of 1688* (London 1957); [Edward Stephens], *The Beginning and Progress of a Needful and Hopeful Reformation in England* (London 1691).

53. CLRO, Rep. 95, fols. 310, 318v–19v, 321v–4v; Rep. 96, fols. 42–3.
54. CLRO, Mansion House Charge Bk., vol. 3, *passim; Proposals for a National Reformation of Manners, Humbly Offered to the Consideration of Our Magistrates and Clergy* (London 1694).
55. CLRO, Jor. 51, fol. 295–5v.
56. *C.J.*, vol. 11, p. 96; for the MS drafts in the same hand of two bills to reform the poor laws and employ the poor in workhouses, one of which deals solely with London, see BL, Sloane MS 2504, fols. 31v–66 (I am grateful to Professor John Phillipps for this reference).
57. PRO, CO 391/9/2–4v, 57–7v, 94v–5, 115v; 388/5/55; SP 44/274/306; SP 44/99/309, 315, 341–2; HMC, *12th Report, Le Fleming MSS*, p. 346; H. Horwitz, *Parliament, Policy and Politics in the Reign of William III* (Manchester 1977), p. 190; I. K. Steel, *The Politics of Colonial Policy: The Board of Trade 1696–1720* (Oxford 1968), pp. 10–32.
58. PRO, CO 391/9/11.
59. PRO, CO 391/9/27–7v, 132–2v, 138; 388/5/78, 79, 83v, 97, 100, 213–14v.
60. PRO, CO 388/5/250–50v.
61. PRO, CO 389/14/127–38, 23 Dec. 1697; *C.J.*, vol. 12, p. 99.
62. CLRO, Jor. 52, fols. 177v–8.
63. CLRO, Jor, 52, fols. 178, 191v; *A Short Account of the Work-House Belonging to the President and Governours for the Poor* (n.p. 1702), p. 2.
64. CLRO, Jor. 52, fols. 221, 222–2v, 228.
65. [Nye], *Life of Mr Thomas Firmin*, p. 38; CLRO, Jor. 52, fol. 191v.
66. CLRO, Jor. 52, fol. 221.
67. GL MS 5386/1, no fol.: 'In the Mayoralty of Sr Humphry Edwyn Anno 1698'.
68. Bucks. Rec. Off., A.4./1 (Clayton MSS): Sir Robert Clayton to Sir Francis Child, 18 May 1699 (I am grateful to Professor Melton for this reference).
69. CLRO, Jor. 52, fols. 273–3v; *At a Court of the Right Honourable The President and Governors for the Poor of the City of London, Holden at Guild-Hall, on Thursday the 25th day of May, 1699* (n.p. 1699): BL, 816 m. 9 (7).
70. *A Short Account of the Work-House* (1702), pp. 2–3.
71. GL MS 5386/1; Bodl. Libr., MS Rawlinson D734, fol. 37; *An Account of the Corporation of the Poor of London* (London 1713), p. 6.
72. *An Account of the Corporation Of the Poor of London* (1713), p. 6; *A Short Account of the Work-House* (1702), p. 3.
73. *London Work-House. Easter, 1703. A True Report of the Great Number of Poor, Vagrant, and other Children* ... (n.p. 1703), broadside.
74. *An Account of the Corporation of the Poor of London* (London 1713), pp. 14–15, emphasis added.
75. *London Work-house. Easter, 1703. A True Report* ... (1703).

76. Edward Hatton, *A New View of London* (London, 1708), vol. 2, pp. 751–2; Bodl. Libr., MS Rawl. D734, fol. 37v; *London Work-House. Easter, 1703. A True Report ...* (1703); CLRO, MS 66.8, fol. 10v.

77. *A Short Account of the Work-House Belonging to the President and Governours for the Poor* (n.p. 1702), p. 3.

78. CLRO, Courts of the president and governors of the poor of London 1702–5, 32B, *passim*.

79. I. Pinchbeck & M. Hewitt, *Children in English Society* (London 1969), vol. 1, p. 154; CLRO, Courts of the president and governors of the poor, fols. 16, 36, 38v, 40v, 58, 61v, 159–60v.

80. CLRO, Courts of the president and governors of the poor, fols. 43–4, 157v, 193v, 246v, and *passim.*; for the annual numbers of vagrants and children discharged, see Table, p. 269.

81. CLRO, Courts of the president and governors of the poor, fols. 10, 17v, 170, 172v–3v.

82. S. and B. Webb, *Old Poor Law*, pp. 369–70; CLRO, Courts of the president and governors of the poor, fols. 244, 246v.

83. CLRO, Courts of the president and governors of the poor, fols. 43, 245.

84. CLRO, Jor. 52, fol. 228; Jor. 53, fol. 387; Jor. 54, fols. 42, 485; Jor. 55, fols. 38–41, 209–12; Jor. 56, fols. 76v–78v.

85. CLRO, MSS 66. 1–13, *passim*.

86. Arthur Baron, Joas Bateman, John Bellers, James Denew, William Disher, Peter Godfrey, Nathaniel Gould, Edward Haistwell, Nathaniel Mason, Arthur Shallett, and Sir William Hedges (the Corporation's treasurer); Clayton, who apparently influenced the selection of many of these men behind the scenes, became a Bank director himself in 1702, and was already a Whig MP, see GL MS 5286/1; Woodhead, *Rulers of London*, p. 48; for biographical data on the fifty-two assistants, see Macfarlane, 'Studies in Poverty and Poor Relief', pp. 360–71.

87. Sir William Hedges, Arthur Baron, John Bellers, Col. James Boddington, Benjamin Brownsmith, Sir William Coles, Sir James Collett, Sir Thomas Cudden, John Deacle, James Denew, Daniel Dorville, Peter Godfrey, Edward Haistwell, Richard Haley, Abraham Hickman, James Hulbart; probable dissenters included Thomas Eyre, William Faulkner, Thomas Fyge, Jonathan James, and Arthur Shallett.

88. Bucks. Rec. Off., A.4./1.

89. Governors of Christ's Hospital were Arthur Baron, Adrian Beyer, Col. James Boddington, Sir William Coles, Sir James Collett, Peter Godfrey, Samuel Jackson, Robert Knight, Thomas Lockington, and Micajah Perry.

90. GL MS 3149/3/243, 30 Aug. 1698 (St Sepulchre Holborn, VMs).

91. CLRO, MS 66.1: St Giles Cripplegate, St Dunstan in the West, St Andrew Holborn, St Bartholomew the Great, St Bartholomew the Less, St Bride Fleet St., St Olave Silver St., St Mary Staining, St Leonard Foster Lane, St Anne Aldersgate, St Alphage; the others were St James Dukes Place and St Clement Eastcheap.

92. GL MS 3149/3/278, 3 Oct. 1699; CLRO, Mansion House Charge Bk, vol. 4, no fol., 20 Nov. 1699; CLRO, MS 66. 1.

93. The bill was introduced on 5 Mar. 1700: *C.J.*, vol. 13, pp. 265, 273; for the text, see GL MS, 5386/1.

94. *Reasons Humbly Offered to this Honourable House, Why a Bill Pretended to Give Further Powers to the Corporation for Setting the Poor of the City of London and Liberties thereof to Work, Should Not Pass into Law* (n.d. or pl.): BL, 816 m. 15 (49).
95. *Observations Upon a Paper . . .* (n.d. or pl.): BL, 816 m. 15 (50).
96. CLRO, Sessions Minutes, vol. 70, no fol., 8 Apr. 1700; GL MS 5386/1; see also CLRO, Sessions Minutes, vol. 70, 1 July 1700.
97. CLRO, Mansion House Charge Bk, vol. 4, no fol., 24 July 1700; Sessions Papers, August 1700, Augustine Ballowe (secretary to the Corporation) to Thomas Tanner (clerk of the peace), 24 Aug. 1700; Sessions Minutes, vol. 70, no fol., 26 Aug. 1700, presentments nos. 26 & 27. 27.
98. CLRO, MS 66.4.
99. CLRO, MS 66.12.
100. CLRO, Jor. 54, fol. 708.
101. CLRO, Misc. MS 230.18.
102. CLRO, Jor. 55, fols. 192–3.
103. CLRO, Jor. 55, fols. 351–2.
104. CLRO, Sessions Minutes, vol. 79, no fol., 6 July 1713; Jor. 56, fols. 76–8v; for subsequent comment on the reduced state of the workhouse, see Strype (ed.), *Survey*, vol. 1, bk. 1, p. 202.
105. Cf. CLRO, Jor. 54, fols. 707–11; Jor. 55, fols. 41v–42v, 191v–193v, 350v–352; Jor. 56, fols. 43–44v; and *The Poll of the Livery-Men of the City of London* (1710), in GL; see also G. A. Holmes & W. A. Speck (eds), *The Divided Society: Party Conflict in England 1694–1716* (London 1967), p. 128.

Index

Index

Index